DATE			

Wilberforce

Wilberforce at the age of 29 in June 1789,
from the painting by John Rising
now at the Wilberforce House Museum, Hull

JOHN POLLOCK

Wilberforce

ST. MARTIN'S PRESS   NEW YORK

for

MICHAEL ALISON

Contents

Illustrations

In the text

Acknowledgments

During the six years this book has been in the making, many people have helped me in one way or another.

I give my warm thanks to those who kindly allowed me to consult and in many cases quote from manuscripts owned by them: the late 16th Duke of Norfolk, E.M., K.G. (and his Archivist Mr. F. W. Steer), the Duke of Devonshire (and his Librarian, Mr. T. S. Wragg), the Duke of Westminster (and Mrs. E. Berry, City Archivist of Chester); the Marquess of Lansdowne; the Earl Bathurst, the Earl of Buchan, the Earl Fitzwilliam, with the Trustees of the Wentworth Woodhouse Estate and the City Librarian, Sheffield, the Earl of Gainsborough, the Earl of Harewood (and the Archivist, Leeds City Library), the Earl of Harrowby, the Earl of Lonsdale, the Earl Waldegrave, K.G.; Viscount Thurso, the late Lord Egremont, Lord Kenyon; Sir Peter Roberts, Bt., Brigadier Sir Richard Anstruther-Gough-Calthorpe, Bt.; Mr. John Spencer-Bernard, Miss Constance Biddulph, Mr. Richard Gurney, Mr. David Holland, Mr. Charles Jewson, the Rev. T. H. Levesley, Dr. Wilmarth Sheldon Lewis, Brigadier A. W. A. Llewellen-Palmer, Col. A. B. Lloyd-Baker, Mrs. Edward Noel, the Rev. J. S. Reynolds and Mr. C. J. Wilson.

I am specially grateful for the kindness and hospitality of Lord and Lady Buchan, Lord and the late Lady Harrowby, Lord and Lady Waldegrave, and Brigadier and Mrs. Llewellen-Palmer.

I wish to thank also the Trustees of the Bodleian Library, Oxford, for permission to quote from manuscripts, and the Keeper and staff (especially Mrs. M. Clapinson) of the Department of Western Manuscripts, and those of Rhodes House Library; the Trustees of the British Museum, for permission to quote, and the staff of the Students' Room, Department of Manuscripts.

The Library at Duke University, Durham, North Carolina is the pleasantest of places for research, and I should like especially to thank Mr. Paul I. Chestnut and Mr. William R. Erwin, Jr., for their guidance and encouragement, and Duke University for permission to quote freely from their vast collection of manuscripts. I owe a special debt to the Trustees and staff of Wilberforce House Museum, Hull and wish especially to thank the then Director, Mr. John Bartlett (now Director of Sheffield City Museum) and the Keeper, Mr. W. H. Southern.

For permission to consult and quote from manuscript material I also wish to thank the University Library, Cambridge (and the staff of the Anderson Room), St. John's College, Cambridge (and Mr. N. C. Buck, Sub-Librarian); Trinity College, Cambridge (and Mr. Trevor Kaye, Sub-Librarian); Oriel College, Oxford; British and Foreign Bible Society; Church Missionary Society; Friends' House Library; Lambeth Palace Library.

The List of Manuscript Sources shows how much I am indebted to Record Offices, public and academic libraries in Britain and overseas. I am grateful to all who enabled me to consult manuscripts, and would specially like to thank the County Archivist of North Yorkshire, Mr. M. Y. Ashcroft, for his help when I researched the Wyvill Papers; and the staff of the Henry E. Huntington Library in California for the trouble they took in getting me microfilms.

Miss Felicity Ranger, the National Registrar of Archives has helped throughout with my numerous enquiries.

For permission to reproduce pictures in their possession I am very grateful to Lord Gainsborough, Lord Annan, Mrs. C. R. Maxsted, the late Mrs. Arthur Hankey, and the Trustees of the British Museum.

For information regarding Wilberforce's various homes, I am indebted to Mr. John Patterson of Windermere; the Librarians of Lambeth, Westminster and Merton; Mr. Peter Bezodis of the Greater London Survey; the Secretary of the Royal Commissioners for the Exhibition of 1851; and the Keeper of the Muniments, Westminster Abbey.

For guidance on medical details I am indebted to Dr. H. Durston-Smith of South Molton, Mr. Paul Fairbairn of the Department of Ophthalmic Optics, City University, and Mr. Robin Price of the Wellcome Institute of the History of Medicine.

I should like to express my very warm appreciation of encouragement and information from the History of Parliament Trust through the Secretary to its Editorial Board, Mr. E. L. C. Mullins, and the editor of its volumes for 1790–1820, Mr. R. G. Thorne.

The Anti-Slavery Society for the Protection of Human Rights encouraged me, through its Secretary, Col. J. R. P. Montgomery. It continues very active work throughout the world from 60 Weymouth Street, London, W.1.

Professor Ian R. Christie of London University and Mr. John Erhman very kindly allowed me to tap their great knowledge of the period, and so did Professor Roger T. Anstey of the University of Kent at Canterbury, the historian of the Slave Trade. Professor Thomas Pinney of Pomona College, California, and Dr. R. Robson of Trinity

College, Cambridge sent me extracts from the MSS diaries and letters of Lord Macaulay. Professor Frederick Pottle of Yale sent me notes of Boswell's relations with Wilberforce. Mr. E. J. Miller, Assistant Keeper, the State Paper Room, British Museum, guided me about Proclamations against vice. Mr. John Leighton-Boyce gave me the benefit of his wide knowledge of 'the Banking Smiths'.

I am most grateful to those who read the draft and made many helpful suggestions: Professor Roger Anstey; Sir Richard Barrett-Lennard, Bt., my father-in-law; Mr. David Holland, formerly Librarian of the House of Commons; Mr. C. E. Wrangham.

Mrs. J. E. Williams deciphered my handwriting, and among many others who helped in various ways I should mention the following: the Librarian of Windsor Castle (Sir Robert Mackworth-Young); the Archivist (Mr. C. W. Schooling) of the Moravian Church; the Clerk to the Governors, Pocklington School; the Librarian of the Royal Institution, the Archivist of Saint Bartholemew's Hospital, and the secretaries of Boodle's, Brookes's and White's Clubs; the House of Lords Record Office; the Centre of African Studies, Edinburgh University; Devon County Reference Library; Exeter City Record Office; India Office Library; and the London Library. The Duke of Northumberland, the Marquess of Normanby, Sir Robert Birley, the editor of the *Church Times*, Miss Carol Croshaw of Washington, D.C., the late Father Stephen Dessein, Dr. John Dinwiddy, the Rev. F. T. Dufton, Canon Michael Green, Canon Michael Hennell, Mr. Edward Ingram, Mr. Timothy Lodge, Mr. Robson Lowe, Mr. Neill Mackay, Dr. David Newsome, Mrs. S. Palmer and Mr. John Todhunter.

Finally, a very warm thank you to Mr. Michael Alison, M.P. for suggesting the subject; and to my Literary Agent, Miss Felicity Bryan; and to my publisher, Mr. Benjamin Glazebrook and his colleagues.

Preface

Twelve days after William Wilberforce's burial in Westminster Abbey on 3 August 1833, Thomas Babington Macaulay, the future historian, wrote to his sister Hannah: 'Robert Wilberforce is writing his father's life – I suppose in order to turn a penny: and that in the process he may save a penny, he has written to me begging that I will receive and frank all letters, parcels, proofsheets and so forth relating to this work. I answered him, for his father's sake, with great civility. I mean to send him two old coats and a shocking bad hat when I leave London, though my clerk will grumble, I fear, at losing his perquisites.'[1]

Macaulay's sarcasm was unfair, for Robert and his brother Samuel, who joined him in authorship, were devoted to their father's memory. Their *Life*, published in five volumes in 1838, became one of the standard works of the nineteenth century, although several of Wilberforce's surviving friends criticized it as an incomplete and in some respects misleading portrait.

It was very much a book of its time. Letters, for instance, looked complete from greetings to farewells, without any hint that too private or supposedly damaging sentences had been expunged, according to recognized custom. Thus in April 1793 shortly after Louis XVI's execution, when the increasing use of the guillotine in France caused mounting fears of revolution in Britain or its Empire, Wilberforce wrote in a private letter: 'If I thought the immediate Abolition of the Slave Trade would cause an insurrection in our [West Indian] islands, I should not for an instant remit my most strenuous endeavours.'[2] The sons suppressed this revolutionary sentence.

No further biography of importance emerged for eighty-five years, until Sir Reginald Coupland's famous *Wilberforce: A Narrative* (1923). Coupland did not gain access to original sources in the hands of descendants, except for one early diary, nor did he research the extensive deposits of Wilberforce letters already in the British Museum. His standpoint of benevolent imperialism was natural enough to a British writer of his period but makes him less valuable after half a century, especially as those regions of the world most influenced by

Wilberforce have dismissed this author, and his subject, in favour of the Marxist view of the Abolition of the Slave Trade and Slavery set forth in 1944 by Dr. Eric Williams, afterwards Prime Minister of Trinidad. Dr. Williams' handling of evidence has been strongly challenged by subsequent historians.

The third notable biography came out in 1974, *William Wilberforce* by Robin Furneaux, now Earl of Birkenhead, the first Life since 1838 to go back to the Wilberforce Papers. Although I cannot agree with his statement that the biographer of Wilberforce must lean heavily on the printed sources, Robin Furneaux puts all students of the subject in his debt. His long, affectionately written book began the process of restoring Wilberforce to his true place and demolished the weak dull character imagined by Eric Williams.

My own book is from a rather different angle, and draws on a considerable amount of fresh manuscript material, ranging far beyond the Wilberforce Papers; many essential manuscripts lie among those of his contemporaries, whether friends or opponents. Through the courtesy of private owners and public institutions I researched a great deal which was not available to his sons and has not been consulted by later writers, in over one hundred manuscript collections from more than eighty locations in Britain, the United States and Australia.

As Professor David Brion Davis remarked in his masterly *Slavery in an Age of Revolution*[3] (1975), 'Few biographical subjects are so treacherous as William Wilberforce.' The manuscript letters and papers newly come to light provide vital evidence to widen the picture and to resolve many of the 'contradictions of a liberator'.

Some of the new discoveries are copious enough to fill out forgotten aspects, such as Wilberforce's stand as the first political independent in the modern sense of the term, or his attempt to destroy the Portuguese and Brazilian slave trades which continued openly long after the British trade had been outlawed. Other new insights hang on single threads; when, for instance, the aged Lord Carrington, last survivor of a circle of young M.P.s, recalled in 1838 the doggerel verse and appalling pun perpetrated by Wilberforce as they celebrated the current Toast of the Town one evening in the early seventeen-eighties, it is not surprising that the story has no other source.

To keep this book to a reasonable size I have restricted the historical background to a minimum, all the more so because Professor Roger Anstey's definitive study, *The Atlantic Slave Trade and British Abolition 1760–1807* (1975) has appeared since the last biography of Wilberforce, overturning many previous conclusions and providing a full account which needs no exhaustive repetition. To Wilberforce, Abolition was of course 'the grand object of my Parliamentary existence'. But he commands attention on many other grounds. For instance, his efforts to improve the economic condition of the poor are little understood, while his ideas of penal reform and Parliamentary reform have never been properly explored. The range of his religious sympathies, the depth of his spiritual convictions, and his concern for the moral climate of an age which in many ways was like our own, add to his interest and relevance when they are placed in perspective. I believe that my book offers a fresh starting point for historical debate.

The general reader should be as much entertained as I have been, by a Wilberforce neither politically repressive nor personally dreary, but exciting, lovable, delightful, with faults which must have maddened his friends.

JOHN POLLOCK

Rose Ash

Devonshire

PART ONE

The Young Member
1759–1788

CHAPTER ONE

Two Guineas a Vote

A huge bonfire blazed beyond the walls of Hull on the night of 24 August 1780. An ox roasted whole. Citizens danced, ate, got drunk, and roared huzzas for their host, the young head of the house of Wilberforce, whose coming of age feast begged their votes in the imminent General Election.

No one round the bonfire that summer evening, least of all himself, could have guessed how William Wilberforce would achieve his fame. To seek election so very young was strange for one of his background, for the Wilberforces were mercantile men. They came from Wilberfoss near York to Beverley in the mid-sixteenth century, and flourished modestly until young William's grandfather, also named William, who was born in 1690, pushed the few miles south to Kingston upon Hull to build a great fortune in the Baltic trade.

Hull was the fourth port of England, ranking after London, Bristol and Liverpool (which was growing to greatness by the Slave Trade) and this earlier William Wilberforce had a red brick mansion in the High Street. The other front overlooked the staiths on the River Hull a few hundred yards from its outflow into the Humber; he could watch his ships unload hemp and timber from Riga and St. Petersburg, and iron ore from Sweden, and load again with every kind of Yorkshire product, from Sheffield knives to ponies.

Alderman Wilberforce owned land in three parishes around Hull and, through his mother, the estate of Markington near Harrogate, which had tenant farms but no country house. He was a man of very vigorous mind who became mayor of Hull at the early age of thirty-two and, in 1745 was mayor a second time: had the Young Pretender come that way he would have been confounded by the old civil war ramparts repaired and manned; the volunteers even had muskets. The Alderman married into another prosperous Hull family in the Baltic trade, the Thorntons, and had two sons and two daughters. The elder son, William, married his first cousin Hannah Thornton and joined

3

his father-in-law, a great Russia merchant, director of the Bank of
England and Member of Parliament, in London. The second son,
Robert, stayed in Hull and became managing partner, probably at the
age of twenty-seven in 1755 when the Alderman, at sixty-five, handed
over the High Street mansion and counting house and went to live
nearby at North Ferriby on the Humber.

Robert Wilberforce married Elizabeth Bird from London; and his
sister married her brother; and the Birds and the house of Wilberforce
were even more confusingly intertwined since Elizabeth's sister had
married the other partner in the firm, Abel Smith, a younger son of the
banker of Nottingham whose numerous descendants have been important in banking ever since. Abel founded two banks himself, in Hull
and in London, which were ancestors of the National Westminster. His
large family included Bob Smith, Pitt's friend whom he ennobled as
Lord Carrington.

Thus, when the third child and only son of Robert and Elizabeth
Wilberforce was born in the Wilberforce house at Hull on 24 August
1759, and christened William, he had a network of uncles, aunts and
cousins.

The eldest sister died, and another who had followed William after
a long interval; only Sarah (Sally) survived childhood. William's early
days at Hull were normal enough for a rich merchant's son, despite puny
size, indifferent health and weak eyesight, offset by a hot temper, a kind
heart, and mental and physical energy. In 1767 he went to Hull Grammar School as a dayboy. That same year his grandfather foisted on the
mayor and corporation a new and young headmaster, a poor weaver's
son of Leeds named Joseph Milner who had won the Chancellor's Medal
at Cambridge and was curate of North Ferriby. Milner's large, uncouth
eighteen-year-old brother Isaac, on the path from the woollen trade to
an academic distinction even more marked than Joseph's, came too as a
temporary usher. Isaac would one day influence William Wilberforce
profoundly, but their paths crossed only briefly at Hull Grammar School.

Next summer when William was turning nine, his father died at the
age of forty. Abel Smith became head of the business; the firm changed
its name to Wilberforce and Smith, and William's life changed too.
Not merely because he would be independent and quite rich when he
came of age, but because he was sent, a year after his father's death, to
live with his childless uncle and aunt, William and Hannah Wilberforce,
at their Wimbledon villa in the Surrey countryside and their London
house in St. James's Place. They put him to boarding school at Putney.
'It was one of those little schools,' he would tell his sons long afterwards, 'where a little of everything, reading, writing, arithmetic, etc.
is taught: a most wretched little place. I remember to this day the
Scotch usher we had, a dirty disagreeable man. To show what kind of
place it was, there were charity boys there, only they lived at the top of

the house, we at the bottom.'[1] Vacations were enjoyable, for he adored the uncle and aunt.

They 'were great friends of Mr. Whitefield', the first 'Methodist' (in the usual eighteenth-century sense before any denomination existed) who had sparked an evangelical revival in Bristol and London at the age of twenty-two, a full year before the conversion of John Wesley. The two evangelists were close friends though disagreeing on points of doctrine, but George Whitefield made more impression among the richer London merchants than Wesley, and in 1754 he had won a convert in Hannah's half-brother, John Thornton, whom the Secretary of the Treasury afterwards described as 'very rich, in great credit and esteem, and of as much weight in the City as any one man I know'.[2] Thornton was one of the most generous men of his day, though considered rather vulgar, and he lived just south of the Thames on the country estate which his father had bought at Clapham, the village linked more than any other with the names of Thornton and Wilberforce.

Hannah probably took her small nephew to Clapham but almost certainly he never heard Whitefield, who in the early autumn of 1769, at about the time of William's coming south, left for his sixth and last visit to America, where he died. William remembered a younger Evangelical, John Newton, the parson of Olney in Buckinghamshire who often preached in London and was soon to be famous as a hymn-writer. A boy could hardly fail to be impressed by this jolly, affectionate ex-sea captain and slaver, who as a youth had been flogged in the Royal Navy for desertion and later suffered as the virtual slave of a white man's native mistress in West Africa. Wilberforce listened enthralled to his sermons and his stories, even 'reverencing him as a parent when I was a child'.[3]

Mrs. Robert Wilberforce became alarmed. By William's letters and his behaviour on visits home he might be 'turning Methodist'. She was more churchgoing than many of her circle but shared the widespread prejudice against any form of Enthusiasm, whether the Whitefield brand or the Wesleyan; and after consulting the Alderman she took a coach to London and rescued her son 'before I should imbibe what she considered was little less than poison, which indeed I at that time had done. Being removed from my uncle and aunt affected me most seriously. It almost broke my heart, I was so much attached to them.'[4]

His mother did not return William to Hull Grammar School since the Master, Joseph Milner, had unexpectedly turned 'Methodist' too, and preached afternoon sermons in the parish church at variance with his vicar's in the morning. Instead she chose the grandfather's old school at Pocklington, a small town thirteen miles from York at the foot of the Wolds; the hill behind the town provided a fine view of York Minster.

Here William spent the next five years, 1771–1776, as a boarder. Founded in 1514, Pocklington had risen by the mid-seventeenth century to be a grammar school of 125 boys, and in the twentieth century is an independent school of 300. In Wilberforce's time, however, attendance had dropped to about thirty, ranging in age from six to seventeen, and the fees were exorbitant. He sums up the place succinctly: 'The Master was a good sort of man and rather an elegant scholar but the boys were a sad set. . . . I did nothing at all there.'[5] The Master was a former Fellow of St. John's, the Reverend Kingsman Baskett, who had been at the school seventeen years and would stay another thirty-six, by which time it lay even more in the doldrums.[6]

Wilberforce's quick mind masked his idleness. He grew into a fair classicist, stuffed his memory with much classical and English verse, and learned to write a good hand: even before worsening eyesight in middle age forced him to use black ink and a bold script, his handwriting was clearer than most of his contemporaries so that the manuscripts remain easier to read than Pitt's less rounded hand or the hasty large scrawl of Dundas, or scores of others. Only his diaries, written very small, presumably by using a glass, are difficult to decipher.

In the holidays the Wilberforce family began to scrub William's soul clear of Wimbledon and Clapham, a slow process: he wrote manfully to his uncle of endurance under persecution, and of increasing 'in the knowledge of God and Christ Jesus whom he sent, whom to know is life eternal.'[7] The Theatre Royal manager described Hull as the Dublin of England for its 'hospitality, plenty of good cheer, with too much welcome'; and if stage plays distressed pious William at first, in time he enjoyed the visits to the family box at Finkle Street and the Assembly Rooms in Digger Lane. He was taught to play cards, young as he was, for this was the normal practice among the gentry. Fashionable Hull dined at two. When business shut at six 'we went up and drank tea: after tea we played cards till nine: then there was a great supper, game, turkey etc. This used to go on all the time I was at home.'[8]

Hull was more than a mercantile town, since county families wintered there and William mixed with them on easy terms. Out of season when the county returned to its estates, 'we were the aristocracy of the place' – that is, the Wilberforces, along with the eccentric Sir Henry Etherington, a warm-hearted baronet who never went out in an east wind and who allowed his servants a table even more luxurious than his own; and the Joseph Sykes of West Ella. Sykes was a native of Leeds who had secured the lease of the white-iron mines in Sweden which produced the best ore for Sheffield steel, and owned the ships to carry it. The Sykes and the Wilberforces were in and out of each other's houses until William looked on the numerous Sykes children, little Marianne especially, as half-brothers and sisters.

He developed a fine singing voice of considerable range. He had quick wit, a merry affectionate nature, and charm. 'In this idle way did they make me live. . . . I was naturally a high spirited boy and fiery. This pushed me forward and made me talk a great deal and made me very vain. This idle way of living at home, of course, did not dispose me for exertion when I returned to school.'[9]

In late November 1774 Alderman Wilberforce died, aged 86, and was buried at St. Mary's, Beverley. Uncle William of Wimbledon nearly followed him into the grave the next week, but on 9 December Bob Smith wrote from London, 'Mr. Wilberforce was yesterday declared to be out of danger from his carbuncle; he mends very fast, but his friends are a good deal alarmed at his dropsical symptoms.'[10] Had the uncle gone, William would have been a rich youth indeed.

In October 1776 at the age of seventeen, small in size but a young man in mind and manner, William went up to Cambridge, the first of his name, and entered St. John's College, with which Pocklington had links, as a fellow-commoner.

'The first night I arrived at Cambridge I supped with my tutor and was introduced to two of the most gambling vicious characters perhaps in all England. There was also a set of Irishmen of this sort to whom I was introduced. There I used to play at cards a great deal and do nothing else and my tutor who ought to have repressed this disposition, if not by his authority at least by his advice, rather encouraged it: he never urged me to attend lectures and I never did. And I should have done nothing all the time I was at [Cambridge] but for a natural love of classical learning, and that it was necessary for a man who was to be publicly examined to prevent his being disgraced. . . .'[11] The tutor was William Arnald, then aged about thirty. He was appointed sub-preceptor in natural science to the Prince of Wales and in 1782 went mad.[12]

Within a few years Wilberforce would bitterly regret that Arnald and his colleagues never taught him to work hard or systematically. Eighteenth-century dons allowed men of independent means, if not reading for the Church or the Bar, to treat a university as a place to acquire a little civilization and a smattering of classics and mathematics. Fellow-commoners were exempt from lectures, yet Wilberforce's good memory and quick intellect enabled him to pass examinations, if without glory: in December 1776 he was not classed with the Honours men but received a place, which would have been higher 'if he had prepared himself in Stanyan [*Grecian History*] as well as he had done in every other subject'.[13] In his first year's examination in June 1777 he was again not classed but received a mention with five other unclassed men, and again in the following December, when he was reported to be 'good in the Classics'.[14]

The man in the neighbouring set of rooms on his staircase was a Harrovian, Thomas Gisborne, a Staffordshire squire's son reading for holy orders, who won the Chancellor's Medal in classics and was placed Sixth Wrangler in mathematics. Men would say behind Wilberforce's back but meaning him to hear, 'Gisborne is very clever, but then he fags, whereas Wilberforce can do as much without working at all.'[15]

Gisborne in old age recalled Wilberforce as the most agreeable and popular man of his year although (Gisborne was too polite to mention it) an ugly little fellow with a tipped-up nose too long for his face – his portraits would generally be painted full face to disguise it. He had hazel eyes and never grew taller than perhaps five foot three or four – his surviving clothes show a chest measurement of about thirty-three inches.[16] Gisborne would see his diminutive short-sighted friend in 'the streets, encircled by a set of young men of talent, among whom he was *facile princeps*. He spent much of his time in visiting, and when he returned late in the evening to his rooms he would summon me to join him by the music of his poker and tongs – our chimney-pieces being back to back – or by the melodious challenge of his voice. . . . He was so winning and amusing that I often sat up half the night with him, much to the detriment of my attendance at lectures the next day.'[17]

Wilberforce loved entertaining and had 'unlimited command of money from the time of my going to the University'. He loved singing, and listening to instrumental music, and conversation. Books meant less than friends idling their time away, fortified by a great Yorkshire pie. Two of his friends came from the Lake District where Wilberforce visited them: William Cookson (Wordsworth's uncle), and Edward Christian, who had a brother named Fletcher Christian. Wilberforce must have seen Fletcher Christian before the boy entered the Navy and later sailed with Bligh to the South Seas, and it would be to Wilberforce that a horrified, puzzled Edward turned for comfort on learning that Fletcher Christian had led the mutiny on the *Bounty*.[18] Earlier, Edward had borrowed £510 off Wilberforce.[19]

At Pembroke was the younger Pitt, three months older than Wilberforce. They knew each other only slightly because Pitt's set was more studious, and his tutor, George Pretyman, had a quite different view of his duties from the tutors at St. John's. One close Johnian friend, Gerard Edwards, was already an extensive landowner in Rutland and Leicestershire by the death of his father, descended in the female line from the seventeenth-century Huguenot who had made a fortune by draining the fens. His mother was a sister of the bachelor Earl of Gainsborough and Edwards was his heir and expected to be created an earl when he inherited. He was not. But this amusing, unstable character would be a rather improbable yet strong link in the chain of events which led Wilberforce to take up the Abolition of the Slave Trade.

Wilberforce did not join in sexual adventures nor drink as hard as some of his friends. His happy nature, his charm and especially his wit allowed him to set stricter limits without seeming a prig. The wildest parties left him rather miserable and in his second year he shook off the fastest members of his set, and at high table sat with the Fellows instead of giggling with fellow-commoners at the other end.[20] He continued gay. Many years later another M.P., Charles Long, would tease the moral leader of England by recalling their Cambridge 'dissipations': Wilberforce would look grave, then roar with laughter and cap the memories by others.[21]

He continued indolent too, ignoring mathematics but browsing in the classics: 'Edwards and Wilberforce were both good in the Classics' runs the report for the December 1777 examination, but neither was classed.[22] He was too idle to win an Honours degree. Looking back in old age Wilberforce felt he had some excuse: 'Now though I am sure I would be the last to extenuate waste of time,' he told his sons, 'I must say that in my case it was as much extenuated as is possible. When you think that all those without exception who ought to have been urging me on to diligence and exertion were leading me into scenes of idleness and dissipation you must see what I mean. I'm sure that as much pains were taken to make me idle as were ever taken to make any one else studious.'[23]

The dropsical uncle William died in 1777 leaving Wilberforce even richer; he need not earn a penny when he went down from Cambridge. He had no leanings to study or to scholarship and certainly none to the family business, which would mean submitting himself to his Smith cousins. They were typical of their breed, combining assiduous attention to the counting house with the life of a country gentleman and eventually a seat in Parliament, though they entered the Commons younger than most mercantile men, Bob Smith at the age of twenty-eight. But he always put his banking first.

Wilberforce, in contrast, began to dream of a life devoted to politics, of entering public life as soon as he came of age. He passed the summer vacation of 1779 in agreeable idleness and country house visiting. In the autumn he was in Cambridge off and on, for Gerard Edwards wrote to his mother, Lady Jane Edwards, on 7 November: 'Mr. St. John and Charles have taken their degrees. I am to have mine in about a fortnight with Lord [*illegible*] and Mr. Pratt. Mr. Wilberforce is in College, I am going to play a rubber of whist with him.'[24] Wilberforce postponed taking his degree for two years.

That winter of 1779–80 he was much in London, idle, but frequently watching debates from the gallery of the House of Commons, often with William Pitt. Acquaintance ripened into friendship and Pitt, reading hard for the Bar but determined on a political career, encouraged Wilberforce to join him in the House as soon as they could get seats.

It was ironic that the indolent amateurish Wilberforce should enter the House before the professionally-minded Pitt. In the spring of 1780 when Wilberforce came home, the card table gossip predicted an early General Election. He conceived the daring ambition of standing for Hull, one of the twenty largest borough electorates in Great Britain with about 1,100 electors out of a population of over 15,000. Most of these electors were hereditary freemen who differed little from their survivors and descendants described by the Municipal Commissioners in 1835: 'The freemen are generally persons in a low station of life, and the manner in which they are bribed shows how little worthy they are of being entrusted with a privilege from which so many of the respectable inhabitants of the town are excluded.' Two Members were returned, so each elector had two votes. In 1780 the bribe ran at two guineas a vote, which many of the electorate regarded 'as a sort of birthright'.[25]

Government could expect to secure the return of one Member by the votes of the garrison and excise officers: their man for the past thirty-three years, who would stand again, was a now elderly general, Lord Robert Manners, uncle of the Duke of Rutland. The great Whig houses of Yorkshire led by the Marquess of Rockingham and Sir George Savile, managed the return of the other Member for Hull: in 1774 they had squeezed in, by 65 votes, the eccentric David Hartley.

Hartley was the son of a philosopher. He invented a fireproof house. He wore peculiar clothes and did not powder his hair. He suffered, like Wilberforce, from weak eyes and secured his spectacles by a band round the top of his head, being no gentleman: Wilberforce had to abide by fashion and use only an eye-glass on a riband. The length and dreariness of Hartley's Commons speeches were said to make him an 'absolute nuisance', even to his friends. He was an ally of Benjamin Franklin and after steadily opposing the American war he had put to the House a compromise, by which the Colonies should receive independence on a basis of mutual citizenship and trade. His hour would come in 1783 when he signed the treaty of peace with the United States. Meanwhile his advocacy of the rights of the Colonists annoyed Hull, and Wilberforce might profit from this, although his own political views, in so far as they were formed, approximated to Hartley's distrust of Lord North and dislike of the American war.

North had been defeated in April 1780 on Dunning's famous motion that 'The influence of the Crown has increased, is increasing and ought to be diminished'. He had recovered, and was believed to be considering whether to run against custom and hold a General Election more than one year before it was due, in the hope of increasing his support in a House where Party meant little and each Administration was, in effect, a coalition of varying interests.

Wilberforce could count on a measure of influence as the head of his family, especially since their money had helped lately to finance Hull's first dock. He began to canvass in May, and some of the replies of outvoters have survived, such as that from one William Bethell, who said he was committed to Manners. A certain helpful W. St. Quentin at Scampston reported canvassing another freeman: 'His answer was very civil, but . . . he still persists in voting as Lord Rockingham shall direct.'[26]

Early in June the Hull mob took up the theme of the recent Gordon Riots and burned down the new Roman Catholic chapel in Posterngate, the first to be built since the Reformation; and because the anti-Popery fury of 1780 had its origin in a limited Act for Catholic Relief which Sir George Savile had introduced, Hartley as Savile's friend lost still more popularity. One of his concerns, however, became a link between Wilberforce and his unforeseen life work. Four years earlier in 1776 Hartley had introduced a motion which 'should lay the foundation for the extirpation of the horrid custom of Slavery in the New World'. A year later he attacked slavery again. Hartley's sentiments, at a time when the Slave Trade and slavery were viewed as unpleasant but scarcely mentionable necessities, could have been the reason why Wilberforce asked a friend who was going to the West Indies to send back details.

In old age Wilberforce recalled that 'I expressed my hope to him that the time would come when I should be able to do something on behalf of the slaves'. This scarcely implies any settled conviction in 1780, but it remains the first authenticated expression of his interest. For if (as a school contemporary claimed after Wilberforce's death) he had written a letter to a York newspaper from Pocklington School deploring the 'odious traffic in human flesh', neither the *York Chronicle* nor the *York Courant* published it and the story is probably apocryphal.*

Wilberforce coaxed the electors all summer with his charm and his purse – he spent the then great sum of nearly £8,000 on the election. A sudden rumour of a Dissolution before his twenty-first birthday nearly dashed his hopes, but Lord North delayed his decision until the very day of Wilberforce's birthday, though the news could not have reached Hull until after the ox-roast.

'I was happy to hear of your great encouragement,' wrote a freeman living in Reading who would not come to Hull unless sent the usual extra £10 for expenses. He added: 'Though I have not the pleasure of knowing your particular sentiments, yet I would hope your parliamentary efforts are, for supporting the rights, liberties and commercial interests of the people; and that you mean to discharge the trust which may be reposed in you with zeal for the real happiness and glory of the

---

* In a letter to the London *Sunday Times*, 9 June 1974, the President of the National Secular Society cited this letter as 'one proof' that Wilberforce became an Abolitionist before 'conversion from atheism. . . . It was during his schooldays in France, among the French freethinkers, whose scepticism he then shared, that his abolitionist ideas were formed.' No evidence was offered for this assertion nor indeed could be; Wilberforce first visited France as a man of 24. For the question whether he was ever an 'atheist', see below, chapter IV.

British Empire.' The candidates went to the hustings on September 11 to make their speeches amid jeers and cheers, and a little throwing of stones. By the following evening every burgess had publicly declared his vote at the Guildhall.

The result was extraordinary: William Wilberforce had secured precisely the same number of votes as the other two candidates added together: Wilberforce 1,126; Manners 673; Hartley 453. Wilberforce and Manners elected.

The ox-roast had been worth it. Yet the man more than his money had won. And by a majority which, as one supporter assured him, 'indicates your superior pretensions, and confirms the character given of you by our friends. . . . You have moreover engaged so much popularity in your favour among the burgesses, as with a moderate attention on your part, which you will be well-disposed to pay them, will secure your elections for the future.'[27]

CHAPTER TWO

Man About Town

Wilberforce took his seat in St. Stephen's Chapel on 31 October 1780 on the Opposition back benches. Behind the Speaker's chair Wren's windows showed the riverside trees in their autumn tints.

Pitt had been defeated for Cambridge University and entered the House in January for a Lowther close borough, but Wilberforce had not yet spoken when Pitt made his maiden speech, an unforgettable performance acclaimed by the whole House, and by Wilberforce with special feeling for the man who now was his closest friend, his hero. The second time Pitt spoke, Wilberforce voted against him. Even in late middle age Wilberforce could recall the pain he felt when personal admiration, held with 'all the warmth and freshness of early youth',[1] conflicted with conviction, and he stayed with Lord North in the Chamber while Pitt went with Burke into the Lobby.

Wilberforce's first recorded speech was on 17 May 1781 during the committee stage of a Bill for Preventing Smuggling. He had presented a petition from Hull and spoke against spirits being confiscated from a ship carrying more than the permitted amount.[2] His maiden speech may actually have been ealier: entire debates went unreported before Hansard, and Lord Carrington (Bob Smith) vaguely recalled in 1838 that his cousin first spoke on a question relating to the Public Accounts;[3] but this refers probably to a debate at the end of May, his second (and unrecorded) effort.

The first major intervention came seven months later – a boyish effusion during a thinly attended debate on naval shipbuilding. Following a speech by Lord Mulgrave, of the Board of Admiralty: 'Mr. *Wilberforce* lamented that he should have his feelings irritated by men in office endeavouring to impress despondency on that House. He declared all that the noble lord had said on the subject of the marine of Great Britain being in former reigns inferior to that of the House of Bourbon, went to harrow and tear up by the roots all those ideas of glory of this country, which he had been taught to adopt in his infancy,

13

and which made every Englishman's breast glow with ardour, whenever he heard of Great Britain being involved in a contest with France and Spain.'[4] He took the opportunity to praise the shipbuilders of Hull.

Captain Lord Mulgrave, R.N., the Arctic explorer, physically a whale to Wilberforce's minnow, snubbed him: two of those Hull ships had sunk on a calm summer's day. Thereupon Charles James Fox laughed at Lord Mulgrave's 'unanswerable reply to Mr. Wilberforce' by reminding the House that a ship from a royal yard had gone down at the same time. Thus Fox rallied to Wilberforce's aid at the very beginning of their time together in Parliament. Before long they stood at opposite poles of their world, yet it would be Fox, near the very end of his life, who would enable Wilberforce to carry Abolition at last.

Wilberforce became at home in the House. Of little consequence politically if very ambitious, he was no time-server but one of the many independents who generally voted against 'the noble lord in the blue ribband' (the Treasury bench wore court dress, with orders) while refusing to be tied to Rockingham or Shelburne or Fox. He attended regularly, spoke seldom, soaked himself in procedure and watched the protagonists; he could soon mimic North to perfection. He relished the anecdotes and reminiscences of the Lobby, the coffee rooms, and Bellamy's kitchen where foreigners would be astonished to see rich legislators, often the owners of great mansions, eating chops and pies in the very place where they were cooked.

More important to his career were the exclusive clubs of St. James's. As a man of the mercantile class Wilberforce would never make his way in the Commons without full acceptance in the clubs. He told his sons of the first time he entered Brooks's, a greenhorn from the provinces who knew scarcely anyone above the rank of private gentleman or baronet; how he stood uncomfortably watching the faro, a complicated form of betting on cards which was not a game of skill like whist or piquet, and started gaming from shyness more than pleasure. An acquaintance who had not heard of his election to the club came in and said he was glad to see him. 'Oh, don't interrupt him,' said old George Augustus Selwyn, the well-known wit, who was keeping the bank and thus stood to win the most. 'He is very well employed.' 'They considered me as a fine fat pigeon whom they might pluck,' chuckled Wilberforce.[5]

It was a good story. But in fact he was not elected one of the three hundred members of Brooks's until 7 April 1783 when he was fully established as a popular young man about town, though it is possible he had not played faro. He was already a member of White's across the street, since 1781: later he became its chairman.[6] By his own account he joined Boodle's too, probably in 1782, but his name does not appear in the club archives. His election to White's proved that he had overcome Society's contempt for fortunes founded in 'Trade' rather than the land,

and the elderly Duke of Norfolk did not think it odd to lose £100 to the merchant's son.[7]

Little Wilberforce won his welcome to the luxurious clubs and the great private houses because he was rich, he was amusing, could turn a *bon mot* and had a keen sense of the ludicrous;[8] and he could sing. The Prince of Wales is said to have told the Duchess of Devonshire he would go anywhere to hear Wilberforce sing. George Selwyn was leaving the House of Commons one night when he passed a roomful of young men 'who made me, from their life and spirit, wish for one night to be twenty. There was a table full of them drinking – young Pitt, Lord Euston, Barkley, North, etc. etc. staging and laughing *à gorge deployée*. Some of them sang very good catches: one Wilberforce, a M.P. sang the best.'[9]

On another night Bob Smith, Wilberforce and several other bachelors were dining together when someone happened to eulogize a pretty girl, Barbara St. John, the unmarried sister of Lord St. John of Bletso, a college friend. Wilberforce immediately spun a doggerel poem about her beauty, ending with the appalling pun:

'And if you continue to torture poor us
'You are no longer Barbara but barbar*ous*.'

The youthful host of the evening, a bachelor, drew himself up. 'That,' he said, 'is the mother of my children.'[10]

Like all his set, Wilberforce went to the Opera, the play, the pleasure gardens of Vauxhall and the rotunda at Ranelagh. A comic sidelight on this period comes at third hand through Thomas Babington Macaulay, whose Journal for 16 May 1850 records a conversation when Wilberforce's son Samuel, then Bishop of Oxford, was one of six guests at breakfast at Macaulay's London house: 'I was surprised at the Bishop's telling us that his father when young used to drink tea every evening in a brothel – Not, said his lordship from any licentious purpose – His health alone would then have prevented that. But it was the mode among young men. I should have kept the secret from my son, if I had been Wilberforce senior, and from the public if I had been Wilberforce junior.'*[11]

Wilberforce was healthy enough for a brothel: however, as he recalled to a correspondent more than a quarter of a century later, 'I certainly did not then think as I do now but I was so far from being what the world calls licentious that I was rather complimented in being better than young men in general.'[12]

He took rooms within a stroll or chair-ride of St. James's where dinner at Boodle's would be laid on the table at 4.30; supper at 10.45, with the bill brought at midnight. The evening would pass while

---

* Macaulay first wrote 'old Wilberforce' but crossed *old* out and inserted *sen*.

bottle after bottle went round. Cards and gaming were allowed upstairs but men went to Boodle's primarily for drinking and chat.[13]
They went to Brooks's for gambling, and by 'gambling and playing
with dukes and earls I might have ruined myself,' Wilberforce comments. Fox lost all his money. Pitt gave up gaming because he sensed
its fascination. Wilberforce never was a compulsive gamester and he
abandoned hard play for high stakes after a night when he had won
a big sum and noticed the annoyance of the losers, who as heirs or
younger sons could not really afford to play. His heart was too tender
to fleece his friends.

And thus he became friendly with the former Lord Chancellor
Camden, famous as a champion of the constitution and of the liberty of
the subject. Wilberforce recalls: 'When I was a young man, he was a
very great one. He took a great fancy to me because, I believe, when all
the others were wasting their time at cards or piquet we would come
and talk with him and hear his stories of the old Lord Chatham, etc.
On this account he talked very freely to me and talked amongst other
things on religious subjects. . . . His views were very dead, he quite
disbelieved Religion.'[14] He also disliked mimics. Wilberforce obediently stopped, although even in middle age he could not quite resist
mimicking public figures when chatting about them.

Twenty-five Cambridge contemporaries took over a club in Pall Mall
run by a former coffee-house owner named James Goostree, and Pitt
and Wilberforce dined there nearly every night they were in London.[15]
'Dear Wilberforce,' runs an undated note, 'We have just escaped with
our lives from Brighthelmstone – and dine to-day at Goostrees. Yours,
W. Pitt. Thursday.'[16] Wilberforce knew the hidden side of Pitt, his
warmth and kindliness and good humour. He could detect when Pitt's
coldness to strangers sprang from shyness, when from pride, or a
deliberate protective pose. He thought Pitt the 'most truly witty man'
he ever knew, whose wit was both systematic and controlled.[17]

'The Gang,' as Wilberforce called the Goostree set,[18] deepened other
friendships which would be important in his life. Henry Bankes had
already inherited the fine Dorset mansion of Kingston Lacey, where his
descendants still live, and the ruins of Corfe Castle and its town, the
family's close borough for which he now sat. Nearly three years older
than Wilberforce, Bankes was a slow speaker with an engaging
modesty but a 'stiff and lofty' way of carrying himself: he once con-
vulsed the House when leaving his place to go to the Opera, wearing
the usual full court dress, by accidentally impaling his neighbour's wig
on the tip of his sword and marching out unawares.

Edward Eliot, Pitt's particular friend, was another west countryman.
Precisely one year older to the day than Wilberforce, he was eldest son
of the Member for Cornwall, a politician of some consequence. Wilberforce's nickname for Edward Eliot was Sir Bull,[19] possibly because of

his sexual prowess, for when Eliot married, Wilberforce would no longer use it, 'particularly when I recollect the epigram on which your old name was founded.' This epigram cannot be identified; perhaps a dog-Latin tag. In 1785, after overcoming his father's opposition, Eliot married Lady Harriot Pitt, the sister nearest to William Pitt in age. Harriot wrote to her mother on 1 June 1781: 'To-day I dine with Lady Middleton and in the evening I go to Vauxhall with Lady St. John. William, Mr. St. John, Mr. Wilberforce and Mr. Eliot are to attend us, so we count on a prosperous party.'[20]

This Lady Middleton was the mother-in-law of Wilberforce's Johnian friend Gerard Edwards, a member of the Goostree 'Gang' but not yet in Parliament. Edwards had married Diana Middleton when both were very young, an odd match because her father, Captain Sir Charles Middleton, Comptroller of the Navy, and his wife were Evangelicals. Their country home was in the parish of Teston in Kent, where the parson was a former naval surgeon of the Captain's, James Ramsay, who had been ordained for the West Indies and hounded out of his living on St. Kitts because of his compassion for the slaves. Apart from once meeting Ramsay at dinner at the Edwards', when the conversation turned to negroes, Wilberforce knew little about slaves or Evangelicals: he does not appear to have followed up the enquiries into slavery which he had made during the Hull election, and he had long drifted from the Evangelical fervour which had characterized his uncle and aunt, William and Hannah.

Yet under his gaiety and his indolence and his intense ambition, his friends detected an almost indefinable difference about him, which he barely understood himself. Gerard Edwards (by no means an Evangelical like his father-in-law) put it into light-hearted words in a note on a December day, probably in 1782: 'I was very sorry not to be able to pass a few more remarks with you in Bond Street, but I was engaged to meet my lawyer to give him instructions to make my *Will*, lest I should break my neck in hunting unprepared. My friendship for you, therefore, may be troublesome to you as I have taken the liberty of having you as a Trustee. I thank the gods that I live in the age of Wilberforce and that I know one man at least who is both moral and entertaining. I think I almost make love to you. The truth is that I think myself extremely happy on the subject. . . .'[21]

Wilberforce played his small part in the bringing down of Lord North's Government on the snowy evening of 20 March 1782, and was invited with Pitt and other young men to attend a meeting with Fox and Shelburne who were forming a new Administration under Lord Rockingham, although each of the three mistrusted the others.

Pitt refused a subordinate position and Shelburne could not get a boy of twenty-two into the Cabinet. Wilberforce circulated on the fringe of

2

the Ministry and attended Fox's dinners. Gossip predicted a junior post
and a peerage, and in Cambridgeshire the antiquary William Cole took
down one of the twenty alphabetical manuscript volumes in which he
was compiling notes for an *Athene Cantabrigiensis*. Cole, who died from
gout at the end of that year, waxed a little satirical: 'Wilberfosse: 1782.
A promising young Fellow of St. John's and much caressed by the
patriotic faction. The Marquess of Rockingham patronizes him and
says that he is one of the most judicious scholars he knows.'[22]

Rockingham died in July, and when the King offered the premiership
to Shelburne, Fox resigned with most of his group. Pitt became
Chancellor of the Exchequer and Leader of the House. Wilberforce
hoped ardently for office, however junior, but he represented no
interest, was owed nothing, and he had resolved never to ask his bosom
friend a favour for himself; personal distinction, not greed for a fat
sinecure, was his primary object.[23] Like Pitt he was driven by genuine
love of his country. Unlike Pitt he was vague in his political views. He
had a further limitation, which Lord Carrington could recall long afterwards: 'Mr. Pitt had a great kindness towards him. . . . But as to his
fitting office his careless and inaccurate method of doing business
rendered him wholly unfit for it.'[24]

Carrington ignores one factor which irritated and handicapped the
young Wilberforce: eye trouble. This was not solely short-sightedness.
The eyes sometimes stopped him reading altogether. The symptoms
are never sufficiently described at this stage of his life for any modern
diagnosis, but within a few years the doctors may have unwittingly
inflicted further distress on his eyesight; and never realized what they
had done. Equally unwittingly, the doctors in saving his life would
seem to have been responsible for deepening the streaks of indolence
and muddle in his character.

In the light of these well-meaning medical efforts his future achieve-
ments are astonishing.

CHAPTER THREE

'Bravo, Little Wilberforce!'

Lauriston House stood in five and a half acres on the south side of Wimbledon Common, a few hundred yards from Rushmere Pond. Built in 1724 in the squarish Queen Anne style with tall windows on both the main floors, it had been bought in 1752 by Wilberforce's Uncle William who later commissioned Angelica Kauffman, who arrived in England in 1766, to paint the staircase walls and ceiling.[1] He left it to his widow for life but she preferred Blackheath; Wilberforce had had Lauriston House at his disposal since 1777, and on the forming of Shelburne's Administration it came into its own.

Wimbledon, eventually to become synonymous with genteel suburbia, was in 1782 a village of rural Surrey. In spring and summer, rather than sleep in Downing Street Pitt preferred to cross Westminster Bridge after business, or when the House rose, and ride down the Kingston road some seven miles to Wilberforce's, who rearranged the house to provide eight bedrooms, one of them known as 'Pitt's Room' through many changes of ownership until the building's demolition in 1958. 'Eliot, Arden and I will be with you before curfew,' runs an undated, unsigned note from Pitt, 'and expect an early meal of peas and strawberries. Bankes I suppose will not sleep out of Duke Street but he has not yet appeared in the
House of Commons
Half-past four.'[2]
Arden was Solicitor-General. His very prominently deformed nose was said to be the result of a childhood collision with a tin trumpet.

Often Pitt and Wilberforce were alone. Pitt could unburden himself and shake off the *gravitas* which masked the Chancellor of Exchequer's youth.[3]

Before Pitt came into office they had spent the Easter vacation at Bath and Brighthelmstone (Brighton) but Wilberforce could not drag the Chancellor from his desk that summer of 1782, so he planned a Continental tour with St. Andrew St. John. He abandoned it when the death of the elderly Manners caused a vacancy for Hull's other seat. Wilberforce's cousin and near-contemporary Henry Thornton contemplated standing against David Hartley. Wilberforce told his college friend Lord St. John on 30 July, that if they proceeded to a contest, 'which I am told is their intention, I fear my friends will think it necessary for me to begin foyning* also; in whose opinion right or wrong, in matters of these sort it is generally prudent to acquiesce. I sometimes however indulge myself in far more pleasant prospects and I am not without all hope of enjoying myself on the Banks of Windermere, where if my good star should draw your Lordship it will give me the greatest pleasure to shew you some of the more *Private Parts* and more retired beauties which are likely to escape the notice of a traveller.'⁴

In the event, David Hartley came in unopposed because Thornton refused to bribe electors; he won a tough bye-election at Southwark later in the year without bribery. Wilberforce went to Windermere, where he had a seven-year tenancy of a small early eighteenth-century manor house, Rayrigg, on the lakeside a short distance from the town.

His love never wavered for the Lakes, 'the Paradise of England', where a man might enjoy (if it did not rain) the 'most delicious scenery in the most delicious weather'. He boated on Windermere, rode or walked over the passes and up some of the fells, empty then save for shepherds and their flocks, for he liked occasional solitude. Too much of it bored him. St. Andrew St. John therefore stayed at Rayrigg for weeks, and later came Mrs. Wilberforce and Sally, with Mrs. Joseph Sykes and her young daughter Marianne, who thought Mr. Wilberforce 'riotous and noisy';⁵ while the beautiful Duchess of Gordon, the political hostess, whose extra-marital affairs made her no suitable caller on Mrs. Wilberforce, sought him out on her road to Scotland.

The Lakes brought Wilberforce one of his greatest friendships, although presumably they were first acquainted in the Commons, with Colonel John Pennington. Nearly fifty years old to Wilberforce's twenty-three, and heir to Muncaster in Eskdale with its splendid view of Scafell from the terrace, he had entered Parliament the previous year and would shortly be created Lord Muncaster in the Irish peerage to satisfy a promise made to his father by the Duke of Grafton. Lord Muncaster, though a fervent admirer of Pitt, became an infrequent attender at the House, and it was to 'My dear Muncʳ' that Wilberforce wrote his longest series of letters on current affairs. Muncaster always replied: 'My dear Wilber.' This seems to have been Wilberforce's name to such few of his intimates who did not follow custom in using surnames among close friends. No one, except perhaps his mother and Sally, called him 'William'. Even his wife would call him 'Wilber'.

In mid-autumn 1782 Wilberforce went south to King George's

---

* Contesting, duelling (physically or with words). A quite commonly used word at the time.

favourite watering place of Weymouth, where he announced to Eliot in Cornwall: 'Me voici, as the French say, and so mild is the climate and so calm and clear is the sea that on this very fifteenth day of October I am sitting with my window open on its side and am every moment wishing myself up to the chin in it. . . . Come then, my Genius, come along. . . .'[6]

Dull constituency matters took a little time on his return to London for the brief December sitting of Parliament. 'Mr. Wilberforce presents his compliments to Mr. Hartley and begs leave to inform him that Mr. W. did himself the honour of calling in Golden Square this morning to speak with Mr. Hartley. . . .'[7] It was all a matter of a Memorial from the grocers of Hull. 'Mr. W. is not much versed in matters of this sort,' but would join whatever course his fellow Member preferred. It was more amusing to do a good turn for young Thomas Thompson who now managed Wilberforce and Smith. Some difficulty with Customs had made Thompson despatch a discreet gift in a right direction, while Wilberforce obtained the interest of his friend the Chancellor. Pitt replied: 'I wrote a letter to you this morning, which I put in my pocket, and which has somehow or other escaped from thence, the Lord knows where; in consequence of which I send this duplicate to tell you that (thanks to the Chestnut Colt) Mr. Thompson will I doubt not, have the preference he wishes from the Commissioners of the Customs, application having been made to them for that purpose.'[8]

During the Recess the Administration had negotiated peace with France, Spain and the United States against a backdrop of British sea victories which made the Treaty look an untimely surrender. Early in 1783, while rumours spread that Fox would unite with his enemy North to turn out the unpopular Administration, Pitt invited Wilberforce to second the Address to the Crown to ratify the Treaty. He spent a bad night contemplating the ordeal of speaking to a full House, and walked nearly four hours after church on Sunday before going to Townshend's house to hear the Address read.[9]

Tommy Townshend, one of the two Secretaries of State, wrote to the King that the Address was '. . . very well seconded by Mr. Wilberforce.'[10] They were beat by sixteen on 17 February. Four nights later, after a debate in which Wilberforce spoke again and listened admiringly to Pitt ('one of the finest speeches ever delivered in Parliament') they lost by seventeen. Shelburne resigned, but the King, in his dislike of 'this unnatural and factious coalition' of Fox and North, refused to send for the figurehead who would serve as their First Lord of the Treasury, the Duke of Portland. On the following Monday Pitt told Wilberforce at dinner in Downing Street that the King had offered the premiership to himself, not yet twenty-four: 'the very surprising propositions', as Wilberforce described them in one of his brief diary entries.[11] Pitt declined. Wilberforce never suggests that Pitt sought his opinion. While the King held out against Fox, whom he detested for his politics and his ruin of the Prince of Wales's morals, the ministerial vacuum lasted throughout March. Wilberforce's eyes were bad but he kept abreast of every ebb and flow of the crisis until at last on March 31 the King gave way. Pitt resigned the Chancellorship and the Fox–North coalition came in.

Pitt threw off the cares of office. Wilberforce dined with him in Downing Street on the evening of his resignation, went to Goostree's for supper, and to bed at 3 a.m. Pitt and other friends followed him down to Wimbledon. 'Delicious day,' recorded Wilberforce. 'Lounged morning at Wimbledon with friends, foyning at night, and ran about the garden for an hour or two.'[12] Pitt was a boy again: the Angelica Kauffman murals resounded to the laughter and shouts and horseplay of the man who had delivered such grave and memorable orations in Parliament. The friends 'foyned' with singlesticks in the garden, they 'foyned' verbally indoors, and probably this was the time when Pitt got up early to sow Wilberforce's flower beds with bits of the dress hat belonging to Dudley Ryder, the future first Earl of Harrowby who had become a close friend of both. Pitt, Wilberforce and Eliot went boating and fishing on Rushmere Pond. Lord Shelburne, down in Wiltshire, heard of 'some little excess' which had alarmed the neighbours in Wimbledon. Nobody had made ill-natured reflections upon a mere frolic: 'It has only been pleasantly remarked that the rioters were headed by Master P.— late Chancellor of the Ex—, and Master Arden, late Solicitor-General.'[13]

In London Lady Harriot Pitt regaled her mother with Wilberforce calling early to get a ticket for a duchess's ball, 'which circumstance rather prolonged our breakfast'; and how a few days later Wilberforce and Lord Mahon, Pitt's first cousin, were laughing so noisily 'that I really hardly know what I write'.[14]

Wilberforce relished London's small, close-knit world of politics and fashion. He pushed his puny and protesting frame through a round of gaieties interspersed with some quite hard exercise: he thought nothing of walking five hours and then drinking much wine at Goostree's while playing faro with Pitt, Bankes and Camden's son, John Pratt. After dining with Henry Dundas another day they talked the whole night through. He saw Kemble in *Hamlet* and Mrs. Siddons, and the opera, and played cards at the Duchess of Portland's when the Prime Minister entertained friends and opponents at Downing Street. Henry Dundas, who controlled much of the Parliamentary representation of Scotland and would hold high office and become a thorn in Wilberforce's side, took him to sup with Mrs. Siddons. He danced till the small hours at Lady Howe's ball.[15]

Parliament rose and Wilberforce went down to Yorkshire, where his mother and his witty but neurotic sister made him irritable: the society of Hull seemed insufferably provincial and the charm that delighted his friends wore thin. But he refused Pepper Arden's invitation to Durham for the assizes. Arden had a rich niece, rather past her bloom, who had rejected the advances of John Villiers because he was merely an earl's second son. Arden told Wilberforce: 'If you now had taken a fancy to her, which I do believe you would for she is really a charming girl in every respect, I know of no objection but one, and that is her age, which to use her own expression to Villiers and me, for she is very open, is "half past five".'[16] Wilberforce preferred to remain what he called 'that isolated unproductive and stigmatized thing, a Batchelor'.[17] And the niece was a silly girl because Villiers eventually succeeded to the Clarendon earldom and estates.

In September Wilberforce met Pitt and Eliot at Bankes's place in Dorset, where the others teased him with having nearly shot Pitt as they walked partridges.[18] The three friends crossed to France, to Rheims, but they had forgotten to obtain proper letters and their only introduction turned out to be 'a very little grocer'. They were rescued by an abbé after a police official had reported them as suspicious characters, and soon they enjoyed the hospitality of the Archbishop, Talleyrand's uncle, a jolly man who played billiards.

They followed the court from Paris to Fontainebleau where a laughing Marie Antoinette twitted them about the grocer of Rheims, and Wilberforce thought Louis XVI in his clumsy boots so strange a being that it was worth going a hundred miles to see him. They met Lafayette and Benjamin Franklin. In an arrogant English way Pitt, Wilberforce and Eliot always made up a supper table with compatriots instead of mixing with courtiers who spoke only French.[19]

The holiday ended abruptly in late October when a special messenger urged Pitt's return to England, followed two days later by Wilberforce.

The Fox–North Coalition rode high in November 1783, until Fox's India Bill precipitated a political crisis.

A less corrupt method of governing the East India Company's vast possessions had been sought for years, but this Bill would transfer the Company's rule, patronage and property to a Board of seven commissioners sitting in London, who would all be Coalition supporters. Pitt and his friends saw Fox gaining enormous patronage and with it unlimited power over British politics, whatever happened in India. They therefore assailed the Bill night after night.

Wilberforce could not match Pitt's lucidity and debating skill but he ranged his eloquence at Pitt's side. 'Mr. Wilberforce,' runs the record of the debate for 20 November, 'answered Mr. Burke, and with humour and ability compared the seven Commissioners and eight Directors to seven physicians and eight apothecaries come to put the patient to death *secundum artem.* After laughing with this idea he became more serious and said he wished that in the end, if the present Bill passed, we might not see the Government of Great Britain set up in India, instead of that of India in Great Britain.'[20]

By now the City, and many of the provincial squires and merchants who in political terms constituted 'the people', were so alarmed by the implications of Fox's India Bill that Lord North's former party manager, who had deserted him, drew up lists of M.P.s who might support an alternative administration. The India Bill passed the Commons but the Lords threw it out on the direct intervention of the King. Next day, 18 December, the King dismissed the Coalition and sent for Pitt, who became Prime Minister at twenty-four in a hostile Commons.

Pitt did not dissolve Parliament while his support in the country grew, for many Members would return whenever he dissolved and he needed to strengthen his position in the House. All his friends rallied to this work. Three days before Christmas Wilberforce drove about London, paying calls. 'So your friend Pitt means to come in,' sneered Mrs. Crewe. 'Well, he may do what he likes during the holidays, but it will only be a mince-pie Administration, depend upon it.'[21] Wilberforce attended a meeting of Pitt's supporters and then spoke very well, in his own opinion, when the House sat on Christmas Eve. He ate Christmas dinner at Lord Chatham's and spent Boxing Day closeted with Pitt, and on New Year's Day 1785 he posted to Cambridge to canvass for Pitt, who had decided to stand for the University at his re-election upon taking office.

In the first quarter of 1784, while Pitt fought for his administration's survival, Wilberforce was his close confidant and frequently his host, with a rôle more important than junior office. As he recalled long after: 'For weeks and months together I have spent hours with him every morning while he was transacting business with his secretaries. Hundreds of times, probably, I have called him out of bed. . . . As he knew I should not ask anything of him, and as he reposed so much confidence in me as to be persuaded that I should never use any information I might obtain from him for any unfair purpose, he talked freely before me of men and things, of actual, meditated or questionable appointments and plans, projects, speculations, etc., etc.'[22]

The House defeated Pitt's motions but the King retained him and the people sent a flow of petitions in his support. He had Wilberforce's melodious voice and rapid delivery to help repel the Opposition; the Member for Hull was playful and sarcastic at Fox's expense and praised the patriotism of Pitt: 'Mr. *Wilberforce* pursued his panegyric for some minutes in terms of great eloquence.' On other nights he would be grave, expounding the correctness of the King's dismissal of 'despotic faction,' his refusal to bow to a 'corrupt majority' who aimed to destroy the Crown's prerogative and the Constitution's balance.[23]

But the extraordinary situation in which the King and his Minister defied the House – 'the quarrel between the House of Commons and the Crown'[24] as Wilberforce termed it – could not long continue before Pitt must go to the country.

Wilberforce began to harbour an astounding ambition, which would equally serve Pitt, the King, and his own career, yet looked too absurd even for Pitt's private ear: to return to the new Parliament as one of the Knights of the Shire for Yorkshire, the two most powerful County Members in England.[25]

The two Members for Yorkshire represented the entire county except for York itself and thirteen older boroughs. Sir George Savile had called Yorkshire a 'little kingdom', and because the new industrial towns such as Sheffield, Leeds, Halifax and Bradford had no representatives yet, Savile and his fellow-Member, Henry Duncombe, had been the Parliamentary mouthpieces for manufacturers and artisans as much as for squires, yeomen and their labourers.

The vast expense of a contest had usually enabled the county magnates to settle the nomination among themselves, though they could not put up a candidate disliked by the squires and the mercantile men; but the thirty-five-year-old Earl Fitzwilliam who had inherited the Rockingham lands and political interests, and the Dukes of Devonshire and Norfolk (both great landowners in Yorkshire) were all Whigs who had supported the late Coalition. Wilberforce would not get in as their man. The squires, however, whose favour would be essential to any candidate hoping to oppose them, would look askance at a merchant's son, for as Wilberforce recalled in later life: 'Contemptuous ideas of merchandize were then very strong.'[26]

The highly respected Savile had retired in November 1783, dying soon after, and his nephew by marriage, Francis Foljambe, disappointed those who had returned him unopposed. Meanwhile the influential Yorkshire Association which had grown up a few years earlier, to petition for constitutional reform, had split when its leader Christopher Wyvill, and the county member whom it supported, Henry Duncombe, came out for Pitt. Wilberforce knew Wyvill slightly; he was a clergyman who had succeeded to his family estate at Constable Burton near Bedale by marrying a cousin.

Wyvill determined that Yorkshire should join the counties and boroughs who were addressing the Throne for a General Election, which ought to give Pitt a majority; and he secured sufficient names for the High Sheriff to summon a General County Meeting of Freeholders for 25 March 1784, to be held in the extensive grassy yard of York Castle. The Whig lords and other supporters of Fox and North were equally determined to persuade the County Meeting to reject such an Address, since rejection by Yorkshire could be disastrous for Pitt. Wilberforce feared that these Whigs had an unbreakable hold on

2*

the county but he left London on 21 March to do all he could for Pitt, whom he kept in ignorance of any ambition beyond a speech to the County Meeting.

Wilberforce counted for little in the city of York: the only resident of consequence whom he knew was a Canon of the Minster, William Mason, a native of Hull, a man of letters and minor poet whose plays were performed at Covent Garden. Mason had sided with Pitt and lost London friends 'by detesting Charles Fox and his vile Coalition'.[27] Wilberforce stayed with him, and they helped Wyvill to draft the Address. It attacked the late Coalition for attempting to seize such vast patronage by the India Bill that the balance of the Constitution and the liberties of the people would have been destroyed; it congratulated the King for dismissing his former ministers, and called for an appeal to the nation. Wyvill's intense desire for Parliamentary reform was expressed by a passing reference to 'the present manifold defects of our National Representation'.[28]

As hundreds of Freeholders converged on York, Wilberforce walked alone in the countryside, knowing that his speech at the Meeting next day could decide his future.[29] Thursday, March 25 came bitterly cold and windy with hailstorms. Wilberforce watched as each great lord alighted at the Castle Yard from his magnificent coach and four: the Duke of Devonshire and his brother, Lord John Cavendish, Member for the City of York, who had been the Coalition's Chancellor of the Exchequer; Lord Surrey, the Duke of Norfolk's son and heir, who had renounced the Roman Catholic faith to enter politics but claimed in his cups to be a good Catholic still. Three other earls supported Fox against the Crown, while the Earls of Effingham and Fauconberg opposed him, a curious reversal since Fauconberg was a descendant of Oliver Cromwell, and Fox of Charles I.

More than 4,000 Freeholders assembled. A wooden canopy protected the speaker from the weather while a table served for platform. The *York Chronicle* described the County Meeting as 'more numerous and respectable than any ever held upon a similar occasion.' Nearly all those present had landed estates or mercantile riches. The mob was not admitted.[30]

From mid-morning until late afternoon the Freeholders listened without heckling or tumult, a tribute to their political consciousness as much as to the gravity of the national crisis, though the cold may have frozen some ardour; the wind certainly prevented those at the back from hearing several of the speakers. Duncombe spoke in Pitt's favour. His colleague Foljambe would have spoken against Pitt and the Address, but his betters did not put him up. Twelve long speeches included a memorable attack by Lord Fauconberg on his fellow-aristocrats when he asked sarcastically: 'Whether it is George III or Charles Fox to reign? . . . Let the people decide.' By now the 'people' were wearying, having listened in the open for over five hours: it was after 4 p.m., nearing dinner time, and during Lord Surrey's criticism of Pitt many drifted away.

As Surrey stepped down a slender, small young man mounted the table briskly. Few knew him by sight. His voice immediately reached to the farthest edge of the crowd. A newspaper reported: 'Mr. Wilberforce made a most argumentative and eloquent speech, which was listened to with the most eager attention, and received with the loudest acclamations of applause. It was indeed a reply to every thing that had been said against the Address; but there was such an exquisite choice of expression, and pronounced with such rapidity, that we are unable to do it justice in any account we can give of it; we shall however give a few particulars: He said these persons, of whom he was one, that opposed the undue influence of the Crown, should be the foremost in support of its Prerogative, to shew they acted from principle not from party spirit, or personal antipathy to any Minister. He dwelt long on the odious East-India Bill; read several clauses of it. . . . He alarmed the Freeholders, by shewing that it might have been a Precedent for exercising the same tyranny over the property of every Man in the Kingdom. . . .'

Among the audience stood James Boswell, on a journey between Edinburgh and the ailing, aged Samuel Johnson. Boswell does not mention Wilberforce in his diary nor in the long account he wrote for the *Edinburgh Advertiser*, but eight years afterwards Wilberforce heard from Boswell's own lips what he had said to Henry Dundas at breakfast five days later: 'He saw a little fellow on a table speaking – a perfect shrimp. But presently the shrimp swelled into a whale.'[31]

Wilberforce arraigned the Coalition 'with keen severity, as a union of men who disagreed, not only as to the American War, but had never agreed in any one principle; who mutually imputed to each other the loss of America, and one of whom had been branded by the other with the most ignominious epithets. . . .' He was still speaking after nearly an hour when a King's Messenger who had ridden express from London alighted at the Castle Yard, pushed through the crowd and handed up a letter to Wilberforce. Wilberforce paused, read it, and announced with Pitt's authority that Parliament had been dissolved that very day.

Pitt had dated his letter in Downing Street at 12.30 the previous afternoon. Considering the distance to York the King's Messenger had staged a most dramatic moment, and Wilberforce was able to conclude with an earnest appeal for support to Pitt in the imminent General Election. 'We are now to decide upon a solemn crisis; you are now upon your trial; we have heard much of an Aristocracy; if there is any such bias on your minds, let no little consideration weigh against the public interest. If you approve of those Ministers who have fought, and

I hope I shall say have conquered, in support of the Constitution, come forth and honestly say so. – That distinguished person who has done so much in your cause will esteem your approbation his best reward.'

The final speaker, Lord John Cavendish, failed to offset Wilberforce. After some confusion while the High Sheriff could not decide the show of hands, the Meeting approved the Address. The Foxite Freeholders then dispersed to a public dinner at Bluitt's and the Pittites to the York Tavern in St. Helen's Square, the chief coaching inn.

Despite gratifying shouts of 'We'll have this man for our County Member', Wilberforce had far to go to displace the Foxite Foljambe as fellow-candidate with Duncombe. Pitt's letter, indeed, when exhorting Wilberforce to hold their friends together and tear the enemy in pieces, had suggested quite another name.

Events again played into his hands. The more the Pittites drank into the night, the more their unity cracked.

Tory clothiers who had thrown over Lord North had little in common with Whig aristocrats who had thrown over Fox, while many Freeholders who wanted Pitt's victory disliked Wyvill and the Yorkshire Association. A violent quarrel broke out between Buck, Recorder of Leeds, and another. As the diary of Walter Spencer Stanhope of Horsforth records laconically: 'Much squabbling later. Some people drunk.'[32] Men began to say they could not agree and had better separate.

Wyvill and Wilberforce restored harmony. When the party broke up at midnight, intending to disperse from York next mroning, Wilberforce leapt to his feet, saying he would now sleep in peace because their glorious triumph had not been tarnished by a quarrel among themselves. At that, Harry Pierse of Bedale, his hand on the doorknob, impulsively turned round and shouted, 'Bravo, little Wilberforce! And I tell you what, I will give £500 towards bringing you in for the County!'[33] The room echoed with cries of 'Wilberforce for ever! Wilberforce and Liberty!'

Fauconberg during the dinner had tentatively commented to Wilberforce that the rival groups might unite behind him, and at Pierse's impulsive shout the Pittites agreed not to disperse to their homes but to meet again. However, the morning apparently had brought a hangover, for Walter Spencer Stanhope opened proceedings by emphasizing the expense of a contest.

Richard Milnes interrupted him; they had £10,000 in that room alone, he shouted. Milnes being only a young man of Wilberforce's age they hesitated still, until the Fitzwilliam party sent across an offer of a compromise: that the present Members should be returned, a Pittite Duncombe and a Foxite Foljambe. The meeting promptly rejected this as a Fitzwilliam dictation to the County, and adjourned. The same evening a much larger, and prolonged, Pittite meeting closed the breach between those who favoured and those who hated the Yorkshire Association; they united to back Wilberforce and Duncombe. Over at Bluitt's Fitzwilliam and the Cavendishes chose William Weddell and Foljambe.

Duncombe would get in anyway but Wilberforce must secure his retreat. When General Elections spread over several weeks many Members kept funk-holes in case they lost the seat they coveted. Pitt had Bath if Cambridge University turned him out, as Wilberforce expected; Fox sat for a Scottish seat until his Westminster victory was confirmed after long scrutiny. Wilberforce therefore must win Hull again. He drove over at once for a whirlwind canvass in continued cold weather and falls of snow, with his cousin Samuel Thornton standing also, against a David Hartley more unpopular than ever as Fox's friend. Wilberforce came top of the poll at a cost of £8,807. During the triumphal chairing some snowballs flew, and believing that this aggression arose from resentment at his preference for the county seat he dashed from the chair to his old nursery window and won over the mob below.*

At Hull Wilberforce had to pay all but £1,000 of the bill.[34] For the County election Wyvill had secured such massive subscriptions that neither candidate was allowed to give a penny. Peers who could sway voters wrote Wilberforce letters of support: Lord Hawke and Lord Grantley would be absent but 'certainly wish well to your nomination and your meeting',[35] while Lord Fauconberg expressed his dislike of Foljambe 'and Mr. Waddle'.[36] On April 3 the nomination meeting's show of hands looked plainly in favour of Duncombe and Wilberforce, but their opponent's supporters demanded a poll, to begin four days later.

It was not, however, the heavy excitement of the canvassing tour through Sheffield, Barnsley, Halifax and Leeds, with speeches in cutlers' halls and cloth halls, which ensured the Pittite victory; but the county-wide network of committees which the Yorkshire Association had set up several years earlier to project a stream of petitions to Parliament for constitutional reform. Wyvill put this, one of the earliest constituency organizations in British politics,[37] behind Duncombe and Wilberforce, who afterwards tried to express to Wyvill 'some little of what I felt towards you for all your zeal and friendly assiduity in my support'.[38]

The two candidates returned to the York Tavern on Tuesday afternoon, 6 April, the eve of the poll, knowing that the canvass promised them 11,000 votes and more, against a mere 2,500 for the Foxites,

---

* It may have been here with the family beside him (and not at York as Croker states in the *Quarterly Review*, April 1838) that among the huzzas and shouts of 'Wilberforce for ever!' someone yelled, 'And Miss Wilberforce for ever!' Sally shouted back: 'Not Miss Wilberforce *for ever*, I hope.'

who had been unable to improvise an organization to rival that of the Association. That afternoon, after Lord John Cavendish and his Foxite colleague had lost the York City election, the Whig lords acknowledged that a County poll would be an expensive waste of money. At 8 p.m. a message came from Bluitt's.

Wilberforce exulted in all directions. 'Keep your Cornish Boroughs to yourself,' he scrawled to Edward Eliot, who presumably had jocularly offered one of his father's pocket boroughs if Wilberforce were beaten for Yorkshire. 'I'll have none of them. I am or at least shall be tomorrow (our enemies having this evening declared their intentions of declining a Poll)

Knight of the Shire for the
County of York.'*39

---

* On the letter Eliot scribbled 'Ld. J. Cavendish and Sir W. Milner are beat at York. Pitt for ever!' And also the current State of the poll (on the day of receipt presumably, 8 April) for the long drawn-out Westminster contest. Fox was then at the bottom.

CHAPTER FOUR

Unexpected Horizons

'I think . . . nothing can be more essential than a Yorkshire meeting,'
wrote Fox to William Windham many years later. 'The Meeting in that
County certainly gave the tone *for* us in the year 1780 and *against* us in
the year 1784.'[1] Wilberforce's success resounded through the nation as
the General Election continued, and helped to sway it for Pitt.

His election brought immense prestige to the new Member for
Yorkshire. He became a man of some consequence; which, according to
a Fitzwilliamite member of the Sykes family at Hull, soothing the angry
earl, had been his chief aim all along: to force Pitt to reward him. 'He
has always lived above his income and it is certain he is now in expectation of a lucrative post from Government of which he is in the utmost
need.'[2] Sykes misconstrued the aim and exaggerated the financial
plight, but not the ambition, though no office came. Instead Wilberforce was pre-eminent in the second line, behind ministers and the
scions of great houses. He emerged as one of the leading debaters,
Wraxall in his famous Memoirs marvelling that such an ugly
undignified little man could speak 'with great perspicuity as well as
fluency.'[3]

His oratory owed much to the peculiar sweetness and exceptional
range of his tones, which a Parliamentary reporter described in Wilberforce's middle years as 'so distinct and melodious that the most hostile
ear hangs on them delighted. Then his address is so insinuating that if
he talked nonsense you would feel obliged to hear him.'[4] His speeches
were not contrived; generally he spent little time preparing elegant
phrases but talked from the top of his mind in a conversational style
more like that of a much later age. Contemporaries therefore never
judged him equal with Burke or Windham, though warmth of feeling,
expressed in face and gestures as well as by voice, offset the lack of
marshalled argument. He spoke fast (and was often misreported)[5] and
he had a gift which was rare, and rather awkward in a politician, for
exploring both sides of a question.

Wilberforce could summon up great pathos, and had also a devastating

31

sarcasm. Afterwards he seldom employed it but in the first sessions of the Parliament of 1784 he attacked with a sarcasm and a bitterness that made Fox hate him for a time.[6]

Pitt won complete ascendency in the Commons. Wilberforce and Bankes opposed him occasionally,[7] which made no difference to mutual affection; sometimes Pitt encouraged their independence. Wilberforce supported Pitt's desire for Reform and classed himself as 'a hearty and zealous well wisher to a Parliamentary reform',[8] which indeed he was bound to be, as one who had been returned for the County through the efforts of the Yorkshire Association, though his feelings were genuine. Fox mischievously brought forward this question of Reform in June 1784 before Pitt was ready, knowing that the Minister and the two Members for Yorkshire would dare not prevent him doing so for fear of being called reactionary.[9] The Commons debated, noted and shelved; and the first short Session ended.

Wilberforce planned for his mother and sister and himself to spend next winter on the Franco-Italian Riviera for Sally's health, together with her delicate cousin Bessy Smith, Bob Smith's sister who afterwards married the West India merchant Henry Manning (she died young: it was his second wife who was mother of Cardinal Manning). The three women and a maid would travel in the coach and Wilberforce in his post-chaise. He wanted a travelling companion and invited an Irishman living in Yorkshire, who declined. Wilberforce had no one else in mind when the family went to Scarborough, Yorkshire's fashionable watering place, for the summer season. Here he fell in with the huge Isaac Milner, his former usher at Hull Grammar School who now was a tutor of Queen's College, Cambridge. On impulse, apparently, Wilberforce invited Milner, all expenses paid.

They knew each other slightly, and Wilberforce did not discover until long after that his grandfather had once considered Milner as a tutor for a possible grand tour. Though a clergyman, like every college Fellow Milner appeared 'very much a man of the world in his manners', so Wilberforce recalls, 'and was lively and dashing in his conversation', with no sign of the Evangelical influence of his brother Joseph. Wilberforce would not have invited an Evangelical.

After some delay in securing leave of absence from his college, Milner accepted. Wilberforce meanwhile had stayed briefly in the Lake District, where it rained and his eyes were too bad for reading and his reader failed to arrive at Rayrigg. No one amusing passed through. He stood leaning his forehead against the chimney piece in gloom and wretchedness.[10]

He spent his twenty-fifth birthday at York races; the County Members were always stewards and he owned a racehorse. He then went south to catch up on the immense correspondence of a Member for

Yorkshire, which included a letter from the persistent Pepper Arden, just married, again urging matrimony. Now that Bankes, Pretyman and himself had 'shown you the way, I hope that you will be the next of Pitt's friends who will enter that state of Marriage. I think it absolutely necessary for your health as well as happiness, and I beg you will seriously attend to the advice.'[11]

The party crossed[12] from Dover to Calais on 20 October 1784 (seasick on a smooth sea) and drove through France to the Rhône at Lyons, where they put their carriages on boats, and Wilberforce wrote Pitt a 'picturesque and poetical epistle'.[13] They toured the Marseilles region and the Côte d'Azur and settled at Nice, a favourite winter haunt of the English.

On and off through France, Wilberforce and Milner argued. They had begun it right back in Scarborough. The name of James Stillingfleet, rector of Hotham, north of the Humber, happened to be mentioned, who was an Evangelical and an assiduous pastor. Wilberforce dubbed him a good man who took things too far. Milner, to Wilberforce's astonishment, disagreed. 'No,' he said. 'How does he carry them too far?'[14] They argued the point on the sands.

Wilberforce having buried the impressions formed by the Wimbledon uncle and aunt during his childhood, supposed that their views usually were held only 'by vulgar or at least uninformed enthusiastic persons'. His friends reckoned Wilberforce moral and religious; an opinion which he afterwards used as an evidence of the low standards of religion in the 'fashionable' world of the early 'Eighties. To humour him Pitt and Arden sometimes came to Wimbledon parish church. In London he had a sitting at the Essex Street chapel founded by Theopilius Lindsey, the 'father' of modern Unitarianism, one of the few clergy of the Church of England who had shown courage and principle enough to resign their livings on abandoning, like so many, a belief in the divinity of Jesus Christ. Lindsey still preached the Christian ethic and read the Church services, and his chapel attracted several eminent men: Wilberforce rated him London's only fervent preacher,[15] since the Evangelical or 'methodistical' preachers he had enjoyed with the uncle and aunt were now outside his pale.

In the chaise across France Wilberforce ridiculed to Milner the views of 'Methodists' such as the beloved aunt and her brother John Thornton the banker, or Thomas Thompson, manager of Wilberforce and Smith at Hull, whom one day he would describe as 'a true Christian as well as a man of great acuteness and tried integrity'.[16] Thompson's wife was a granddaughter of the Kentish rector who wrote the great Methodist hymn, 'All Hail The Power of Jesus Name'. Wilberforce also fired off 'sceptical notions' of the sort labelled Socinian then and Unitarian now. In no sense was he an atheist. Lindsey's disciples at Essex Street worshipped the Deity, a benevolent Providence in some way also the judge of man's actions, but they rejected Christ's divinity, the Christian view of the Atonement, and the authority of Scripture.

Milner, in contrast to his usual jocularity, would reply: 'Wilberforce, I don't pretend to be a match for you in this sort of running fire. But if you really wish to discuss these topics in a serious and argumentative manner I shall be most happy to enter on them with you.' Milner was a mathematician and scientist with a brilliant mind. If he never quite fulfilled the promise of his Cambridge examiners' verdict, *Incomparabilis*, he 'possessed in a marvellous degree,' so a pupil recalled, 'the faculty of bringing abstruse subjects within the reach of ordinary and youthful comprehension.'[17] He brought this gift into use with Wilberforce; for though nothing about Milner's habits or behaviour at that time suggested the 'serious' Christian, he had a clear grasp of the intellectual heart of Christianity. His explanations made little impact during the outward journey or on the Riviera.

At the turn of the year Wilberforce received a long, affectionate letter from Pitt, begging him to be back by the day he would introduce Parliamentary Reform.[18] It was decided that the ladies should stay in the sunshine while the men returned overland to England. Shortly before they set out again in the chaise, Wilberforce casually picked up a book which belonged to Bessy Smith. It had been given to her mother by William Unwin, an Evangelical clergyman in Essex, son of the Unwins who had befriended and inspired the poet Cowper. Wilberforce leafed it over and asked Milner's opinion. Milner replied: 'It is one of the best books ever written. Let us take it with us and read it on our journey.'

The journey had its adventures. Climbing a frozen hill in Burgundy Milner and Wilberforce walked behind while the postboy led the horses. The chaise slipped on the ice and pulled the horses back, the boy could not hold them and it would have toppled over a precipice had not Milner held it by sheer brawn until the horses regained their footing: it was a chaise, not a heavy coach, and contained only the baggage; nevertheless none but a man of Milner's bulk could have saved it.

In calmer moments they read Bessy's book. It was *The Rise and Progress of Religion in the Soul* by Philip Doddridge, who published it in 1745 and died in 1751. He is still remembered for hymns such as 'O God of Bethel', 'Hark the Glad Sound', and 'O Happy Day that fix'd my Choice'. He was a Dissenter, one of the old Independents like Isaac Watts who, indeed, suggested to him the plan of the book. Doddridge had taught his students in Northamptonshire the great Reformation doctrine of Justification by Faith before Whitefield and Wesley recovered it for the multitudes in Hanoverian England. His book is a reasoned, elegant exposition suited more to parlours than to market crosses or hillsides; Doddridge was a man of broad sympathies and charm, whose published *Travel Letters* were popular in polite society. One of his surviving friends told Hannah More, 'he never knew a man of so gay a temper as Doddridge.'[19]

Wilberforce's subsequent accounts of his long drawn out Conversion or perhaps Re-dedication to the Christ of his boyhood faith – are somewhat contradictory, but he gives a prime share to his reading Doddridge's book with Milner.[20] They possibly looked up relevant passages in the Bible, for Wilberforce says he adopted his religious principles from 'the perusal of the Holy Scriptures and . . . the instruction I derived from a friend of very extraordinary natural and acquired powers.'[21]

By the time Milner deposited him on 22 February 1758 at Number 10 Downing Street, Wilberforce had reached intellectual assent to the Biblical view of man, God and Christ. He thrust it to the back of his mind and resumed his social and political life.

Two subjects dominated the Commons in the next four months before Wilberforce returned to the Continent; Parliamentary Reform and Ireland.

Wilberforce and Wyvill helped Pitt draw up his modest ill-fated Reform Bill, wherein the thirty-five boroughs with the smallest electorates would be bought up by consent, giving eventually seventy-two seats for redistribution around London, Westminster and those counties which included the large new towns of the Industrial Revolution. The Bill would also widen the franchise slightly. Wilberforce's speech on 18 April 1785 showed that he already disliked the politics of 'Party'. By destroying the rotten boroughs, he said, which were used by powerful men to control votes in the House, 'freedom of opinion would be restored, and Party connexions in a great measure vanish'. He wanted to see a time when he could come into the House and give his vote 'divested of any sentiments of attachment'. Since he already did this, he was speaking in general terms of a time when no Member would vote to please a patron.[22]

Wilberforce never thought himself a Party man, certainly not a Tory; the Tories when he entered the House adhered to North. Wilberforce was a Pittite because he believed in Pitt's policies, as against an Opposition which he reckoned 'as unprincipled and mischievous as ever embroiled the affairs of any country'.[23]

He was prepared to act independently of his constituents. The Irish Propositions, by which Pitt hoped to soothe discontents and alleviate economic distress, included one clause which West Riding woollen manufacturers believed would unfairly strengthen the competition of Irish textiles. They demanded that their County Members should oppose it. But Wilberforce viewed the Propositions as a whole: a contented Ireland would advance, not retard the West Riding. During the all-night sitting on 12 May Lord Surrey accused the two Members of suppressing a petition against the Propositions, whereupon '*Mr. Wilberforce* rose to satisfy the House as to his conduct in respect to the fact stated by the noble lord; and . . . was proceding to state, in glowing terms, his sense of gratitude to his constituents; but overcome with sensibility, the fatigue of having sat in the House so many hours, and with the pressure of infirmity, he sunk upon his seat.'[24]

He did not relish constituents' displeasure. 'Your letter,' he wrote to a Mr. Clapham two days later, 'has laid a weight on my mind which I cannot remove; the situation of a Representative disagreeing with his constituents on a matter of importance must ever be a situation of pain and embarrassment; it is particularly distressing in my case, for they with whom I have the misfortune to differ are persons whose utmost efforts were exerted to place me in the honorable situation I now fill. . . .' He showed in detail why he disagreed, and why 'Ireland has a claim to be regarded by us in a very different light from any other nation.'

He concluded a long letter: 'However you may conceive my opinions erroneous, I trust you will believe that I am not influenced by private friendship or Party spirit, but that I am actuated by a sincere regard to the public good.'[25]

In the end Pitt's Propositions came to grief in the Irish House of Commons.

Wilberforce left England again with Milner in late June 1785 before the end of the Session. This time he was not sick on the Channel but conversed with the Captain, Sharp, who assured him 'there never was a week when quantities of wool and live sheep were not smuggled over to Boulogne.' Wilberforce passed the information to Pitt: 'There is no way by which you can render yourself more popular, and more deservedly so amongst my clothiers than by putting a stop to this practice, of which Sharp declared himself an eye-witness.'[26]

Joining his mother and the girls at Genoa, they proceeded by easy stages through Savoy and Switzerland, where Interlaken's famous view, a cloudless Jungfrau, entranced Wilberforce. And mile after mile the two men read and discussed the New Testament in Greek, until Mrs. Wilberforce complained of too infrequent visits to the other carriage; she irritated him anyway, he admits.[27] Wilberforce pressed 'my various doubts, objections and difficulties',[28] which Milner answered one by one. Slowly intellectual assent became profound conviction: 'I got,' Wilberforce recalled in old age, 'a clear idea of the doctrines of Religion perhaps clearer than I have had since, but it was quite in my head. Well, I now fully believed the Gospel and was persuaded that if I died at any time I should perish everlastingly. And yet, such is man, I went on cheerful and gay.'[29] In early September they settled for nearly six weeks at the resort of Spa in the Austrian Netherlands. He joined in the cosmopolitan junketings with the old abandon except that he would not go to the theatre or travel on Sundays; he sang glees and catches, he danced, he ate and drank his way through the enormous meals with which society passed much of its time.

In this he was behaving as a man of the world. In the 1780s the gulf between the 'worldly' and the 'serious' lay wide. The 'serious' man might be as cheerful as John Thornton and his home happy like Lauriston House in the days of Uncle William and Aunt Hannah; but serious men did not go to the theatre or to balls as Wilberforce did at Spa. The thought obtruded on him therefore that 'in the true sense of the word I was not a Christian,'[30] and he began to sicken of the profligacy and selfish luxury of the rich, of the hours they wasted in eating. By September 28, when he congratulated Edward Eliot on his marriage to Lady Harriot Pitt, who brought no fortune, he said he had never before felt such contempt of money. If a man has enough it 'seems to me a perfect madness'[31] to torment himself to get more.

By the third week of October 1785 the 'great change', as he afterwards termed it, had driven Wilberforce to rise early each morning to pray. Soon spiritual anguish engulfed him. His friends might regard him as a moral man but the futility and selfishness, the 'shapeless idleness'[32] of the past appalled him. 'I was filled with sorrow. I am sure that no human creature could suffer more than I did for some months. It seems indeed it quite affected my reason; not so as others would observe, for all this time I kept out of company. They might see I was out of spirits. . . .'[33]

His crisis bears the stamp of a classic Christian tradition. Again and again the rebirth of a soul in confrontation with Christ has involved pangs of spirit – Augustine, Luther, Cromwell, Pascal, Bunyan; each refer to darkness preceding dawn. For Wilberforce, the crisis hung on the dilemma that if he became a Christian he must be fully at God's disposal; and then he would become the odd man out in his circle, might lose his popularity and friends, perhaps must abandon political ambition. He had to choose between Christ and the world. He wanted both.

Lady Harriot Eliot wrote to her mother Lady Chatham from Downing Street on 10 November 1785: 'In the evening we were agreeably surprised by a visit from Mr. Wilberforce who is come home remarkably well.'[34] Out of her sight the anguish continued as he blanched at his ingratitude to God, fought his pride, and struggled to yield his stubborn will.

By late November he had decided that if he would live for God he must withdraw from the world. He wrote to several friends and especially to Pitt, warning him that he could no longer be in any sense a Party man; and that he intended to go away by himself. The letter is lost but it does not seem to have shown clearly how fast he was becoming what his set would call 'a Methodist'. On 2 December he received Pitt's long reply, full of kindness and without hint of flippancy, but written in alarm that 'You are nevertheless deluding yourself into principles which have but too much tendency to counteract your own object, and to render your talents useless both to yourself and mankind.' Since Wilberforce had assured him the character of religion was not gloomy, why then, asked Pitt, 'this preparation of solitude, which cannot hardly avoid tincturing the mind either with melancholy or superstition?'[35] Next day they had two hours uninhibited discussion at Wimbledon. Pitt failed to reason Wilberforce out of his new convictions. Neither did Wilberforce convert Pitt, too absorbed in politics, he supposed, to give much thought to religion.

Wilberforce felt that if he were not to go out of his mind, he must confide in a spiritual counsellor. Though he had read the Bible and Pascal, and Butler's *Analogy*, at Pitt's suggestion,[36] and had sermon-tasted the Evangelicals he once despised, and put himself to humiliations such as travelling between Wimbledon and London by stage coach instead of a chaise, he remained in a tumult of emotions and hopes. He turned to his boyhood hero, John Newton, now sixty years old and Rector of St. Mary Woolnoth in the City.

To posterity Newton is honoured for 'Glorious Things of Thee Are Spoken', 'How Sweet the Name of Jesus Sounds', 'Amazing Grace', and many other hymns; and as a possible original of Coleridge's Ancient Mariner. The fashionable world of 1785 looked at him and other Evangelicals with the contempt, suspicion and ignorance that Soviet Russia reserves for its Jewish and Christian Believers. This explains Wilberforce's 'ten thousand doubts' about making the approach to Newton; the precautions taken to prevent whispering among his friends; the plea to Newton for secrecy, the walking twice round Charles Square, Hoxton, before he could persuade himself to knock at the door of Newton's home, more than a mile from his church, at the appointed time.[37]

Newton did not disappoint Wilberforce, who found 'something very pleasing and unaffected in him'. Still humorous and quaint yet with the mark of sainthood, the old ex-sailor, ex-lecher, ex-slave trader was not one to be grim towards a young man of fashion; nor to be surprised at questionings and doubts and the lack of any sudden, total shaft of spiritual illumination. His own conversion had been even slower.

Newton calmed and guided Wilberforce. More especially he urged him not to cut himself from his present circles or to retire from public life. Some words Newton wrote to him nearly two years later may well echo what he said in his Hoxton house that 7 December 1785: 'It is hoped and believed that the Lord has raised you up for the good of His church and for the good of the nation.'[38] Wilberforce did not follow Newton in all his theology but he followed him in this, and the advice was all the more important in that most Evangelicals shunned public life as worldly. Therefore to Newton, as well as to Pitt, belongs credit for keeping Wilberforce in politics.

The old parson sent him away – he was going down to Pitt's newly-bought country house, Holwood in Kent – with a less burdened conscience. Wilberforce did not climb clear from his slough of despond at once. Weeks passed before glimpses of the peace and love of God opened into a more settled serenity. 'But then after a while,' as he put it in old age, 'I was comforted.'[39] The awareness of being redeemed, bought at great price from the slavery of sin, became stronger than the sense of guilt.

At Easter-tide, in mid-April, he drove by post-chaise into Essex to stay with William Unwin, rector of Stock near Billericay, the donor of Doddridge to Bessy Smith's mother, for teaching and advice. Soon after sunrise on Easter Day, 1786, the Member for Yorkshire took to the fields to pray and give thanks 'amidst the general chorus with which all nature seems on such a morning to be swelling the song of praise and thanksgiving.'[40]

CHAPTER FIVE

Between Two Worlds

The gaiety of spirit which had delighted his friends returned in good measure. Throughout 1786, however, Wilberforce was a man between two worlds, between the old life and the new, trying to find himself, seeking the purposes for which Providence had called him, and outlets for the compassion which welled up inside.

The Warren Hastings case had begun to dominate the political scene. At the end of April 1786 Lobby rumour reported that Wilberforce and Bankes had urged Pitt to send the Resolutions for Impeachment to the Lords,[1] but early in June Wilberforce spoke against impeachment on the first charge, the conduct of the Rohilla War. Pitt did not regard the question as a straight issue between Opposition and Administration, more a matter of Members' consciences, though personally he defended Hastings. On 13 June, during Fox's passionate attack over the second charge (the deposition of the zemindar of Benares) Wilberforce saw Pitt 'listening most attentively to some facts which were coming out . . . he paid as much accurate attention to it as if he was a juryman'. Fox sat down and Philip Francis rose. Pitt turned in his seat and beckoned to Wilberforce. They went behind the Speaker's Chair.

Pitt said: 'This really looks very ill, does it not?' 'Very bad!' They returned to their places, and Pitt delivered his famous speech throwing up Hastings' defence.[2]

During that summer Session of 1786 Wilberforce moved two measures, the first being somewhat bizarre. The previous year the eminent Leeds surgeon, William Hey, had given Wilberforce as County Member the heads of a Bill to advance the cause of anatomical research and to outflank the body-snatchers. Most anatomy teachers could obtain corpses only by surreptitious encouragement of (in Hey's words) 'a set of the greatest rascals whose nightly employ is to commit depredations, sometimes on the living and sometimes on the dead'.[3] By an Act of 1752 the bodies of executed murderers might be

40

sold for dissection; these were comparatively few and Hey suggested that the Act should be extended to cover criminals executed for any other capital offence: 'Why should not those be made to serve a valuable purpose when dead, who were a universal nuisance when living?'

Wilberforce also had been with the rising lawyer Samuel Romilly, whose pamphlets and later his Parliamentary work make him the greatest of the earlier advocates for humanizing the penal law. Romilly had drawn his attention to the fact that women convicted of high or petty treason were still sentenced to be burnt, though by custom they were hanged first. In this year of 1786 20,000 people watched the burning of Phoebe Harris outside Newgate.

Wilberforce, in his first attempt at humanitarian reform, lumped the two subjects together, to produce a 'Bill for Regulating the Disposal after Execution of the Bodies of Criminals Executed for Certain Offences, and for Changing the Sentence pronounced upon Female Convicts in certain cases of High and Petty Treason'. He had the Law Officers vet the Bill. Seconded by Walter Spencer Stanhope, who had succeeded him as Member for Hull, it passed the Commons but was thrown out by the Lords in July 1786 after Lord Loughborough, chief justice of the common pleas and future Lord Chancellor, had castigated 'raw, jejeune, ill-advised and impracticable' schemes for altering the execution of criminal justice.

Wilberforce believed that Loughborough opposed him out of political enmity against a friend of Pitt. To support the burning of women seems indefensible, even for a still brutal age, but Loughborough claimed that an execution with horror made a stronger impression 'than mere hanging', while additional pain was not inflicted; the hangman never lit the fire until life appeared extinct.

Loughborough took firmer ground in throwing out the dissection clause. Wilberforce approached the matter purely from the surgeon's view; but the law had little interest in the surgeon. It held dissection to be a strong deterrent to murder because the prospect terrified criminals, partly owing to popular belief that the 'resurrection of the body' at the Last Day meant the flesh rising to life from the churchyard, and partly because of the hope of 'resurrection' of another sort – the revival of an apparently dead malefactor if his friends could intervene between the gallows and the surgeon's knife. Wilberforce proposed extending dissection to those executed for rape, arson, burglary and robbery. Loughborough asked whether it were wise to put these offences on the same level as murder 'by making the deprivation of the rights of burial a common and an ordinary consequence of every conviction of almost every capital offence.' It would, he said, increase murders committed in the course of burglaries.

Wilberforce's inexperience as a humanitarian had muddled him into linking separate causes. The burning of women, offensive already to many, was a straightforward issue; but not the disposal of criminal corpses. If these had been delivered privately to anatomists the Wilberforce Bill might have won support, but a surgeon often dissected publicly as a spectacle; in the prevailing indecorum the Bill's provisions would have widened the horror. Anatomical studies, however, remained crippled; body snatching continued. As late as 1816 Wilberforce looked back wistfully to this Bill's defeat, when asking Sidmouth as Home Secretary to intervene in the case of a respectable young doctor fined for obtaining a corpse; he urged the finding of a solution to anatomy's impasse. In 1829 the murders committed by the Edinburgh body-snatchers, Burke and Hare, highlighted the problem until it was resolved in 1832 by the Act for Regulating Schools of Anatomy.[4]

Wilberforce's other measure of 1786 expressed his continued interest in Parliamentary Reform.

His radical, rather peculiar friend Lord Mahon (Pitt's brother-in-law) had drawn up a Bill to provide that all Freeholders entitled to vote in a constituency should be registered, nor merely scrutinized by the returning officer at the poll; and to provide that the poll be taken simultaneously at different places, not at the County town over several days. When Mahon succeeded as 3rd Earl of Stanhope on the death of his father he asked Wilberforce to take over the Bill. Wilberforce invited Duncombe to second it, for he liked to 'consider my colleague and myself a sort of double headed shot that came out of the piece together and must continue for ever inseparable'.[5]

They introduced their Registration Bill on 15 May 1786. The largest County needed it most, yet Yorkshire disliked the clause which would concentrate the entire poll on one day, and on 29 June Duncombe wrote gloomily to Wyvill, for whom Registration was a pet project: 'Our Bill at last has passed the Commons and I confess I shudder at the thoughts of what it may produce.' He believed it a 'very ill-advised measure' and admitted he supported it against his conscience. He rather hoped it would fail in the Lords; otherwise 'the odium we have incurred by it will . . . be quite decisive of our fate at the next General Election. With regard to myself I am not much anxious concerning that event but I think the County couldn't have a more honest nor so able a Representative as my Colleague. . . .'[6]

The Lords threw out the Bill, since neither the high Tories nor many Whigs liked it. Stanhope urged Wyvill on 8 July: 'If you should see Wilb. or Duncombe or should have occasion to write to them, try to make them persevere.'[7] Wilberforce leaned more to Stanhope's enthusiasm than to Duncombe's gloom, but suggested that the proposal for a Register of Electors be separated from any change in the current method of polling. Wyvill wanted to increase the number of polling places in Yorkshire: Wilberforce wanted to drop that clause, which he believed might hinder a revised Registration Bill he wanted to bring forward at the right moment.[8]

After 'so much broiling and bustle in Parliament Street',[9] Wilberforce got away to the North in early July, and joined his mother, sister and the Sykeses at Scarborough.

His mother had heard alarming rumours that he had turned melancholy mad, since he no longer went to theatres (or even to the Ancient Musick since he did not wish friends to think that the musical Wilberforce was merely bored with plays).[10] His cheerfulness, his consideration and the absence of quick temper surprised her. Certainly he displayed a 'serious' outlook which echoed the Clapham religion she disliked, but his sunny nature no longer clouded over in her company; it warmed her. Mrs. Sykes remarked: 'If this is madness, I hope that he will bite us all.'[11] The new influence on his character showed all the more impressive in that 'the sea and heat and dust so disordered my eyes that I have seldom known them so bad.'[12]

From Scarborough the Wilberforces settled near Nottingham for a long stay with the Samuel Smiths at their almost new mansion, Wilford House. Here over the next two months Wilberforce set out to educate himself, to recover ground lost by indolence at Cambridge. He read history, economics, literature, philosophy, even some science. The idle undergraduate began to disappear into a politician much better read than many; in Montesquieu, Adam Smith, Blackstone, Locke and Pope, and with a particular delight in Dr. Johnson: when Boswell came out some years later Wilberforce read him at breakfast, lingering long after he knew he should be getting down to work.

At each well-staffed home where he stayed, for a month or two every summer until marriage, he would study nine or ten hours a day: breakfasting alone, taking his walks alone, dining with the host family and other guests but not joining them in the evening until he 'came down about three-qarters of an hour before bedtime for what supper I wanted'.[13] 'You would be as much the master of your own hours,' he wrote to a friend when inviting him to Rayrigg, 'as I claim myself the privilege of being whenever I quarter myself in another's man's house, and that is saying a good deal, let me assure you.'[14] Some years he quartered himself in the rectory of his college friend Cookson, for whom he had obtained a living in Norfolk; often he stayed with Gisborne, now a squarson at Yoxall Lodge in Staffordshire. He sat at their feet.

When travelling he would enquire about conditions, listing questions in a notebook; 'I should ask for facts rather than opinions,' he advised a young friend later who wondered how best to observe on tour.

Wilberforce trained his alert, inquisitive mind:[15] only towards the end of his career, burdened by poor eyesight and other infirmities, did he become notorious in his circle for depending on information supplied by others.

He never eradicated the butterfly mentality acquired at Cambridge. Concentration flagged; he jumped from subject to subject; the pleasures of conversation deflected him. Despite intelligence, a quick grasp of facts, an excellent memory which he now took steps to improve, he might have made no mark without a demanding cause. A country squire's duties, had his inheritance been larger and more compact than the scattered estate near Harrogate and Hull, which agents could manage, would have tied him when the cause required flits around England. Besides, he was not a true countryman; he loved the country for beauty and for quiet, yet when taken round his tenant farms he remarked: 'My land, just like anyone else's land.'[16] However he made a good landlord, who in the coming time of depression would actually lower rents though he needed the extra money; for which William Hobson, Robert Herdsman, Jonathan Laybourn and other worthy Yorkshire farmers were presumably grateful.[17]

He worked hard to strengthen not only mental but spiritual stamina. He saw himself embarked on a pilgrim's progress, not idling in green pastures beside still waters; for with awareness of God's presence went a sense of 'the strictness and purity of the Christian character',[18] a desire not only to do good but to be good, never content with attainment.

The Bible became his best loved book and he learned stretches by heart. He made rules for himself – and generally broke them, for in venial matters he had a charming inability to live up to his rigid standards; foibles and failings kept him human. In great matters he did succeed in mastering his passions and ambitions, not without struggle and time. Milner had embarked seriously on a pilgrim's progress too. They mutually agreed to act the candid friend and 'exercise the *invaluable* practice of telling each other what each party believes to be the other's chief faults and infirmities'.[19] It would seem that Milner did most of the telling. At one time each promised to pay a forfeit, presumably to charity, on breaking one of their rules;[20] but when the guineas began to drift rapidly from Wilberforce's pocket, already lightened by philanthropies, this ploy seems to have stopped.

Wilberforce adopted rigorous self-examination. A warmly impulsive man who lived for the moment, fully absorbed in action or conversation, he gave little thought beyond it until he withdrew to the seclusion of his room. With paper in front of him he would examine his motives, conduct and words. He had kept a brief daily journal; now he would often insert spiritual comments or confession, agonizing over his sins with almost illegible scrawling. From time to time, especially on Sundays, he would take a loose piece of paper and examine himself more fully and add extempore prayers. What a Roman Catholic confessed orally, Wilberforce, a compulsive note-jotter, wrote down. 'I have often kept written on a small slip of paper,' he informed one of his daughters when advising her on spiritual improvement, 'a note of my chief besetting sins against which it was especially necessary that I should be habitually watching and guarding; of the chief Christian graces which I wished to cultivate, of the grand truths which I desired to bear in remembrance; and I used to look over the paper at my seasons of prayer or of self-examination.'[21] He generally needed to add further expressions of penitence. He would also list names of friends and relations needing prayer.

These brief daily diary entries and meditations were for his eye alone. They reveal an important side of his character: the attitude of penitence, the self-questioning in the sight of God. But in printing them by the yard five years after his death his sons gave the public a view of their father which lacked perspective, for none of the playfulness of his letter writing obtruded into the diary, nor the exuberance and joyousness which delighted his friends. Though political or social conduct is ruthlessly examined, entries often concern trivial failures. Wilberforce had avoided the grosser habits of the age, and if warm blooded kept himself strictly towards women; nor had he lined his pockets by socially accepted peculations. He certainly had ambition, and the diary reflects his struggle to contain it. More usually as he noted the day's doings, any confession would be of idleness, or 'dissipation' of time, or self-indulgence (by his standards) in food and wine.

A confession which survives among the Bodleian manuscripts provides an example of Wilberforce's private introspections. It illuminates the difficulties of remoulding his character in the image of Christ; and though merely sensual failures are concerned it is moving in its simplicity, disclosing also a little of a time when public men waded through enormous meals and drank themselves stupid.

After dining alone with Pitt, a single thought dominates Wilberforce as he withdraws to his room, takes a sheet of paper and dips his pen: once again, he has fallen to 'temptations of the table' and broken his rules. Sins of the table, however trivial in themselves, 'disqualify me for every useful purpose in life, waste my time, impair my health, fill my mind with thoughts of resistance before and self-condemnation afterwards,' and deflect him from thoughts of God. 'Sometimes it is an excess in wine and sometimes in eating, or in dessert as to-day. May God Almighty forgive me – I see Bob Smith who is influenced by inferior considerations, I see Pitt, too, and others of my friends practising self-denial and restraint in these respects, and if they exceed tis at seasons of jollity; whereas I do it merely from the brutal sensuality of animal gratification.

'I trust I shall better keep than I have done by the resolutions of temperance that I make at this moment: no dessert, no tastings, one thing in first, one in second course. Simplicity. In quantity moderate. . . . Never more than six glasses of wine; my common allowance two or three. . . . To be in bed always if possible by eleven and be up by six o'clock. In general to reform in accordance with my so often repeated resolutions. These are now made in the sight of God, and will I would humbly hope be adhered to. I will every night note down whether have been so or not, and . . . at the end of every week set down on this paper whether in the course of it I have in any instance clearly transgressed.'[22]

He looked at the paper a fortnight later at Bath after stopping at friends' houses on the road from London. He added: 'Arrived last night. On Monday the very day after that in which I had tasted the pleasantness of the ways of religion, I gave in to intemperance and this was the beginning of a week that has been spent in one vicious course or another, leaving my mind at this moment in a state of life-lessness and complete ineptitude to spiritual things.' Even allowing for the hyperbole, his hosts would have been astonished at this secret confession by cheerful little Wilberforce with his happy ways and sparkling talk.

Yet this cheerfulness was not the humbug of a man gloomy at heart who pretends to be happy. In Wilberforce, interior severity helped create the joy which he considered a mark of genuine Christianity. Many years later after Bob Smith (Lord Carrington) had apparently expressed mistrust of joy, Wilberforce wrote to him: 'My grand objection to the religious system still held by many who declare themselves orthodox Churchmen . . . is, that it tends to render Xtianity so much a system of prohibitions rather than of privilege and hopes, and thus the injunction to rejoice so strongly enforced in the New Testament is practically neglected, and Religion is made to wear a forbidding and gloomy air and not one of peace and hope and joy.'[23]

The secret buffetings of the flesh sometimes took even a Catholic form such as putting a stone in a shoe. They were a disciplining of himself for the better service of his Saviour whatever it should prove to be. For Wilberforce wanted to subject not merely his appetites but his politics to Christ: 'A man who acts from the principles I profess,' he told a constituent three years after the conversion, 'reflects that he is to give an account of his political conduct at the Judgement seat of Christ.'[24] This strong sense of accountability was turning Pitt's once easy-going supporter into a new force in British politics.

In the autumn of 1786 Wilberforce, at Wilford, did not want to go to Yorkshire. County Members were expected to junket together through their constituency now and again, patronizing race meetings, balls, and dinners at which they must eat eight or a dozen courses and drink two or three bottles at least, besides proposing, hearing and downing numerous toasts. Once his constituents realized that Wilberforce had turned 'serious' or 'Methodist' they might deride or pity but they would excuse his cutting balls, shying off racecourses and refusing potations; until they realized it, as he pointed out to Wyvill, his behaviour might appear cold and reserved: 'I should excite disgust rather than cordiality.'[25] A friendly, open manner and faithful discharge of Parliamentary duties would not weigh against his cold-shouldering what he called 'jollity and conviviality'. Fortunately Wyvill did not think a progress necessary when the Government was popular and trade flourished. Henry Duncombe had fled to his estate, Copgrove, and Wilberforce gratefully did nothing in Yorkshire except a brief dash to the Sheffield Cutler's Feast, returning to his studies at Wilford.

Study and fasting had increased his usual aches and pains and worsened his eyes. He went over to Leeds to consult Hey the physician and surgeon, already one of his regular political correspondents. Hey was a friend of John Wesley, though adhering to the Established Church when the break came, and thus was in sympathy with Wilberforce's new outlook though their characters contrasted, for Hey lacked humour. He was personally austere, but warned Wilberforce that a poor physique could not stand fasting and 'low living'. He found nothing basically wrong and advised a course of Bath waters.

Wilberforce returned to Hull with his mother and Sally for October before returning south. 'We had the honour of a call from Mr. Wilberforce the day he left Hull,' wrote Kitty King, daughter of an Evangelical merchant, to her brother George at Trinity College, Cambridge, on 1 November 1786. 'I was much shocked to see him, he looks so emaciated and altered – he enquired very kindly and particularly after you and regretted not seeing you, he asked if you was stronger and said he did not know whether it was to be wished, for that a delicate constitution often preserved a young man from many snares and that with *care* they might enjoy all the *comforts* of life; he spoke in a very pretty and feeling manner. There is a prospect of his being a very useful member of society if his life is preserved. He has been very active here in promoting two spinning schools and eight [*illegible*] schools and has left orders with his mother that the church at Drypool which used to have duty only once a month be every Sunday supplied with a faithful minister.'[26]

A 'prospect of being a very useful member of society' had indeed opened.

Shortly before Wilberforce's call on the Kings he had received and answered a letter from Captain Sir Charles Middleton, M.P. for Rochester, father-in-law of his Cambridge friend Gerard Edwards. Middleton suggested that Wilberforce should bring forward in Parliament the subject of the Slave Trade.

Wilberforce in His Prime, 1808
from the etching by H. Edridge; engraved by J. Vendramini, 1809

Captain Sir Charles Middleton, Bt., R.N., afterwards Vice-Admiral Lord Barham from the painting by his wife

Lady Middleton from a self-portrait

CHAPTER SIX

The Cause of the Slaves

Captain Sir Charles Middleton, R.N., M.P., afterwards Admiral Lord Barham,* was one of the two Members publicly regarded as Evangelicals, the other being comic little Sir Richard Hill. Henry Thornton, Wilberforce's cousin and soon to be his closest friend did not yet range himself with the religious interests of his father, John Thornton, whom he secretly despised. Nor was Sir William Dolben, the elderly burgess for Oxford University, more than friendly to the religious revivals.

Wilberforce became fond of the Middletons through friendship with their feckless, extravagant, always amusing son-in-law, Gerard Edwards (afterwards Noel) and now began to look on the old sailor, who at sixty was still in his prime, as almost a second father. He loved their Kentish home, Barham Court at Teston near Maidstone.

Middleton's importance in naval history lay obscured for nearly a century after his death in 1813 but is now widely acclaimed. At the height of the American War he became Comptroller of the Navy and head of the Navy Board, where he reorganized an archaic system of supplies, introduced new guns and new methods of shipbuilding and repair. He tried to eliminate corruption, and resigned in 1790 because Pitt delayed further reforms recommended by a royal commission. By then Middleton had effectively prepared the Navy for the Revolutionary and Napoleonic Wars. His finest hour came at a great age when he was appointed First Lord of the Admiralty in the dramatic circumstances of April 1805 and, as Lord Barham, personally directed the strategy which culminated in Trafalgar.

Lord St. Vincent, who loathed him professionally and personally, dubbed him a 'Scotch pack horse', 'a compound of paper and pack thread'.[1] Middleton (a lowland Scot, first cousin to Henry Dundas)

---

* Pronounced *Bare'*m; not *Bar'*m as the Royal Navy pronounced capital ships named in Lord Barham's honour. The last battleship *Barham* was torpedoed with heavy loss of life in 1941.

3

was certainly dry and shy, though a kindly old salt to his intimates. As a young lieutenant he had fallen in love with his Captain's niece, Margaret Gambier, and married her in 1761 on returning with prize-money won by putting down privateers in the West Indies. He had also put down sodomy, swearing and drunkenness on his ships, the brig *Speaker* and then the frigate *Arundel* – an incredible achievement if his claim be substantiated.

His wife was a notable character, being an accomplished painter and musician, the friend of Reynolds, Garrick, Johnson and Hannah More. Margaret Middleton had become an Evangelical in early life, probably under the influence of George Whitefield, and Middleton said he owed to her perseverance 'all I possess of religion'. Beilby Porteus, Bishop of Chester and then (1787–1811) of London, wrote in a manu-script memoir that 'the great and distinguishing feature of her character was an active and indefatigable spirit of benevolence, which extended even to the brute creation, and which kept her mind so constantly on the stretch in seeking out opportunities of promoting in every possible way the ease, the comfort, the prosperity, the happiness temporal and eternal, of all within her reach that she seemed to have no time left for anything else and scarce ever appeared to bestow a single thought upon herself. . . .'[2] A room at Barham Court was kept for sick cottagers, tramps, discharged sailors or anyone in distress who passed that way.

Barham Court actually belonged to Lady Middleton's lifelong friend 'Mrs.' Bouverie, a rich spinster. When yet girls these two had set up house and easels together with another, now known as 'Mrs.' Twysden, a shadowy, sentimental person. Middleton settled down in this unusual household while on half-pay for eleven years before the American War, and turned the manor farm into a showpiece of the agricultural revo-lution.

A short walk down the hill, past the new orangerie, stood Teston church and the red-brick vicarage occupied by James Ramsay, who had talked about Negroes when Wilberforce had met him dining at the Gerard Edwardses in Curzon Street in 1783. It was not fortuitous that Ramsay held the living. Like Middleton an Aberdonian, this sensitive parson with his sad smile, bluish eyes, rather equine face and nostrils, had been the surgeon on *Arundel*. On 21 November 1759, sixty-four leagues north-west of Antigua, Middleton had ordered Ramsay to board a slaver (*Swift* of Bristol) recaptured from the French after a chase. Plague raged aboard and he never forgot what he saw of the blacks. He was invalided out of the Navy after breaking a thighbone, took holy orders and settled in the island of St. Kitt's as a rector and as medical supervisor of plantations. His horror at corporal punishments of slaves, and his disgust with the slave market when fresh cargoes landed, helped to sway his mind against the whole system. His efforts to ameliorate the conditions of Slavery made him increasingly unpopular with the whites until in 1781, after a spell as Naval chaplain, he accepted Mrs. Bouverie's presentation of the living of Teston. He moved there with his wife and daughter and his black servant, Nestor. 'By robbers torn from his country and enslaved,' so runs Nestor's memorial on Teston churchyard wall, 'He attached himself to his master. . . . His neat dress, his chaste, sober life, his inoffensive manner subdued the prejudice his colour raised. . . . From his humble state he fixed his faith in Christ and looked up to heaven for happiness.'*

Lady Middleton and Bishop Porteus urged Ramsay to write against Slavery. After much hesitation because of what it would bring on his head he published in 1784 a long *Essay on the Treatment and Conversion of Slaves in the British Sugar Colonies*. Convinced that men will not respond to lessons on eternal redemption from those who enslave them on earth, or about heaven when kept in hell, he urged humane treatment with a reasonable prospect of freedom, which he admitted could not come at once without chaos. He proposed steps to total Emancipation, and suggested that free labour would yield more profit to plantation owners.[3]

His intention was 'to convince and conciliate, not to inflame', but his book produced a storm of paper abuse in the Caribbean and angered the West India lobby in Britain. The *Monthly Review*, however, discussed it in friendly tones reflecting the current view of the Enlightenment that Slavery and the Slave Trade, like pain in surgery or childbirth, were deplorable necessities for which no answer had been discovered. The reviewer complained that Ramsay advocated the abolition of Slavery yet seemed a friend to the Slave Trade. Ramsay, horrified, immediately wrote a second, shorter book, *An Inquiry into the Effects of Putting a Stop to the African Slave Trade, and of Granting Liberty to the Slaves in the British Sugar Colonies* (1784), which attacked the Slave Trade for its revolting 'degree of barbarous cruelty and oppression'. He propounded a thesis that the best way to abolish the Slave Trade was to civilize Africa; ships now carrying slaves would transport free immigrants to work in good conditions in the West Indies. Sugar might in fact be grown in Africa itself. He added: 'The improvement of Africa is a compensation which we owe for the horrid barbarities we have been instrumental in procuring to be exercised on her sons.'[4]

This second book by Ramsay is almost ignored by historians yet had very considerable influence on Wilberforce and Pitt, especially Ramsay's insistence that Britain owed compensation to Africa.

Wilberforce may have read neither of these books on their publication in 1784. Two years later, when he drew close to the Middletons as a fellow-Evangelical, and dined or conversed at their house in Hertford Street or Sir Charles' official rooms in Somerset House, 'Africa'

* As Nestor died in December 1787, aged 36, his epitaph must be one of the earliest public references to colour prejudice in England.

was their atmosphere. He always maintained that his concern began with hope of improving the condition of slaves in the West Indies. He passed next to the state of Africa, and only then to the Slave Trade.[5] The three strands were already intertwined in the thinking of the 'Testonites', as Hannah More called them. Wilberforce also saw much of John Newton at this period, who always brought in some remorseful reference to his time in the Trade[6] and spoke of the African coast where he had once been 'a servant of slaves'.

Right to the end, Africa had a large place in Wilberforce's thought. 'My grand arraignment of this most detestable and guilty practice, the Slave Trade,' he said in a public speech of 1819 when the Trade, killed by Parliament twelve years since, was only too much alive, 'is because it is chargeable with holding in bondage, in darkness and in blood, one-third of the habitable globe; because it erects a barrier along more than 3,000 miles of the shores of that vast continent, which shuts out light and truth, humanity and kindness.'[7]

In July 1786 the Middletons called an informal conference at Teston by inviting Bishop Porteus of Chester, a Virginian by origin who hated Slavery and all its excretions such as the Trade, to meet Benjamin La Trobe, a leader among the Moravians, the sect made famous by Count Zinzendorf. The Moravian Brethren were the only missionaries among the slaves. La Trobe fell ill on the night of his arrival – probably the onset of cancer – and lay for fifteen weeks at Teston Vicarage slowly worsening but able at first to impart much information. The Middletons sent for his wife and one of his sons, Christian Ignatius La Trobe, who on returning from teaching music at a Moravian college in Germany had become a Moravian minister and now was about to become Secretary of their missions. They stayed at Barham Court the entire period.[8]

Another guest now came to Teston Vicarage, a young red-headed clergyman of St. John's College, Cambridge named Thomas Clarkson. Clarkson's Cambridge prize *Essay on the Slavery and Commerce of the Human Species* had just been issued in 1786 by Ramsay's Quaker publisher, who sent him a copy, yet so scattered were opponents of the Trade that Clarkson had never heard of Ramsay or even of Granville Sharp, whose winning from Lord Mansfield in 1772 the Somersett judgement (that English law does not recognize Slavery; therefore a slave who sets foot in Great Britain becomes free) is often regarded as the effective starting point of the Anti-Slavery movement in England. Ramsay invited Clarkson to spend a month at Teston, giving some help in the parish.

At dinner one afternoon at Barham Court Clarkson renewed publicly his vow, made privately by the wayside near Ware as he rode up to London, to devote himself to the cause. He was thus the first to offer his whole time. Ramsay had his parish; Porteus, back in Chester, his diocese. Middleton had the Navy Board, and the Quaker merchants in the City who had been pioneers in Anti-Slavery had their businesses, and Granville Sharp his philanthropies, intellectual pursuits, and music. Clarkson left Teston with the intention of stirring up public opinion by distributing copies of his Cambridge Essay.

Public opinion alone would do little. Ramsay and Middleton must have long realized that only Parliament, or an international treaty ratified in Parliament, could kill a trade important to the economies of Britain, France and Spain; yet even so great a Parliamentarian as Edmund Burke believed Abolition a chimerical hope. Lady Middleton, however, at last forced her husband to face facts, when the Testonites sat round the breakfast table one autumn day some weeks after Clarkson's departure: the conversation is ignored in his two-volume *History of the Abolition of the Slave Trade*, a book concerned primarily with his own part.*

'Indeed, I think, Sir Charles,' Lady Middleton exclaimed, 'you ought to bring the subject before the House, and demand a Parliamentary enquiry into the nature of that hideous traffic, so disgraceful to the British character.'[10]

Sir Charles, who had made two speeches in two years, both on Navy Board subjects, replied that the cause would be in bad hands if he took it up. They considered other M.P.s. Wilberforce emerged a strong possibility and it was then that Middleton wrote to him the letter he received in Hull. Ignatius La Trobe recalls the Captain reading out the reply a few days later: 'Mr. Wilberforce wrote to the following effect; "That he felt the great importance of the subject, and thought himself unequal to the task allotted to him, but yet would not positively decline it; adding, that on his return to town he would pay a visit to the family at Teston, and consult with Sir Charles and Lady Middleton etc. on the subject." '[11]

Wilberforce's letter from Hull is not extant as evidence, for Middleton burned it according to his usual practice;[12] but La Trobe always felt that the honour of launching Wilberforce belonged to Lady Middleton. The Wilberforce biographers quote their father as saying that the Middleton letter was 'just one of those many impulses which were all giving to my mind the same direction'.[13] In 1815, however, La Trobe wrote that when he mentioned the incident 'to Mr. Wilberforce some time ago, he said: that though so many things had intervened that his ideas respecting dates and particular occurrences had become confused, he believed my statement to be correct, and himself to have received the first direct application from Teston.'[14]

Wilberforce duly spent time with the Testonites in Kent in the early

---

* For instance, it skips the entire period of his temporary retirement. For Wilberforce's considered verdict on the book, see References and Notes.[9]

winter of 1786–7. Back in London he called on Ignatius La Trobe at the urging of Middleton, who then forgot to make the appointment, so that when Wilberforce called at Roll's Buildings, Chancery Lane, La Trobe's chambers were being turned out. The two young men sat in the bedroom and the fire smoked. Wilberforce would not let him open the window: 'I can bear smoke better than the tooth-ache!'[15]

He also consulted West India merchants and Members of Parliament and found them open and unguarded as yet. He probably mentioned the subject to Pitt, for in 1806 Wilberforce recalled reading Burke's African Code 'one day in Downing Street, but I did not take it away with me. The plan was drawn up, as much at least as 20 years ago, before the Slave Trade had engaged the attention or investigation of Parliament, a circumstance to Mr. Burke's honour.'[16] The Code aimed to improve conditions for the negroes in the slave ships and on plantations, and to introduce civilization to Africa; Abolition and Emancipation were politically impossible in the foreseeable future, Burke feared, and his Code would be the best substitute.

Shuttling between a villa in Wimbledon and lodgings in London wasted time and money. Wilberforce put up Lauriston House for sale and bought from Philip de Crespigny the nearly new lease of Number 4 Old Palace Yard, property of the Dean and Chapter of Westminster. He moved in at Christmas 1786. He did not find Lauriston House easy to sell; it was still on the market when he slept there the night of 20 May 1787: 'all the furniture is removed and I was fain this morning to wash my hands in a slop basin.'[17]

4 Old Palace Yard stood exactly opposite the King's Entrance to the House of Lords, one of a block of old houses re-fronted in Georgian style near Poets' Corner of Westminster Abbey.[18] The next-door neighbours for most of Wilberforce's tenancy were Henry Bankes on the south and William Eden, Lord Auckland, in the larger house to the north ('very kind and pleasant . . . a most happy family')[19] while Sir William Dolben lived round the corner. The house eventually became solicitors' and agents' offices and was pulled down in 1896, the site being now a grassy plot next to George VI's statue.

There was one little difficulty. Number 4's stables were less than two hundred yards away at the bottom of Abingdon Street but the House of Lords had ordered that no carriages, drays or carts pass through Old Palace Yard during the Session between 1 p.m. and one hour after the House rose. To reach his front door from the stables Wilberforce's carriage had to go round, as he complained with pardonable exaggeration, 'almost by Ranelagh, Hyde Park Corner and Charing Cross'.[20] After three weeks' inconvenience he wrote to General the Marquess of Lothian, Colonel of the Life Guards, and Gold Stick, for a pass. Lord Lothian had no authority to waive an Order of the House of Lords, but evidently forwarded the request since no further complaint appears.

Here at 4 Old Palace Yard, early in the new year of 1787, Thomas Clarkson left a copy of his Essay on Slavery. He called a few days later. Wilberforce received him with open arms. The first discussion between Thomas Clarkson and William Wilberforce is a focal point in the Abolition movement.

Clarkson assumed that Wilberforce had never heard of him until presented with the Essay. It is hardly possible the Testonites had not mentioned him but Clarkson tended to regard himself as prime mover in any undertaking. Thus, though recording that Wilberforce, when thanking him for the gift of the Essay, said he had thought about the subject often and it was near his heart, Clarkson convinced himself that it was he who first supplied details; and he who made Wilberforce aware of Newton. Even more absurd, Clarkson believed he introduced Pitt to the question in 1788, and stuck to the story in old age though confronted with evidence that Pitt and Wilberforce had been negotiating with France on Abolition for several months before Pitt interviewed him. Words which Wilberforce wrote to Zachary Macaulay (in 1811, when they were all trying to get a ship's master suspended for slaving) are echoed several times across the years in Wilberforce's letters: 'Clarkson's conduct . . . is certainly very far from the simple plain proceeding of a fair mind; though I would hope that vanity has more to do with it than any more deeply laid . . . plot.'[21]

Wilberforce never grudged Clarkson the merit of being first in the field, or denied 'the obligation under which all who took part in the Abolition must ever lie to you for your persevering exertions by which you so greatly contributed to the final victory.'* No defects in Clarkson could justify Robert and Samuel Wilberforce's portrayal of him, last of the pioneers alive, as having been a sort of hack to Wilberforce and the Abolitionists. This provoked much ill-feeling and a dreary pamphlet warfare, neatly summed up by T. B. Macaulay in a letter to his sister on 2 January 1839: 'By the bye how curious it is to observe how much more we owe to our enemies than to ourselves. Clarkson has been writing himself down all his life. And then come the Wilberforces, and write him up. He made himself ridiculous by over-rating himself. They have made him a person of prodigious importance by under-rating him.'[22] They made it up in the end.

In the early months of 1787 Clarkson called each week at Palace Yard to exchange information and evidence. He suggested that Wilberforce summon like-minded friends for regular meetings, and at the first of them, when Middleton, Ramsay, Sir Richard Hill, Granville Sharp and others were present, he read a paper.

* From Wilberforce's letter of 20 May 1808 (Boston MSS) thanking Clarkson for a copy of his 2 Volume History.

Wilberforce studied Clarkson's evidence and pursued his own researches. At length an inescapable fact confronted him: the high death rate on the 'Middle Passage' between Africa and the Caribbean. Since every dead slave lowered the traders' profit, this high mortality 'speaks for itself. . . . As soon as I had arrived thus far in my investigation of the Slave Trade,' he would eventually tell the House, 'I confess to you, so enormous, so dreadful, so irremediable did its wickedness appear that my own mind was completely made up for Abolition. . . . Let the consequences be what they would, I from this time determined that I would never rest until I had effected its Abolition.'[23] He was harassed in mind by warnings from merchants and planters that he would ruin the West Indies. The alternative, the Trade or ruin, looked dreadful; but he could not believe that Providence, however mysterious his ways, had so constituted the world that the prosperity of one part depended on the depopulation and devastation of another.

Clarkson reported his conferences with Wilberforce to the Quaker merchants in the City. Not knowing about Lady Middleton's initiative the previous autumn they urged him to corner Wilberforce into a clear promise that he would move Abolition in the Commons; this would be their signal for founding a committee to lobby Members and stir up petitions, a form of political pressure at which Quakers excelled. Clarkson promised, but shyness stopped his mouth. It should have been obvious to an obscure young clergyman that no busy M.P. would grant frequent consultations unless he contemplated Parliamentary action, but the rather devious Clarkson plotted with a sympathetic mutual acquaintance, Bennet Langton, an immensely tall, rather lazy Lincolnshire landowner, to hold a dinner party at which Wilberforce should be offered opportunity to affirm his intention.

The party took place on Tuesday 13 March 1787. By Clarkson's account the other guests were Middleton, Isaac Hawkins Browne, M.P., William Windham, M.P., Sir Joshua Reynolds, and James Boswell – Langton had been a close friend of Dr. Johnson. Clarkson says that after dinner 'the subject . . . was purposely introduced', that he, Clarkson, was questioned and showed them samples of African cloth. Sir Joshua Reynolds, Boswell, Windham and Hawkins Browne made comments condemnatory of the Trade, and their host then put the question to Wilberforce 'in the shape of a delicate compliment. The latter replied that he had no objection to bringing forward the measure in Parliament, when he was better prepared for it, and provided no person more proper could be found. Upon this Mr. Hawkins Browne and Mr. Windham both said they would support him there.'[24]

Clarkson possibly lays too much significance on this dinner, for although Wilberforce's first public avowal, however tentative, must be important in retrospect, it may not have seemed so to the other diners. The only immediate account is in Boswell's diary and he does not even mention Wilberforce: 'Dined at Langton's with Sir Joshua, Malone, Windham, and Rev. Mr. Clarkson. I was dull.'*[25] Boswell was depressed at this time and his diary entries are brief. Windham's diary entry for 13 March is lost but when he dined at Wilberforce's with Burke and another guest on 25 April, they talked about India, not 'Africa'.[26] There is no reason to doubt the conversation at Langton's nor that Clarkson secured Wilberforce's permission to report it to his Quaker friends in the City, but nearly two months passed before, on 22 May, a Committee for the Abolition of the Slave Trade was formed with Granville Sharp in the chair. Wilberforce did not come, nor join the Committee for the present, to preserve freedom of action, and his attendance is not recorded until 21 December 1791.[27]

Meanwhile Bishop Porteus of Chester (he was not translated to London until November) had received strong evidence in support of Ramsay. 'This morning,' wrote Porteus in his Occasional Journal on 13 April 1787, 'I had a visit from Mr. Stuart, a clergyman of the Church of England, a man of credit and character', who had spent two years in St. Kitt's in Ramsay's time and had read his books.

Stuart 'declared to me repeatedly', wrote Porteus, 'in the strongest and most solemn manner that Mr. Ramsay's representation of the state and the treatment of the negro slaves in the British W.I. Islands was literally strictly true, and that their labour, their clothing [?] and their punishments were strictly what he had described. He said that Mr. Ramsay had not aggravated a single particular, that he would recollect; but on the contrary had suppressed and softened many acts of cruelty which he might have mentioned, and printed in much stronger colours. . . .'

Stuart showed letters from another West India clergyman which provided similar evidence. Porteus then asked a question which is of particular interest because some of Wilberforce's later critics would assert that day-labourers in England, those paid by daily, not weekly wage, suffered much worse than negro slaves and that he should have begun his charity at home.

Porteus asked Stuart 'particularly whether he thought the situation of the negro slaves *in general* better and more comfortable than that of the day-labourers and peasants in England. He said nothing could be more false and that the lowest of our labourers were infinitely happier than the negro slaves in the W. Indies. And in general he declared that the two pamphlets published against Mr. Ramsay and in the W. Indies were full of the grossest falsehoods and misrepresentations.'[28]

Whether or not Porteus communicated Stuart's report, the pressures mounted on Wilberforce to declare himself, until his decision came at last on a day in the late spring of 1787, warm enough to lounge out of doors (Wilberforce family tradition sets the date as 12 May), when he,

* Boswell does not mean 'bored' but felt he had been a dull dog.

3*

Pitt, and Pitt's first cousin and eventual successor as Prime Minister, William Grenville, sat under an oak tree on the Holwood estate, just above the steep descent into the Vale of Keston: three young men in their twenty-eighth year.[29] Wilberforce did not like Grenville particularly at that time: 'a shabby man bent upon amassing money'.[30] Later they would move close, and Wilberforce always admitted Grenville's political sincerity and freedom from the vice of flattering Pitt.

Under his oak tree Pitt brought Wilberforce's hesitations and prevarications to the sticking point. 'Wilberforce, why don't you give notice of a motion on the subject of the Slave Trade? You have already taken great pains to collect evidence, and are therefore fully entitled to the credit which doing so will ensure you. Do not lose time, or the ground may be occupied by another.'

Wilberforce does not record his answer, nor whether it disclaimed the motive of personal credit which Pitt, knowing him of old, seemed to suppose still dominant. But this was the incident, not the dinner at Langton's, which Wilberforce would recall when asked in old age why he took up Abolition. 'I distinctly remember,' he would say, 'the very knoll on which I was sitting near Pitt and Grenville.'[31]

The oak stood for another hundred years, known as 'Wilberforce Oak'. Its stump is still to be seen, marked by a plaque.

CHAPTER SEVEN

Remaking England

Early in 1787 when feeling his way towards Abolition, Wilberforce outlined to Bishop Porteus a plan which had nothing to do with slaves.

Too many men and women in England were hanged, Wilberforce felt. And crimes which led to the gallows flourished for two reasons especially: a widespread contempt for lesser laws, and lack of adequate law enforcement in a land without proper police; Pitt's Metropolitan Police Bill in 1785 had been killed by public hostility. For Wilberforce, the answer now lay deeper. If he could reform the morals (or 'manners') of England he would help empty the prisons and cheat the gallows.*

No one in Britain in the 1780s regarded a man's morals or religion as purely private: the Crown was the guardian of the Christian faith and the Statute Book should enshrine a Christian moral framework, even if 'free Britons' cheerfully flouted laws which governed moral behaviour. A new Sovereign on his accession always issued a Proclamation, 'for the Encouragement of Piety and Virtue; and for the preventing of Vice, Profaneness and Immorality'.[1] Most were treated as a mere form of words, but Wilberforce discovered that William and Mary's Proclamation (issued late, in 1692) apparently had succeeded in its purpose more than others because local 'Societies for the Reformation of Manners' were formed to assist magistrates in the detection of crime, and the Commons had appointed a committee to consider moral reformation. Under the Hanoverians, libertines regained the initiative.

In the eighteenth century the Crown did not usually prosecute. Although criminal offences were 'against the King's peace, Crown and dignity' it was more often the victim, or his representative, who brought the prosecution or left the alleged offender unindicted: a fact

---

* The problem is perennial. Wilberforce might almost have used the very words spoken by Lord Chancellor Hailsham on 12 May 1972: 'I do not believe that the motivation of crime and the criminal can be isolated or detached from the behaviour and moral climate of individuals in society at large. The climate of permissiveness generally has, I believe, a far bigger influence on society in general and therefore on crime and the criminal, than the criminal courts and the police put together.' *The Times*, 13 May 1972.

vital to an understanding of Wilberforce's attempts at reform. He puzzled how to deal with offences which were not directed at person or property but against the general good of the people. The moral reformation of King William's time showed that a Society might prosecute where an individual hesitated, for fear of slander, ridicule, expense or the imputation of false motives, yet it could only function effectively if encouraged by the State. Wilberforce therefore resolved to persuade George III to re-issue the Proclamation which had marked his Accession. This was the Plan he disclosed to Bishop Porteus.

Porteus recorded in his manuscript book of *Occasional Memorandum and Reflexions*: 'The object was, principally to check as much as possible that deluge of vice and immorality which was overflowing this country, to enforce the execution of the laws against drunkenness, lewdness and indecent prints and indecent publications, disorderly public houses, and the various profanities of the Lord's Day; to give support, and activity to the magistrates in the prosecution and punishment of offenders against good manners and public decency.

'The design appeared to me in the highest degree laudable, and the object of the greatest importance and necessity; but I foresaw great difficulties in the execution of it unless conducted with great judgement and discretion, especially in the first outset. My advice therefore was to proceed in the beginning cautiously and privately, to mention the Plan in confidence, first of all to the leading men in Church and State, the Archbishop of Canterbury and Mr. Pitt* to engage their concurrence by [illegible] and then by degrees to . . . obtain if possible the assistance of the principal and most respectable characters among the Nobility, Clergy and Gentry in and about London and afterwards throughout the Kingdom.'[2]

Throughout the spring of 1787 Wilberforce drove his plan for moral reform in double harness with his studies for Abolition (the chronology disproves the impression left by the official *Life*, and followed by Coupland and Furneaux, that his concern to check vice and immorality preceded his concern for the slaves). Porteus noted: 'Mr. Wilberforce, who took a very active part in this business, and pursued it with indefatigability and perseverance, made private application to such of his friends of the Nobility and other men of consequence.' He secured the 'entire approbation' of Pitt and the Archbishop, Dr. Moore, and communicated the Plan to Queen Charlotte. The Archbishop told him he had 'opened the subject' to one greater than himself, who could only be the King, and had found him deeply impressed.[3] Moore probably raised it verbally as no record appears in the Royal Archives. Wilberforce himself deliberately covered his own tracks by an 'amiable confusion'.

---

* These names were crossed through, probably by Porteus himself, at a later date.

On 1 June 1787 George III gazetted a 'Proclamation for the Encouragement of *Piety* and *Virtue*. . . .'[4] Few who read it in newspapers or on walls knew that the moving spirit was the twenty-seven-year-old Member for Yorkshire, without rank or office, but determined to change the moral climate of the age, no less, and thus to reduce serious crime: his motive was humane, not repressive.

The Royal Proclamation used the normal form drafted in 1692 and issued at the Accession in 1760. Only the lengthy Preamble differed: 'GEORGE R. Whereas we cannot but observe with inexpressible concern, the rapid progress of impiety and licentiousness, and that deluge of profaneness, immorality, and every kind of vice, which, to the scandal of our holy religion, and to the evil example of our loving subjects, have broken in upon this nation: We, therefore, . . . have thought fit, by the advice of our Privy Council, to issue this our Royal Proclamation, and do hereby declare our Royal purpose and resolution to discountenance and punish all manner of vice, profaneness and immorality, in all person, of whatsoever degree or quality, within this our Realm, and particularly in such as are employed near our Royal Person. . . .'

The next eight customary paragraphs, if taken literally as Wilberforce intended, would make Georgian England and its 8 million inhabitants very different from top to bottom. All persons of honour or authority were to set a good example themselves and to help reform 'persons of dissolute and debauched lives'. The King prohibited his loving subjects from playing dice, cards or any other game whatsoever on the Lord's Day, whether in private or public, and they should attend the worship of God. Judges, sheriffs, justices and indeed all were to be 'very vigilant and strict in the discovery and the effectual prosecution and punishment of all persons who shall be guilty of excessive drinking, blasphemy, profane swearing and cursing, lewdness, profanation of the Lord's Day, or other dissolute immoral or disorderly practices'; they must suppress all public gaming, disorderly houses, unlicensed places of entertainment, and 'all loose and licentious prints, books and publications dispersing poison to the minds of the young and unwary and to punish the publishers and vendors thereof. . . .'

The statutes preventing commerce on Sunday were to be enforced. The clergy were to read the Proclamation publicly at least four times a year immediately after divine service. On 23 June 1787 the Secretary of State for the Home Department, Lord Sydney (the former Tommy Townshend) sent six copies of the Proclamation to the High Sheriff of every county with the King's command to carry it out.[5]

Wilberforce could be encouraged as he watched the effect. Sir William Dolben, for instance, wrote to his son at the family estate of Finedon near Northampton: 'As the King's Proclamation has been much attended to by the magistrates of London, Middlesex, Westminster and Surrey, as well as many other parts, I hope it will be properly noticed by the Bench at Northampton. . . . The Archbishop of Canterbury is zealously active upon the occasion, and I believe the King himself has it very much at heart. Several of the highest rank in the Nobility as well as the Church have taken the matter up warmly, and together with many of the other House and other respectable characters mean to support the execution of the laws, and countenance those worthy persons in the inferior stations of life who will have the courage to stand forth as in King William's time. . . .' Sir William described various efforts and concluded: '. . . I have now filled my paper and must go to Tea. All join in love and good wishes to you all. . . .'[6]

Wilberforce next put into operation the second part of his Plan. On 7 June the dull, unworldly, unexceptional Earl of Ailesbury, a lord of the bedchamber, called on his elder brother, the Duke of Montagu, Master of the Horse, a cold and weak man in Horace Walpole's opinion.[7] Ailesbury wrote in his diary: '. . . I went in coach to Whitehall, and had dish of tea and bit of bread and butter at Duke of Montagu's, whom I found Mr. Wilberforce with and asking him to be president of a society for carrying into execution the proclamation of last Saturday's Gazette for the Observance of Sunday etc.'[8] The two brothers then went to a charity sermon in the City which lasted fifty minutes of a two-hour service. Ailesbury haggled over what to put in the plate.

On 13 June Ailesbury himself received Wilberforce and recorded: 'He proposes certain rules which arise out of proclamation, and a committee of five persons, one of which was Sir Charles Middleton, who was a man of business and in town a good deal officially.'[9]

All that summer Wilberforce circulated his Plan to men of influence or rank asking them to create local associations. He enclosed to Wyvill an impressive list of supporters: 'There can be no plainer proof of the sense of men in general on this point than the names you will read, of those who have come in to my idea. The barbarous mode of hanging has been tried too long and with the success which might have been expected from it: the most effectual way of preventing the greater crimes is punishing the smaller, and endeavouring to repress that general spirit of licentiousness which is the parent of every species of vice.'[10] He admitted that regulating external conduct did not necessarily change hearts, but removing temptations would help.

George Pretyman, Pitt's former tutor and secretary whom he had just promoted Bishop of Lincoln, approved although he had little time for Wilberforce's new religious opinions and influenced Pitt against them. The Duke of Manchester wrote warmly to Wilberforce of 'the laudable plan you have formed. . . . It gives me pleasure to find that you join in the ideas of many humane and thinking men, in reprobating the frequency of our executions and the sanguinary severity of our laws. . . . If you and other young men who are rising in the political sphere would undertake the arduous task of revising our code of criminal law in its [?] severity,* I mean largely the number of capital punishments, I am satisfied it would go far towards bettering the people of this country.'[11]

When Parliament rose, Wilberforce bowled along dusty, bumpy pre-macadam roads to visit bishops and great men, in such a hurry that on 6 July he missed Windham in Norwich by an hour, to the chagrin of Windham who had not replied to Wilberforce's note since he had planned already to be in the city and could carry him back to Felbrigg.[12]

Wilberforce called on his old adversary Earl Fitzwilliam, 'a very unexpected visit,' so Fitzwilliam wrote to his political ally, the elderly parson Henry Zouch, who had in fact established a somewhat similar society in Pontefract the previous year. Fitzwilliam laughed in Wilberforce's face, agreeing there was a great deal of debauchery and very little religion, but in a wealthy nation it would never be otherwise. The only way to reform morals was to ruin purses, 'and I promised him a speedy return of purity of morals in our own homes, if none of us had a shilling to spend in debauchery out of doors.' The earl then turned serious and begged Wilberforce to think twice before involving respectable persons in upholding laws concerning moral behaviour, since half of these laws were absurd and the other half 'a still greater disgrace on account of the partial, time-serving and hypocritical motives, which have given rise to them'. Wilberforce's Plan would lead to another round of Gordon Riots. 'For giving Mr. W all credit for sincerity, which I really do,' if ever such a Society rose into authority, all its power would quickly be out of his hands, 'and presently be in those of men of another description. . . .' Fitzwilliam scented a Pittite political plot behind the idea, but even if there were not, 'I dislike it for itself'.[13]

He put his finger on a danger already clear to Wilberforce: encouragement of hypocrisy and malicious prosecutions. To forestall this, Wilberforce intended to restrict membership of his Society to men of substance, not admitting all and sundry as in the earlier societies. He was not dissuaded by Fitzwilliam. Nor by another nobleman who took him to a painting of the Crucifixion as an example of the fate of young would-be reformers.

The Plan raised a further problem, neatly put by Daniel Defoe in 1698: the laws against immorality, he said, were 'cobweb laws, in which the small flies are catch'd, and the great ones break through'.[14] The rich, symbolized in Wilberforce's day by the gaming clubs of St. James's, could debauch with impunity.

Wilberforce had resigned from his five clubs in one day. He gave much thought to reforming their members and on 27 September 1787 he wrote to Dudley Ryder, who with his father, Lord Harrowby, sympathized with the Plan. 'In the first place,' wrote Wilberforce,

* The ducal writing is illegible at this point.

'don't imagine that I am about to run amuck and tilt at all I meet. You know that on many grounds I am a sworn foe to the Clubs, but I don't think of opening my trenches against them and commencing open war on such potent adversaries. But then I honestly confess to you that I am restrained only by the conviction that by such desperate measures I should injure rather than serve the Cause I have in view; and whenever prudential motives do not repress my "noble rage" I would willingly hunt down vice whether at St. James or St. Giles's. Indeed it is one of the main objections that I expect to hear urged against the plan, that it attacks petty criminals only and suffers the greater offender to go on unmolested. . . .'

The rank of the high born lifted them virtually above the law except for the most heinous crimes. Wilberforce would try a different mode: he would make goodness fashionable. They would then no longer pretend to be worse than they were, for hypocrisy did not run one way. 'When a profession of Religion opens the road to respect and power,' he reminded Ryder, 'there is always a great deal of religious hypocrisy; we have now an hypocrisy of an opposite sort, and I believe many affect to be worse than in principle they really are, out of deference to the licentious moral [*sic*] of the fashionable world.'[15]

He intended to change the attitudes of the ruling class. To turn 'eighteenth-century' gentlemen into 'nineteenth-century' gentlemen.

The reforming movement was not specifically religious. The Duke of Montagu was not known as religious. The Duke of Manchester (at least according to Wraxall) had 'very dissipated' habits; he died the next year from a cold caught watching cricket. Wilberforce enlisted any grandee of good will, indeed he commented to a friend during August 1787 'that from the situation in which I now am, my appearing to the world in the light of a man over-religious might be prejudicial to interests of the first importance'.[16] His most active colleagues in the proposed Society, however, were religious. And he was strengthened by the accession of two very different recruits.

Hannah More, the playwright, wit and blue stocking, one of the 'Nine Living Muses of Great Britain' in the famous print, had slowly moved towards an Evangelical outlook through her friendship with Lady Middleton and Bishop Porteus and the counsel of John Newton. She reached full sympathy with Wilberforce, and although they did not agree in all points of doctrine or politics she worked hard to further his reforming zeal, both for the Abolition of the Slave Trade and the moral regeneration of the age. She grew equally concerned for the poor and for the upper-class patrons who had welcomed her into their *salons*.

In 1787, after conference with Wilberforce, the Middletons and Porteus[17] she published her anonymous *Thoughts on the Manners of the Great*. Its impact was all the stronger in that no one could discover the author; some assumed it Wilberforce. Hannah More's book sought to help the poor by reforming the rich, persuading them to think of their inferiors. For instance, she attacked the custom whereby servants supplied the playing cards out of their own pockets, fresh packs nightly, receiving generous tips from the guests; she said this gave a vested interest in securing places in 'dissipated' households. She attacked the convention whereby a master ordered servants to tell callers, 'Not at home', when he meant 'Busy' or 'I don't want to see you'. She said it taught servants to tell lies. Wilberforce dropped it after his man complained that a caller had looked at him long and hard, as if to say, 'You know you are lying'.

Hannah More attacked the usual Sunday 'routs' and assemblies because fashionable women could not attend without having elaborate coiffeurs professionally arranged immediately beforehand; thus hairdressers must miss church and their time at home, or lose custom, and they would get no compensating day off during the week. Sunday, Hannah More wrote, should be a domestic day. She did not quite like to denounce the royal Sunday Drawing Rooms but these remained a running sore to the reformers. Four years later Porteus, by then Bishop of London, recorded on returning from an audience of the King in his Closet, that 'Among other things . . . I also expressed my humble wishes to his Majesty that the Sunday Drawing Rooms might be discontinued; as I knew they gave offence to many serious people and kept many of the Nobility and gentry and all their servants and hairdressers from going to church on those days. The King received my representation very graciously and promised that he would take the several subjects mentioned to him into consideration.'[18] His Drawing Rooms continued on Sundays until ceasing altogether with his illness of 1805.

Wilberforce's other recruit came out of tragedy. The marriage of Edward Eliot, the former 'Sir Bull', to Pitt's sister, Lady Harriot, had proved blissful. She was described as 'a very beautiful woman and possessed every quality which would make her attractive and respectable'.[19] In September 1786 she gave birth to a daughter and died a few days later, leaving Pitt and Eliot in 'a state of dreadful agitation'.[20] Pretyman told Addington next day that Pitt had recovered a little: 'Eliot is I think more composed, but still suffers bitterly.'[21]

Wilberforce's sympathy became one of Eliot's chief props in the months that followed, until he grew to share Wilberforce's faith. 'I was little better than an infidel,' Eliot commented some years later, 'but it pleased God to draw me by [the bereavement] to a better mind.'[22] Eliot never quite recovered his earlier buoyancy: he lived under the shadow, touchingly devoted to his little child, Harriot: 'no father,' wrote Wilberforce, 'ever loved a daughter better.' A year after Eliot's early death when Harriot was eleven, Wilberforce told her how glad he was 'to look back upon the hours I have spent with my excellent

friend, to cherish the memory of his valuable and amiable qualities.'
He reminded her of her father's kindnesses, his diligent cultivation of
every Christian grace, his 'deep conviction of the unrivalled importance
of eternal things.' Eliot would often withdraw from the crowd to com-
mune with Christ and, Wilberforce hints, with the dear departed.[23]

Eliot and Wilberforce attended together at the Lock Chapel, an
austere building near Hyde Park Corner built in 1764 by the governors
of the Lock Hospital for curing prostitutes (of venereal diseases and
sins) which had become famous for its Evangelical chaplains. The
incumbent since 1785, Thomas Scott the Biblical commentator,
unpolished but forceful, always preached for exactly an hour, scarcely
two minutes more or less. Wilberforce and Eliot 'thought him the
best minister we ever heard'.[24]

The two could open their hearts to each other. Both knew the difficulties
of walking with God when pressed by the rush and other temptations
of political life. 'Pray for me, my dear friend,' Wilberforce urged Eliot,
'as I do for you; we can render each other no more effectual service.'[25]

Eliot had hesitated when Wilberforce first outlined his Plan for 'a
Society to Enforce the Kings Proclamation', but joined him on 28
November 1787 for the first committee to settle the outline, the subscription, and the secretary; the others present were Middleton and
three bishops: Pretyman of Lincoln, Barrington of Salisbury (later of
Durham) and Porteus, whom Pitt had just translated to London on the
death of Lowth.

Wilberforce did not want a flourish of trumpets to launch the
'Proclamation Society', as men soon dubbed it. He merely circulated
a list of six dukes, eleven lesser peers and nineteen archbishops and
bishops, together with a dozen commoners. 'Nothing is to be announced
to the world of a society,' he told one of them, Sir Lloyd Kenyon,
Master of the Rolls, 'only that the gentlemen mentioned have felt the
necessity of attending to his Majesty's call and have agreed to assist in
carrying the Proclamation into effect.'[26] Not until nearly three months
after the preliminary meeting did Wilberforce actually convene a
meeting of notables at the Duke of Montagu's house in Whitehall. By
then his movement to change Britain had gathered momentum: the
Proclamation Society being only one of the thrusts.

In planning moral reform he showed awareness that politics are
influenced more by the climate of an age than by the personal piety of
statesmen and politicians. Wilberforce believed, nonetheless, that
England's destiny lay safest in the hands of men of clear Christian
principle, and that submission to Christ was a man's most important
political as well as religious decision.

Very early in his own pilgrimage Wilberforce set out to bring his
friends to Christ. He would agonize about them in his diary and his

prayers, he would think out phrases or subjects ('launchers', he termed them) which might turn the talk to religion, whether at table or tête à tête. He adapted his approach to his friends' characters: sometimes 'when I have appeared gay and unthinking I have been secretly influenced by a desire of promoting their dearest interests',[27] but staying with one solemn fellow Member he read Doddridge aloud and had 'grave discourse'.[28] He urged regular family prayers. He liked them short but very reverent, the whole household attending. Family prayers had been customary among Methodists but the spread of the habit in the upper classes, until it became a feature of Victorian England, stems chiefly from Wilberforce.

Before long he had a circle about him, some of them disciples, some described better as sympathizers. Since he encouraged converts to continue in their callings,[29] not to quit the armed services or Parliament to enter the Church (as he had wished to do himself until John Newton stopped him) several of them constituted an incidental factor in his political power. They were not associated with Clapham in the public mind yet; four who later would be among his chief 'Clapham' colleagues lived overseas, still unknown to him, and the only contemporary nickname was 'The Saints'. They never formed a tight-knit homogeneous group. Some hardly answered to the name of Evangelical.*

His faith spread to his relations, including his sister and several of the Smith cousins. Bob Smith, Lord Carrington, thought he was proof, for all their cousinly affection: 'He knew he could not convert me.'[30] As late as 1829 when both were seventy Wilberforce tried once again in a long conversation while staying at Carrington's home, Wykeham Abbey.[31] But something of the piety of the one brushed off on the other, and the Smith girls were ardent disciples.

The Smiths were unimportant politically, whereas Edward Eliot's political significance might have grown strong had he not died at the age of thirty-eight; Pitt intended Eliot, not Mornington, to succeed Shore as Governor-General of India. Far more important politically was Dudley Ryder whose dress-hat Pitt had scattered round the Wimbledon flower-beds. As 2nd Baron and 1st Earl of Harrowby he held Cabinet office for many years. His clerical ancestor had been ejected from his living in 1660 for conscience sake, and he himself married one of the Gowers of the famous Romney painting 'The Gower Children': both she and her sister, the 'Good' Duchess of Beaufort were strong Christians and philanthropists. The Harrowbys founded an Evangelical dynasty.†

---

* A fundamental weakness of Ford K. Brown's huge study, *Fathers of the Victorians*, is his assumption that Evangelicals were a tight-knit pressure group. And his theory that they took up Abolition as a lever for the moral reform of England does not fit the chronology.

† His descendant the present Earl of Harrowby, who has made a close study of the 1st Earl's papers, feels that his faith could be ascribed mainly to family tradition and less to external influences, of which Wilberforce might be the chief.

In 1788 Lord Muncaster lost his young son and heir. The news brought to the Lake District a letter very different from Wilberforce's usual political budgets. The crawling handwriting shows his emotion as 'I take up my pen instinctively, yet what can I say but recommend you to the tender mercies of our Heavenly Father who in all his chastisements has a gracious meaning and who has promised that all shall work together for good to them that love him. Oh, Muncaster, He so loved the world that he gave his only begotten Son to die for us etc. . . .' The consolation of friends could effect little 'in the first moments of your agony, but several of us would sit by you and be with you and talk with you about your little darling from whom I trust you are only doomed to sustain a temporary separation. I hope it pleases God to enable Lady M. to bear this severe stroke as a Christian ought – *God bless you.* For many days you have been remembered in my most solemn moments and you will continue to be so. *God bless you* once more.'[32]

The papers of other friends, such as Lord Apsley (afterwards 3rd Earl Bathurst) and Henry Addington (Sidmouth) contain letters urging or encouraging them to religion, while those to Lord Belgrave, M.P. (afterwards Earl Grosvenor and finally 1st Marquess of Westminster), lend some substance to Cobbett's complaint to Windham: 'He is completely under the control of Wilberforce.'[33] He was the chief spokesman in the House for the Proclamation Society. 'I wish you could find someone . . . who could at all supply your place,' Wilberforce wrote when Belgrave went to the Lords.[34]

Matthew Montagu, M.P. and his wife laughed when Wilberforce suggested saying grace before meals. By 1790, however, Wilberforce is writing as one Christian to another. 'My best wishes and earnest prayers are poured forth for your welfare. . . . I doubt not my dear Montagu that you also can derive pleasure from the reflection that at this moment perhaps I may be experiencing the benefits of your kind remembrance of me at the Throne of Grace. Thus may we go on, hand in hand, whilst we travel through this life, mutually strengthening each other. . . .'[35]

Wilberforce had his rebuffs and failures, such as Pepper Arden, who replied to urgings about eternal destiny: 'I hope things are not quite as bad as you say. I think a little whipping will do for me, not with any severity, I assure you.' Later Arden admitted he should have attended more to such things when younger 'But now I am in for it.' 'You are not in for it, my dear Pepper. No. Now if you will seek for it you will be received and blessed of God.'[36] Wilberforce wept when Arden (Lord Alvanley) died. His son became a notorious rake.

Failure to win Pitt grieved the most. Pitt was not entirely irreligious but behind him stood Bishop Pretyman to whom he left the ordering of his religious views: Wilberforce considered the Bishop far too complacent about the state of Pitt's soul, and was disappointed that Pretyman blocked almost all Wilberforce's recommendations for ecclesiastical preferment. More important he blocked Pitt's conversion to a thorough-going Christian faith, which would have led, Wilberforce believed, to Pitt governing by principle rather than by influence, and to Parliamentary reform, and incalculable benefit to Britain.[37]

One contemporary from the days of the Goostree's 'Gang' remained an intimate to the end of Wilberforce's life: Henry Bankes. As next-door neighbours in Palace Yard they corresponded little; Bankes kept out of the public eye, his papers are lost and the evidence is scanty on how far his affection and admiration included a sharing of faith. They were certainly described as birds of a feather in the satirical political poem *Criticisms on The Rolliad* (the fourth edition, second part, 1790).

Presumably as a somewhat involved satire on their comparative youth and their reforming zeal, they are shown as dirty little school-boys pushing open the door of a w.c. and discovering Jenkinson, chief Parliamentary spokesman of the Liverpool Slave Traders (afterwards Lord Hawkesbury, and Prime Minister as Earl of Liverpool):

> As Wilberforce and Banks,
> Late in the Lobby play'd their usual pranks,
> Within a water-closet's niche immur'd
> (Oh that the treacherous door was unsecur'd!)
> His wig awry, his papers on the ground,
> Drunk, and asleep, Charles Jenkinson they found.
> Transported at the sight, (for oft of late
> At Pitt's assembled on affairs of state,
> They both had press'd him, but could n'er prevail,
> To sing a merry song or tell a tale).
> In rush th'advent'rous youths: – they seize, they bind,
> Make fast his legs, and tie his hands behind,
> Then scream for help. . . .'[38]

If not accustomed to scream, little Wilberforce might well feel the need for help when he contemplated his diary entry for Sunday 28 October 1787: 'God Almighty has set before me two great objects, the suppression of the Slave Trade and the Reformation of Manners.'[39]

CHAPTER EIGHT

'No Doubt of Our Success'

Thomas Clarkson called at Palace Yard on a summer's day of 1787 before setting out on his arduous, and at times dangerous, fact-finding tour of the Slaving ports. He found the Member for Yorkshire ill once again, with Sir Richard Hill beside the bed, no doubt cracking the dry jokes which Wilberforce dubbed 'Hillisms'; despite which he recovered.

His purse was a trifle sick too. His fortune, 'never so great as the world imagines',[1] had been reduced by the two contested Elections at Hull, where supporters did not raise funds as in the County. Since his Conversion he had given much to charitable and religious causes and he loved giving presents. He kept open house for Members, not lavishly but it 'made me extremely popular',[2] and he had set aside £10,000 to the support of his mother and Sally.[3]

Bob Smith offered a form of sleeping partnership in Wilberforce and Smith which would increase income, but also make Wilberforce nominally a 'merchant'. Therefore he asked Wyvill whether the proposal might damage him 'in the County. In the W. Riding clearly not; but might not the squires deem the County of York degraded by having a merchant for its Representative? . . . It must be remembered that it is not as if a Knight of the Shire were to go into business who had been elected on the footing and had been viewed in the light of a County gentleman. Mine is known to be a commercial family: the greatest part of the fortune I enjoy was got in trade and I dare say many imagine I have been or am personally concerned in it from the name of Wilberforce being still continued in the firm.'[4]

Wyvill replied he was 'glad you are at last to have the profit', having long had the criticism, for their opponents 'worked upon the silly pride of several of our squires'.[5] However, no more seems heard of Bob Smith's scheme.

That summer of 1787 Wilberforce had the unpleasant experience of attempted blackmail. A Wimbledon man of his acquaintance, Anthony Fearon, who had used violent language and written abusive letters now threatened to publish a libel. Its nature does not emerge from the manuscripts but Wilberforce's nervousness ('*at all events he must not be permitted to publish*')[6] suggests it was richer muck than the 'strange story' which Lord Mornington heard and passed to Grenville, 'that Wilberforce had married his sister's maid. Can it possibly be true?'[7] It may have been the libel which circulated for years, that Wilberforce had been an absentee owner of West Indian slaves until he sold them, at a handsome profit, on taking up the cause of Abolition: a story still told in Jamaica.[8]

Wilberforce reacted to Fearon in a way that was becoming characteristic. Though the man was impoverished and malicious, he was not mad. 'It is very painful to me to think that his family may want the necessities of life.' Wilberforce knew that Fearon must have a guilty conscience. 'Poor creature! The sensations of his own mind must be too painful for one not to wish to alleviate his misery.' To send relief openly would appear as buying him off, just as any anxiety in public 'is the way to subject myself to the perpetual impositions of an unprincipled and artful man'. Wilberforce therefore asked Henry Addington, Pitt's rising protégé, to find Mrs. Fearon suitable employment. Fearon died three years later.[9]

Wilberforce was now digging deep foundations for the assault on the Slave Trade.

He aimed at an entire end to Slavery itself. Thirty years later he stressed this picturesquely in a letter to the young Quaker, Joseph Gurney: 'It is most true, that it has ever been and still is, both the real and the declared object of all the friends of the African race, to see the W.I. slaves GRADUALLY *transmuted* into a free Peasantry; but this, the ULTIMATE object, was to be produced progressively by the operation of multiplied, chiefly moral causes; and to appear at last to have been the almost insensible result of the various improvements: not to have been an object all along in view, and gradually but slowly advanced upon (like an obelisk at the end of an avenue) but like the progress of vegetation which appears to have gradually changed barrenness and desolation into virtue and beauty. . . .'[10]

Wilberforce knew that to secure sudden emancipation from Parliament was politically impossible. Moreover he accepted the general belief that, as he wrote in 1787, it 'would be productive of universal anarchy and distress'.[11] The immediate aim therefore was to stop the supply of slaves, for this would both force the planters to treat their present slaves better, as irreplaceable stock, and alleviate the cruelties practised in the course of the Trade in Africa. Clarkson's enquiries and his own reading convinced him that these were worse than any in the West Indies.[12]

Wilberforce hoped that Abolition might come swiftly by international agreement. William Eden, whom Pitt had sent to Paris with the rank of minister to negotiate the highly advantageous Commercial Treaty with France, was the Archbishop of Canterbury's brother-in-law. Wilberforce extracted from him at the Archbishop's house a promise to sound the royal French Government privately on the subject. At first, Eden did nothing.[13] Then both the Treaty and the hope of Abolition ran into danger because the French intervened in the internal affairs of Holland, and thus acted counter to a fixed point of British diplomacy: that France must never control the mouth of the Scheldt. Public opinion expected war.

Wilberforce believed that any war, however essential for the protection of British interests, must be a disastrous setback for national reform and for the slaves. The Cabinet mobilized the fleet and raised Hessian mercenaries, but on the other hand sent Grenville as special envoy to Paris. On 22 September 1787 Pitt wrote to Wilberforce: 'Things are at last come to a crisis. . . . There is a fair prospect of success, on terms both honorable and advantageous. We must however be ready for either alternative. You will imagine I write without much leisure, but I knew how anxious you would be to hear.'[14]

By early October war had been averted. Grenville returned from his special mission in Paris, and brought Wilberforce news that the French foreign minister, de Montmorin, might be friendly to the cause of international Abolition. Wilberforce sent Eden a gentle prod on 20 October, shrewdly emphasizing Pitt's interest in the subject and offering to travel to Paris himself. Eden remained silent until Pitt added his own prod on 2 November.

Six days later Eden reported to Wilberforce a favourable discussion with de Montmorin, who asked urgently for facts. A typical Wilberforce delay then made Eden beg Pitt to prod the other way. Wilberforce wrote at last on 23 November with 'utmost pleasure. . . .' He had been waiting for someone, presumably Clarkson, who was making enquiries, and had intended to spend that morning writing to Eden but a caller had 'detained me from my desk till it is just dinner time, and at last sends me to it so fatigued that I can scarcely hold my pen or keep my eyes open'. He wrote a very long letter, which is important on wider grounds as showing the state of his enquiries by the end of 1787.

He told Eden, that the annual export 'from the Western coast of Africa by all nations, somewhat exceeds 100,000. . . . Some are criminals but as might be expected the laws have been framed with a view of the Slave Trade and are every day more accommodated to it, as slaves become scarcer which by the way they do in a considerable degree. . . .' Some were prisoners of war; Wilberforce knew of wars provoked between good neighbours by slave merchants. When the ships come in 'rum etc. are temptations too powerful to be resisted and hostilities were commenced under the influence of them. Indeed one may be sure this must happen. Arguing from the general principles of human nature. Perhaps the African merchant himself would allow us to regret the *waste* of human flesh in this mode of obtaining slaves, for you may fairly reckon that for every single negro bought sound and hale to the market two or three are killed in the action or rendered unserviceable.'

Wilberforce's conclusions, based largely on the work of the American Quaker Benezet, have been on the whole confirmed by modern research, as against the trader and traveller Robert Norris, whose *Short Account of the Slave Trade* soon afterwards claimed that all sold into slavery were genuine criminals, saved thereby from execution. Norris was more accurate in portraying Western Africa in a state of barbarism, whereas Wilberforce told Eden: 'All these proceedings take place in a country the inhabitants of which are an honest, peaceable, cheerful, social set of beings, and which the police and administration of justice, except that this abominable Trade has in some measure affected them, are remarkably regular and exact. In proof of this *vide* Benezet's two treatises, whose statements are confirmed to me by creditable witnesses who have been resident in different parts of Africa.' However, the barbarism described by Norris is now recognized to have degenerated from a higher, more peaceful civilization as a result of three centuries of Christian Europe's slave trading.

Wilberforce did not give Eden facts about the Atlantic voyage, the 'Middle Passage', but continued: 'As to the treatment of these poor wretches when they get to the W. Indies, though to our shame be it spoken, we use them more barbarously than any other European nation, it is in all extremely inhuman. The African Captains have told me that they have been shocked to see it, whilst indicating at the same time the humanity of their own conduct. . . . I have made enquiries among the best-informed and most disinterested men respecting the truth of Ramsay's assertions; they say that his account is substantially true, though perhaps some particulars may be a little exaggerated. But we must have other, must I say better grounds on which to rest our cause than those of humanity. This Trade instead of being like others, a nursery of seamen, may be rather termed their grave; it consumes annually about 1/4 of those engaged in it. . . .' And the French, with larger ships requiring a long stay on the fever-ridden coast to fill their holds, lost proportionately more.

He added that on West Indian estates which were already cultivated the stock of negroes could be kept up by breeding: this 'is proved to me beyond all question'. Abolition would therefore relieve planters of expense, though the French, having much territory to reclaim in San Domingo, might find more difficulty. 'We are all of us clearly of opinion that the best measure is a direct prohibition of the import of any slaves from Africa, which must be made a capital crime. Many expedients might be devised for ameliorating the condition of these poor creatures in the islands, but without this grand preliminary these would be ineffective; with it they will be unnecessary. . . .'

Wilberforce ended his letter to Eden: 'I am persuaded that it will require all your address to produce a favourable issue. However, if you allow the Englishman to speak out, I think you know these French fellows and can mould and shape them to your purpose; you really do have good stuff to work with, for they are a good-natured and ambitious people.

'Your words "the very short time I shall stay at Paris" are my determining motive for sending you this hasty scrawl, which I believe would otherwise help to keep me warm this very cold weather.'[15]

Eden replied with pessimism. Wilberforce wrote him on 7 December another very long letter, agreeing that the French had more to lose and urging him to push the negotiation fast but strictly in private: 'The less the measure is made a subject of common town talk the more likely it is to be adopted by your kings and ministers and gentry of that description; one would be glad that mankind should always act from the purest principles but we must be content to avail ourselves of such as we can get. If in this case the splendour of the measure dazzles one, would not this effect be diminished and its operation proportionately weakened, if the Court seems rather to follow the general opinion than to lead it?'[16]

Wilberforce thought now that an agreement with the French had better wait until Parliament abolished the British Slave Trade. He believed this would happen speedily: 'As to our probability of success; I assure you I entertain no doubt of it. The evident, the glaring justice of the proposition itself; Mr. Pitt's support of the measure and the temper of the House, the disposition of which I know rather better than I wished at so early a period, through the indiscreet zeal of some very worthy people who have been rather too chattering and communicative.'[17]

Soon after Christmas, 1787, a few days before the Recess, Wilberforce gave notice in the House of Commons that early in the new Session he would move the Abolition of the Slave Trade. Fox rose in his place to assure him of support, saying he had often intended to raise the matter himself. Other Members were equally kind.

Eden met resistance in France. On 5 January 1788 de Montmorin told him that Abolition would ruin the French islands, especially as other nations would carry on the Trade. Nevertheless, Louis XVI and his ministers earnestly desired to make the attempt if – as de Montmorin frankly doubted – the British abolished the Trade too. Eden suggested a compromise, that France, Spain and Britain should mutually denounce the Trade and promise to abolish it as soon as practicable.[18] This idea was icily received by all concerned: by de Montmorin, who pointed out that to announce a future intention would morally bind his Government to stop the Trade at once: 'it would be disgraceful . . . to maintain so detestable a commerce';[19] by Pitt, who told Eden that a temporary interruption would be difficult and inconvenient and probably defeat its object, as well as compromising the principle of humanity and justice.[20] Wilberforce wrote much the same; he had reverted to his earlier belief that success in Britain would largely depend on agreement with France to abolish together.[21]

Eden next reported renewed French disquiet lest having pledged themselves, they would find the British reject Abolition and seize the French share of the Trade. Wilberforce dismissed the fear. The feeling in the House and out of doors continued in his favour. 'On the whole, therefore,' he wrote on 18 January 1788, 'assure yourself that there is no doubt of our success.'[22]

His assurances, and the rise of a French Abolitionalist movement headed by Lafayette,[23] did not stop Louis XVI's ministers diverting the question into official channels, and losing it to sight after Eden left Paris for Madrid.

Wilberforce's optimism was not shared by another zealous ally, the veteran John Wesley. Wesley's pamphlet of 1774 (*Thoughts on Slavery*) had been one of the very first against the Trade and he now sent Granville Sharp a warm, wise letter dated 11 October 1787 which, like his later letter to Wilberforce, was not made public. He wrote: 'Ever since I heard of it first, I felt a perfect detestation of the horrid trade. . . . Therefore I cannot but do everything in my power, to forward the glorious Design of your Society. And it must be a comfortable thing to every man of Humanity to observe the Spirit with which you have established yours on. Indeed you cannot go on without more than common Resolution considering the opposition you have to encounter. All the opposition which can be made by men who are not encumbered by either Honour, Conscience or Humanity and will rush on . . . through every possible means, to secure their great Goddess Interest.'

Wesley warned Sharp that opponents would not spare money or a thousand arguments, and would raise 'every possible objection against you'. Therefore the Society might be wiser not 'to *hire* or *pay* informers'. He felt that the matter would finally turn on the question of 'the Interest of the Nation', and that the mortality of seamen in the Trade would be considered.

'In all these difficulties,' he concluded, 'What a comfort it is to consider (unfashionable as it is) that there is a God! Yea, and that (as little as men think of it!) He has still all power, both in Heaven and on Earth! To Him I commit you and your Glorious Cause, and am, sir, Your affectionate servant *John Wesley*.'[24]

Sharp probably showed Wilberforce this letter. Meanwhile James Ramsay had been working at Teston and sent to Wilberforce two days after Christmas 1787 a paper afterwards published as *Objections to the Abolition of the Slave Trade, with Answers*. 'I offer them to you in hopes that they may find a leisure hour to be the object of your consideration', because apparently insuperable objections often emerged 'of no consequence when more fully considered. . . . I am sure of the principles of the business; nor do I fear any possible objection, which I have had time to consider. The only use I can be of in the business is as a pioneer to remove obstacles; use me in this way; and I shall be happy. . . .'[25]

Wilberforce, still preparing his case, applied to Principal William Robertson of Edinburgh, a leader of the Enlightenment and the pre-eminent historian of the day until Gibbon overshadowed him; his *History of America* contained material about Slavery, and he was completing a book on the European trade with India round Africa. Wilberforce did not know Robertson personally, but begged for 'such facts or observations as may be useful to me in the important task I have undertaken of bringing forward into Parliamentary discussion the situation of that much injured part of the species, the poor negroes. . . .' He told him that while 'the main object I have in view is the prevention of all further exports of slaves from Africa', he needed to study the best and swiftest ways of ameliorating their state in the West Indies, and also what might happen after the Abolition, 'both in Africa and the Western World, and this not only in our own case but in those of other European nations, who might be induced to follow our example; all these come into question, and constitute a burden too heavy for one of powers like mine to bear, without calling for help where it may be so abundantly afforded.' He added a request for information on the enlightened and progessive Jesuit institutions in Paraguay, 'which it has long struck me might prove a most useful subject of investigation for anyone who would form a plan for the civilization of Africa.'[26]

On the same day as his letter to Robertson, 25 January 1788, Wilberforce told Lord Stanhope that Pitt and he were both urgent that 'petitions for the abolition of the trade in flesh and blood should flow in from every quarter of the kingdom'.[27] Led by the town of Manchester, over thirty petitions had come by late January, and this normal way of conveying public views to Parliament took on a new depth of conviction and urgency. Liverpool, not surprisingly, petitioned in favour of the Trade. Meanwhile the press teemed with Abolitionist pamphlets.

The West India lobby did not reply. As Stephen Fuller, the elderly Jamaican Agent in London, wrote to his masters in Kingston, 'We have nothing as yet but a Phantom to contend with.'[28]

Wilberforce intended to bring on quite soon his 'motion in favour of the poor Africans. I perceive with joy,' he wrote to a constituent, 'that their cause begins to interest the public, and I trust a flame is kindled that will not be extinguished till it has done its work. . . . Nothing is more desirable than to excite such a general feeling against it as may render it *insufferably* odious; thus it will be attacked on all points, and so assailed it cannot but give way.'[29]

Pitt at this time was hot for Abolition, but he perceived more clearly than Wilberforce how the opposition would mount as the West India and the Trading interests awoke. Recognizing that accurate information alone could rebut the planters and slave traders, he somewhat highhandedly ordered the Privy Council, by its standing Committee for Trade and Plantations, to investigate the Slave Trade and the whole subject of British commercial intercourse with Africa.

Pitt meanwhile threw dust in the enemy's eyes. Early in February 1788 Fuller heard a very strong rumour 'that Mr. Wilberforce had opened his plan for the abolition of the Slave Trade to Mr. Pitt, and that Mr. Pitt had declared his resolution to give him his full support', and he asked Lord Sydney to discover the facts. Sydney returned from conference with Pitt saying 'the report was not true. But that on his [Pitt] first being acquainted with Mr. Wilberforce's intentions it struck his feelings, that it would be well if it could be brought about; but that there were so many points of the greatest consequence to this country involved in the question that he should never think of supporting any plan, until after the fullest investigation.'[30]

Fuller reported to Jamaica his continued conviction that Pitt would support Wilberforce, and that agitation in the Commons might be fatal to all the islands, 'but ours in particular'. He impressed this on Sydney, who if happy as Home Secretary to forward Wilberforce's plans for England's morals had no sympathy with Abolition. Fuller added they were being unfairly kept in the dark to give time for petitions to mount up. He concluded: 'The more I look into it the more I am convinced of the absurdity and impossibility of abolishing Slavery; and if we do not avail ourselves of the labour of slaves, our enemies will, to our certain undoing.'[31] His reference to Slavery indicates his belief that Wilberforce indeed aimed at Emancipation as well as Abolition.

The original date for Wilberforce's motion, early February 1788, proved impracticable. He still hoped to introduce it within five or six weeks, although the passage of an Abolition Bill would be painfully slow since objectors must be heard by their counsel at the bar of the House. Then a new factor intervened.

He had fallen sick on 10 January but resumed his place in the House after two days. His load might have crushed a fit man. On 31 January he met Ramsay. On both 6 and 7 February Sir Lloyd Kenyon, Master of the Rolls, records dining in Wilberforce's company,[32] and the names of those present suggest that they discussed the imminent launching of the Proclamation Society on 12 February, when numerous peers and bishops attended and 'Mr. Wilberforce opened the business', Porteus recorded, 'with stating the design and object of the Society and proposing some resolutions, and ballotting for a sub-committee. What passed afterwards I know not. . . .'[33] The Right Honourable the Lord Bishop of London had to leave early for St. James's Palace, for the first meeting of the Privy Council committee for examination of the Slave Trade. And here, day after day, Wilberforce must brief counsel and members for cross-examination of witnesses. On top of this, and his attendance at the House, he was discussing a fresh measure of Parliamentary reform, a new Register Bill.

One week later, on 19 February, exhaustion, fever and loss of appetite overcame him. Sleepless nights and feverishness forced him on 23 February to consult his doctor, James Pitcairne, the Scottish physician with such a high reputation in London that Wilberforce meekly went by carriage instead of sending for the great man. Pitcairne failed to dispense an effective remedy and Wilberforce retired to bed. Milner abandoned his Cambridge lectures and fussed around, dearly loving to play the doctor.[34] Wilberforce refused to stop work entirely, although as he wrote to Kenyon on Leap Year's Day: 'I . . . am still a close prisoner, wholly unequal even to such little business as I am now engaged in: add to which my eyes are so bad that I can scarce see how to direct my pen.'[35]

On 4 March Pitt urged him into the country air of Clapham, to John Thornton's, where Wilberforce had been given a room of his own since leaving Wimbledon. He returned next day, better, but under doctor's orders to drink the waters at Bath. Before he set out for Bath he suffered a complete relapse on 8 March; debility, loss of appetite, feverishness, and recurrent diarrhoea: in modern medical terms the symptoms suggest a case of ulcerative colitis, which is caused by stress. Lord Muncaster and Matthew Montagu took on themselves the rôle of chief nurses. Seeing him wasting away they sent hurriedly for his mother and Sally, and called in Dr. Richard Warren, who had made a name treating the Prince of Wales and soon would earn more than any physician in England. Warren was a gloomy man; later this year he said the King could never recover (from what everyone supposed insanity) and maintained this opinion until confounded by the rival Dr. Willis. Warren reported of Wilberforce: 'that little fellow with his calico guts, cannot possibly survive a twelve-month,'[36] while a consultation of the doctors produced an even worse verdict: 'that he had not the stamina to last a fortnight'.[37]

On 24 March Lord Fitzwilliam in Yorkshire heard rumour of Wilberforce dying: an agent suggested Fitzwilliam could recover the County seat at the consequent bye-election if he put up Viscount Downe, young grandson of a former Member: 'his social rank is in his favour because some of Wilberforce's supporters sometimes wish he were of more social consequence.'[38]

No bye-election came. Wilberforce passed the crisis. On 27 March Bob Smith could write to Wyvill 'with infinite satisfaction . . . that there is now the greatest reason to hope that his valuable life will long be preserved to his friends and the public. The state of his health a month ago was indeed very critical. But within the last fortnight he put himself under Dr. Warren's care, and his strength has been restored during that short period beyond all expectation. Little now is wanting for his recovery but repose of body and mind. On this his physician lays more stress than medicine, and I must do Wilberforce the justice to say he seems entirely disposed to follow orders.'[39]

Warren and Pitcairne had ordered Wilberforce a favourite late eighteenth-century medicine: opium. As Bob Smith, Lord Carrington, commented dryly half a century later: 'It is extraordinary that his health was restored by that which to all appearances would have ruined it, namely the constant use of opium in large quantities.'[40]

Opium has become so associated with addiction and drug-pushing that the later twentieth century can hardly comprehend how to the England of 1788 it was merely a medicine or 'pure drug'.

No moral issue crossed the mind of doctor or patient (despite tales of opium smoked in the East) and every medicine cupboard held an opiate, more usually in the liquid form (laudanum) though Warren prescribed it dry, in pills, for Wilberforce. The profession disputed over opium's medical value, some considering it too powerful for household use, but because eighteenth-century physicians treated symptoms rather than causes, opiates were obvious remedies for such ills as severe pain, loose bowels, sleeplessness or distraught nerves. Opium was as normal as 'cupping' or bleeding, and in the prevailing state of medicine it probably offered the best available treatment if Wilberforce's malady were ulcerative colitis.[41]

By 1838 when the official biography appeared, the first questionings had been aroused by de Quincey's anonymous *Confessions of an Opium Eater* and the gossip about Samuel Taylor Coleridge's excesses. The Wilberforce sons seem somewhat coy in their reference to opium, and their choice of phrase leaves open whether their father increased his dose at times of stress. The medical view of Wilberforce in 1788, however, was much that of the Ipswich doctor in 1790 who put the parson-poet Crabbe on a lifelong course of opium after he had complained of vertigo and had collapsed in the street: 'There is nothing the matter with your head. . . . Let the digestive organs bear the whole blame; you must take opiates.'[42]

It was known that the side effects of opium could be distressing, and contemporary attitudes would suggest that this, rather than the moral doubts his sons imply could have been the root of Wilberforce's hesitation when Warren and Pitcairne put him on opium. He seems to have wanted to stop a few years later. Milner, already heavily on opium after a severe breakdown, thereupon sent him a frank letter about a cure for bowel trouble which, from the context, must be opium: 'However be not afraid of the *habit* of such medicine, the *habit* of growling guts is infinitely worse. There is nothing injurious to the constitution in the medicines and if you use them all your life there is no great harm. But paroxysms of laxity or pain leave permanent evil.'[43]

Wilberforce's opium eating was perfectly open because neither he, his doctors nor his friends linked it with shame or moral weakness. It was not bracketed with tobacco or over-indulgence in alcohol, and the drug was bought at chemists or druggists as openly as other medicines.

When Lord Harrowby (Dudley Ryder) was Foreign Secretary in 1804 and fell down the Foreign Office stairs on to his head, he complained of so many headaches 'as to make me frequently unable either to see my paper or guide my pen. Would to God they were over or I out!' Wilberforce replied: 'Do you try laudanum? or what I always find far preferable when either of the two are necessary, opium (it does not sicken so much, and the slower is far more durable in operation) for your headaches? Dr. Perceval told me he obtained great relief from it, so has the Dean of Carlisle [Milner] or Dr. P. said the Black Drop, which he recommended though a Quack medicine, being prepared by a surgeon he knew, would produce the effects of opium or laudanum (of which it is composed with some acid) without sickening. Excuse this Quackery I am really *much hurt* on your account.'[44]

Modern clinical studies have proved that opium does not in itself destroy character if tensions are absent and the personality sound. A danger of any drug must lie in the body's demand for ever increasing doses to achieve the required remedy; Wilberforce, like Crabbe, successfully resisted the craving; except possibly on occasions he maintained the dose at a constant, low level, though with the years he had to increase it. In 1796 during a severe bowel complaint he took five grains daily[45] but in April 1818, thirty years after the first prescription, Wilberforce noted in his diary that his dose 'is still as it has long been', a pill three times a day (after breakfast, after tea, and bedtime) each of four grains. Twelve grains daily is a good but

Wilberforce's house and Old Palace Yard, 1792, print by Thomas Malton

KENSINGTON GORE

Gore House Kensington—formerly the Residence of the Countess of Blessington—

*Gore House, Kensington Gore, some twenty years after Wilberforce's time,
from the sketch by T. H. Shepherd*

'Bewilderforce's Rhapsodies on Peace', a cartoon of 1795

not outstanding dose and very far from addiction after such a length of time. Occasionally in very cold weather he took a little more but did not like to do so 'and don't commonly exceed my regular allowance'. By 1818, when lung trouble had added to his ailments, if he forgot to take his night-time dose he would feel ill in the morning, 'forced to lie in bed, great sneezing and other signs of spasm', with sweating.[46]

It never occurred to opponents looking for mud to fling, to attack him on the ground of his opium eating; indeed Coleridge once defended his own habits by exclaiming: 'Who has dared blacken Mr. Wilberforce's good name on this account?'[47] Yet effects there must have been. Wilberforce certainly grew more untidy, indolent (as he often bemoaned) and absent-minded as his years went on though not yet in old age; it is proof of the strength of his will that he achieved so much under a burden which neither he nor his doctors understood. Drugs at that period were not standardized. Although dried opium has a tenth of the power of morphine extract, neither druggists nor doctors knew that its potency varied with factors such as the season in which the plant had been collected. Thus one day the chemist might unwittingly wrap up thirty pills of a dangerous drug, while the next order might be harmless.

Wilberforce in later years frequently mentioned as the 'peculiar complaint of my eyes', that he could not see enough to read or write during the first hours of the day. This is a symptom of a slow build up of morphine poisoning.

Warren and Pitcairne had saved his life. Wilberforce now entered a 'Dark Night of the Soul', if a small red leather notebook[48] is his, which passed down in the descendants of William Spooner his brother-in-law, and has no name, merely: March 1788. The handwriting strongly resembles Wilberforce's at that date (it changed somewhat as he grew older) and though authorship remains unproven the Spooners held it to be his. Possibly it was left behind on a visit after frequent removals and the loss of a settled home had put all his papers in a muddle; or, less likely, given to the sympathetic William Spooner as a keepsake.

Changes of quill suggest that he filled the notebook gradually over a period. It contains prayers from the Book of Common Prayer and other sources, a few literary quotations, and several informal prayers which can only be his own composition. 'Lord,' runs the first of these, 'thou knowest that no strength, wisdom or contrivance of human power can signify, or relieve me. It is in thy power alone to deliver me. I fly to thee for succour and support, O Lord let it come speedily; give me full proof of thy Almighty power; I am in great troubles, unsurmountable by me; but to thee slight and inconsiderable; look

4

upon me O Lord with compassion and mercy, and restore me to rest, quietness, and comfort, in the world, or in another by removing me hence into a state of peace and happiness. Amen.'

His system's reaction against the side-effects of the drug would have depressed him, but the next prayer suggests that he dreaded the fight for Abolition. Contemplating the opposition, the possibility of physical assault, and of losing friends like Sir William Young, who owned 1,300 slaves in three islands, Wilberforce prayed: 'Almighty God, under all my weakness and uncertain prospects give me grace to trust firmly in thee, that I may not sink under my sorrows nor be disquieted with the *fears* of those evils which cannot without thy permission fall upon me. . . .'

The deepest point is reached when, perhaps, the opium threatened to set him on the road which Coleridge and de Quincey trod. Wilberforce cries out: 'Corrupt imaginations are perpetually rising in my mind and innumerable fears close me in on every side. . . .'

The later prayers strike a different note: 'O Lord our God, thou hast said unto us I will never leave you, nor forsake you . . . thou *hast* supported my spirit in the days of trouble, and hast given me many intervals of refreshment, renewing thy loving kindness day by day. . . .' By the time he stops using the notebook his prayers ask calmly for grace to do his duty, freedom from worldly motives, from desire for applause and from the temptation to depend on human aid alone. The final choice of quotation suggests that spirit and mind had suffered worse than the body; it had been partly a nervous breakdown.

Writing from Bath on Monday, 7 April 1788 Wilberforce begged Pitt to take over his Abolition cause in the House. Never did he forget the kindness of the prompt reply and warmth of promise. On 9 May Pitt moved that the House should investigate the Trade: a less definite motion than Wilberforce had meant to move, and introduced by a speech of studied neutrality; but the Privy Council Committee had still not reported.

By then Wilberforce had left Bath for Cambridge where he stayed a month at St. John's. 'I trust I mend daily,' he wrote to Addington. 'The regularity of a college life well suits a convalescent.'[49] He spent much of the summer and autumn with his mother and Sally at Rayrigg. Out in Windermere lay the islet of Woodholme. Taking the smallest of his three boats he would row alone the few hundred yards and sit under its lee reading the Bible and praying 'early in the fine autumn mornings when the lake used to be as calm as so much glass, and all the mountains, shrouded with vapours, compassed me round like so many sleeping lions, and the sun shining on the varied enclosure in the nearer foreground used to present a scene I never saw surpassed.'[50]

Meanwhile Sir William Dolben had introduced his Slave Limitation (or 'Middle Passage') Bill. An empty slaver in the Thames had revealed to him the cruelly small space for each slave, thus exploding the ingenious pretence of the Traders that slave ships really were larger than officially listed (and thus able to carry their slaves in comfort) because owners dishonestly entered a smaller tonnage to avoid higher port dues. The Traders fought Dolben's Bill, provoking Pitt into threatening to vote for 'utter Abolition' immediately. Dolben commented to his son: 'They have hurt their own cause by their conduct in opposing this Bill, which has been very disingenuous and uncandid.'[51] Wilberforce feared it would be lost in the Lords until Lord Stanhope piloted it successfully.

When Parliament rose, Rayrigg and Windermere soon filled with friends; Pitt himself hoped to stay but never found the time. Local tradition claims that the Abolition Bill was first drafted on Wilberforce's dining-room table, but the stream of guests eating up the hours with congenial chat sent him into his usual remorse about 'dissipation'. He did not renew the Rayrigg lease when it fell in next spring.

Many of the guests had passed through Yorkshire and warned him of the gossip there that his health would never let him stand again for the County. He issued therefore an 'advertisement' in appropriately flowery language announcing his recovery; 'and so long as my Constituents shall be disposed to continue to give me the important charge with which they have intrusted me, I feel too highly gratified by such mark of their confidence not to be desirous of retaining it, however conscious I may be of the little right I have to so flattering a distinction.'[52] The disappointed Viscount who had hoped for the seat consoled himself with the general belief that the twenty-nine-year-old Wilberforce would not live 'more than six years or so'.[53]

Wilberforce went south by Hull, Lincoln and Cambridge to Bath to complete his cure. Even in the post-chaise his mind dwelt on the negroes. Pitt having consulted him on whom to appoint Master of Trinity, he urged the claims of Milner (who had just been elected Resident of Queens') and then went on to 'another topic of far more importance, I mean the Slave Question. I trust in God our efforts in behalf of these poor wretches will in the end be effectual, but the argument of other states taking up the Trade if we relinquish it operates powerfully against us.' He urged Pitt to cultivate the friendly disposition of the Courts of Europe 'and bring it to some point. Remember me most kindly to Eliot: would it be possible to tempt him over to Bath for a day or two. . . . I beg also my respects to Lady Chatham. . . .'[54]

Wyvill dragged Wilberforce back protesting to Yorkshire for the centenary celebrations of the Glorious Revolution of 1688 on 5 November: his presence at this Whiggish affair was essential because 'we are misrepresented by our opponents as inclined to Tory principles'.[55] Wilberforce then drove post all the way down England again on the November roads, reaching Bath only to learn of the King's illness. With the Opposition demanding a Regency, which would bring them in, Wilberforce hurried to London to support Pitt in the Chamber for the first time since February.

Fully recommissioned, if frail and reduced, he sat on the Commons' Regency Committee, beside Fox who had travelled so fast from Italy that his legs were swollen. Wilberforce remarked that the long sittings suited them, as invalids, better than fit Members who missed their exercise. Fox replied that he was used to sitting up all night gaming at Brooks's and sleeping through the day, under the influence of laudanum when necessary.[56] Wilberforce's reply is not recorded.

PART TWO

Sorrows of Africa
1789–1807

CHAPTER NINE

The Commons Turns Aside

Milner said to Wilberforce when they were discussing Abolition, 'If you carry this point in your whole life, that life will be far better spent than in being Prime Minister many years.'[1] The remark hardly implies ambition in Wilberforce for the premiership, but he dropped hints enough in his private journal that he aimed at high office. The unlikelihood of his reaching it, when all factors are considered by hindsight, does not detract from the sacrifice he had made by devoting himself to the slaves.

Early in 1789 he was preparing to raise the question in the House at last. He went through the report of the Privy Council Committee with Dundas in January: it included no recommendation, but to Wilberforce the evidence formed an unanswerable case for killing the Trade. To Traders and the West India interest, on the other hand, the evidence made no more than a case for regulating abuses. 'The pamphlets you sent me,' wrote a Bristol shipper that January to Sir William Codrington of Dodington in Gloucestershire, whose fortune derived from slave plantations, 'are indeed replete with ignorance and falsehood. I at first laughed at the attempt of the Manchester fanatics,* but now find it is a serious business, taken up warmly by Mr. Wilberforce and others. . . . They do not require any modification of the Slave Trade but a total Abolition.'[2]

Wilberforce was strengthened in his view by meeting a strikingly handsome Scottish lawyer, James Stephen who was returning to St. Kitt's, where his practice would have evaporated had he owned publicly to a hatred of slavery. He promised to furnish further evidence. Neither man could have realized as they breakfasted at Palace Yard on 31 January 1789 that they would become close friends, colleagues and brothers-in-law; and that at the last it would be Stephen's genius which outflanked and routed the entrenched defenders of the Trade.

Wilberforce overworked himself preparing the case, until he slept

* Manchester had led the way in petitioning against the Trade.

badly. Meanwhile the House debated the Regency Bill day after day. Fox was absent sick. 'You cannot imagine,' commented Wilberforce to Lord Kenyon on 12 February, 'how insipid and vapid our debates are without Fox: they serve us up the same tasteless mess day after day till one *loaths* the very sight of it. . . .'[3] The King recovered suddenly. Pitt excused Wilberforce the Thankgsgiving Service at St. Paul's in April for he was by then at Teston with Middleton, Clarkson, Ramsay and others of 'the Anti-Slavery junta' as their ally Hannah More termed it. He had found time, however, to call on the veteran John Wesley (24 February). 'A fine old fellow,' Wilberforce told his diary, while Wesley told his: 'An agreeable and useful conversation. What a blessing is it to Mr. P. to have such a friend as this.'[4]

Pitt postponed the debate to give Wilberforce more time, and together with Grenville (now briefly Speaker but soon to succeed Sydney as Home Secretary) they drew up twelve Resolutions arising from the Privy Council Report, which Pitt urged Wilberforce to move at the end of his speech; once the House had entered these Resolutions in the Journal a general motion for Abolition could be built on them. Early in May Wilberforce stayed with Pitt at Holwood. On Monday May 10 he returned as far as Matthew Montagu's at Shooter's Hill for a final discussion with Montagu, Ramsay and Lieutenant John Clarkson, R.N., Thomas Clarkson's younger brother. Next day, 11 May, the morning of the debate, he arrived in London feeling unwell.

Wilberforce rose in his place soon after 5 p.m. The House resolved itself into Committee to consider the Report of the Privy Council, the petitions for Abolition, the evidence accumulated in the past year, and related matters. Speaker Grenville vacated the Chair for Sir William Dolben, chairman of Ways and Means.

Wilberforce spoke for three and a half hours. Since most uncommitted Members vaguely shared the Enlightenment's rejection of Slavery as inhuman, he had a House predominantly friendly, yet uneasy lest tampering with the Trade should damage British commerce and ruin the British West Indies. Some, like Charles Grey, the future Earl of Grey of the Reform Bill, were worried that if Britain abolished unilaterally, other nations would take over the British share. (Urging Grey not to abstain, Wilberforce told him confidentially that during the Parliamentary discussions 'I mean to press for a negotiation's being opened with the Courts of France and Spain, particularly the former.')[5] Granville Sharp had warned Wilberforce of a further worry: if Parliament enacted Abolition a strong movement might arise in the West Indian colonial assemblies to declare independence and to federate with the United States.[6]

Wilberforce knew therefore that passionate polemics would not achieve his aim. He was not making a speech of protest before the general public, which counted for little in 1789; nor one designed to sway newspaper readers next day, nor a disquisition for posterity. His audience was not a debating society but a body of men elected to maintain and strengthen British interests and (if they would admit it) the interests of their class, the men of land and commercial property. Wilberforce was on his feet with no other intention than to persuade a majority in this most critical and powerful legislature to take a particular action – to vote *aye* to the proposed Abolition.

His speech created all the stronger impression for its moderate unsensational tone, free from gibes or bitterness or windy rhetoric: he had prepared no fine phrases but had simply numbered his points on sheets of paper (now in the Bodleian)[7] and spoke extempore out of months of deliberation. Burke said later in the evening with pardonable exaggeration that 'principles so admirable, laid down with so much order and force, were equal to anything he had ever heard of in modern oratory; and perhaps not excelled by anything to be met with in Demosthenes'.[8]

Wilberforce urged Members to approach the subject without passion: 'I ask only for their cool and impartial reason. . . . I mean not to accuse anyone but to take the shame upon myself, in common indeed with the whole Parliament of Great Britain, for having suffered this horrid trade to be carried on under their authority. We are all guilty – we ought all to plead guilty, and not to exculpate ourselves by throwing the blame on others.'

He said that the Slave Trade, when examined, had proved to be what any man of reason would have expected. 'For my own part, so clearly am I convinced of the mischiefs inseparable from it that I should hardly want any farther evidence than my own mind would furnish by the most simple deductions. Facts, however, are now before the House. . . .' He then took them through the printed Privy Council evidence as he saw it, discussing first the effect on Africa, next the miseries of the Middle Passage. The pleasure cruise which Robert Norris had pictured in his oral evidence and in print became a voyage of terror and sorrow as Wilberforce disposed of Norris item by item, without naming him. The high mortality rate, considering the fact that no slave was bought unless sound in wind and limb, afforded damning evidence against the Middle Passage: he told the House how this point above all had thrust him into taking up the subject.

Wilberforce in his speech reached the West Indies. Shrewdly he allowed that absentee slave owners sent out admirable orders and that managers did not generally intend to be cruel. They looked on slaves as a different species; they could have no sympathy for them, 'and it is sympathy, and nothing else than sympathy which . . . is the true spring of humanity.' He made the point that stopping the flow of new slaves would oblige planters to treat existing stock better: stronger, healthier slaves would work harder and procreate more, thus building up a

4*

labour force without any outlay on new purchases: far from being ruined, the sugar islands would prosper, freed from the strange tendency of planters to depreciate their assets merely because visits to the slave market were less nuisance than good feeding and careful grading of work. Wilberforce breathed no word of his desire for the entire abolition of slavery itself: he was a politician, trained in the art of the possible. His ideal must wait.

He dealt with the arguments of opponents: that Liverpool would be ruined, that the French would step in, that the Trade performed an essential service by nurturing seamen for time of war; and that any inhumanities could be removed by regulation without total Abolition. 'It is not regulation, it is not mere palliatives, that can cure this enormous evil: total Abolition is the only possible cure for it. . . . I trust I have shown that upon every ground the total Abolition ought to take place.' But, he said, motives of policy or self interest which he urged on the colonies and traders were not 'my own leading motives. . . . Policy, Sir, is not my principle, and I am not ashamed to say it. There is a principle above everything that is political. And when I reflect on the command that says, "Thou shalt do no murder", believing the authority to be divine, how can I dare set up any reasonings of my own against it? And, Sir, when we think of eternity, and of the future consequences of all human conduct, what is there in this life which should make any man contradict the principles of his own conscience, the principles of justice, the laws of religion, and of God?

'Sir, the nature and all the circumstances of this Trade are now laid open to us. We can no longer plead ignorance, we cannot evade it, it is now an object placed before us, we cannot pass it. We may spurn it, we may kick it out of our way, but we cannot turn aside so as to avoid seeing it. For it is brought now so directly before our eyes that this House must decide, and must justify to all the world, and to their own consciences, the rectitudes of their grounds and of the principles of their decision. . . . Let not Parliament be the only body that is insensible to national justice. Let us make reparation to Africa, so far as we can, by establishing a trade upon true commercial principles, and we shall soon find the rectitude of our conduct rewarded by the benefits of a regular and a growing commerce.'

He then proposed his twelve Resolutions. This move, though suggested by Pitt, was probably an error of judgement; as Fox implied, it left issue less clear cut. Having brought the House to a peak where it viewed total Abolition, Wilberforce let it wander down into a maze where his opponents could regain the initiative.

In the debate the leader of the West India lobby, Lord Penryhn, and the Member for Liverpool, Bamber Gascoyne, accused Wilberforce of misrepresentation; and Alderman Nathaniel Newnham, a former Lord Mayor of London who had extensive sugar refinery interests, forecast the ruin of the City if Abolition passed. Pitt, Burke and Fox supported Wilberforce. But most of the House were still uneasy; swayed by Wilberforce's facts yet worried lest Abolition would be an economic disaster.

When therefore the debate was adjourned about 11 p.m. and resumed nine days later, the opponents of Abolition found a tactic: Alderman Sawbridge, an advocate for regulating but continuing the Trade asked Wilberforce whether he intended to call more evidence. Wilberforce replied that he had not the least intention: they had evidence enough already. Sawbridge thereupon made a long speech to persuade the House that they could not proceed to 'so rash and impolitic measure as the unqualified Abolition' without hearing evidence at their own bar; even Thomas Powys, a Foxite country gentleman who had listened sympathetically to Clarkson at Wilberforce's house the previous year, said he could not make up his mind on the present evidence. Despite pleas from Fox and Burke, Wilberforce's Resolutions never were discussed. The House clutched gratefully at the argument of the mischief-making Lord Maitland, self-constituted watchdog of its rights, that to proceed on Privy Council evidence would be demeaning to itself. Wilberforce's question was lost.

The House resolved itself into a Committee which heard further evidence on nine days of that summer and then adjourned the matter until the next session. 'We can no longer plead ignorance,' Wilberforce had said, 'we cannot turn aside.' But that is what the House did on 23 June 1789.

The sole gain of the summer was the renewing of Dolben's Slave Limitation Regulations. Even this cost a compromise. Dolben hoped to increase the pitifully small space allowed each slave in the ships but the Liverpool lobby threatened to prevent any renewal if he pressed the point. He told his son on July 3: 'I yielded . . . at the instance of almost all the principal characters that have taken up the cause of the Negroes. Mr. Wilberforce, Pitt, Grenville, Sir Chs. Middleton etc. . . . .' Since opposition stood adamant in both Houses, the Abolitionists agreed not to ask for an increased allowance of space immediately, for 'in this situation it was certainly wiser to give way in some degree and get a little, than to be persevering to no purpose. I flatter myself therefore,' concluded Dolben, 'that if the Abolition does not take place next year, a regulation Bill will at last be carried that will give great comfort to the slaves in the mean time.'[9]

Wilberforce no longer wanted an international treaty because the prolonged negotiation would freeze all efforts of individual nations to abolish their own trade. Hoping to persuade France to abolish theirs, Wilberforce decided to visit Paris in July 1789. After the Fall of the Bastille on the 14th he had second thoughts and on 17 July wrote his excuses to de la Jeard, the abbé who had rescued them at Rheims: '. . . But though the hope I had entertained of speedily seeing you is hereby disappointed, yet I trust I shall be able to realize it ere it be very long: in the meantime bear me in remembrance, and believe that I sympathize warmly in what is going forward in your country, particularly where my personal feelings are called forth by my friends being concerned. . . .'[10] No one in England realized that the Bastille presaged the French Revolution. Clarkson went to Paris instead of Wilberforce to stir the French Abolitionists.

While one of the pioneers thus went to France another was removed by death. James Ramsay's integrity had been venomously attacked in the debate of May 21 by Crisp Molineaux, a planter of St. Kitts who lived in Norfolk. Middleton had risen to his defence but Ramsay's fragile health broke under this public calumny. At Teston in July, Wilberforce heard that Ramsay had died in Middleton's London house.

In August Wilberforce took his sister to Bath. This visit had a surprising sequel when they were enjoying a few days with Hannah More at Cowslip Green on the edge of the Mendips, where she and her three sisters had a summer cottage away from their school for young ladies in Bath.

He could relax with the devout and witty Mores, all of them clever except Betty, who did the housekeeping and was the soul of kindness. The youngest, Patty, a high Tory who thought Wilberforce too liberal, had pretensions to beauty, with soft blue eyes. Sally More looked a little severe but she had a strong sense of the ludicrous, just like Wilberforce, and her jokes could be seen in her dark expressive eyes before she spoke.[11]

The More sisters sent him sightseeing to Cheddar Gorge with a picnic lunch. He returned hours later with his cold chicken and wine untouched, appalled by the destitution of the Mendip people who seemed as savage as their remote countryside, and without education or pastoral care. He discussed their plight with Hannah and Patty More far into the night, and volunteered that if they would do something, he would pay for it.[12]

Hannah More worked out a plan in the next weeks for establishing a school to teach them to read, which should be a centre of charity too. Wilberforce approved and sent a first draft for a considerable sum. Hannah More replied: 'I joyfully accept the honourable office of your almoner, on condition that you will find fault with me and direct me with as little scruple as I shall have in disposing of your money. . . . What a comfort I feel in looking round on these starving and half-naked multitudes, to think that by your liberality many of them may be fed and clothed; and O if but one soul is rescued from eternal misery how we may rejoice over it in another state! where perhaps it will not be one of our smallest felicities that our friendship was turned to some useful account in advancing the good of others. . . .'[13]

Hannah More soon found that the farmers hated her for attempting to educate and raise the living standards of people they treated almost as serfs: 'We shan't have a boy to plough or a wench to dress a shoulder of mutton.' She persevered. Through all vicissitudes and growth her schools remained one of Wilberforce's favourite charities.

By the time Hannah More accepted his commission Wilberforce was at Buxton in Derbyshire, Dr. Hey having recommended the new spa laid out by the Duke of Devonshire. Hannah More had accompanied the Wilberforces on their tour up the Wye Valley to view the ruins of Tintern Abbey, then brother and sister drove on into Shropshire to stay with Sir Richard Hill at Hawkestone. On 31 August Hill took Wilberforce over to dinner at Lord Kenyon's seat, Gredington, and the Lord Chief Justice dined at Hill's two days later. Wilberforce and Kenyon presumably continued their discussions on penal reform which they had begun in Somerset the previous month, after Wilberforce had sat on the bench as Kenyon's guest and had been upset to hear five criminals sentenced to death.[14] The Lord Chief Justice, as a committee member of the Proclamation Society, shared his friend's desire for a less barbarous system but had to administer the law as it stood.

At Buxton Wilberforce drank the waters, disliked the company and endured the horrible treatment of Skin Rotations, a massage bath in which he lay on a flat dish of copper while masseurs directed douches of thermal water at his body and manipulated the affected parts. After a fortnight's break at the Gisbornes he returned to resume the Rotations, a proof, he wrote to Montagu, 'that I believe myself to have benefited from my former ones, for no human being that could find refuge in any other quarter of the globe (let me rather confine myself to England) would come here a second time'.[15] The benefit dragged him back to Buxton each autumn of the early seventeen-nineties, to 'the barrenness and tumult of this crowded wilderness'. [16]

Before returning to London for Christmas and the new Session he spent nearly a month in Norfolk continuing his education with the William Cooksons at Forncett Rectory where Dorothy Wordsworth, Cookson's niece, thought him 'one of the best of men'. Her friend Jane Pollard of Halifax suggested Dorothy might marry him. Dorothy retorted: 'Mr. W. would, were he ever to marry, look for a Lady possessed of many more accomplishments than I can boast, and besides he is as unlikely as any man ever to marry at all as any I know.'[17]

Unknown to Dorothy, he had recently been in love. The girl was possibly the only sister of Henry Addington's wife Ursula, and co-heiress of the late Leonard Hammond of Cheam. Addington, who had succeeded Grenville as Speaker, evidently expected the match; for when he broke to Wilberforce the news in the Speaker's Room that she

Wilberforce's handwriting in 1789 from a letter dated 17 May to Charles Grey.

had accepted another man he assumed that Wilberforce's hearty approval disguised a broken heart. Wilberforce evidently had been smitten, but he realized the incompatibility of 'Miss H.' and himself. At the time of her wedding he wrote to Addington to assure him 'with great pleasure' that the expression of approval at her engagement had remained 'the abiding sentiment of my heart. The delicacy and frankness of Miss H's whole conduct I shall ever esteem; and I will also add, that (tho there is no guessing how far a more intimate acquaintance and frequent intercourse might have produced by degrees a coincidence of sentiment), yet that I believe there was *then* the difference in views and Plans of Life, which remaining unaltered, two people of as much sensibility as she and I could not have been happy together. . . .' He held opinions which were 'so much the result of deliberate conviction' that he could not alter them without self blame, 'and probably she might in part be able to say the same. It is my frequent prayer that God may bless her – and as the Orientals have it, what can I say more?

'It is very likely I shall never change my condition; nor do I feel solicitous whether I do or not.'[18]

For Wilberforce, the decision not to propose to 'Miss H.' was a sacrifice. And a warning too. It taught him that sexual passion was the only force which might be strong enough to deflect him from the faith and purpose to which he had surrendered himself. The affair had shown, he told Addington in this same letter, 'that when Love comes into question, or even approximation to it, I should find it very difficult if not impossible to preserve that composure which I have found nothing else so efficacious in disturbing.'*

When Wilberforce resumed 'the Hurley Burley of my Palace Yard life',[19] with the opening of the new Session in January 1790, his opponents reckoned that if a Committee of the whole House continued to hear witnesses, as in the previous summer, the pressure of other matters and the boredom of Members not directly interested would supervene before too much hostile evidence.

To thwart them he proposed that the question be sent upstairs to a Select Committee. On 25 January Bamber Gascoyne, Sawbridge and others urged the House to deny him even the opportunity to move in the matter. They failed, and in the main debate on 27 January Wilberforce showed his political skill: his opponents claimed that a Select Committee would deny all Members their rightful opportunity to examine witnesses; Wilberforce outflanked them by saying that his Committee should be an open one which any Member might attend. He knew that for some days they might stew in the heat of bodies crowding the Committee room; then only the few who cared would come. This ploy satisfied the House. Wilberforce had acted much as he described to a critic in another matter years later: 'I softened my language and my proceedings for the very purpose which I obtained, of producing an unanimous support of my propositions.'[20] Some might call this deviousness, others adaptability; it was a much-used weapon in Wilberforce's political armoury.

The Select Committee involved a sentence of hard labour for Wilberforce and William Smith, Member for Sudbury, the Unitarian wholesale grocer who lived at Clapham and was his chief coadjutor in the

---

* The first sentence quoted from this letter runs in full: 'I have great pleasure in being able to assure you that the Declaration I made you (I think in your Room at the H. of C.) when you first acquainted me with the Event, was not merely a fine thing, in which the consciousness of it being such is what alone supports one in saying it, but the abiding sentiment of my heart.' W. to Addington (Sidmouth MSS) from Buxton, N.D. (probably 1789, possibly 1790 or 1791). It is a pity this curious new light on Wilberforce cannot be dated because I cannot discover details of Ursula Addington's sister or identify another 'Miss H.'.

House at this time. For weeks and months they helped examine witnesses, alongside 'that keen sour Stanley',[21] Member for Hastings and Agent for Nevis, an opponent; and Philip Francis, the scourge of Warren Hastings and reputed author of the Junius Letters: he was for Abolition but Wilberforce, when reminiscing to Smith nearly forty years later, recalled him as coarse and ponderous and a bit of a buffoon.[22] Witnesses for the Trade were heard first. They assured counsel that the high mortality on the Middle Passage stemmed entirely from epidemics. Some of the witnesses grew heated as Wilberforce and Smith punctured their claims, especially Captain Robert Norris with his pleasure cruises for slaves. When Wilberforce formally impeached his credibility Norris grew so threatening that Wilberforce positively feared murder.

Evidence on behalf of the Trade finished in April.[23] Its friends tried in the House for a snap decision before evidence against the Trade could be heard. Wilberforce got wind of this and drummed up allies after ensuring that Pitt and Fox would be in their places. The debate went Wilberforce's way. It also brought a witty dig from Fox about Wilberforce's steady support of Pitt: 'It had been remarked that the honourable gentleman (Mr. Wilberforce) by bringing the question to an immediate discussion, should atone as far as he could, for the mischief he had occasioned by ever bringing it forward. He was himself of an opinion far different, and thought that the honourable gentleman, by agitating this question, had atoned in a great measure for the general tenor of his political conduct!'[24]

Wilberforce carried without a division his motion to continue the hearing of evidence. Spring passed into summer, witnesses came and went, the clerkly transcripts of evidence had reached ten thousand folio pages (all apparently burned in the fire of 1834), when early in June 1790 Pitt decided to go to the country, nearly a year before he must.

Wilberforce would now discover whether his change of principles since the last General Election, and his devotion to causes beyond Yorkshire, had cost him his seat.

CHAPTER TEN

I Shall Never Relinquish
Their Cause

Wyvill wanted Wilberforce to show the constituents he was the same person whose cause they had espoused in 1784. Wilberforce replied: 'I cannot say that I am by any means exactly the same person. I can assert with truth that I have a higher sense of the duties of my station and a firmer resolution to discharge them with fidelity and zeal,' (he knew that Wyvill would not consider this arrogance) 'but it is also true, that I am under many restraints as to my conduct to which I was not then subject, and that my religious opinions are very different. Not that I would shut myself up from mankind and immune myself in a cloister. My walk I am sensible is a public one, my business is with the World, and I must mix in assemblies of men or quit the post which Providence seems to have assigned me. . . .'[1]

He had resigned his stewardship of York races, diverting the subscription to a hospital; he avoided Grand Juries because of boozy junketings which followed.[2] But his political enemies could not deny his 'fidelity and zeal' in constituency affairs. Looking back to 1784 and hopefully to the next Election a political opponent in Leeds, John Beckett, had said of Wilberforce that 'though he came in in consequence of a fine speech of his own and through the momentary delirium of the County of which he could not avail himself again,' he had strengthened himself by his conduct. His constituents were visited, he attended assiduously to their letters and cultivated their good opinion.[3]

Wilberforce did not visit his constituents as much as Beckett believed, but he was always open to them, if sometimes he wished for less of them and their letters: 'I am . . . in the most charming retreat you can imagine with a friend or two to relish it,' he once wrote lightly to Matthew Montagu from Barham Court. 'I have ten times more leisure than in London though my constituents still pursue me; nor, thanks to the improvements in these refined days, is there that lurking hole into which they will not dive after you; however I call to them as it were "de profundis" and I can at least keep them at arm's length.'[4]

Although in a sense he 'attended assiduously' to his constituents' letters they, like all his correspondents, had to wait, sometimes for months. Wilberforce was incorrigibly tardy. All political figures in the eighteenth century from the Prime Minister downwards had to spend hours in quill driving, since to dictate a letter when addressing an equal, except on the most formal matter, was to insult him: Wilberforce's eyesight forced him to use amanuenses more than most, with suitable apology, but many letters were too confidential or intimate; even a dictated letter he often finished in his own hand. He wrote remarkably neatly despite his short sight and must have used a frame-ruler, for his lines never wander on the page, even when written in a carriage or at dusk. He ends one neatly lined letter with: '. . . so I will waste none of your lordship's time or my own eyesight in making apologies. *Eyesight* is rather an improper word: it is power of feeling, for it has long been too dark for me to see my way well along my paper. . . .'[5]

Eyestrain increased his ingrained reluctance to face his huge correspondence. He was always 'incurring a sad epistolary arrear (for I am an universal defaulter)'.[6] He likened his letter-writing to that of a hunted creditor straining to pay his debts while more mount up.[7]

He deployed a whole battery of charming excuses for his indolence. Often the first page and a half of a letter went in explaining why he had not replied sooner. To Mornington, when Governor-General of India, he was quite picturesque: 'Were you ever unfortunate enough to have put yourself into the power of that foul fiend Procrastination? If so you will not hesitate to compare its tyrannical hold to the firm grasp of that cow-like old fellow who bestrode poor Sinbad the Sailor in the Arabian Nights, and could not be shaken off by his utmost efforts. Again and again I have resolved to write to you. . . .' In that letter he covered two sides, then left it for weeks, atoning eventually by a long despatch of news and comment.[8]

He chafed Muncaster in Cumberland: 'Another and another and another post you will say, and no letter. . . . Indeed, my dear fellow, I am not to blame. In intention I have written to you again and again. But again and again has the progress of this *Intention* into *Act*, been interrupted.'[9] He claimed (with justice) that his time had been frittered away by engagements and matters converging on him whereas Muncaster had the privilege of country solitude. Muncaster knew such excuses as: 'I have been writing to you in Idea every day almost, for some time past. . . .'[10] Thomas Gisborne gave Wilberforce as good as he got, and once wrote: 'Considering the multiplicity of your business I always let good intentions stand for something on your side of our correspondence account. Yet I can no more subsist wholly on your

Ideal letters than I could on the imaginary puddings and legs of mutton
which the cook might tell me she had been for weeks intending to set
upon the fire for my dinner. At present I do thank you for a very substantial meal. . . .'[11] With constituents or other occasional correspondents Wilberforce added to his difficulties by being unable to
remember whether he had replied or not. A younger friend claimed
that in later years Wilberforce would keep a letter for weeks and then
send answers three days running.[12]

His letters were always lively. He was one of the best letter writers
of his age but posterity never realized this because of his sons' editing.
He seldom premeditated but wrote, as he once put it, 'with all the
unguarded haste of intimacy'.[13] He wrote as he spoke and not in neatly
composed literary sentences; as in conversation, he could not resist
going off at a tangent to pursue any thought that crossed his mind.
Playful touches broke through serious discussion. He specially loved
nautical allusions, oddly for a man who hardly went on the water.
When willing to make a journey: 'I will ride at *single anchor* ready to
put to sea at a moment's warning.'[14] When asking whether a friend's
son would like to hear a Commons debate: 'If so, I should be very glad
if he would make Palace Yard a post to touch at and wood and water
etc.'[15] And when he wanted to discuss the blackmail case with Addington, whom he believed to be 'hovering in the neighbourhood' of Bath,
he pretended he had ordered him to be brought into port complete with
his valuable prize-cargo of wife and daughters.[16]

Like any assiduous Member, only on a necessarily larger scale,
Wilberforce presented petitions from constituents, put forward the
names of applicants who were known or recommended to him for
places or promotion in the armed services or the Excise ('And I am
always extremely on my guard not to give expectations without seeing
my way perfectly sure')[17] and piloted Bills like the Rotherham Road
Bill, when he tried to bend the rules of the House by winding up, in the
absence of supporters, a debate which he himself had opened: Speaker
Addington refused to let him. The Bill was lost.[18]

Wilberforce especially welcomed opportunities to intercede for
convicts if there were grounds for saving them from the gallows or
Botany Bay. In the summer of 1790 Lord Hawke wrote from Yorkshire
on behalf of one Shepherdson, condemned to the hulks, asking that he
be allowed the slightly more merciful punishment of compulsory enlist-
ment on a man-o'-war. Wilberforce looked up the judge's remarks at
sentencing (unfavourable) and sent them to Hawke, while begging
Scrope Bernard M.P., Under-Secretary at the Home Office, to have
Lord Grenville urgently review the case. Grenville could not see his
way to recommend the lighter sentence. Informing Wilberforce of this,
Bernard added: 'I wish I could send you better news on a subject on
which I know you are so anxious.'[19] Wilberforce's friends would tell

him of cases, as in a note from Burgh: 'Wilber, there is now in the city of York a man under sentence of death whose guilt, though pronounced by his jury, I understand is in some way doubtful. . . .'[20]

In greater matters, the vast constituency of Yorkshire proved a natural base for Wilberforce's continuing interest in Parliamentary reform, which historians have largely ignored.

After the failure of his Register Bill in 1786 he and Duncombe continued to share Wyvill's concern. Early in 1787 the three worked out a scheme by which the constables in each parish of Yorkshire would draw up a list of Freeholders entitled to vote, similar to the list of those liable to jury service. Wilberforcè passed the plan to Pitt and enlisted a young lawyer to draft a Bill, who unexpectedly died before finishing the work. Meanwhile that ardent reformer Lord Stanhope prepared to oppose them, because he preferred that Freeholders should themselves be responsible for placing their names on a central list of voters. Wilberforce recognized difficulties in both schemes: Freeholders would forget to register under Stanhope's; his own might lead to muddle or corruption where a voter owned land in different parishes and appeared on several lists. In May 1787, immersed in Abolition and in the Proclamation business, he decided with Duncombe to defer the Register Bill for a year, because no time remained in that Session for the necessary lobbying.[21]

Wyvill pressed Stanhope to withdraw his opposition but Wilberforce, on 8 February 1788, shortly before his complete breakdown, wrote that he was not 'bigotly attached to our own Plan'[22] and would bring forward Stanhope's rather than see the reform lost through disunity: however, he thought that only a man of Stanhope's energy would get it through the Commons and no one would get it through the Lords.

But Stanhope successfully introduced a Register Bill in the Lords that summer and called on the convalescent Wilberforce to rejoice with him. Stanhope proposed next year to bring in a Bill to divide the whole kingdom into polling districts, instead of confining the scheme to Yorkshire. Wilberforce and Duncombe disagreed, certain that the Country Members would throw it out, and the Register Bill be lost with it.[23]

Nothing further had happened by October 1789 when Wilberforce told Wyvill that Duncombe and he still hoped to bring in their Yorkshire Register Bill some day. They now favoured polling by districts but felt they had better receive fresh instructions from the County before taking further action. Wyvill replied tartly: he had understood that the two Members had promised to adopt the Bill during that Parliament and thus win the public's gratitude, by success or strenuous efforts, before the next General Election. 'I do not say . . . that without such adoption you and Mr. Duncombe will lose your seats; I only mean to declare my opinion, that if you wish your Re-election to be carried with as much eclat as your first Election, you must jointly exert yourselves to promote the measures in question; without which the zeal of many friends will abate. Ill health for some time reduced you to a state of inactivity which was unfortunate, but too surely unavoidable: since the re-establishment of your health, your Constituents have not repined that their immediate business was postponed and your talents chiefly employed in pleading the cause of the oppressed Africans. But after having done that generous service to the most despised and injured race of men you seem to have leisure. . . .'[24]

This was a trifle unfair in that the new Session would bring the labours of the Commons Committee on the Slave Trade. And Wyvill not only wanted Wilberforce and Duncombe to carry a Register Bill and a District Polling Bill but, in effect, to jump right through to 1832 and win 'the emancipation of Copyholders and unrepresented Freeholders by imparting to them the Right of Suffrage'.[25]

Wilberforce replied on 24 November 1789 that he would try first for the District Polling Bill, whereby polling would take place simultaneously throughout the Country instead of in York only; this would discourage fraudulent voters, 'because the battle would be decided before the danger of defeat staring either Party in the face should stimulate it to bring forward the Ragamuffins of the Camp which is usually done at the close of a hard contest'.[26] It would have to wait another Session. Opportunity never came before Parliament was dissolved.

In the General Election of June 1790 the Foxites were determined to recover one of the seats at Hull, and the Pittites to outwit them. Fitzwilliam's agent, William Hammond, complained that the writs were being concealed, 'and it is given out that Duncombe, Wilberforce etc. are to be here to-night. Duncombe is gone off to Bank Top to Wilberforce and the plot is there to be hatched. How it will turn out, God knows; expense excepted I have no dread of danger and *be reflecting* my good Lord what resentment for such behaviour requires. . . .'[27] Whether Hammond was accurate or not about Pittite machinations, Fitzwilliam's nominee, Lord Burford, defeated Wilberforce's friend Spencer Stanhope and came in for Hull with Samuel Thornton.

In the County it went the other way. A three weeks' canvass up and down Yorkshire showed Duncombe and Wilberforce favourites and they were returned without the expense of a poll. The election cost Wilberforce little except for a nasty carriage accident on the Bridlington road:[28] he was unhurt, but this and other escapes may have been the reason for his nervousness in later years whenever he knew one of his family to be on the road. He welcomed each safe arrival as a singular providence.

After the 1790 Election Wilberforce returned to Hull and took his mother to Buxton to join several of the Sykes family. Also at Buxton was Henry Thornton, who met Marianne Sykes for the first time but did not fall in love with her at once.

Henry Thornton was now Wilberforce's dearest friend. They had drawn close when Wilberforce had accepted John Thornton's offer of a country niche at Clapham. Henry, prim and rather pharisaical as a young man, had been a little repelled by the ardour of his uncouth father, some of whose associates pursued business methods out of tune with the easy pieties on their lips. Henry found his bachelor cousin 'Wilber' different. 'I owed much to him in every sense', Thornton wrote near the end of his life, and emphasized Wilberforce's breadth of mind, his piety and his affectionate understanding.[29]

The cousins, who would work together so closely until Thornton's premature death, were opposites. Henry weighed a subject with deliberation where Wilber leaped by instinct, not always to the right decision. Distress summoned Wilber's immediate sympathy and he could be gulled. Henry, no less sympathetic under the skin, went thoroughly into a case. In the Chamber or the Lobby the Member for Yorkshire persuaded by graphic word-pictures, the Member for Southwark by meticulous explanation. Wilberforce liked to consider himself a 'political economist' but Thornton really was one, and became a pioneer of currency reform by his book on Paper Credit. 'Allow me,' wrote Wilberforce, introducing Thornton to Bishop Pretyman, 'to express a wish that your Lordship would not suffer his hard, cold, unpromising exterior to prevent your becoming acquainted with his internal worth. . . . Sweetest fruit hath sourest rind, was never more fully exemplified, if for sour one should read frigid or cold or dry.'[30]

Thornton did not accompany Wilberforce, Mrs. Wilberforce and Marianne Sykes from Buxton to their next stop, Yoxall Lodge in Staffordshire, the comfortable home of Thomas Gisborne, Wilberforce's intellectual neighbour of college days who now was an Evangelical squarson. Yoxall stood deep in the woody part of Needwood Forest with beautiful views and no close neighbours except an abundance of deer, but for Wilberforce it would not be a holiday place. He had a rendezvous to prepare for publication a digest of the evidence given before the Commons Committee on behalf of the petitioners against the Slave Trade; to consolidate the statements of witnesses, and thus to rebut for Members and the public the evidence given earlier that Slavery was mild and the Middle Passage comfortable and the Blacks worse off in Africa. The Abolitionist evidence, on the contrary, was well epitomized by Captain Thomas Wilson R.N., H.M.S. *Racehorse*: 'It is a Trade evidently founded on injustice and treachery, manifestly carried on by oppression and cruelty, and not infrequently terminating in murder.'[31]

Already arrived at Yoxall were Mrs. Gisborne's brother and sister-in-law, the Thomas Babingtons. Babington was squire of Rothley Temple in Leicestershire, which his ancestor had acquired when the Knights of St. John of Jerusalem were suppressed at the Dissolution of the Monasteries. He had been at St. John's Cambridge, with Wilberforce and Gisborne, and was one of Henry Thornton's intimate friends. His wife was a Macaulay, daughter of a Scottish Presbyterian minister. She had a young brother, Zachary Macaulay, who had gone out to Jamaica to make his fortune but in 1790 was an overseer of slaves, hating himself for enjoying tyranny, and looking for opportunity to return home. Yoxall Lodge, therefore, was forging the link between the names Babington and Macaulay and Wilberforce. Babington and Wilberforce worked against time to condense the Select Committee evidence. Marianne wrote to her mother that they 'have never appeared downstairs lately except to take a hasty dinner and for half an hour after we have supped. The Slave Trade has occupied them for nine hours daily. Mr. Babington told me last night that he has 14 hundred folio pages to read to detect the contradictions and to collect the answers which corroborate Mr. Wilberforce's assertions in his speeches. . . . The two friends begin to look very ill, but they are in excellent spirits and at this moment I hear them laughing at some absurd questions in the examination proposed by a friend of Mr. Wilberforce's.'

'Every corner of this house,' Marianne prattled on, 'is crammed with books, and people are free to read or go out or come in and do exactly as they like. I have left Mr. Babington reading to Mr. Wilberforce in the corner of the room. Mr. Gisborne correcting the proof sheets of his book in another and Mrs. Babington, Mrs. Gisborne and I have been "discussing" in the middle of it. We all have supper at eight o'clock, and a little after nine wonder that we should sit up so late, and retire to our own rooms.'

Wilberforce's mother hated the early hours. She grumbled that if she adopted such habits she might as well give up living in the world. The plain Mrs. Gisborne, mistaking her meaning, replied piously that she herself did not want to live 'in the world' at all. 'Mrs. Wilberforce replies that Enthusiasts call it a wicked world but that she never will.'[32]

Marianne found Wilberforce much changed since 1784. 'He is now never riotous nor noisy but always very cheerful, and sometimes lively but he talks a great deal more upon serious subjects than he used to do. Eating beyond what is absolutely necessary for his existence seems quite given up. He has a very slight breakfast, beef or mutton and nothing else for dinner, no more that day except some bread about ten o'clock.' Wilberforce would not have awarded himself such good marks. At Yoxall later that autumn he vowed not to spend more than one and three quarter hours over dinner and one and a quarter over supper, and compiled a secret chart on which to assess his conduct and thoughts. He looked at it a week later and scrawled 'bad' or 'baddish' against every head.[33]

Sally Wilberforce had not joined the Yoxall party because she had become engaged to the Vicar of Hull, Dr. Clarke, a middle-aged widower. Wilberforce, just a trifle worried as to Clarke's suitability, social and religious, gave her away in September, having settled £9,960 on her, which Clarke and his heirs should inherit if she died childless.[34] Describing the wedding to Matthew Montague, Wilberforce let his pen run away at a typical tangent. 'My dear little fellow, the interesting nature of the subject on which I am writing seems to call forth a double measure of my affection for yourself and I would my pen could express half of what my heart feels of my best wishes for your happiness. May every blessing attend you and your dear little woman. May it please God to render you a mutual comfort to each other in this life and a mutual help in what regards your everlasting state. . . .' He concluded with a doxology from the Book of Revelation, but returned to earth with a bump: 'P.S. I have been at Buxton for some time and my Bowels have received benefit. I am going in a few days to join the new married couple on the Welsh sea coast.'[35]

Marianne went to Carnarvon, too, with the Wilberforces, the Babingtons and the newly weds. Clarke read to his wife while she drank her coffee, and for the first time since Marianne had known her 'she seems free from sorrow. Sometimes I believe that men are lovers only before marriage but Mr. Clarke reverses the matter and is infinitely more lover-like now than formerly. Mrs. Wilberforce is pretty well and seems happy in her daughter's happiness but tutors her as much as ever. Mr. Clarke is the happiest being I ever saw, amuses me extremely by calling his lady Miss Wilberforce perpetually. . . .'[36]

As for Wilberforce, Marianne may have been a little in love: 'To me he appears truly angelic.'[37]

Wilberforce now concentrated his nervous and physical energy on the coming Parliamentary battle for Abolition. 'I cannot help expressing my surprize at its having been reported I had given up the Business,' he wrote to James Currie, the Scottish doctor who maintained an almost lone Abolitionist front in Liverpool, having once been a tobacco factor in Virginia. '. . . In truth you do me no more justice in believing that the principles on which I act in this Business being those of Religion not of sensibility and personal feeling, can know no remission and yield no delay; I am confident of success. . . .'[38]

He dared not be positive about immediate success. Some of the signs seemed good. Clarkson in Paris (where the revolutionary spirit enlarged his ideals of liberty) wrote that Mirabeau had promised to move Abolition in the National Assembly. Wilberforce told Pitt that he heard it said that three negroes from San Domingo were allowed to sit and vote, pending a decision whether to admit them permanently. 'If so, my three Blacks take their places as regularly as the whitest Frenchman amongst them. Though one can't build on the circumstances as strongly as if the Assembly were in its *quiet mind*, yet I trust it is likely to operate in support of our cause.'[39] These were actually six mulattos, intent on securing equality with whites whether or not the Assembly should decide to apply the first of its Rights of Man ('Men are born free and remain free and equal in rights') to slaves in French colonies.

Wilberforce hoped to re-start his Select Committee at once in the new Parliament, and on 14 December 1790 he defended Pitt's Spanish policy so heartily that Windham complained he virtually labelled any opposition as wicked.[40] Wilberforce may have hoped that this partisan speech would melt Pitt into allowing the Slave business precedence over the Budget debates, for he was inwardly angry when it did not, but the Select Committee delayed its hearings until February 1791, resuming after Wilberforce had resisted an attempt by the Slave lobby to stop the evidence.

Then came news of a serious though abortive slave rebellion in the West Indian island of Dominica. Lord Carhampton, the Irish adventurer, asserted in the House of Commons that the slaves believed 'the Governor had the authority of the British Parliament and of *Massa King Wilberforce*' that they should only work three days a week, and be paid.[41]

The Dominica rising helped to deepen the doubts of those uncommitted Members who were worried by the ferment in France, who believed that any upset of an accepted situation would precipitate unrest. In the West Indies the planters saw hope. 'Surely,' wrote a slave owner's agent in Antigua, 'the Enthusiastic rage of Mr. Wilberforce and his friends can never prevail in a matter of such consequence to the Colonies and the Mother Country'.[42] The Jamaica Agent in London was not so sure; he had too healthy a respect for Wilberforce. 'It is necessary to watch him,' wrote Fuller, 'as he is blessed with a very sufficient quantity of that Enthusiastic spirit, which is so far from yielding that it grows more vigorous from blows, and I fear he has art enough with power at his elbow to do us much mischief, without doing the least good to his ostensible objects.'[43]

Wilberforce once again was 'up to the chin in slave papers',[44] analysing the evidence, now at last completed. In the midst of the turmoil he received the encouragement of old John Wesley's oft-quoted letter, one of the last he wrote, aged eighty-seven, the day before the onset of his brief final illness: '. . . unless God has raised you up for this very thing, you will be worn out by the opposition of men and devils. But if God be for you, who can be against you. . . .'[45]

The debate came at last on 18 April 1791. Wilberforce approached it in a spirit of prayer, looking to God for 'wisdom and strength and the power of persuasion, and may I surrender myself to him as to the event with perfect submission and ascribe to him all the praise if I succeed, and if I fail say from the heart thy will be done.'[46] The subject loomed so vast now that when he rose in his place at 5 p.m. he felt sadly unprepared despite the months of study and cross-examining.

He spoke for over four hours until past nine, basing his case squarely on the mass of evidence, and concluding with an expression of strong conviction that the country stood behind him. The cause of the slaves began to prosper and he had 'no doubt that his present application would succeed. "But whatever may be its success," said Wilberforce, "I have attached my happiness to their cause, and shall never relinquish it. Supported as I have been, indeed, such a desertion would be most despicable. I have already gained for the wretched Africans the recognition of their claim to the rank of *human beings,* and I doubt not but the Parliament of Great Britain will no longer withhold from them the rights of *human nature!*"

'Mr. Wilberforce, after a most impassioned and emphatic appeal to the feelings of the Committee, concluded with moving: "That the Chairman be directed to move for leave to bring in a Bill to prevent the farther importation of African Negroes into the British Colonies and Plantations." '[47]

The Chairman was Sir William Dolben. During the debate, which continued until 11 p.m. and resumed next day, he could not make notes. When the printed unofficial report of the week's proceedings came to hand he wrote down his comments as he read over the speeches he had heard. The debate occupied eighty-five pages of this, *The Senator* (Clarendon's Parliamentary Chronicle), with Wilberforce himself taking twenty-five. Even Sir William Dolben's manuscript,[48] eight foolscap pages, is too long to quote in full but these private reflections of an elderly man of compassion, on what he had heard addressed to him at the Table, bring to life the long hours of debate on those April evenings of 1791.

Dolben makes little comment on Wilberforce: 'His preface is such as I should think would lay fast hold on the attention of every man who had ears to hear, and a heart to feel. His clear, circumstantial and plain account of this dreadful business, with the vouchers he produces in proof of his aspersions are sufficient to baffle all contradiction, and the whole of his strong arguments are urged with a peculiar gentleness and modesty.' The one omission was any mention of the masters' cruel neglect of worn-out slaves.

'Colonel Tarleton comes next.' (A wounded hero of the American War, a rich man-about-town who kept the Prince of Wales's discarded mistress and was the subject of a famous Reynolds; he was the new Foxite Member for Liverpool, an inveterate opponent of Abolition.)

'He begins,' recorded Dolben, 'with saying the ingenuity, the amplification, the pathetic eloquence of the Hon. Gentleman had worked *no* conviction on his mind. I laid down the book, I could not bear it, and though I took it up again in the evening I could not persuade myself to go on till the next day. His arguments are only, that the Trade had been sanctioned by Parliament and they could not give it up without break of faith; the value of the Trade; and then digressed into a downright vulgar scold of the Ministers . . . that the men who would destroy the Trade are fanatic dreamers.' (Banastre Tarleton's recorded words were: 'A religious inspiration seemed to have got possession of the other side of the House, and a revelation of it was partly communicated to some of those amongst whom he had the honour to sit.') Dolben dismisses Tarleton's concluding remarks as proving nothing but that the Trade was profitable to Liverpool.

A Grosvenor uncle of Wilberforce's young friend Lord Belgrave spoke third, arguing that the Trade was nasty but necessary; in Dolben's summary: '. . . The wisest thing we can do is to shut our eyes, stop our ears and run away from the horrid sounds without enquiring about it, or words to this effect.'

A speaker in support of Abolition (James Martin, Tewkesbury) sounded 'a truly humane religious Christian'. Next the impassioned advocacy of Philip Francis pleased Dolben 'exceedingly. Though Mr. Francis is interested in the West India trade he is one of the most strenuous advocates for the Abolition of the African Slave Trade. He observes that though many plead in its behalf that it is politic and expedient, yet, not one had denied its being criminal.' Francis brought out two further grisly instances of cruelty.

When the debate resumed on the Thursday Sir William Young expressed his conviction that immediate Abolition would lead to the loss of the Colonies. He conceded that Abolition must come, but at present the other nations would simply seize the British share. Dolben comments: 'If others choose to be guilty of murder, is that a reason why we should?' Matthew Montagu uttered a brief burst of loyal support for Wilberforce and then the Attorney-General for the Leeward Islands (John Stanley) claimed that Providence intended one set of men always to be slaves of another. Dolben dryly remarks: 'I cannot find that in the New Testament. . . .'

Late in the debate Pitt spoke, emphasizing the injustice and the impolicy of the Slave Trade. Dolben summarizes his speech as 'sensible, just, clear and persuasive'. It was Fox, however, who impressed Dolben: 'truly *Samsonic*: strong, bold, and powerful'. Fox said that those who now opposed Abolition could do so only from hardness of heart. If the House voted *No* it would give Parliamentary sanction to rapine, robbery and murder. He knew they did not want to hear further tales of cruelty 'but the House shall hear them. Mr. Fox then related two shocking instances of barbarity. He observed, the tales were so horrid that they could not listen to them without shrinking. Will the House then, said he, sanction enormities, the bare recital of which is sufficient to make them shudder?' Dolben noted words which ring out more clearly from *The Senator*'s report of Fox's speech: 'Humanity, Sir, does not consist in a squeamish ear. It belongs to the mind as well as the nerves, and leads a man to take measures for the prevention of cruelty which the hypocritical cant of humanity contents itself in deploring.'

Fox concluded with assuring the friends of Abolition of his undying support; and Dolben, good Pittite that he was, could not resist a dig at Fox's usual political activity: 'What a pity it is this man should ever exert his abilities to mislead and confound the judgement of his hearers.'

It was now about 2 a.m. A new Member, J. T. Stanley, was forced down by cries of 'Question!' calling for the vote to be taken. Pitt intervened, Stanley got a hearing and revealed that he had come to the House against Abolition but found the arguments for it irresistible. Dudley Ryder also confessed that his indecision had been resolved by the arguments. Edmund Burke rejoiced at these conversions, and then old Drake of Shardiloes, Member for Amersham, suddenly rose in the stale atmosphere of the Chamber. 'Mr. D. opposed the question violently,' noted Dolben. 'He seems to be just awaked out of his sleep and yawning and stretching to cry out, like Mrs. Thursby's parrot at the card table. O law! O law! What are ye all about.' Next came Lord Sheffield (John Baker-Holroyd, Gibbon's friend) the eminent political economist. Since becoming Member for Bristol he had switched from pro-black to pro-Trader. Sheffield's manner made Dolben exclaim: 'Mercy on us, what an explosion! Why this is a volcano brim full of combustibles, I wonder it did not set the House on fire. He could trace nothing like Reason in the debate, it was all frenzy. There is no arguing with gunpowder.'

Shortly before 3.30 a.m. in the early morning of 20 April 1791, Wilberforce made a short reply to the debate. The House divided. Slightly less than half the Members were present to vote, and they voted in the way that Drake of Shardiloes (whose speech had reminded Dolben of Mrs. Thursby's parrot) had predicted: 'The leaders . . . were for the Abolition. But the minor orators, the dwarfs, the pygmies . . . would this day carry the question against them.'

Sir William Dolben as Chairman could not vote. Sadly he recorded on his manuscript the figures: '*Noes* 163, *Ayes* 88. Majority against the Abolition, 75.'

CHAPTER ELEVEN

Serving Africa

One January day back in 1790 Wilberforce had called at the Treasury on an errand from Granville Sharp. Sharp wanted the gift of a ship, the *Lapwing*, having understood that vessels in the Condemned Hole at Wapping, seized for smuggling, would be burnt. Wilberforce learned, however, that they would be sold, half the proceeds going as prize money to the seizing officer and half to the Crown, but he could tell Sharp, 'I think it probable I may be able to get the Treasury to make a present of their half. . . .'[1]

Sharp wished to send the *Lapwing* to the West Coast of Africa, to Sierra Leone where he had founded, by proxy, a 'Province of Freedom'. In 1787 he had been approached by the leaders of London's 'Black Poor', the freed slaves and unemployed black servants who wandered about the city. With Treasury help he shipped them to form a self-governing community at the discarded trading stations of the small mountainous peninsula of Sierra Leone, an experiment which Wilberforce approved on more than philanthropic grounds: it served his strong sense that Britain owed compensation to the areas from which slaves had been seized, and it fed his lively curiosity as to the true conditions of the African interior. Wilberforce was one of the early members of the African Association, founded in 1788 to send out explorers such as Mungo Park and Ledyard.[2]

A peaceful commerce to replace the Slave Trade could be a sure method of compensating Africa. When Sharp reinforced his 'Province of Freedom' by forming the St. George's Bay Company (the grand name implying analogy with the great Hudson's Bay Company) to trade from Sierra Leone, Wilberforce and Thornton attended the first meeting of shareholders in February 1790. But before the *Lapwing* could sail, Granville Sharp heard that his Settlement's capital, Granville Town, had been burned down by the local chieftain in revenge for an outrage by unruly settlers. The Treasury refused further help. The

Company needed a broader financial base and in the process the unbusinesslike Sharp ceded the chairmanship to Henry Thornton. Slaver opposition stopped the grant of a royal charter, but in the summer of 1791 an Act of Parliament authorized the establishment of a new Sierra Leone Company. It would trade, except in slaves; and all under its flag would live free and equal, regardless of colour, with free education for their children and the protection of English common law.[3]

Thornton and Wilberforce each put up considerable shares of the capital. 'I came up hither to qualify for the Directorship of the Sierra Leone Company,' Wilberforce wrote to Eliot after leaving Pitt at Holwood on 2 August 1791, 'and am somewhat uncomfortably dangling about this hot town – in two or three days I expect to be released from this obligation to stay and shall bend my course for a very short visit to Cookson . . . and then sit down for *good* at Babington's in Leicestershire. . . .'[4] Thirteen directors were elected including Babington, and also Thomas Clarkson who could have put up only a token share, and a new ally, Charles Grant. Lately arrived from Calcutta, and soon to be elected a Director of the East India Company, Grant had been born while his father was out in the Forty-five, and named in honour of Bonnie Prince Charlie. He had gone as an official to India where he and his wife had become strongly Evangelical and tried to secure for Christian Missions a toe-hold in Bengal. His administrative skill made Grant an obvious director for Sierra Leone.

Thornton organized offices near his bank and did most of the drudgery. Wilberforce raised money from friends, persuaded the great Sir Joseph Banks to find a botanist for the new colony,[5] and eased relations with Pitt and the Government. He was no sleeping director, however, and a special opportunity came very soon.

An escaped slave from the American South who had served with the British in the late war reached London early in 1791 from Nova Scotia, complaining that more than a thousand black loyalists and Christians shivered in the cold, and virtually in Slavery because they had been denied the land to which they were entitled as old soldiers. This barely literate Thomas Peters (or Petters as he probably pronounced it) had crossed the Atlantic to seek redress for his miscellaneous community in the Maritime Provinces after hearing about the 'Province of Freedom'.[6]

The new Company and the Treasury saw these Nova Scotia blacks, with their churches and pastors, as obvious reinforcements for Sierra Leone. Henry Dundas, who had lately become Home Secretary (the department included Colonial affairs) on Grenville's accession to the Foreign office, thereupon sent instructions to the Governors of Nova Scotia and New Brunswick. The Admiralty offered ships.

Clarkson's younger brother John, twenty-eight years old, a naval lieutenant on half-pay, volunteered to command the expedition from Canada to Africa. Wilberforce knew the task would not be easy and from Leicestershire on 8 August 1791, six days after qualifying as a director, he sent John Clarkson a long letter of advice. It indicates the atmosphere of hostility around 'friends of Africa', and also Wilberforce's wiliness when officials needed to be persuaded.

'My dear Admiral,' he began playfully, and then set down instructions rather in the manner of a Pitt or a Grenville sending a negotiator abroad. The first: 'Don't talk about the Abolition of the Slave Trade, except where you are *sure of* your company.' He amplified this in a postscript: 'I mean, that you should not give the Governors reason to believe you entertain any *jealousy* of them. If it was my own case, I would not enter very much into the *particulars* of the business, still less talk with them on the ill-usage the Blacks had received, which would nettle the Governors; but recollecting and always keeping in view that it may be of great consequence to you to *appear to have their judgements*. I advise you to be as civil to them as you can, which will produce civility on their part, and don't call on them except when it is absolutely necessary to take part in the conduct of the transactions; but obtain their confidence and a kind of general discretionary power to act for yourself. . . .'

He told John Clarkson to 'Keep yourself as distinct from Petters [*sic*] in the general estimation of men as you can: hereby, you will not be implicated in any errors he may fall into, and even acting ever so prudently, I foresee he may justly or unjustly be liable to censure.

'3. Make up at once to the Governors and talk with them in *your open* way so far as discretion shall render proper.' If they complained that Clarkson's distribution of printed invitations to Sierra Leone was a deliberate attempt to provoke discontent, he should reply that the measure was indispensable, in all fairness, 'to prevent the negroes being deceived by the high flown exaggerated reports they might receive of our transatlantic settlement, etc. etc.' He warned Clarkson that Nova Scotian employers who may 'wish to hinder the poor fellows getting away' might say they could not go because they owned money. Wilberforce cannily told John not to hurry to disclose the method which his brother Thomas had devised for settling these debts but to draw the opposers onward until their whole case rested on this one ground, 'and then by coming forward and cutting it from under them, every difficulty will be at an end'.

With similar cunning, Clarkson was to rush the Governors into spending money on the expedition, because if local opposition produced cold feet they could be reminded that 'what may have been already spent will be so much thrown away'. Finally, 'I trust you to behave with the utmost temper and prudence. You'll have many enemies on the watch to take advantage of any little faux pas. I have given you a high character to the Governors for discretion; I shall lose all credit if you fail in coming up to it. . . .'[7]

Wilberforce did not lose any credit; Lieutenant Clarkson proved an admirable choice. Even before the expedition left Nova Scotia for Sierra Leone with 1,900 emigrants Wilberforce wrote congratulations and urged him to accept the Superintendency of the Settlement. Two clergymen were going out 'who will feel the poor Blacks are their fellow creatures and will labour to bring them to that state of happiness where all distinctions will be forever done away'. The two were of the Established Church but sympathetic to the varied Methodism they would find in their flock. Then Wilberforce told his 'Admiral': 'I conceive it probable from your having left England so suddenly, that you may not have carried with you many of those little conveniences in which *you Naval gentlemen* generally *abound*, and I send you by one of the ships that are now going out a writing desk which is fitted out for dressing of which I beg your acceptance, as a token of my affectionate remembrance. The Cabinet Maker says you must keep it as much as possible both from damp and heat, but if it is injured by the climate it can be restored when you return. . . .'[8]

Through all the vicissitudes of the faraway infant Settlement, Wilberforce remained optimistic and encouraging. 'Notwithstanding I regret the jarrings that have happened,' he wrote to Clarkson in July 1792, 'I cannot say I am very much surprised at them, human nature will be human nature, and except where it has been worked into the mind by a course of long discipline there is no quality so rarely found as disposition to obey, and to be moderate and acquiescing in the exercise of authority. . . . We will look out for an assistant to you. I don't like to call him a successor, with all possible diligence. Meanwhile we cannot spare you; take courage, my dear John, I trust God will support you and give you health and spirits to undergo all your trials. . . .'[9]

It was as an assistant to Clarkson that they sent out young Zachary Macaulay, who thereby comes into Wilberforce's circle where he was to shine with such lustre after his final return to England. Macaulay had left Jamaica with a troubled, gloomy spirit which his sister and brother-in-law, the Babingtons, restored and redirected while he stayed at Rothley Temple. Sierra Leone brought out Macaulay's brilliance as an administrator. It gave him Wilberforce's undying affection, which soon was mutual although Macaulay's severe, humourless character, and insatiable appetite for intellectual industry, would be tried by Wilberforce's jollities and jumps.

Sierra Leone's subsequent troubles would hurt Wilberforce. Day by day details matter little to his story but Carrington, one of the shareholders who never saw a dividend, considered that Thornton and Wilberforce mismanaged 'in a most ignorant manner'.[10] Wilberforce himself ascribed the near-failure to the delay in abolishing the Slave

Trade (the slavers tried to stifle a settlement devoted to peaceful commerce) and partly to the cost of defence, and the ruin caused by the French assault in the coming war.[11] Added to this the directors saw through a glass darkly. Wilberforce's imagination doubtless furnished a lively picture of Sierra Leone but neither he nor Thornton knew what a tropical palm tree looked like or ate a banana. They tried their best to understand the situation. Indeed one factor which led them eventually to withdraw confidence from John Clarkson and not send him back for a second term, was a belief that he had withheld essential information about the mortality rate.[12]

Sierra Leone, for all the mistakes, represented a dream. Wilberforce loved it as a token of his desire that England should devote public and private money to promoting 'the civilization and happiness of Africa in proportion to the degree in which we had been the chief instruments in prolonging their misery and barbarism'.[13] Pitt shared his enthusiasm, in theory at least, and 'used often to indulge in speculations',[14] (so Wilberforce told Grenville after Pitt's death) as to the best steps.

Wilberforce, from the start, saw Sierra Leone as a base for distant exploration, civilization, 'and still more bringing them acquainted with the great truths of Christianity'.[15] He knew nothing of the highly organized Muslim emirates south of the Sahara, and being a man of his age he equated civilization with the best European ways; but that does not spoil the splendour of his dream. He urged John Clarkson to make contact with the far interior, and suggested, ingenuously, that 'Mohametan priests' could be paid to bring in 'promising young men' to be educated and 'domesticated' by the African settlers from Nova Scotia. He and Thornton hoped to found a settlement similar to Sierra Leone on the Gold Coast.

For Wilberforce, Africa was the continent of the future. 'We know,' he wrote on 28 December 1791 in words that foreshadow Livingstone's vision, 'there are some considerable talents in Africa, and if we could once establish a connection with them, it might be productive of the most intensive benefit. . . . I think this idea of providing the means of *probing* the interior is never to be lost sight of; it may be attended by the most *splendid* and the most blessed consequences.'[16]

Africa, its future happiness and Europe's atonement for past oppressions, formed the theme which Wilberforce impressed on Pitt as they conferred on the morning before the next great Abolition debate. Pitt transmuted the theme into one of the most eloquent passages ever heard in the House of Commons.

Every 'friend of humanity', in Dorothy Wordsworth's phrase,[17] had lamented the defeat of 1791. William Smith and Granville Sharp organized a boycott of West Indian sugar; Clarkson stumped the

5

country distributing Abolitionist literature. As for Wilberforce, he was full of suggestions: 'The subject in question is one on which so many ideas crowd into my mind, that it is difficult to avoid being diffuse on it whenever I enter on it at all.'[18] His chief plan lay in mobilizing 'the virtue and humanity of the People'.[19] Soon after Parliament opened at the end of January 1792 he would give notice of a fresh Abolition motion. This would 'be the signal for the commencement of Action to all our numerous and widely dispersed friends',[20] so that when the debate came on, the Table would be loaded with petitions. It was. Even the Livery of London sent one.[21]

Another tide was rising, however: from France. Though Louis XVI still reigned, part constitutional monarch, part prisoner, Revolutionary violence had strengthened the distaste of propertied Englishmen, great or small, for high-flown conceits of liberty. They identified 'democracy' with mob rule. Even more than in 1791 they dreaded lest Abolition, by tampering with recognized rights, might encourage the Jacobin spirit. Fox gloried in the Revolution; William Smith, as a Unitarian, welcomed it; Thomas Clarkson returned from France full of it. Wilberforce found advisable, when giving notice on 9 March of his motion, to disclaim any intention to proceed from Abolition of the Trade to Emancipation of the slaves.[22] This was disingenuous and not quite honest and in his opening speech in the debate next month he backtracked, admitting his hope that slaves in the distant future would become free peasants.

More dangerous to the cause than fear of Jacobins stood the stark fact of Sainte Dominique (San Domingo). This most developed and prosperous French colony had been ruined by the rising of the mulattoes aided by the blacks, with much carnage of white settlers. San Domingo warned Englishmen what might happen in the British West Indies, since the rising had been provoked by disappointed hopes of political equality. So strong were Parliamentary feelings that Pitt had prevented Wilberforce moving Abolition at the end of the previous Session; Pitt had acted for Wilberforce's good, believing he would damage his cause if he moved at that moment, but the action strained their friendship.

Wilberforce refused pleas of others to drop his motion altogether until a more expedient time, for the flood of petitions for Abolition had proved the national feeling. Shortly after 6 p.m. on 2 April 1792, in a House where humanity struggled with expediency, he rose to move that 'The Trade . . . ought to be abolished', the motion which must precede leave to bring in an Abolition Bill.[23] The debate continued all night, culminating in Pitt's great speech, one of his most famous. As the early morning sun broke through the windows of the Chamber he seized the moment with a brilliant impromptu, quoting an apt couplet of Virgil from which he appealed to the House to bring a sunrise of happiness to Africa.

Burke a few days later called the Abolition debates 'the greatest eloquence ever displayed in the House',[24] but it was not Pitt's eloquence which decided the issue, nor Fox's, nor Wilberforce's own long and able opening speech with its moments of high emotion: ' "Africa! Africa!" exclaimed Mr. Wilberforce, "your sufferings have been the theme that has arrested and engages my heart – your sufferings no tongue can express; no language impart." '* The House heard them all with rapt attention. And followed a way out suggested by Dundas, who had now replaced Wilberforce as Pitt's closest friend. Saying he sought to bring extremists to a middle ground, though probably he was swayed by desire to postpone upheavals in the colonies for which he had assumed responsibility, Dundas suggested that the Abolition motion should pass with an amendment of one word: *gradual*. He talked of ten or fifteen years. He even threw in a scheme of gradual Emancipation. (Long years later, Wilberforce bitterly reproached himself for not calling Dundas's bluff and demanding Emancipation.) Speaker Addington supported Dundas. Mr. Speaker in 1792 could still give his private views when the House was in Committee and he not in his Chair; Addington seized on this 'middle path' whereby the crime of the Slave Trade might be condemned without a rash upset of the West Indies.

The House accepted Dundas's amendment; and by 230 votes to 85 resolved that the Slave Trade ought to be gradually abolished.

The Trade stood condemned; Wilberforce's friends congratulated him.[26] His first reaction was to be hurt and humiliated by failure to win the immediate Abolition he had aimed at since 1787. On reflection he felt a little encouraged. 'I cannot help regretting we have been able to do no more,' he wrote to John Clarkson in Sierra Leone, 'yet on the whole we have reason to be thankful for what we have obtained.'[27]

The word *gradual* had many meanings. Wilberforce and his friends determined that it should mean *very soon*. Fox hustled Dundas into prompt resolution by emphasizing: 'Whilst the House paused, the work of death was not suspended on the Coast of Africa.'[28] Dundas agreed to introduce his definitive resolution at the end of the month, but Burke, whose views of liberty had been moderated by the French Revolution, urged on him[29] an adaptation of his own original African Code of the early 'eighties, in which Regulation, Abolition and Emancipation should proceed slowly together. Wilberforce knew it unworkable, depending too much on the co-operation of Traders and on the Colonial legislatures, whose members rejected Abolition of any kind as 'totally subversive'.[30]

On 27 April 1792 Dundas proposed that Abolition should take effect

---

* Young Lord Wycombe, M.P., heir to Lord Lansdowne, wrote to his father in a long account of the debate '[Wilberforce] intended probably to be moderate but I could not help taxing him in my mind with exaggeration.'[25]

in 1800, seven years ahead, three years earlier than the Gradual Abolition recently enacted by the King of Denmark for the tiny Danish colonies. Richard Wellesley, Lord Mornington, for whom Wilberforce retained a real affection despite Mornington's wayward morals, proposed the date should be altered to *1 January 1793*, a mere eight months ahead. Wilberforce seconded the amendment. The House compromised with *1 January 1796*.

The Resolutions, however, were diverted by the House of Lords into the quicksands: the Lords demanded fresh evidence.

Wilberforce had a further humiliation. Captain John Kimber, a Bristol slaver whom he had named when pressed by the House, for flogging to death a menstruous negress, had been arrested on the strength of Wilberforce's word and put on trial for murder. The ship's surgeon and a seaman who had produced the story gave their evidence badly and two boys who had helped at the flogging never appeared. The Admiralty judge, Sir James Marriott,* leaned heavily towards the defence throughout the trial. The jury acquitted Kimber and the judge committed the prosecution witnesses for perjury. Kimber wrote to Wilberforce demanding a public apology, £5,000 and a government post. He followed up with menaces and harried Wilberforce, now and again, for two years.[31]

Kimber was a mere pinprick beside the humiliation of gradual Abolition. Wilberforce no longer had the hopes of quick success which had buoyed him since 1787. 'I daily become more sensible that my work must be affected by constant and regular exertions rather than by sudden and violent ones.'[32] Whenever he should revive the question, Dundas or others might divert it to Gradualness, a coward's answer which could postpone Abolition indefinitely. Wilberforce never harboured grudges; but it is debatable whether the disillusionment with Dundas's character in 1792 lingered in his mind to influence subconsciously – certainly not consciously – his judgement in 1805 which brought Dundas to ruin.

---

* Marriott was simultaneously Master of Trinity Hall, Cambridge, and disliked by the Fellows so much that he stayed away for years. (DNB.)

CHAPTER TWELVE

The Coming of War

In the spring of 1792 Henry Thornton suggested to Wilberforce that they set up a 'chummery' at Battersea Rise, the small estate which Thornton had bought in Clapham. Each would pay his share of the housekeeping.

Battersea Rise became Wilberforce's real home for the next five years, a small squat Queen Anne house to which Thornton added wings; Pitt is reputed to have designed the oval library which looked across lawns shaded by old elms and firs and tulip trees. Clapham Common lay immediately to the north.[1] Wilberforce considered it a 'poor mimicry of the real (live) country',[2] for Clapham village had a population of 2,700; but it was refreshing after the bustle and soot and fogs of the capital. Number 4, Palace Yard, became more a perch and an office, and like the houses of most public men had a room for those who sought audience. Their extraordinary variety made Hannah More dub it a Noah's Ark, full of beasts clean and unclean. (Wilberforce had once told her naughtily that the House of Commons was like Noah's Ark – many beasts and a few humans.)

Thornton built two smaller houses on the edges of his estate: Broomfield Lodge, which Edward Eliot rented, and another which Charles Grant bought and named Grant Glenelg. Thornton relations and William Smith already lived in the village; Stephen, Macaulay and Teignmouth settled there from overseas at the turn of the century. Clapham thus acquired its special flavour and repute, though the misleading term 'Clapham Sect' never was applied in Wilberforce's lifetime.* For their parson, Thornton secured shy John Venn. In his early thirties, like Wilberforce and Thornton, and married to the

---

* The origin of 'Clapham Sect' may be the essay title of James Stephen the Younger's review of Milner's *Life* and Lord Teignmouth's *Life*, published in 1844. Sydney Smith is sometimes credited with the term but he referred only to 'the patient Christians of Clapham'. The church historian Michael Hennell believes it may have been used in the *Record* church newspaper before 1844.

Kitty King from Hull who had commented in 1786 that Mr. Wilberforce would be a useful member of society if his life were preserved,
John Venn attracted such large congregations that canny late-comers
in winter could sit by the vestry fire listening through the open door.
'Quite a first rater,' was Wilberforce's verdict to Hannah More, and
he told Eliot: 'I like him very much, and if I am not greatly mistaken
indeed, you will grow inordinately fond of him. . . . Really, I think
Pitt would do well to make him a bishop.'[3] Pitt did not.

Venn profited much from Wilberforce when they went on a summer
tour, Venn told his father, the distinguished Evangelical who had
been vicar of Huddlesfield, that he had very seldom met with a person
who appeared to be more devoted to God: 'He is no common Christian:
his knowledge of divine things and his experience of the power of the
Gospel are very extraordinary.'[4] Old Henry Venn, who did not know
of Wilberforce's temptations to indolence, ascribed to his influence
John's conquest of slothfulness.

Battersea Rise was in fact a place for delightful waste of time as
much as for the industry, conclaves and mutual self-criticism which
Thornton, Babington and Wilberforce considered so important.
Wilberforce could never resist prolonging a chat. 'My neighbour
[i.e. Thornton] declares we had a tête-à-tête of above $\frac{1}{2}$ an hour
on the stairs and was very eloquent on the subject,' he scribbled in a
postscript to Bishop Pretyman;[5] while Thornton noted in the 'spiritual'
diary he kept very spasmodically: '. . . . talked with Wilber and G.N.
grew tired and rather out of temper at the length of our conversation. . . .'
And a day or two later: 'Talked with Wilber a few hours on politics
gaining much information from him. . . . Hurried off to dine with
Dr. Milner and Wilber – talked two or three hours. . . .'[6]

If Clapham and Battersea Rise, 'that honoured and almost hallowed
spot' as he described it in old age to Venn's son,[7] became one pole of
Wilberforce's existence in the 1790s, the other was Bath.

Several times a year he would travel the Bath Road. His log of
miles in a year, whether to and from Bath or elsewhere and everywhere, was amazing in an age when public figures usually progressed
in an orderly annual round between London, their country estates
for the shooting, then Bath or Cheltenham or Buxton for the waters.
Wilberforce knew his restlessness or 'volatility' might be a fault;
he assured Wyvill that ill health had mercifully curbed it[8] but five
years later he told Eliot: 'I hope in time to be a less volatile, unsteady
being.'[9]

Down and up the Bath Road he would bowl by post chaise, or sometimes by his own carriage and slow 'job horses'. His 'varlet',[10] as he
spelt and presumably pronounced valet, and Mr. Craggs 'a sort of
secretary'[11] (rather useless) would accompany him. Wilberforce would
sometimes steal by in a 'thievish kind of proceeding . . . without

calling on any of the friends which are sprinkled around my line of march.'[12] More often his carriage would turn off the highway up some avenue of lime or elm and soon Wilberforce would be savouring his constant pleasure of conversation, with Addington at Woodleigh or Bob Smith at Wycombe Abbey, and always if possible with Montagu at Sandleford Priory, the gothic show place inherited from his aunt Elizabeth Montagu, the first 'Bluestocking'.

It was on one of these Bath journeys that he visited his friend and political opponent Sir William Young, just back from his slave plantations with much to report, at Salt Hill near Slough, and Boswell joined the supper party. The *Life of Johnson* had been published the previous year making Boswell famous. He had been to Eton to pick up his boy Alexander and came into supper half drunk, so Wilberforce thought. 'Suddenly he started and said, we have not said grace. I determined not to let him off and spoke to him next morning seriously. He was evidently low and depressed and he appeared to have many serious feelings.'[13] At supper Boswell had boasted being a rabid anti-Abolitionist. They discussed this and Dr. Johnson's religion and Boswell's soul. In a rare mysterious mood Boswell announced he would go off on a walking tour to the West, and departed with *The Spirit of Athens*, a book by Sir William Young, under his arm. Perhaps Bozzy was throwing Wilberforce off the scent for he walked no farther than Taplow, where he had arranged to call on Lord and Lady Inchiquin, and next day came back to London[14] – not a Wilberforce convert.

Wilberforce would pretend to himself that he went to Bath for solitude and study after the turmoils of the Session, but he always wanted a friend. Inviting Eliot he wrote: 'Spa water in company will do better for me than Bath water in solitude, which (entire solitude I mean) though not unpleasant to me occasionally, is certainly injurious to my health.'[15] His health was never endangered by solitude at Bath: the hurry and noise of his rented house in Queen's Square or (in the broiling summer of '93) on Claverton down, drove his sister and Dr. Clarke to take a place for themselves.[16]

One of the benefits of Bath for Wilberforce was Hannah More. Their Cheddar charities continued in full swing from Cowslip Green and the sisters now had a house in Bath, having sold their Bristol school. Hannah More helped him resolve the inward conflict which still obtruded between piety and gaiety of heart. 'I declare,' she assured him, 'I think you are serving God by making yourself agreeable . . . to worldly but well disposed people, who would never be attracted to religion by grave and severe divines, even if such fell in their way.' His happy ways were an 'honest bait' by which acquaintances who were dead and buried in luxury and indulgence might be awakened. They would realize he was not driven to religion by lack of relish for enjoyment and wit, and they would better discern the power of the

Christian faith when they reflected that gaiety did not seduce him from 'the rigour of your principles and the severity of your morals. . . .'[17] Wilberforce accepted her counsel. As the years passed, for all his private self-examinations, he looked on joy as one of the choicest fruits of the Spirit which he loved to share.

His 'honest bait' became well known at Bath and attracted its share of misunderstandings and sneers. Conversing in the spacious Pump Room a general and he happened to disagree on the wording of a Latin tag from Horace. Wilberforce had a Horace in his pocket and they consulted it as they strolled. A newspaper gossip thereupon recorded: 'Behold an instance of the Pharisaism of St. Wilberforce! He was lately seen walking up and down in the Bath Pump Room reading his prayers, like his predecessors of old, who prayed in the corners of the streets, to be seen of men.'[18] Wilberforce felt indignant, to judge by his diary note of contrition, but Hannah More, much amused, bid him not take his prayer book to Bath next time.

Two fishes from these apostolic nets were important for Wilberforce's wider work: the widowed Countess Waldegrave and her mother, who was Duchess of Gloucester by her second marriage and thus, to his royal displeasure, sister-in-law to the King.

The Duchess, once a great beauty, had herself been a widowed Countess Waldegrave, with three daughters, when the Duke of Gloucester fell in love. They kept their marriage secret for years. The King then acknowledged it – grudgingly because Maria was not only non-royal but illegitimate, one of the three bewitching bastards of Horace Walpole's brother by a Pall Mall milliner. The Gloucesters' marriage preceded the Royal Marriage Act and Maria was an un-doubted Royal Highness (even her Waldegrave daughters had to address her as such) though cold shouldered by the Court. Her eldest daughter married her cousin the 4th Earl Waldegrave and was left widowed with a large young family; Lady Waldegrave's life became a succession of tragedies and bereavements.

When her eldest boy drowned at Eton Wilberforce sent the news to Hannah suggesting she offer comfort. She replied: 'By return of post I received a long letter not from poor Lady Waldegrave but from the Duchess of Gloucester, so humble and respectful that you would have thought I had been the Princess and she the Cowslip Green woman.'[19] The Duchess's letter (now among the present Lord Waldegrave's papers) accepted Miss More's offer and added: 'I shall derive the utmost satisfaction from the visit, as your exemplary piety will give her all the consolation she *can* receive at present. Give me leave, dear Madam, to subscribe myself, your very great admirer. . . .'[20]

A rewarding friendship began, of great influence on the Duchess. She had been a shrew who made her husband's life so miserable that they had almost parted in 1787, seven years before Hannah More came into her life. But when the Duchess died in 1807, two years after the Duke, Hannah More (who was not given to exaggeration even about princesses), mourned 'her piety, her strong trust in God, her ardent gratitude for his mercies, her thorough conviction of his goodness.'[21] Even the King had lost his dislike of her.

Wilberforce had met the Gloucesters in the South of France but it was not until nearly a year after Hannah's visit that he became a friend of the family. 'Mr. Wilberforce was with me Saturday evening,' the Duchess told her. 'If he liked us as well as we liked him he will come again: he is very agreeable, and very good; I wish all young men were like him. He has a very great respect for you. . . .'[22]

The Gloucesters had two children, Princess Sophia and Prince William Frederick. Unlike his first cousins the King's sons, the Prince had morals and a knowledge of religion which much impressed Bishop Porteus when he examined him for Confirmation.[23] He was nineteen when Wilberforce became a family friend and he soon looked on Wilberforce as his hero.

Prince William, as 2nd Duke of Gloucester and Edinburgh, was to prove a stalwart friend to Wilberforce at the height of the Abolition crisis when the other Hanoverians opposed him.

Wilberforce had every need of a firm base and faithful friends as Britain entered the French Revolutionary War, for he drew nearer to the loneliness of a true political independence.

Wilberforce was not a pacifist. Some years after Waterloo Thomas Clarkson asked him to support a pacifist society and he replied that Scripture allowed defensive wars; moreover if he had proclaimed himself 'a condemner of war universally, I should have put it out of my power to contribute my aid towards preventing my Country engaging in war, in any particular instance'.[24] Before the outbreak of war in February 1793 he indeed did all in his power, being imbued 'with a sense of the extreme inexpediency of war in the present situation of the country'.[25]

Unlike Wyvill he had no sympathy with the attempts of Tom Paine and others to transplant the French Revolution and to ferment the unrest caused by the recent disastrous harvest. Wilberforce told a sympathizer of Paine: 'Surely the disposition to fall in with such doctrines as are contained in the writings of these miscalled champions out for *freedom* is, at bottom, pride and fullness bred of irreligion.'[26] He did not, however, share Burke's desire to oppose the Revolution root and branch. When the Convention made him an honorary citizen of France he never publicly repudiated the embarrassing honour, to the disgust of high Tories,[27] and he thought Burke a menace to peace: 'O that I could transport Burke to some fertile island in the Great South Sea.'[28]

5*

To the last minute Wilberforce worked strenuously on Pitt, knowing and approving Pitt's secret efforts to end the hostilities on the Continent. Wilberforce had agreed by voice[29] and vote that Britain must honour her treaty obligations to restrict the navigation of the Scheldt to Dutch shipping (a treaty to British advantage) but he believed Pitt would stop the French invasion of the Low Countries if he now made public his negotiations, on a basis of France giving back her conquests while Austria and Prussia allowed her to become a republic.[30] In the vital debate of 1 February 1793 Wilberforce tried to catch the Speaker's eye to say so. Pitt sent Bankes to beg him stay silent because his intervention could do 'irreparable mischief'.[31] He had no further opportunity to speak before the French declaration of war reached London.

Pitt did not withdraw friendship or confidence because of this dissent, but it angered Wilberforce's Tory supporters, such as Dr. Hey of Leeds, who hated the Revolution, or the West Riding manufacturers who scented quick profits. Christopher Wyvill, on the other hand, whose sympathy for the Revolution had extinguished his ardour for Pitt, was cross because Wilberforce did not denounce the ministers as warmongers. Wilberforce replied: 'I own to you I cannot quite acquit Administration of *all* blame, or I should rather say, I don't believe I should have acted quite as they have done; yet from my heart I declare I cannot condemn them. . . . My dear sir, independently on [*sic*] all considerations of policy what a dreadful, what a monstrous idea is that of two great Kingdoms using all the talents which God gave for the promotion of general happiness, for their material misery and destruction. May the mercy of the Great Disposer of all human events watch over us, and not us only, but over those poor misguided French who so greatly deserve our pity.'[32]

Wilberforce deplored the war for many reasons. He foresaw the freezing of moderate Parliamentary reform. He did not want radical reform of the Constitution and used unnecessarily vigorous language against a Sheffield petition for short Parliaments and a wide franchise,[33] nor did he vote with the small minority for Grey's famous motion; but he wanted to end abuses of the electoral system. Pitt had no such intention after a few months of war, and Wilberforce admitted to Wyvill a streak of personal cowardice in himself: 'This whole subject is one on which I neither could nor can talk with Mr. Pitt without pain and perhaps mutual recrimination, therefore I avoid it.'[34] He believed war would also set back his 'reformation of manners'.[35] In this he prophesied wrongly, for the national crisis in fact created a new seriousness among sizeable sections of the upper classes, appalled by the fate which overtook the self-indulgent and luxury loving aristocracy of France.

As for the slaves, Wilberforce had quick and grievous evidence of the war's effect when he attempted to revive the question in the Commons on 26 February 1793, and thereby to prod the Lords into a decision on Gradual Abolition. He was recovering from a heavy cold in the head and entered the Chamber dubious of success, knowing he was to be opposed by his slave-owning friend Sir William Young. A thin House threw out the motion by eight votes and thus effectively reversed the Resolutions of the previous year.[36] The Lords discussed the question some six weeks later on a prevaricating motion by an anti-Abolitionist peer, a debate enlivened by the maiden speech of the young Duke of Clarence, the future Sailor King, who had served in Jamaica where by his own private admission he lived 'a terrible debauched life'. The royal duke 'asserted that the promoters of the Abolition were either fanatics or hypocrites, and in one of those classes he ranked Mr. Wilberforce'.[37] ('In my opinion,' commented the Prince of Wales, 'Republican at heart.')[38]

Two days later, on 13 April, Wilberforce scotched rumours that he was fainting in his course. 'Nothing,' he assured James Currie of Liverpool, 'is farther than the truth'.[39] It was a calumny such as every public man must expect (this was a gentle dig at Currie who had lately abused Pitt in a widely read anonymous pamphlet, Wilberforce being one of the very few in the secret of the authorship). Explaining why he never could give up, this private letter of 1793 reveals the steel spring within the feeble exterior, the reason why, as Fuller complained, Wilberforce jumped up whenever they knocked him down.

'In the case of every question of political expediency,' he wrote, 'there appears to me room for the consideration of times and seasons – at one period, under one set of circumstances it may be proper to push, at another and in other circumstances to withhold our efforts. But in the present instance where the actual commission of guilt is in question, a man who *fears God* is not at liberty. To you I will say a strong thing which the motive I have just suggested will both explain and justify. If I thought the immediate Abolition of the Slave Trade would cause an insurrection in our islands, I should not for an instant remit my most strenuous endeavours.* Be persuaded then, I shall still less ever make this grand cause the sport of caprice, or sacrifice it to motives of political convenience or personal feeling.'

In that spirit he tried another tack towards total Abolition. On 14 May 1793 he sought leave to bring in a Bill to prohibit the carrying of slaves in British ships to foreign territories (short title: The Foreign Slave Bill). Both sides found difficulty, so late in the session, in mustering supporters, and it was a very thin House which chuckled at Lord Carhampton's portrayal of Wilberforce as a bit addled by five years'

---

* When the letter (*Currie MSS*) was published in the Wilberforce official *Life* of 1838 (II, p. 22) this was the revolutionary sentence imperceptibly expunged, referred to in my preface.

close application to a single subject: 'He therefore advised him to brush up his person a little, send for a hair-dresser, put a few curls on those straight locks, go to the play – first to Covent Garden then to Drury Lane – if they were shut up, let him go to Sadler's Wells, and in time he should be glad to have the pleasure of seeing him with a female friend under his arm strolling at night round Covent Garden.' According to the gossip of two or three Members to Hannah More, Wilberforce took it with great patience and turned the laugh 'with a degree of wit, gaiety, and good humour which delighted the whole House.'[40]

And Wilberforce won, by 7 votes in a House of only 79 out of the full complement of 515. Elated, and noticing several opponents slip away, he immediately sought leave to bring in another Bill, to regulate the number of slaves which might be imported into British colonies, but he miscalculated. Enough of his friends had gone to supper or bed to cause a defeat by 10 in a House of 64. He was left with the Foreign Slave Bill, which he introduced eight days later only to lose its Third Reading by a mere two votes, again in a nearly empty House.

Had it passed, Wilberforce knew it would never have got through the Lords in the nine days left of the Session. Stephan Fuller the Jamaica Agent, however, was alarmed.[41] Sir William Young and several other planters had supported the Bill, believing that if slaves could not be imported into foreign islands the price of slaves in the British would fall. Wilberforce had driven a first thin wedge between planters and merchants.

Early next Session, in February 1794, he brought in the Foreign Slave Bill again. Thornton reported to Macaulay in Sierra Leone: 'Pitt and Fox spoke admirably and Wilberforce's reply was admirable too. Though we beat them by a majority of 22 [actually 23] I fear there is much doubt and difficulty remaining as to our clearing the Bill even through the House of Commons. It is however great news for Africa. May God grant that it may be a prelude to happier days on that continent.'[42] Young opposed it, but several Planters voted with Wilberforce: Stephen Fuller complained they had given 'more help than they ought to Mr. Wilberforce's scheme of promoting a division between the Planters and the African Merchants'.[43] Fuller knew it would be fatal if these natural allies fell out.

Wilberforce, however, had a new and formidable antagonist, the first holder of the newly created office of Secretary of State for War and the Colonies, Dundas. He had ended a letter to Wilberforce the previous autumn, 'But you my dear little fellow, take care of yourself, and oblige all your friends, none more than yours most affectionately, *Henry Dundas.*'[44] But now having despatched a force to seize the French West Indian islands he wanted no upsets in the British. He replied to a private appeal from Wilberforce to support the Foreign

Slave Bill: 'I don't dispute that a great deal of very good reasoning can be offered on the principles you state, but I know with absolute *certainty* that your Bill will be considered by the Colonies as an encroachment upon their legislative rights and they will not submit to it unless compelled. Upon that ground I have used all the influence to prevent any question on the subject being agitated during the war at least. . . .' And having failed, he would stay silent; even that would be difficult 'if I did not believe that your Bill would not pass the House of Lords, and of course the mischief which I dread from it will be postponed'.[45]

News came that the French Republic had abolished Slavery in a desperate and successful attempt to stop the blacks in San Domingo supporting the British invasion of the island. The French part at least of the 'Foreign Slave Trade' might appear to be dying of its own accord. At the Second Reading on 25 February Pitt urged the House to support Wilberforce in case it should revive.

At the vote the Noes must stay in the Chamber, the Ayes go out to the Lobby. Sheridan, who had come down to the House drunk, intended to vote for the Bill but lay full length snoring on an empty bench and the Abolitionists could not get him out. He was however unwittingly paired by John Dent, a firm Slaver, who was not quite so drunk and stumbled into the Lobby not knowing what he did.[46] Wilberforce won by 18.

Sharp disappointment followed. Lord Grenville, the Foreign Secretary, wrote to Wilberforce that he saw no point in pushing the Foreign Slave Bill in the Lords because it would give the dominant Slaver interest the opportunity to delay consideration of the larger question. He would speak to that effect while expressing approval of 'any attempt to diminish that which I wish utterly to abolish'.[47] Wilberforce felt 'half-vexed' with Grenville though prepared to be patient. Soon, in Fuller's expressive phrase, the Bill was 'fast asleep in the House of Lords'.[48]

There it remained. And that summer Thomas Clarkson retired, pleading ruined health and empty pocket; Wilberforce and others subscribed to buy him an annuity and he disappeared into the country for the twelve years which are ignored by his *History of the Abolition*. But if one strong man fell out, another arrived, who, for the task that remained, would prove the more apt and powerful. James Stephen returned from the West Indies for good, with three turtles in his luggage, the best being for Wilberforce, who passed it on to a bishop for a charity dinner.[49] He joined the Admiralty bar, quickly made his name and fortune, and with brilliant legal mind and enormous intellectual energy became a formidable recruit for Abolition.

CHAPTER THIRTEEN

The Independent

Wilberforce reconciled himself slowly and questioningly to 'a war more bloody I fear than any in modern times (except that there have been few great battles) and more ferocious in its principles; one cannot . . . contemplate this afflicting and humiliating scene, without grief and shame and disgust.'[1] He could not stomach bellicose Britons who talked of military glory and toasted 'death to the French'; for him, it was 'one of the most horrid aspects of war that it extinguishes all the kindly feelings of the heart and makes men tigers and wolves to each other'.[2] On the other hand he would not join the witch-hunt against sincere critics of the war.

By January 1794 the French had grown not only more determined abroad but tyrannical at home, sweeping away the Christian religion and curtailing private liberty. Hoping that France might turn out Robespierre and try an American-style Constitution, Wilberforce would have preferred British withdrawal from the Continent into a kind of armed isolation, rather than a formal treating with the Convention, which 'would be most probably productive of far worse calamities than . . . the continuance of the war.'[3] It might even bring revolution to England. He therefore approved Pitt's suspension of Habeas Corpus in May 1794. Pitt continued to treat him almost as a member of the Cabinet, certainly as if he had taken the oath of a Privy Councillor, and discussed state affairs freely 'under a tacit and implied though not an expressed injunction of secrecy'.[4] Were a Privy Councillorship or ministerial office ever offered, Wilberforce refused.

At midsummer Lord Howe's fleet returned victorious to Portsmouth from the Glorious First of June, and Wilberforce acquired first-hand experience of enemy attitudes. 'Would it not have surprised you,' he wrote jauntily to Muncaster from Portsmouth on 30 June 1794, 'when the wind had a little cleared away the smoke in which the royal salute had enveloped the skies, to have seen Harry Thornton and C. Grant and your humble servant perched on the poop of the *Queen* at Spithead. Yet so it was. We thought Portsmouth might be a highly useful as well as an interesting spectacle, and accordingly went thither a couple of days and should have stayed longer (I at least) if the Royal Family's being there had not made the place so very bustling and kept away some persons we principally wished to see. We found matter of lasting reflection. . . .' The wounded of both sides and the French prisoners stimulated 'many ideas' for the relief of war sufferers, which remained one of Wilberforce's concerns right through until after Waterloo. He was also shocked by the revolutionary sentiments of the French: 'One man said to me with vehemence and eloquence, words I shall never forget. *La Liberté est mon dieu: c'est même pour moi avant Dieu.*'[5]

He found even more matter for reflection when news arrived in the late autumn that Freetown in Sierra Leone had been sacked on 28 September by a pitiless if raggle-taggle French force.

Soon Wilberforce began to harbour serious doubts about prolonging the war. Hope of counter-revolution had receded; France would not collapse from starvation since the grain fleet had slipped through while Howe fought the Glorious First of June; royalists and the Continental Allies had failed in their military operations and the Duke of York would shortly be isolated in Flanders with his back to the sea. Robespierre's fall and the gradual end of the Terror produced an over-optimistic impression that the French might abandon their ambition to carry the Revolution through Europe, so that to Wilberforce the war appeared to have no further object than the aggrandizement of Prussia and Austria and the British conquest of sugar islands, each one reverting to slavery when seized, thus providing more markets for slavers. He believed that Pitt's continued zest for war derived partly from the pressure of his new Portland Whig colleagues, wishing to prove themselves, and much from the ambition of Dundas for colonial conquest.

Wilberforce sought counsel of friends.[6] He was told by Pitt that Britain could possess no security until France lay crushed, whereas 'Citizen' Stanhope begged him to denounce the war outright. He did not contemplate, however, going further than proposing exploratory negotiations towards an honourable peace. Even this agitated Pitt. The price of Wilberforce's open dissent might be a parting of friends of fifteen years. Pitt's attitude disclosed the strength of Wilberforce's position in the country: Pitt could brush aside as party politics the opposition of Fox and Grey and Sheridan, not of Wilberforce. Too many thousands throughout Britain looked to him for moral leadership, especially those Dissenters who hated the war but supported it as a grim necessity so long as Wilberforce did.

Three days before Christmas and eight before the opening of Parliament, Wilberforce wrote in anguish to Eliot, his dear friend and Pitt's brother-in-law, who had not yet come up from the West Country:

'I don't think you'll be much surprised, knowing what has formerly been the state of my mind, but I am sure your affectionate heart will be not a little hurt, to hear that I fear I must differ from Pitt on the important point of continuing the war . . .' They were to confer again, 'but I fear he has nothing to urge which will convince me of the soundness of his conclusion. I am sure that (praying to be enabled to decide aright) I have pondered over this subject most seriously, coolly and fully, and I am more and more convinced that we ought to make a *general* peace if practicable, on equitable terms (preparing meanwhile for the most vigorous exertions) and that though our offer should be rejected, it would certainly be productive of excellent effects in this country, and very probably might do good in France.

'I need hardly say that the prospect of a public difference with Pitt is extremely painful to me, and though I trust this friendship for me has sunk too deep in his heart to be soon worn out, I confess it hangs on me like a weight I cannot remove, when I anticipate the whole situation. My spirits are hardly equal to the encounter. However, I hope it will please God to enable me to act the part of an honest man in this trying occasion. . . . You and I, my dear friend, have formed, I hope, a connection which will last for *ever*. May it please God to preserve us both and make us partakers of the same eternal blessedness. Meanwhile believe that so far as one can look forward to anything future I shall ever be – most truly and affectionately yours, *W. Wilberforce*.'[7]

On the night before the opening of Parliament, while Pitt held his Cabinet dinner to read the Speech from the Throne, Wilberforce held another in Palace Yard; but his 'Cabinet' was not unanimous. It was agreed he should propose an amendment to the address and Duncombe would second it. Bankes and Thornton were for him, as their speeches showed next night. Muncaster and Montagu could not bring themselves to promise votes against Pitt. Wilberforce slept badly.

On the evening of Tuesday, 30 December 1794, after the young Irishman George Canning had seconded the Address with such vigorous wavings of his handkerchief that he caused Pitt and Dundas to edge apart on the Treasury bench in front of him,[8] Wilberforce moved his Amendment, praying the Throne to try for peace, and to continue the war only if the violence and ambition of the enemy frustrated the attempt.

Anxious neither to embarrass Pit nor to encourage the Foxite Opposition and the 'Jacobins' in the country, Wilberforce felt afterwards that his speech had been 'incoherent'. It made a deep impression on the House. Windham, indeed, now Secretary at War, replied in astonishment and anger while Fox rejoiced, scenting a convert. Pitt spoke long but moderately, without barbs or bitterness, and then had the satisfaction of seeing Wilberforce's amendment soundly beaten by 173 at 4.30 a.m. But, in the Duke of Portland's words a few days later,

'Pitt seemed pretty seriously hurt by it',[9] and during the short night that followed this debate he could not sleep, possibly the single occasion when public affairs robbed Pitt of his sleep.* Wilberforce himself woke up next night worrying, nor could he stop politics running round his head in church on New Year's Day.

To Pitt, Wilberforce's action appeared desertion and betrayal. Neither he nor Fox, who hurried round to encourage Wilberforce to cross the floor of the House, could grasp the situation. Canning showed more perception. He guessed from Wilberforce's speech, and from conversing privately with him in the Lobby afterwards, that having discharged his conscience by an attempt at peace, he and his followers would again support the war. On 5 January 1795, to the disgust of the Foxites, Wilberforce spoke against Sheridan's motion to restore Habeas Corpus, opposing him 'in a few words but very decidedly', as Pitt reported to the King.[10]

In the eyes of the Duke of Portland, who had become Home Secretary when Dundas became Secretary of State for War and the Colonies, this was 'a pretended recantation. . . . It is a ruse which cannot be mistaken,' he wrote to Fitzwilliam in Ireland; and he despised Pitt for not smashing Wilberforce, Bankes and such other 'pretended friends'.[11] The King said to Portland: 'I always told Mr. Pitt they were hypocrites and not to be trusted.'[12]

Wilberforce again spoke and voted with the Opposition on 26 January on Grey's motion for peace with France, although moving his own more moderate amendment. The King apparently considered that this action upheld his verdict on Wilberforce. At the next levée he cut him, passing to the next man without so much as a word or glance, his customary way of expressing his royal displeasure.[13] Thereafter the King opposed Abolition, whereas a few years earlier at a levée he had asked earnestly as he reached Wilberforce, 'How are your black clients, Mr. Wilberforce?' Early in 1795, when the Commons threw out the next Abolition motion, Stephen Fuller wrote to Jamaica that they little realized how much they owed to the King.[14]

The King had a knack of identifying himself with the feelings of the ordinary John Bull, who supported the war and saw Wilberforce rocking the boat at a time of national crisis. 'Great indignation is felt,' noted Farington the portrait painter in his diary for 9 January 1795, 'at Wilberforce having joined the Opposition, or rather at his having moved the Amendment.'[15] And Sir George Beaumont, Wordsworth's patron, told Farington early in February that Wilberforce 'had done much mischief by his motion', which could do no good as he had been sure to lose it; Beaumont thought the man had been prevailed upon by

---

* The Wilberforces believed that the Mutiny at the Nore was the one other occasion, but Croker (*Quarterly Review 62*, p. 274) produced evidence to suggest that news of the Mutiny did not stop Pitt falling sound asleep again.

the Dissenters.[16] In Yorkshire the clothiers were furious at their County Member attacking the war which enriched them. Next summer he was cut by the womenfolk of some of his strongest supporters.

Only a few close friends such as Thornton realized that Wilberforce's conscience drove him towards a new form of political independence. Many Members called themselves 'independents': the term meant almost what a later age would call private member or backbencher, or, at the least, one who did not owe his seat to Administration or to a patron who controlled his vote. The County Members regarded themselves as independents. But they could not always vote as conscience directed if they wished to keep their seats; and they did not expect, as individuals, to influence the course of politics: no independent by himself had secured a major change of policy. To vote for Administration one day and to vote against it a little later, as Wilberforce had done, was unheard of except when an unscrupulous man aimed to rise to power on the ruin of others: Portland and perhaps the King suspected this was Wilberforce's game.

The rare breed of an independent in the modern sense, who genuinely stands apart from the great parties, was coming to birth in Wilberforce. Already, to strengthen his detachment, he had renounced the eighteenth-century politician's use of 'interest' to secure Government favours for friends and relatives. A letter to Pitt dated 6 September 1794 had referred to 'the last case of patronage about which I will ever worry you'.[17] 'This was a hard sacrifice but duty required it,' he told a suppliant twenty years later,[18] and his own mother was cross that he refused to push her brother, or various poor relations. He still suggested suitable candidates for church preferment and occasionally urged Pitt to find a place for someone who had suffered for Abolition principles in the West Indies.[19] He refused any longer to undergird his electoral prospects by soliciting favours for constituents: it took eight years from his Conversion to identify the universal, time-honoured system of 'interest' as a form of corruption, and many long years before his lead would be generally followed. However, a County Member had the duty to suggest candidates for Crown offices such as surveyorships; Wilberforce got round the difficulty by inviting nominations from local magistrates as a means of rewarding them for their voluntary services.

Despite having thus prepared the way, his open act of independence of January 1795 took Pitt by surprise. The breach yawned between them. The thought of it depressed and hurt. Wilberforce grieved at hearing of a 'Party of *the old firm* at the Speaker's, and he not there';[20] but, as he wrote to one of them, 'I feel too much to associate with any of you without embarrassment and pain.'[21] He never forgot 'a most kind letter' Pitt wrote when 'all the hot Pittites would scarcely speak to me'.[22]

The breach was of short duration. On 21 March Bob Smith brought Pitt and Wilberforce together at the dinner table, both a little embarrassed and self-consciously kind to each other. Three weeks later Wilberforce called at Downing Street for the first time since the rupture and they found common ground in abusing Fitzwilliam whom Pitt had recalled from governing Ireland after eighty disastrous days. Then on the last weekend of April Eliot contrived to bring his two closest friends to Clapham, although some constraint remained.

Early in May Wilberforce decided he must oppose the Government's decision to increase, despite the hard times, the Prince of Wales's allowance on the occasion which the King with unconscious irony called 'the happy event of the nuptials of the Prince and Princess of Wales'. This time Pitt did not resent or misunderstand Wilberforce's opposition and when Eliot again invited them to dinner, with Ryder too, the four of them walked, 'foyned', laughed and read verses together in the garden as if nothing had ever come between them.[23]

Dundas stayed sour. Wilberforce wanted to call on him (actually to discuss Admiral Sir Charles Middleton's threatened resignation as a Sea Lord) and Dundas refused to see him. Though claiming unaltered affection, Dundas wrote: 'I have a very decided opinion that some of your late political conduct and the lead you have taken in Parliamentary discussions have done irreparable mischief. . . .' He asserted that unless Wilberforce intended openly to join the Opposition he was behaving rashly and without due information.[24]

Dundas, as the senior minister directing the war, now had reason to be angry. For Pitt had swung round. Pitt could not openly support Wilberforce's next peace motion on 27 May, though the two conferred amicably beforehand and it was he who persuaded him to consult with Fox and Grey; but he had determined to try for peace, as Wilberforce had urged. Pitt's decision also angered Windham, who as Secretary at War had charge of supply and recruiting. During the debate Windham hurled gibes at Wilberforce.[25]

A few days before the end of the Session Wilberforce wrote on 18 June 1795 to the 2nd Earl Camden, his Goostree contemporary who had succeeded Fitzwilliam in Ireland, that by the start of next Session he hoped 'matters will have become so clear one way or the other as to enable me again to support those with whom it must ever be painful to me to differ; and whom, besides all private feelings, I believe one (I need not say I mean Pitt) to be more deeply devoted to his country's welfare than any other political man.'[26]

Wilberforce did not in the least regret his exercise in opposition. He had acted from honest motives and could feel as he told Currie, that '*some* good (I dare not say much) has been done by my own and my coadjutors' endeavours'.[27] Though Pitt's peace feelers failed, the fact of them helped ordinary people to bear the war better. And Wilberforce remained a brake on any headlong rush into conquest for its own sake, even if the more warlike believed that his 'humanity' towards the French, in urging negotiation, had actually prolonged the war by weakening Pitt's resolve. Such men continued to dread Wilberforce's influence, as a private letter from Lord Hawkesbury (the future Lord Liverpool) to the Speaker showed a year later: 'I *am still for war*. . . . I never will doubt of our ultimate success. From the *nexus quis Wilberforcuis* and his party much is I fear to be apprehended, but I hope too much attention will not be paid to them.'[28]

Windham, smarting under the failure of his expedition to Quiberon, went so far as to grumble in December 1795 that the country was 'not governed by Mr. Pitt and others, that we naturally should be, but by Mr. Wilberforce and Mr. This-and-t'other that I could name, and who have not only low and narrow notions of things, but their own little private interest to serve'.[29]

By the end of October 1795 Wilberforce had accepted the impossibility of peace with honour. Holland had changed sides, Spain was about to do so, Bonaparte had emerged. After the debate on the Address George Canning rejoiced that 'Wilberforce and his conscientious followers, the effusion-of-human-blood party, all came back to us'.[30] Despite military failures and a bad harvest Pitt gained strength while Fox and his friends lay farther from power than ever.

The country, however, seethed with discontent. Hunger and war weariness were fanned by agitators who wanted annual parliaments and universal suffrage, wanted to bring in the 'democracy' which gentlemen and yeomen of England believed would lead to terror and bloodshed and the rule of some tyrannical 'Committee of Public Safety', headed by Fox perhaps. In London a great open-air meeting looked like the start of revolution and when the King rode in the State Coach to open Parliament and a stone smashed a window, he believed he had been shot at. After the King had entered the House of Lords the mob badly damaged the coach. The Government immediately introduced two temporary wartime measures, one against treasonable and seditious practices, the other to prevent seditious meetings though not muzzling the Press.

With the great majority in the Commons, which greeted the Seditious Meetings Bill with 'a prodigious *hear! hear!*', Wilberforce believed that the vent for protest should be the House of Commons, not irregular popular assemblies: political meetings in the counties should be summoned in a recognized way by lords lieutenant or sheriffs. Wilberforce said in one of the debates: 'No one was a greater friend to rational liberty than himself: but when clubs and societies talked of introducing a freedom more intolerable than any despotism in Europe, it was high time they should rally round the Constitution. . . . If a large body met in confederacy, if speakers were employed to enforce seditious and dangerous doctrines, it was necessary that magistrates be armed with extraordinary powers, in order to meet the exigence of the crisis.'[31]

The Foxites attacked the Bills. Wilberforce always doubted Fox's political sincerity and ascribed his motive to desire for power rather than love of the people, and believed that he should have allowed animosities to subside when the country stood in danger. Yet Wilberforce would not ridicule and taunt as in the days of their earlier brushes in the House.[32] Even had he not been sensitive to Fox's consistency over the slaves, Wilberforce schooled his political speeches by Christian love, not without cost to his 'natural warmth'. Long afterwards Henry Bankes told Wilberforce's sons: 'I can confidently state from long personal intimacy and accurate recollection that your excellent father's temper in debate partook of the mildness and moderation which governed his whole conduct: and I have known no individual engaged in political controversies upon questions of such high and momentous concern, in whom there was so complete an absence of all rancour, passion, misrepresentation or malevolence. I recollect instances and expressions of his kind feelings with regard to Mr. Fox in particular; and I have often remarked to some of our mutual friends, that all his strictness and restraint was for himself, and all his indulgence for others.'[33]

Wilberforce never retracted his belief in the 'real and urgent necessity'[34] for Pitt's Gagging Bills, as they were nicknamed, and he helped to draft them, inserting a more liberal tone here and there.[35] But Foxites and the new Radicals were not the only contemporaries who shared posterity's view that Pitt over-reacted to the crisis. Duncombe spoke in the House against the Bills, with disastrous effect on his electoral prospects, and at once was answered by Wilberforce. The two Members for Yorkshire mixed themselves in military metaphors, which gave General Tarleton the opportunity to sneer that Wilberforce had 'stumbled over the parapet of prerogative into the ditch of despotism. It was necessary to strip him of that pomp of language, that solemnity of manner which he had effected, those sophisticated sentiments with which he attempted to colour his support of the present measure.'[36]

Out of doors those who saw British liberties threatened by the Bills linked him with Pitt and called him a tyrant; many who had praised Wilberforce's opposition in January abused him in November. At a public meeting in radical Norwich when an alderman spoke up for the Bills, saying he followed 'the example of a man high in the estimation both of God and man, the patriotic Mr. Wilberforce', there was a loud shout from the crowd, 'A hypocrite! A hypocrite!'[37]

In Yorkshire Christopher Wyvill tried to secure a County Meeting to petition against the Gagging Bills. Wyvill had disgusted Wilberforce not long before by wanting to publish part of their private correspondence on public affairs, and afterwards did so in his celebrated *Political Papers.*[38] This was a private dispute; but when the High Sheriff refused to call the County Meeting, though it would have been a legal assembly even after the passing of the Bills, Wilberforce publicly deplored such a foolish suppression of debate.[39]

Wyvill decided to call his own meeting, and in such a way that only those Freeholders likely to support him would attend. He issued on Friday, 27 November, deliberately too late for the public prints, a summons in high-flown language for a meeting in York on Tuesday, 1 December, place unspecified; and circulated it in districts antagonistic to Pitt. Wilberforce, in London, heard rumours but dismissed what he supposed would be a small meeting of Foxites; it was not worth a dash into Yorkshire, especially as he would have to travel on the day he valued as the spiritual oasis of the week.

On Sunday morning he stepped into his carriage at Palace Yard to drive to the Lock Chapel. A messenger who had ridden through the night, express from Leeds, trotted up with an urgent letter from two chief supporters. They told him they were rousing the County to flock into York for Wyvill's meeting on Tuesday. It would be huge and decisive. Wilberforce must come without fail. After seeking Eliot's advice Wilberforce sent his carriage back to the stables to be prepared for a long journey – traces for four horses instead of two – and walked round the corner to St. Margaret's, Westminster, where he endured a 'sad sermon' ('sad' was the usual contemporary euphemism for 'bad' or 'distressing'). He then walked to Downing Street. Pitt and his company were concerned at the news of the impending Yorkshire meeting, which might sway the country as in '84. Pitt said Wilberforce must certainly go, and when a message came that the carriage would not be ready until late afternoon Pitt ordered his own chariot and four, with outriders to clear the way (though at least the road would not be blocked by droves of cattle and sheep so late in the year). One of the Cabinet chaffed Wilberforce: 'If they find out whose carriage you have got, you will run the risk of being murdered.' Feelings in London were high enough for the joke to leave a bitter taste.[40]

Nor could he know what he would find in Yorkshire when he trotted away from Palace Yard at 2.30 p.m. that Sunday.[41] Accompanied by his secretary he sped through Barnet and Hatfield and on up the Great North Road, and spent the night at Alconbury near Huntingdon, probably at the Wheatsheaf Inn. They had covered sixty-seven miles. Starting early next day he dictated his speech despite the swaying and lurching; and what with papers and pamphlets and discarded versions they travelled knee-deep in paper, oblivious of the storm and wind and muddy road, to stop at Ferrybridge beyond Doncaster for Monday night, after a run of 106 miles.[42] They were now 173 miles from London and ten miles short of the signpost where the road to Tadcaster and York branched from the Great North Road. A despatch rider from Downing Street caught up, bringing a further batch of pamphlets breathing sedition and revolution, in Pitt's eyes at least, to strengthen Wilberforce's point when he should address the Freeholders.

Next morning these were in view. For the last twenty miles or so the outriders had to clear the road for Wilberforce to spank through knots of horsemen, most of them evidently clothiers on their pack horses. All the County seemed headed for York but he had no idea whether they were friends. At eleven he drove into the city. As the mud-splashed carriage turned the corner into Coney Street an immense crowd which milled round the Guildhall recognized his head at the window. He was utterly unexpected. A huge cheer went up, hats were flung in the air as he stepped down.

He learned that inside the Guildhall Wyvill's men had seized the platform by subterfuge when they had realized they were outnumbered. All was in confusion. Wilberforce forced his way in and privately urged Wyvill to adjourn to the Castle Yard for a serious debate, as in 1784. Wyvill refused, yet he had summoned the meeting to defend the 'ancient and indubitable right to free discussion'. As Wilberforce wrote to him a few days later: 'I thought it was not using *us* friends of the Bills, and particularly *myself* fairly, to arraign us for having attacked the fundamentals of the Constitution, without giving us an opportunity of vindicating ourselves; and that this conduct was particularly wrong in the case of those who by calling the Meeting, held themselves out as being desirous of free discussion.'[43]

Many of the Pittites (the clothiers carried the nickname 'Billymen' for long afterwards) had already gone to the Castle Yard and here Colonel Ralph Creyke of Marton moved a loyal Address which Spencer Stanhope seconded. Wilberforce then addressed the crowd, estimated at nearly four thousand, in one of the finest speeches of his life. 'Wilberforce spoke extremely well,' is Spencer Stanhope's diary comment,[44] echoed by other contemporaries. Wilberforce had come prepared for a long debating speech which should demolish the arguments of opponents, but since they had refused debate he spoke more briefly, every word clear to the edges of the crowd. He won almost all the uncommitted who were worried by the Gagging Bills.

The loyal Address passed with only four dissentients. A Whig colonel in uniform then made a flaming speech promising that his soldiers would mutiny when the people rose. Freeholders shouted him down. He threw his regimentals to a gathering mob of York rowdies who promptly carried him shoulder high to the rival meeting in the Guildhall. This left the field to the 'Billymen'. Wyvill's refusal of debate had already played into Wilberforce's hand, and the 'mad' colonel's antics completed the victory.

The concourse of Freeholders, far greater than that in the Guildhall, voted unanimously for petitions to both Houses in support of the Bills. To cries of 'The Glorious First of December' Wilberforce despatched a horseman with a triumphant message to Pitt. And on Friday, 4 December 1795, when Duncombe presented the petition sent up by Wyvill's meeting against the Bills, Wilberforce immediately rose in his place. He had arrived back in London the previous evening after travelling some 400 miles in the equivalent of four winter days, and now presented his counter-petition from the Castle Yard. He had no difficulty in demonstrating to a sympathetic and admiring House that the Wyvill petition did not represent the true feelings of the County of York.[45]

CHAPTER FOURTEEN

Prisoners and the Poor

During the years when Wilberforce moved towards political independence, another physically small man became well known for his political thought. Jeremy Bentham, eleven years older than Wilberforce and not yet recognized as one of England's greatest philosophers, had done much work on jurisprudence and law reform. He returned from a visit to Russia enthusiastic about a scheme for humanizing British prison life.

He wanted to replace the hulks in which felons languished in river estuaries by a 'penitentiary house' adapted from the inspection house designed by his brother when building dockyards for the Tsar. Bentham called it the Panopticon. The convicts would live and labour in individual cells in a circular building, unable to see each other yet under the eye of the overseer. Solitary confinement and useful labour would punish and reform at the same time, a humane improvement on the idle communal squalor of county gaols and the hulks.

Bentham sought the support of the Home Secretary and several public figures, among whom Wilberforce was a natural choice, for back in 1786 he had taken a practical interest in Pitt's proposed penal settlement in Botany Bay,[1] a plan humane in conception if carried out with little humanity. Later he had urged Pitt (and the Lord Chief Justice) to establish 'penitentiary houses',[2] possibly after he had talked with or read Bentham, who though not on the committee of Wilberforce's Proclamation Society agreed with it about using common informers as detectives.

When Bentham showed him the model of the Panopticon, Wilberforce lobbied the Law Officers and arranged parties to view it. 'I shall meet my friends at your house at one o'clock today,' he wrote to Bentham on 17 April 1795. 'I hope you won't think I have brought too large a party; they are all good men and true and it seemed quite ill-natured when the subject happened to be mentioned to sit sulky and refuse what I knew would give a friend pleasure.'[3]

The Government passed an Act authorizing the establishment of a penitentiary, engaged Bentham to build and administer it, and planned to buy a small slice of Lord Spencer's Wimbledon Park estate.

The able First Lord of the Admiralty did not relish a large, ugly building peopled by criminals in a corner of his park. Nearly a year later Bentham had spent much and received nothing but broken promises. Wilberforce prodded Pitt and others, assuring Bentham on 2 March 1796, that 'the treatment you have met with grieves and makes me ashamed for those who are the authors of it'.[4] Three weeks later he passed on a scrap of hopeful conversation but early in April the nearly bankrupt Bentham decided to publish the whole story so that his ruin would not be ascribed to imprudence, 'unless it be imprudence to have attributed common honesty to Mr. Pitt. In this crisis,' he told Wilberforce, 'you are my sheet anchor.'[5]

Thwarted by Earl Spencer the Treasury tentatively offered to buy Tothill Fields instead, the marshy land just south of Westminster Abbey owned by the Dean and Chapter.[6] Wilberforce tried to force Downing Street to confirm the offer, writing to Bentham on 20 October 1796, 'I am quite *quite hurt* that I cannot send you any definite intelligence,'[7] and at length, having secured the Treasury's verbal promise, approached Dean Horsley, the proud and prelatical scientist who was also Bishop of Rochester, by letter. The Dean disliked the prospect of criminal neighbours as much as did Lord Spencer.

Horsley wriggled but eventually saw Wilberforce and then Bentham, to whom he asserted that Pitt was not in earnest about the scheme. Bentham burst into tears when telling of this encounter and Wilberforce was 'very much vexed' by the Dean's callousness, and wrote to Bentham afterwards some succinct conclusions regarding character in high places, episcopal and lay: 'I must say, few things have more impressed my mind with a sense of various bad passions and mischievous weaknesses which infest the human heart, than several circumstances which have happened in relation to your undertaking. A little, ever so little Religion, would have prevented it all, and long ago have put the public in possession of the practical benefits of your plan. This is one amongst the many instances I have had occasion to observe, how much a little of this only solid principle tends to the well-being of communities.'[8]

A prince of the Church had refused charity to prisoners. Wilberforce watched with concern the increasing sourness and exasperation of Bentham, and believed, perhaps wrongly, that the utilitarian philosopher first moved towards unorthodox religious opinions, and then to radical politics of the sort which Wilberforce mistrusted, because of his disgust at the prevarications of Church and State.[9]

The two little men had much in common. Wilberforce sometimes called at Queen Square, where Bentham worked in a Wilberforcian muddle of papers and an aroma of hot spiced gingerbread and black coffee. The Panopticon affair dragged on. Once a hurried remark in a shop to a fellow M.P. reached Bentham as Wilberforce's refusal to help further because he 'thought you had been used very ill, and could not keep his temper when he talked on the business'. Bentham shot at him a long involved sarcastic letter complaining that an unscrupulous or oppressive official need only 'screw up the enormity of his guilt to a pitch sufficiently provoking, and on those terms he might make sure of the acquiescence of Mr. Wilberforce. What a lesson! What an encouragement for the advocates of the Slave Trade, for example, were they to hear of this – which perhaps they have done by this time – though certainly not of me! . . . .'[10]

Wilberforce scribbled back a denial from a crowded Committee table the very next day. He reaffirmed his 'earnest desire that you may at length overcome all obstructions and see your ingenious theory realized and your long labours crowned with success. I shall ever be ready and glad to lend my best efforts. . . .'[11]

At last, far ahead in 1810, the penitentiary scheme emerged from the Whitehall labyrinth. Bentham sent Wilberforce a note from Dorset saying he would do nothing for fear of another rebuff from Treasury quarters. Wilberforce fixed a time to meet. 'My dear Sir, don't talk of Treasury quarters. I agree with you – after all you have experienced, unless the way is smoothed and the doors thrown wide for your triumphant passage, I would not have you stir from your chimney corner. But if the House of Commons does awake from its long slumber and wish to establish a system in the highest degree beneficial and humane, surely you will not refuse to lend aid yourself to those who are eager to bring it forward. Nor is it fair to your friends, if you yourself are indifferent to credit, that you should lose the just praise of originating or at least devising the means of carrying into effect, the true principles of penal jurisprudence. I scribble in extreme haste. But I am delighted by seeing in my mind's eye your honour like a great spider seated in the centre of a panopticon.'[12]

Bentham had suffered enough and withdrew, with compensation. Millbank penitentiary opened in 1816 using a modified panopticon design, on riverside land bought from the Grosvenor estate, Wilberforce's friend Belgrave being now Earl Grosvenor. If it did not fulfil expectations, the basic principle strongly influenced penal reform.

Good causes attached themselves to Wilberforce like pins to a magnet.

He took close interest in medical aid for the poor. He had been a governor of St. Bartholomew's Hospital since May 1788 after sending a handsome donation. In the autumn of 1796 he demanded a special meeting of governors; to judge by the minutes, Wilberforce had received evidence that medicines were sold illicitly for private profit instead of dispensed in the wards. He recorded in his diary that the governors found it easy to make new rules, more difficult to punish delinquents. He sat on a committee of investigation but no report reached the minute book and he may have resigned in protest (though this is not recorded) for in 1799 he was again admitted a governor.[13]

He discovered that many of the poor were discharged from large charity hospitals such as the London or St. George's before strong enough to earn a living wage. 'You can scarcely conceive what a source of misery I have now touched upon,' he told a rich woman who sought direction in giving away large sums. 'A poor man or woman's constitution is often weakened for life by returning too soon to hard work.'[14] He encouraged 'Samaritan Societies' founded in this connection.

Wilberforce was interested in the education of the poor, and in the charity school and Sunday school movements which had developed in the last quarter of the eighteenth century. He is said to have founded a 'School of industry' in Bath though he does not appear as founder in surviving city records; he helped Thornton in the education of the deaf;[15] he delighted to help educate 'indigent or friendless' boys such as the sons of dead or ruined clergymen or officers. Thus he assisted a young Scot, Gordon Smith, who became a doctor in the army.[16]

Wilberforce specially liked to further the training of young men who would make good clergy. He supported the Elland Society devoted (in his graphic imagery) to catching colts running wild on Halifax Moor and cutting their manes and tails and sending them to college;[17] and he personally placed individuals under tutors until ready for college, and watched over them until settled in a first curacy; then he would sort out difficulties between a curate and his vicar.[18] Money spent on training the clergy must spread the Gospel and equally aid the poor, because 'such men will always be advocates for them'.[19] Thus it promoted further charity.

His sons claimed that in these years immediately before his marriage Wilberforce gave away a quarter of his income.[20] Much of it went in personal gifts wherever he heard of a need, often anonymously through an intermediary, or by visiting debtors' prisons with his hand in his pocket. Thornton thought him unwise sometimes: 'This . . . is a case in which I think Wilberforce might learn to correct himself in his liberality, as I shall tell him,' wrote Thornton to Hannah More regarding one Martin, a sponger who could always count on a regular £100 or £200 a year 'from Wilberforce, his own scruples forming the only bar to his taking it, Wilberforce never having urged him to make any retrenchment whatever.'[21]

On the other hand, when asked for more alms by Cragg, his ex-secretary, now married, whom he had placed in a clerkship at the new Board of Agriculture, Wilberforce enquired of Lord Egremont, one of the

Commissioners, what sum Egremont had given already; not from curiosity, Wilberforce said, but to prevent himself encouraging extravagance.[22]

The semi-official Board of Agriculture had been founded by a Highlander friend and fellow M.P., Sir John Sinclair. It remained one of Wilberforce's abiding interests, as also the slightly later Society for Agricultural Improvement. Wilberforce was never a man content to ameliorate distress: he sought improvements, and to cure needs by attacking their causes. Early in 1796, as wartime scarcity grew worse, he circulated among his friends a long questionnaire about the rise or fall of wages, about diet, prices and poor-rates and the effect of enclosures; about morals and attitudes among both farm 'labourers' and town 'manufacturers'.[23]

In a few years he would play a significant, if unusual and indirect part in improving the food supply of the country. And in 1796 his support meant much to a new organization: the Society for Bettering the Condition and Increasing the Comforts of the Poor, usually known as the 'Bettering Society'.

It was the brain-child of his friend and fellow-Evangelical Thomas Bernard (afterwards Sir Thomas, 3rd baronet) who was son of the royal Governor of Massachusetts at the time of the Stamp Act. Thomas Bernard had a slight stammer. He had been educated at Harvard and called to the English bar, but gave up his conveyancing practice as soon as he had enough to support himself and his wife – they had no children – and then devoted his organizing skill and fertile brain to improving the lot of the poor.

In April 1796 Bernard, Wilberforce, Eliot, Bishop Barrington of Durham, and other members of the Proclamation Society subscribed together to present to the parish of St. Marylebone a soup kitchen on a system installed by Bernard at the Foundling Hospital. It had been invented by another loyalist New Englander, the ingenious Sir Benjamin Thompson, Count Rumford, and when the parish refused the gift, yet wartime distress and hunger increased, the friends set up 'Rumford Eating Houses' instead.[24]

Four days before Christmas 1796, the Bishop of Durham, Bernard and six others came to Wilberforce's house in the early afternoon to found the 'Bettering Society'. This aimed at scientific investigation of the problems of poverty, and the circulation of information about methods of relief and improvements in living conditions. Local societies would assault local problems and discourage indiscriminate charity. Bernard laid special stress on avoiding the dangers of pauperizing through 'removing the incitement to industry'. Wilberforce's touch is felt through Bernard's words: 'in pauperism as in slavery, the degradation of character deprives the individual of half his value.'[25]

Thomas Bernard has been ridiculed by left-wing social historians for not assaulting inequalities of rank or wealth. This is criticism out of context. The only 'alternative society' in view was the French which the new Radicals might praise but to most Britons, peering across the Channel, looked a chaos of economic and social distress, worse than any in Britain. Moreover, if the Bettering Society had leaned towards Jacobin ideas its usefulness would have been crippled by the antagonism of those whose consciences it sought to stir. There were plenty of political and economic theorists; Bernard, Wilberforce and their friends cared more about immediate practical improvements. The Society put suggestions to country landowners. It attacked the evils of chimney sweeps using small boys to climb up the flues, and tried unsuccessfully to improve their lot; and then formed a separate society to agitate. Montagu and Gisborne studied the conditions of coal miners and tin miners.

Six years after the Bettering Society's birth one of its vice-presidents, Sir Robert Peel, father of the future Prime Minister, pushed through Parliament with Wilberforce's help an Act to limit the excessive hours and to improve the conditions of Poor Law apprentice children working in the new cotton mills which were changing the face of the North. Wilberforce had wanted it extended to cover other manufacturers and all children,[26] but the employers determined to get this first Factory Act repealed. They enlisted Wilberforce's friend Hey, the Leeds surgeon, who reported in favour of children being allowed to work at night. The Bettering Society contested Hey's findings and set up its own committee, which confirmed the value of Peel's Act. Members of the Society undertook to inspect mills and factories.

From a meeting of the Society in January 1799 arose the British (afterwards the Royal) Institution, dedicated to 'diffusing the knowledge and facilitating the general introduction of useful mechanical inventions and improvements; and for teaching . . . the application of science to the common purposes of life'. This great Institution, where Humphry Davy was to perfect his safety lamp and Faraday to discover electromagnetism, is the Bettering Society's lasting claim to fame. Count Rumford took the credit, Sir Joseph Banks the chair, and Thomas Bernard as Secretary kept the British Institution on course. Wilberforce was one of the original proprietors.[27]

Wilberforce knew no bulkhead between philanthropy and politics. Much of his power derived from his regularity of attendance at the House of Commons in an age when the Chamber filled seldom. He went to his place unless sick, or obliged to be more than twenty miles from London.[28] Many of his interventions were on behalf of the poor, such as seconding Rose's Friendly Society Act of 1793, the legal foundation of the mutual benefit societies which became such a feature of nineteenth-century England.[29]

Wilberforce sat on the Select Committee of 1795 which examined the corn supply, and he deplored to the House the Foxites' 'air of concern for the distresses of the poor, while they took no effective part'[30] in obtaining information and suggesting remedies. He urged cheap food for agricultural labourers rather than higher wages, which must increase prices and bring hardship to the 'manufacturing poor'. He spoke and voted against the Game Laws which he considered 'extreme abominations'.[31] And Bentham in a letter of 8 March 1796 applauded (with one caveat) 'the system which through your means is about to be set on foot in relation to the Poor Laws'.[32] This system, whatever it was, does not appear to have been launched.

'The grand object of my Parliamentary existence'[33] remained the Abolition of the Slave Trade. 'Before this great cause,' he wrote early in 1796, 'all others dwindle in my eyes, and I must say that the *certainty* that I am right *here*, adds greatly to the complacency with which I exert myself in asserting it. If it please God to honor me so far, may I be the instrument of stopping such a course of wickedness and cruelty as never before disgraced a Christian country.'[34]

Following the Resolution for gradual Abolition, Wilberforce had been thwarted by the attitude of Dundas and others who claimed: 'We are friends to Abolition no less than you, indeed we best deserve the name,' because his trying for immediate Abolition 'will never bring you to the desired point.'[35] Wilberforce would reply that if he and his friends were 'a set of harmless Enthusiasts,' why was 'the enmity of the Slave Traders . . . directed solely against us?' The Traders looked on Dundas as their friend.

In the spring of 1796 Wilberforce nearly did reach 'the desired point', in the House of Commons at least, and missed victory by a hair's breadth – or, rather, by a comic opera.

Astute tactics had won him through to the Second Reading of his Abolition Bill, to his own surprise. It came up for Third Reading on 15 March. Since Easter 1796 would fall early, several of Wilberforce's supporters had gone down to the country, while that night of the Third Reading a new Italian work, *I Dui Gobi*, which posterity confines to oblivion with its composer, drew many other Members to the Opera House to hear Vignoni, an equally forgotten Italian singer on his first appearance since the outbreak of war. Dundas, however, was in his place in the Chamber. Another voter against Abolition was Scrope Bernard of the Home Office, Thomas Bernard's brother. The House looked no thinner than usual on such a night, yet to Wilberforce's certain knowledge five or six friends of his motion preferred Vignoni's singing. The Third Reading was lost – by four votes: 70 to 74.*[36]

Wilberforce suffered such mortification that he fell seriously ill.

---

* Professor Anstey provides a most interesting list and assessment of the Noes in his *The Atlantic Slave Trade and British Abolition*, 1975, pp. 306–15

Milner again hurried down from Cambridge to apply the medical skill which counted among his extraordinary range of accomplishments. Wilberforce recovered. And that summer, when trying to exchange Milner's distant deanery of Carlisle (held in plurality with the Presidency of Queens', according to very usual academic custom) for a cosy canonry of St. Paul's, he did not mind basing the claim on the importance of Milner to the health of Wilberforce: 'He was the means, if not of saving my life, at least of sparing me a long and dangerous fit of sickness in the last spring. . . . When he is at an *uncomeatable* distance I never have the same sense of security.'[37]

Wilberforce recovered to lose another attempt at a Bill to limit the number of slaves that might be imported. He also failed to deflect Pitt, publicly in the House and by private argument in Pitt's coach all the way to Cambridge,[38] from his policy of further conquests in the West Indies. Several annexed islands had been recaptured by the French, helped by slave risings, so that the patriotic Stephen actually welcomed French victories in the West Indies as Providence's design for ending the 'horrid system'.[39]

Wilberforce's one win of 1796 was Yorkshire at the General Election where he stood as an independent and, to an eye-witness at the hustings, 'appeared to meet almost unanimous approbation'.[40] He then announced to the assembled Freeholders that he would support whichever candidate received their most vocal and visible approval. Duncombe, whom the Billymen now rejected, got more boos than cheers. Fitzwilliam's candidate, Walter Fawkes, looked and sounded popular by the show of hands and the cheers, yet so did Henry Lascelles, a firm Pittite. After a long pause Wilberforce decided that the Freeholders showed preference for Lascelles, nicknamed 'Beau' for his dandified dress and arrogant ways, the heir to the first Earl of Harewood, whose great fortune derived from sugar and slaves.

The defeated Duncombe and the aspiring Fawkes withdrew, leaving a new, ironic partnership for Yorkshire: the slave owner and the Abolitionist.

Wilberforce disappeared to Buxton, where he took the waters, endured the rotary treatment – and laboured with his pen. For Wilberforce was writing a book. It had been three years already in the making.

CHAPTER FIFTEEN

The Heart of the Matter

Far back in 1793 Wilberforce began a little tract to give his friends.

The change in habits and outlook had mystified many: Windham remained so vague that years later he noted with surprise that Wilberforce still believed in the Trinity. Wilberforce wanted a convenient way to explain and advocate, especially since 'the religious system I had embraced . . . is that of the Church of England and of the Bible.'[1]

The tract slowly burgeoned into a full length book. One summer Recess he pleaded literary labours as an excuse to keep out of Yorkshire and stayed at Yoxall, where Mrs. Gisborne, whenever Wilberforce retreated upstairs, would prowl round her drawing-room and conservatory, pick up discarded scraps of paper on which he had jotted phrases or ideas, then arrange them and hand them to him next morning. When he sat with the family sipping evening tea, and the words poured forth as his mind jumped from point to point in that bubbling spontaneous thinking aloud which captivated his hearers, she would seize a pad and afterwards present him with her notes.[2]

He had no gift for systematic theology. He absorbed wisdom from books, sermons or by picking any brain he met, Dean Milner especially being a fount of wisdom as they strolled together, the little wraith-like politician with the tall bulky don, along the Backs at Cambridge or on the lawns of Battersea Rise. 'You might squeeze him and tap him all day long,' Wilberforce once exclaimed, 'and still you would find fresh supplies ready to be drawn off.'[3] Nor was the politician bothered in the least by the preciseness of the mathematics professor, which made Milner 'sometimes appear a little fidgety and particular'.[4]

The chief source of Wilberforce's views was the Bible, 'written to plain unlettered men in a plain popular way not with logical precision or the accuracy of special pleading'.[5] The Bible had changed his life and he found in it the authority and clarity by which he could test the opinions of writers and preachers. 'My judgment . . . rests altogether on the Word of God,' he stressed to a friend. And to a Lieutenant G.

6

Reynolds of HMS *New Zealand* at the Nore, who had written for spiritual counsel, he urged: 'If you read the Scriptures with earnest prayer . . . and a sincere desire for discovering the truth and obeying it when known I cannot doubt of your attaining it.'[6] Wilberforce learned stretches by heart so that he could meditate at night, or should his eyes trouble him, or when needing guidance in his place in the Commons or at committees.[7]

The more he looked at the religion of the New Testament the more he wanted to show how far it lay from the religion of the polite in England, whose blend of a little piety with a little moralizing offered nothing to a man whose inward eye had seen his corruption in the blinding light of the glory of the Lord. Wilberforce once told a Cambridge undergraduate that 'I believe, were I not a Real Xtian (in my belief, I mean, I wish to deserve the name better in my character) I should probably be an Atheist.'[8]

By early 1797 Wilberforce's friends were hopeful that the book might soon be a reality, Hannah More writing that had she not suffered from headache and vomiting she would have called on the way to Teston to ask after his health and how '*the* Book goes on'. He went to Bath and despite incessant callers and calling and much dining out he finished the manuscript in February. Back in London he took it to young Thomas Cadell, who had succeeded his father, publisher of Gibbon and of Blackstone, at the famous shop in the Strand. Cadell gloomily informed him that there could be little market for a religious book, but on being assured that Wilberforce's name would be on it he said they might venture on 500 copies.[9]

During the publishing of a book of 491 pages plus index in a mere two months, a speed which must be the envy of a more technological age, Wilberforce seems to have continued to brush up the text. 'My dear Lord,' he wrote to the Bishop of London on 14 March, 'I want to poach a little in the way of old English Divinity and I believe St. Paul's library abounds in that kind of game. Will your Lordship allow me a morning's thought in your manor and send directions for that purpose. I conceived that the Westminster library would have supplied my wants, but (whether from curiosity or not I cannot say) the Dean desires to know what books I want which is just that which I had meant he should not be apprised of – I hope Mrs. P. and my young friends are well. . . .'[10]*

On 12 April 1797 the book came out, with an immense title in the style of the day: *A PRACTICAL VIEW of the Prevailing Religious system of Professed Christians, in the Higher and Middle Classes in this Country, contrasted with Real Christianity*, by William Wilberforce, Esq., Member of Parliament for the County of York. Wilberforce

* The inquisitive Dean was Bishop Horsley, whose behaviour over Bentham had so disgusted Wilberforce.

sent copies to numerous friends.* The public took it up and within six months it had gone through five impressions, making the then considerable tally of 7,500 copies.[11] *A Practical View* went on to become by the standards of the time a best seller, edition after edition keeping it in print long into the next century in England and America and in five foreign languages.

'I rejoice most on the world's account,' wrote the Calvinist parson Richard Cecil, only four days after publication, 'for I believe it is a pretty well established maxim in this enlightened day that we priests are all Rogues and are no longer to be heard; now if there *should* be found any honest man among us he will rejoice that a man of your character can get a hearing where we cannot, and that the truth should be so clearly and forcibly presented when the motive cannot possibly be suspected.'[12] Thornton wrote to Macaulay in Sierra Leone that Wilberforce's book was exciting a surprising amount of attention, with most bishops and clergy liking it on the whole. 'His gay friends, many of them admire and approve of it. His political friends, and some of gay ones also do but dip into it and find no fault. Several have recognized the likeness of themselves. . . .'[13]

A Practical View is a Biblical view, presented intelligibly if haphazardly. It sets out the essential Christian doctrines by Scripture texts, and then discourses about the imitation which passed for religion in 1797. The very discursiveness which powered the book's impact on a generation rather bored by closely reasoned theologies, makes it wearisome to the modern reader and checkmates literary and theological critiques: it is a slippery eel of a book. Wilberforce's friends called it spoken rather than written, yet his attempt at the accepted classical style of an essayist kills the spontaneity which sparkles in his letters.[14]

The charm and charity of his severest strictures astonished an age used to furious religious arguments, when not so long ago the Calvinist author of 'Rock of Ages' had poured verbal vitriol over John Wesley. In Wilberforce, fervour drove in harness with love for those whose faults he exposed, and he was that rare being, a man of strong conviction who could embrace those who differed. The book was no proud display of learning, no manifesto, nor blast of the trumpet in a doctrinal war, even if it generated a quota of 'replies' from those who disputed its conclusions.

One passage would be manipulated, more than a hundred years later by J.L. and Barbara Hammond in *The Town Labourer*, to damage Wilberforce's position in social history. This passage[15] paraphrased, in effect, the chapter in the Epistle of James which shows that true

---

* The inscribed copy he sent to Bishop Barrington of Durham is in the London Library. The Bishop's prompt thanks, expressing qualified approval of the contents, is in the Bodleian (Bod. d. 13.341) 17 April 1797, as are many other acknowledgments.

religion will teach the rich their social responsibilities, and will ease the sufferings of the poor by sweetening their lives and by the assurance of the eternal glory awaiting the believer. Wilberforce's reference to the poor was torn from context and pilloried as if he taught that they should keep their place and be thankful. One phrase may shock the twentieth-century reader, when Wilberforce writes that the situation in life of the inferior classes, 'with all its evils, is better than they have deserved at the hand of God'. Standing by itself this seems an expression of contempt or callousness, but to the reader of 1797 it merely made the point of Article IX of the familiar Thirty Nine Articles: that in 'every person born into this world', whether poor or rich, the corruption of the flesh wrought by Original Sin 'deserveth God's wrath and damnation'. Thus even the thinnest material blessing is an undeserved mercy for which the very poorest may give thanks. Any distaste in the contemporary reader would have been sweetened on reflection that the words came from the man identified, more than any other public figure of 1797, as the friend of the poor.

A Practical View took the reader on a discursive journey to discover how Christianity should and could guide the politics, habits and attitudes of a nation from the highest to the lowest. Because it diagnosed and prescribed for the condition of Britain, and for many decades was found in every kind of home however poor (the boy David Livingstone would be thrashed by his mill-hand father for refusing to read it) the book helped reverse a national trend. Wilberforce warned that 'the time is fast approaching when Christianity will be almost as openly disavowed in the language as in fact it is already supposed to have disappeared from the conduct of men: when infidelity will be held to be the necessary appendage of a man of fashion, and *to believe* will be deemed the indication of a feeble mind and a contracted understanding.'[16] That this could never be said of the Victorian age, but the reverse, was not a little due to Wilberforce, the man and the book.

For many of his contemporaries the book did more than explain and warn. Wilberforce believed that for clergymen 'the grand business of their lives should be winning souls from the power of Satan unto God, and compared with it all other pursuits are mean and contemptible'.[17] *A Practical View* was his own weapon for 'winning souls', of a steady stream of readers, unknown and known.

Even Edmund Burke told Mrs. Crewe on his deathbed that he had derived much comfort from it, 'and that if he lived he should thank Wilberforce for having sent such a book into the world'.[18] A year or two after its publication, a young rather worldly curate in the Isle of Wight received a copy from a friend who asked his opinion. Legh Richmond sat up late and for the first time understood 'the vital character of personal religion, the corruption of the human heart, and the way of salvation by Jesus Christ. . . . *The Practical View* led me to a study of the Scriptures . . . humbled my heart, and brought me to seek the love and blessing of that Saviour who alone can afford a peace which the world cannot give.'[19] Legh Richmond afterwards wrote one of the most famous moral tales of the early nineteenth century, *The Dairyman's Daughter*.

Richmond, however, was unimportant compared with Arthur Young, the eminent agriculturalist. About three months after the book's publication Wilberforce happened to write a note to Young on an agricultural matter, apologizing for applying to a perfect stranger. He was excited to receive by return of post a long letter in which Young described how he had bought the book while in much anxiety because his young daughter lay dying. He had begun reading with indifference which turned to interest. Parts seemed too hard to understand; he read it again and again 'and it made so much impression on me that I scarcely knew how to lay it aside. It excited a very insufficient degree of repentance and a still more insufficient view of my interest in the Great Physician of souls.'[20] He then put several deep questions to Wilberforce.

Wilberforce replied on 15 August 1797, 'I must have been utterly void of feeling if I could have perused your obliging letter without lively emotion of mind. . . .' It was the start of a long friendship which would have its influence on the state of England, especially on England's poor. For the moment, as he declared to Young, 'the feeling which *abides* in my mind is a feeling of joy to hear that a person such as you are in all respects, has . . . been turned to seek for happiness where alone it is to be found. . . .'[21]

The discursiveness of *A Practical View* makes it less of a guide to Wilberforce's own religion than are his letters and diary jottings, though any attempt to excavate and label his mind may mislead, since he never pretended to be a theologian or philosopher. Certain foundations or pillars, however, stand out.

One was his profound awareness of eternity, of this world being a passage to the next. A man must settle his eternal destiny while on earth, and only if he walked the narrow path which leads to eternal life would his attitude to his fellow men be right. Heaven was real to Wilberforce, a place of conscious joy in the unveiled presence of God, with friends from earth who also had believed, and the whole company of the faithful of every tongue and colour and race and epoch. Those who refused to prepare themselves for heaven would suffer an eternal consciousness of the awful alternative, shut out from the light and joy they had rejected. 'My dear Apsley,' Wilberforce wrote to the future Foreign Secretary Bathurst, 'it is God knoweth my frequent prayer that you and my other friends . . . may not be beguiled by the many comforts you are surrounded with, and be so taken up with the present scene as to forget that which is approaching. We know not indeed how soon we shall be called away and should therefore be always ready. Success is certain if we push forward; delay is death and misery.'[22] Often, as he sat in his place in the Commons, he would pity politicians on both sides 'so hot and eager'[23] for the rewards of this world yet ignoring the far more interesting concerns of the next. He put no faith in deathbed conversion. 'I am always so sleepy when I am unwell I can find it no time to be settling the all important concerns of the soul!'[24]

The door to the heavenly path is Christ, 'our adorable Saviour'. Because Jesus died on the Cross bearing the sin of mankind and rose from the dead, the corrupt and therefore guilty heart of Wilberforce or any friend or opponent or stranger may know pardon, incorruption and immortality. Rottenness is replaced by sweetness, the tendency to evil by an urge to do good, and to think on whatsoever is pure and lovely and of good report; loneliness and alienation give way to the dawning consciousness of the presence of God. Merit cannot achieve this, nor determination, nor effort. A man must be born again. This, Wilberforce urged on Arthur Young, was the 'grand practical conclusion I wish to have impressed on the hearts and consciences of all: that all men must be regenerated by the grace of God before they are fit to be inhabitants of heaven, before they are possessed of that holiness without which no man shall see the Lord.'[25]

The new birth is not an end but a beginning. Just as a baby must grow into a man, so the regenerate Christian must grow as like as possible to Christ who went about doing good. Only the grace of God can achieve this, but the Christian must co-operate by Christ-like actions and, in the strength of the spirit of Christ whom he had admitted to his heart when he believed and was born again, by deliberate cultivation of character. Wilberforce groaned to find how he fell short, especially in the hurly burly of Parliament, which was one reason why he loved to disappear to Bath. 'In spite of all my care,' he told Lord Apsley. 'I find it almost impossible in the World to prevent my mind's becoming too much enslaved by objects which considered in themselves I despise, and which are compelled in my Retirement to assume their just dimensions.'[26] He added he was astonished at himself for being so frequently caught out. 'Tuesday evening 13th January,' begins a loose page of diary. 'Three or four times have I most grievously broke my resolutions since I last took up my pen alas! alas! how miserable a wretch am I! How infatuated, how dead to every better feeling yet – yet – yet – may I, Oh God, be enabled to repent and turn to Thee with my whole heart, I am now flying from Thee. Thou has been above all measure gracious and forgiving. . . .'[27]

Wilberforce lived within a paradox. Like Bunyan's Pilgrim the load of his sins had rolled off his back at the Cross and his conviction of being redeemed formed the bedrock of his life. Yet while he walked through this naughty world, with its vanity fairs and sloughs of despond and all the changes and chances of this mortal life, he was not safe. God's promises were sure and irrevocable, God's grace sufficient to enable him to persevere to the final moment of physical death; yet he would never dare to presume, he must only hope. Unlike George Whitefield, who rejoiced that if a man were saved by faith, he was saved eternally however much he failed his Lord; and unlike extreme Calvinists who believed they were predestined whatever they did, Wilberforce held that he could not count himself safe until the trumpets sounded for him on the other side. In the words of the Book of Common Prayer, he must so pass through things temporal that he finally lose not the things eternal. 'I wish I had been as active as I ought about the poor slaves,' he suddenly exclaimed to Babington in the middle of a long letter on another subject. 'However, the Blood of Jesus Christ cleanses from all sin and there is the comfort which combines the deepest Humiliation with the firmest Hope.'[28] Babington knew what he meant, for he shared his outlook. But such expressions could be misunderstood and may lie behind Coleridge's sneer that Wilberforce did not care a farthing for the slaves, only for his own soul.*

Wilberforce was acutely conscious of the tension between two great principles in the New Testament. On the one hand (he read it in the Greek): 'By grace are ye saved through faith, and that not of yourselves; it is the gift of God.' And on the other: 'Work out your own salvation with fear and trembling. For it is God which worketh in you both to will and to do of his good pleasure.'

'The genuine Christian,' he told his cousin Mary Bird, in a long letter of 1789 which his sons suppressed because it did not fit their religious notions,[29] 'strives not to prove himself guiltless but humbles himself in the dust and acknowledges that he is not worthy of the least of all God's mercies. He takes a survey of his past life and of the state of his temper and affection; these he compares with the law of God and contrasts with the bounty and longsuffering, etc. of his Creator and is ready to despair, when he reads the gracious invitation: Come unto Me all ye that labour and are heavy-laden and I will give you rest, and he reads, God so loved the world that he gave his only-begotten Son, etc. This revives his hopes, but heightens his shame

---

* Not *Clarkson*'s sneer, as is often supposed, which might be damaging. A reference to the punctuation of the original source, Allsop's *Letters and Table Talk of Coleridge* (1834) I, p. 98, shows that the poet had asked Clarkson whether he ever thought of his soul's fate hereafter. 'How can I? I think only of the slaves in Barbadoes!' Coleridge, who never knew Wilberforce personally, then comments in his table talk: 'Does Mr. Wilberforce care a farthing for the slaves in the West Indies, or if they were all at the devil, so that his soul were saved?' Modern readers have been misled by the paraphrase of the passage given in the Diary of Henry Crabb Robinson (see Morley's edition, II, p. 468). Robinson, who was Clarkson's strongest advocate, added: 'This was grossly unjust to Wilberforce.'

and self-abhorrence. His language is "Oh that I might therefore show myself in some sort worthy of this infinite love, infinite condescension and unutterable love".' He goes out from his prayers in this spirit, and if he falls he turns yet again to the Cross, and 'the sight of his expiring Redeemer assures him of the pardon of his iniquities. . . .'

As the penitent sinner gets to know his own heart better, 'how selfish, how ungrateful, how disobedient to Christ's commands', a frame of mind is produced wherein 'the utmost self-abasement [is] mixed with firm reliance on the mercies of God through Christ, and a hatred of sin and a desire to be released from its powers as well as from its punishment. This I trust my dear Mary is on the whole a faithful delineation of your state and I pray God that it may always continue. Look to Jesus. Devote yourself body and soul to His service, I pray to God through Christ to enable you to do this more sincerely, more willingly, unreservedly. . . .'

To preserve their souls' health, Wilberforce himself and several intimate friends endeavoured, very privately, to observe the fast days of the Church of England though his doctors would not let him fast absolutely. He took the Sacrament regularly. On Sundays he went to church twice, and would neither travel nor discuss politics except in gravest emergency. He sought always while a bachelor to spend a part of Sunday in self-examination, a part in acts of kindness to strangers or friends; then after dinner he would 'muster around me in idea my absent friends one by one, to consider how I could do them any good, pray for them individually etc.'[30]

These religious exercises were not in themselves his ladder to heaven. 'The stay and foundation of hope after all,' he reminded Arthur Young, 'is the mercy and love of God through a crucified Saviour.'[31] Wilberforce had not the slightest doubt that the Saviour had risen bodily from the grave, 'and that you may really have that Saviour for a Friend', as he put it to his youngest son.[32] Because Christ was alive, penitence and joy could walk together in Wilberforce. 'By the tones of his voice and expression of his countenance he showed that *joy* was the prevailing feature of his own mind,' wrote a Miss Sullivan to a mutual friend after a long spiritual conversation, '*joy* springing from entireness of trust in the Saviour's merits and from love to God and man.' She added that Wilberforce's joy 'was quite penetrating'.[33]

This too was the impression of the poet Southey, who said he never saw any other man who seemed to enjoy such a perpetual sunshine of spirit. 'There is such a constant hilarity in every look and motion, such a sweetness in all his tones, such a benignity in all his thoughts, words, and actions that . . . you can feel nothing but love and admiration for a creature of so happy and blessed a nature.'[34]

Theologians would list Wilberforce among the Arminians. He did

not use the word. 'There are no narrowing names nor party distinctions in heaven,'[35] he would say, and though 'I myself am no
Calvinist',[36] he urged the claims of Calvinist clergy for bishoprics.
At the Lock Chapel he sat under Thomas Scott, the best of preachers
yet 'one of the most determined Calvinists in England'.[37] He could
even joke to his dear friend Hannah More: 'vile Calvinist you, my
very blood rises at the sight of you.'[38] Wilberforce loathed opinions
which produced hard and sour divinity. 'I think Niceties and Subtilties
are the ruin of religion,' he once commented to Stephen;[39] and he
urged Mary Bird, when in their old age she suffered persecution from
a virulent high Calvinist: 'O whatever else we give up let us retain
love, if we would not abandon our relation to him who states Love
to be the nature of existence.'[40]

Thus Wilberforce built a bridge between warring theological
camps in the Church of England. He was introducing a new spirit of
tolerance among men of conflicting principles and equal sincerity. In
a letter of no less than nineteen pages on church matters to Speaker
Addington, a stiff Churchman, he voiced his unhappiness at religious
divisions: 'God knows, I say it solemnly, that it has been (particularly
of late) and shall be more and more my endeavour to promote the
cordial and vigorous and systematical exertions of all friends of the
essentials of Christianity, softening prejudices, healing divisions and
striving to substitute a rational and an honest zeal for fundamentals, in
place of a hot party spirit.'[41]

A Baptist minister of Norwich, Joseph Kinghorn, wrote in June
1797 to his father in Yorkshire: '*Wilberforce*, Member for your county
has published I hear a *very fanatical* book, it quite raises a hue and
cry, and I begin to imagine by what I hear and what I see in the
reviews that I shall like it in part at least, for there are a set of people
whose outcry is nearly a recommendation.'[42]

A month later young Kinghorn, still waiting on the Library, reported
the hearsay: 'but its subject is Methodism and red-hot Methodism
too as far as I can find, calculated to alarm the conscience, and I am
very glad of it. . . .'[43] When at last *A Practical View* came to hand,
Kinghorn the Baptist did not like Wilberforce's views of Church order.
'But in other things as far as I have read Mr. W's book is excellent. . . .
He will be called undoubtedly a Methodist, probably a Madman but
I think he speaks the words of truth and soberness. What a pity it
is such a man should vote for – war! Especially *this* war!'[44]

A Practical View strengthened Wilberforce's position with Dissenters. He was already in himself a link between Dissent and the
Church of England, to the disgust or puzzlement of many Churchmen. As he once noted, 'They think I cannot be loyal to the Established
Church because I love Dissenters.'[45]

6*

It was a time when relations were in ferment because the 'old' Dissent, which included the emerging Unitarians, agitated for repeal of the Test and Corporation Acts; while the Methodists were reaching the point of formal separation from the Church.

Both problems perplexed him. If he deplored the doctrines of Unitarians ('Socinians') he admired the spirituality and earnestness of Baptists, Quakers and the Independents, or Congregationalists as they were beginning to be called. It was William Jay, the Independent whose Bath chapel he sometimes attended, striking up a warm friendship, who said: 'His preferences in religion were not censorious or exclusive. He had a real and large liberality towards those who differed from him in some of the more external and subordinate parts of Christianity. . . .'[46] Yet his ideal was a formal unity between all Protestant Christians within an avowedly Christian state, rather as in the early years of Queen Elizabeth I. Therefore he opposed the sectarian attitude. When the question of the Test Acts came before Parliament in 1787 he voted instinctively with the majority against Repeal.

Gisborne, however, urged him to change his mind. Wilberforce decided to study the question thoroughly and laid in a stock of books. His friend Beaufoy gave notice that he would raise Repeal in the Session of 1789. Wilberforce by then was 'plunged up to the chin' in preparations for moving Abolition of the Slave Trade. The Dissenters' application came up first, unexpectedly early, before he had briefed himself. He stayed away from the debate, skulking at Holwood among slave papers, and the Dissenters of the West Riding demanded an explanation. He sent a long private reply of which garbled extracts found their way into the newspapers and vexed Wilberforce. 'These little tricks' were an unmannerly attempt to manœuvre him; if he supported the Dissenters when Repeal came up again, he might appear to be voting from fear of their electoral influence rather than 'conviction of the justice of their cause'. He was mortified at hearing a friend say, 'I suppose you dare not offend the Yorkshire Dissenters.'[47]

He entered the debate in 1790 with his conviction unchanged: that to abolish subscription to the Thirty-Nine Articles, and reception of the Sacrament according to the liturgy of the Church of England, would weaken the Christian fabric of the State and encourage looseness of belief. He was intending to make a long exposition immediately after Fox had moved Repeal but Pitt prevented him, possibly to shield him from angering the West Riding again.[48]

The House threw out Fox's motion. Wilberforce rejoiced, yet with qualms. Had the Yorkshire Dissenters then left him to himself he might have come round to Repeal many years before he did, especially as it was he who brought in a Bill to allow Roman Catholics to hold commissions in the Militia.[49] He also supported the Quaker Relief Bill of 1797.[50]

As for the Methodists, Wilberforce greatly admired the Wesleys, both John and Charles, each of whom he met once.* When he learned that Charles Wesley's widow and unmarried daughter Sarah were in reduced circumstances he asked Hannah More to investigate:[51] Hannah replied that the daughter had been 'more a wit than a Methodist' when she had known her some years previously, but both were very deserving.[52] Wilberforce and two of his friends provided an annuity for Mrs. Wesley in August 1792[53] which shamed the Methodist body into raising another.

Wilberforce regretted successive steps which took the Methodist Connexion out of the Church of England, but when they turned to him because of his intimacy with Cabinet ministers he was always ready to help, as a file of letters to Dundas at the War Office reveals: 'I hope amid your many concerns you have found one minute to attend to the fate of my persecuted Methodist suitors in Jersey,' where those who refused to do Militia training on Sundays had been harried by the Governor, General Gordon although they were prepared to pay for extra drills on weekdays, 'and have solemnly engaged to be ready at *all times* and on *all occasions* to take up arms in defence of the island.' Wilberforce harried Dundas and Pitt until the matter sorted itself out.[54]

In April 1797 this, and all the wide influence of *A Practical View*, lay in the future. More immediately, indeed simultaneously with publication of his book, Wilberforce had fallen in love.

---

* The letter of John Wesley 'To a Member of Parliament', July 1790, was probably written to Beaufoy and not to Wilberforce as given in *Letters of John Wesley*, Standard Edition, ed. John Telford, VIII, pp. 230–1.

CHAPTER SIXTEEN

Barbara

Henry Thornton, the complete bachelor, married Marianne Sykes in February 1796. She had consulted Wilberforce and Babington before accepting.[1]

Though intelligent and lively she would have been too highly strung, at least in Zachary Macaulay's view, for Wilberforce, whose 'extreme vivacity and rapidity of thought and action certainly require no small firmness of nerve'.[2] The Thorntons' bliss deprived Wilberforce of a proper home at Battersea Rise, where he dropped in status from part-householder to welcome guest. 'Mr. Wilberforce came to us yesterday,' wrote Marianne to her sister-in-law on 19 September 1796, 'and is as brilliant and at the same time as pious as ever. He looks thin but healthy. . . .'[3] The resolve never to marry, which he had held since the affair with 'Miss H.', began to weaken until, during that winter of 1796–7, 'I began to wish "not to finish my journey alone." '[4]

At Bath he confided in Babington who had a house there. Babington knew just the person. Some young ladies of fashion had recently become ardent Evangelicals and no longer danced the round of balls and assemblies, rather to parental displeasure. He mentioned a certain beautiful Barbara Spooner. Later, by what to Wilberforce seemed a most extraordinary providence but probably owed not a little to a hint from Babington, he received a letter from Miss Spooner requesting spiritual advice. According to the cynical Bob Smith, now raised to the peerage as Lord Carrington, she had fallen in love with his character and set her cap at him, mugging up the Slave Trade in order to effect an introduction.[5] The Thorntons believed that she wrote of her troubles as the sole and persecuted Christian in a worldly family, though they forgot her elder brother William, already 'serious' and in holy orders.[6]

Barbara's letter charmed Wilberforce. On 13 April he discussed her with Babington, on 15 April he met her and fell head over heels in love at first sight.[7]

Barbara Ann Spooner was the third of the ten children of Isaac Spooner, a rich, elderly banker, merchant and ironmaster from Birmingham, who had extended the fortune extracted by his father Abraham from Aston Furnace. Perhaps because of the names Abraham and Isaac, the Thorntons believed wrongly that the Spooners had Jewish blood. Isaac had married slightly above him: to Barbara Gough-Calthorpe, daughter of Sir Hugh Gough, first baronet of Edgbaston (another, even richer merchant) and Barbara Calthorpe, the heiress of a well-connected county family with land in Norfolk and Suffolk: their son, Isaac's brother-in-law, had recently been created Lord Calthorpe.

The Spooners were among the leading citizens of Birmingham. They lived nearby at Elmdon Hall with a second house at Bath which Marianne thought 'the very temple of dullness'.[8] In 1797, however, Barbara Spooner was gay and good humoured and pretty. There would come a time when Marianne said that you would never know how much of the angel there was in Wilberforce unless you had watched his patience with his wife,[9] but this was after her near-fatal attack of typhoid, followed by further childbearing. In 1797 Hannah More had doubts about the family's suitability but she loved 'the sweet woman you have chosen',[10] or so she told Wilberforce. Macaulay, on the other hand, was 'sharp sighted to notice her defects',[11] even before the illness.

It was a whirlwind courtship, with Wilberforce rushing faster than his friends advised, yet trying to check his ardour by keeping a special diary of his feelings. Before he could put the question he received, on Easter Monday, 17 April, a letter by the cross-post from Portsmouth telling of the naval mutiny at Spithead. He hurried round to call on the aged Burke, now retired from Parliament, and there found Windham, Secretary at War, discussing what the Government should do. Wilberforce had expected a mutiny as he knew the seamen's feelings about bad pay and cruel conditions, but firmness was essential now. At half past four he wrote express to Pitt: 'My dear Pitt. . . . I am doubtful whether I shall or shall not hasten to town. Meanwhile for the satisfaction of my own mind, *let me solemnly advise you* I don't much expect you to take my advice, to send for Sir Charles Middleton. . . .'[12] Wilberforce would stand by, to be used unofficially if required.

Admiral Middleton hated the press gang and had worked hard for shipboard improvements but when *Culloden* mutinied in '94 he had prodded a nervous First Lord into preparing to sink her by gunfire, and this threat had snuffed the flame. The situation was more complex now and the present First Lord knew how to combine firmness with finesse. Pitt had no need to call on Middleton for gunfire; nor Wilberforce as peacemaker, which was fortunate for Barbara.

Five days after the news of the mutiny, going deeper into love each time he met her, Wilberforce spent a restless Saturday night unable to sleep for thinking of her. At his prayers on Sunday morning and at church he was agitated whether to propose or resist. A visit to the Pump Room in Barbara's company after church caused the final surrender. He went back to his lodgings and proposed by letter and then told Babington, who urged delay. Wilberforce, with his tendency to be influenced by the last person who talked to him, reluctantly agreed to stop the letter, but it had gone, and that night he received her 'formal favourable answer' and could not sleep for confusion of love and happiness, mixed with anxiety lest he had been swept off his feet.[13]

His friends were deafened with carillons of joy, with Miss Spooner eulogized as 'above all the women I ever knew qualified *in all respects*, to make me a good wife'.[14] They were sworn to secrecy but Hannah More replied that Patty had already sent her the news which was all over Bath. Hannah was amused at his total capitulation. She wanted to tell him how his book went but 'I dare say if I were now to fill up my paper with any other subject but this fair *Barbara* you would think me a dull, prosing, pedantic unfeeling Old Maid who was prating of the book when she should be talking of the wife.'[15] Thornton and Dean Milner were summoned from London to be introduced. They arrived to find Wilberforce preparing to set out for London in obedience to a note from Pitt, who wanted his vote on the Austrian Loan. The message to stop them had missed on the road. Thornton wrote to Marianne that on the whole he did not grudge the needless journey, 'for Wilberforce is full of affection and gratitude to us for coming and will remember it he says for his whole life. . . . I have though been obliged in some degree to impose on myself silence respecting my *wife* that I might allow Wilberforce to talk about his Barbara.'[16]

Wilberforce returned to a London buzzing with rumour that he was helping to foment mutiny in the Army. Pitt asked him the facts. Wilberforce tracked the rumour to a degenerate clergyman named Williams, who in revenge for a written refusal of further alms had gone round the barracks, showing illiterate soldiers the genuine Wilberforce signature and then reading a seditious appeal.[17]

Williams promptly turned his coat. Wilberforce sent him round to help Windham track down the men planning the mutiny. Then Williams disappeared. Pitt begged Wilberforce's aid. A stream of notes from Palace Yard to Downing Street reported attempts to find him: 'Wms. went into the Coffee House in which he wrote to me accidentally having met my servant in the street. It was the Coffee House on the right hand as you enter the Broad Pavement before the door of Westminster Hall.'[18]

By now the Fleet had mutinied at the Nore. Parliament rose for the Whitsun Recess. Wilberforce flung public troubles behind him and doubled back to Bath. On Tuesday morning, 30 May 1797, he married

Barbara Spooner in a quiet wedding, as the custom was, at the parish church of Walcot, Bath. The bridegroom was thirty-eight, the bride twenty.

Many years before he had promised himself that if ever he married he would take his bride, for her first Sunday, to Hannah More's Mendip schools: he said a visit always helped to cure ambition and to rouse him from 'my natural indolence'.[19] After four honeymoon days they arrived at Cowslip Green where Hannah More had rushed down from the wedding of the Princess Royal (Bishop Porteus had secured her a good seat) to conduct them round. The four sisters tactfully squeezed into one carriage, leaving the Wilberforces alone in the other. Mendip poverty and More family philanthropy made a profound impression on Barbara: forty years later, when she tried to compose reminiscences, she wrote pages about it in her manuscript book.[20]

Hannah said she had never seen a poor honest gentleman more desperately in love.[21] Wilber told Montagu after four days of matrimony that his dearest Barbara's mind was disposed exactly as he could wish. 'She wishes to retire as much as possible from the giddy crowd, and to employ herself in "keeping her own heart" and in promoting the happiness of her fellow creatures. I really did not think there had been such a woman. There seems to be entire coincidence in our intimacy and interests and pursuits.'[22] The future did not quite bear out this 'entire coincidence'.

Pitt offered Holwood but they leased Broomfield at Clapham for five weeks from Eliot, whose ill health kept him in the West Country, at £10 a week complete with the admirable Maybach, the butler, a most attentive and intelligent fellow, who refused a tip.[23] Bishop Pretyman must have chuckled at being begged on 10 June to 'present my best respects and my wife's (I love the homeliness of the term) to Mrs. P. and my young friends . . .';[24] and Muncaster to read: 'My dear fellow I long to bring you acquainted with my dearest Mrs W. whom I am sure you will like.'[25] When Parliament rose, the Wilberforces intended to introduce Barbara to the County at the Assizes in York. They were met on the road by news of the sudden death of Sally's husband, Dr. Clarke. He was only forty-five and Pitt had promised him a year ago the Deanery of York in succession to decrepit Dean Fountayne, who had held it for half a century; Fountayne outlived Clarke five years and departed at the age of eighty-seven.

The Wilberforces turned off at once to Hull to comfort his sister and their old mother, who was in 'great decrepitude'[26] and 'a state of great nervous debility'[27] and died the next year. Wilberforce's influence secured Dr. Clarke's vacant living of Hull parish church for Dean Milner's brother Joseph, the Evangelical schoolmaster-historian who had influenced them all. He died within a few weeks.

The saddest death for Wilberforce that autumn was Eliot's. He had seemed to recover, though not fit enough to go out to India as Governor-General in succession to Sir John Shore, another Evangelical. Eliot was never long out of Wilberforce's mind, 'for daily have I thought of you when, on my knees, I number over those friends for whom I am most interested.'[28] When the Wilberforces settled at 10 Pulteney Street, Bath in mid-September they hoped Eliot would come to stay to drink the waters, bringing his little Harriot; their invitation must have crossed the intelligence from Cornwall of Eliot's death. Wilberforce rushed up to London. 'Your very touching account of Pitt's sorrow,' wrote Hannah More, 'has gone to all our hearts, and I did not leave a dry eye below when I came up to write this nor had I anticipated the strong grief of that strong mind. May his stout heart be touched in the way we wish. God grant it!'[29]

Wilberforce himself had 'solid comfort' in Eliot's last letter 'which showed him to have been prepared for the awful change which awaited him'.[30]

Eliot's death altered Wilberforce's life. From Eliot's executors he bought Broomfield, the house Thornton had built near Battersea Rise.[31] With a long carriage drive between an avenue of young trees, it stood four miles by road from Westminster Bridge and a mile and a half from Battersea footbridge (or a quarter-mile less by the fields) and since Barbara soon preferred it to London the sitting of Parliament put her Wilber in a 'constant state of *oscillation* between Broomfield and Palace Yard.'[32]

Barbara had a difficult first pregnancy. 'Poor things,' Wilberforce wrote to William Smith from a thoroughly male standpoint, 'I know how much they suffer while in *this same* state, and how Providence has fitted them kindly to bear patiently what they have to endure.'[33] Their first child, the William who was to bring them such unhappiness, was born on 21 July 1798 (Speaker Addington wrote: 'How did you feel when your ears and eyes first told you that you were a father?')[34] One year later to the very day appeared their first girl, Barbara.

Wilberforce became a doting father, approving his wife's unfashionable determination to breast feed her babies,[35] although she required a wet nurse too. When the four-months'-old first-born and his nurse had stayed on with the Spooner grandparents, Wilberforce ended a political letter: 'Little William to his Mother's great delight, arrived out of Warwickshire a few hours ago fat and well liking – but like his papa not of the rosy order. I must shut up my dear Muncr. I have a frightful arrear of unanswered letters before me. . . .'[36]

Wilberforce sank gratefully into domesticity, struggling only a little at the possessiveness of his wife. He once referred, meaning the phrase admiringly, to her 'excessive affection'.[37] She grudged his absences: her role, by her own casting, was protectress of her valuable husband,

and because her intellectual and spiritual interests were narrower she a little constricted his own; indeed Lord Carrington said, with caustic exaggeration: 'After his marriage the Methodists* kept him wholly to themselves and as he had no hopes of converting me we saw little of each other though we always met with kindness.'[38]

Barbara's protectiveness perhaps prolonged her husband's life, though the physical core must have been tougher than was understood, as often is the case in poor health of nervous origin. More certainly, her hold unwittingly helped him consolidate his political independence.

---

* He was using the term in the non-denominational sense.

CHAPTER SEVENTEEN

Britain at Bay

A few mornings after moving into Broomfield Wilberforce was dressing[1] when Ashley, his secretary, hurried in to say that the previous afternoon, Whitsunday 1798, Pitt had fought a duel on Putney Heath with George Tierney, the elephantine Irish Whig who had thrust himself into the Opposition leadership when Fox and his friends seceded from the Commons in a useless defiance of the Constitution. After Pitt and Tierney had insulted each other in the House Tierney issued a challenge. Dudley Ryder acted as Pitt's second, the Speaker watched from a horse, Pitt fired his second shot in the air and the duellists, unharmed, returned to London in the same coach.

Wilberforce loathed the 'system of HONOUR (what *honour*!)'[2] which hindered a gentleman from telling unpleasant truths to another because 'honour' forbade refusal of the challenge which might follow. Pitt had magnified his fault by duelling on a Sunday, and the idea of the Prime Minister risking life and limb so foolishly shocked Wilberforce into action, especially as the nation took the matter seriously even if a little amused by the absurdity of Pitt, thin as a pole, matched against the huge girth of Tierney. Wilberforce found Westminster much alive about the duel. He put down a motion to outlaw duelling.

Pitt at once objected that 'your motion is one for my removal':[3] to raise duelling that week must censure a particular duellist. Pitt could not brush aside Wilberforce. As one of Fitzwilliam's Parliamentary dependants had complained the previous autumn, echoing a sentiment of Burke: 'Wilberforce, the great little peacemaker and mischief maker . . . is to Mr. Pitt the whole people of England.'[4] Pitt softened his letter with expressions of warm personal affection but he pressed his point, that if the motion passed he must resign. Wilberforce therefore withdrew it, for to him Pitt remained the only national leader and to pillory Pitt for a lawful action, as this motion effectively would do, was a hasty error.

Wilberforce's reaction to the duel illuminated his independence in the years immediately following marriage. A few weeks before, at the crisis of the Spithead mutiny, he had offered Pitt to stand by, 'so far as I can consistently with my duty to God and my Country'.[5] He aimed at this throughout the grim events which closed the eighteenth century, while Britain fought for her life after the French broke off the second round of secret Peace negotiations in the summer of 1797, and smashed the Continental allies until Britain stood alone. These were the years of the first great invasion scare, of the French incursion into Ireland and the attempt on Wales; the years also of the sea victories of St. Vincent, and Camperdown and Nelson's destruction of the French fleet in the Nile.

After the failure of Pitt's attempt at peace, Wilberforce supported the war though he could still provoke taunts of 'humanity' from Dundas and Windham when he protested at the Austrian persecution of Lafayette. As County Member he took part in raising fencibles and yeomanry against the expected invasion, corresponding with landowners such as Grimston[6] in the East Riding and with the Duke of Norfolk[7] as lord lieutenant of the West Riding – two months before the Foxite duke was dismissed for giving a disloyal toast. Wilberforce had already taken up with Pitt the cause of small Freeholders badly hit by the Cavalry Tax, warning him that if he did not exclude them, 'I really believe the most serious discontents . . . will be produced amongst a set of people now well disposed.'[8] He even offered advice on home defence to Dundas at the War Office: the 'hasty scrawl' was addressed 'not to the *Minister* but to the *Man*',[9] and thus it invited no official douche of cold water. But he could not parade with Lord Belgrave, Bankes and other friends in the St. Margaret's Corps because a shower might give him a chill. They made him an honorary member.[10]

His chief war effort concerned what a later age would dub the Home Front. In these dark perplexing years Bonaparte's shot and shell were not the only weapons tearing at the fabric of Britain. Some of Wilberforce's attitudes and actions have been misunderstood because their wartime context is forgotten.

One assault was on the mind or beliefs of Britons, by a determined effort to undermine the Christian religion. Most people in Britain, whatever their personal faith or lack of it, took for granted the truth of the Christian revelation and regarded Christianity as the bedrock of national life. The French Revolution on the other hand promoted an anti-Christian Deism; and in England the prophet of both was Tom Paine.

Paine's new popular-style book, *The Age of Reason*, therefore appeared to be propaganda for the Revolution as much as for the freethinking ideas which caused men to proclaim themselves 'infidels'. It had been adopted as virtually an official manifesto by the mainly working class group, the London Corresponding Society, founded by

Hardy the Piccadilly boot-maker to agitate for Parliamentary reform, but dedicated to republicanism by those who dominated it after his acquittal for high treason. Late in 1796 one of the leading members, Francis Place, the radical tailor of Charing Cross, went into partnership with a poor printer and bookbinder named Thomas Williams for a cheap edition of 2,000 copies of *The Age of Reason*. It sold fast and Williams realized he could make a handsome profit if he reprinted this cheap edition on his own without telling Place. Williams pocketed the proceeds.

Meanwhile counsel's opinion on whether to prosecute him for a seditious and blasphemous libel had been taken by the Proclamation Society, now in its tenth year. The Bishop of London (Porteus), its president from 1793, believed that 'much good has been done by this Society since its institution'. Wilberforce's brainchild had not produced a sweeping national revival, but in the Bishop's view the Acts of Parliament it promoted and the prosecutions it brought had given 'some little check' to vice, 'and things are kept from growing worse which in these times and in such immense places as London and Westminster perhaps is as much as can be expected, till Christian zeal and piety become a little more prevalent and fervent than they are at present.'[11] The Bishop adhered firmly to the view that the state was the nation's moral guardian. The Society stood in high favour with the judiciary, and with reformers like Patrick Colquhoun, who worked towards the founding of a properly organized police.

The prosecution of Williams enraged the Radicals but brought a very large measure of contemporary approval, as even Place admitted in his unpublished autobiography.[12] The Proclamation Society retained the leading advocate of the age, Thomas Erskine, which was a scoop because in prosecutions for sedition, and in trials which threatened freedom of the Press, Erskine usually appeared for the defence; he had won several notable acquittals. Erskine's parents, the 6th Earl and Countess of Buchan and his late sister, Lady Anne Erskine, had been fervent converts of George Whitefield the evangelist, but Erskine himself was not an Evangelical. Francis Place, who was furious at losing him for Williams' defence, reckoned him a hypocrite.

The trial came on before Lord Chief Justice Kenyon on 24 June 1797. Erskine made two brilliant speeches, one being his famous vindication of the truth of Christianity, and Williams was found guilty and remanded to Newgate without sentence. Throughout the Long Vacation Francis Place exerted all possible pressure until Erskine felt uneasy at successfully prosecuting a Radical, and on 23 November went to a meeting of the Proclamation Society: 'Erskine,' runs Wilberforce's diary entry, 'wanting to waive bringing up Williams for judgment – said he would not compromise his character for any set of men. We firm.'[13]

According to Radical legend, Erskine immediately threw up his brief and returned his retainer, in disgust at the Society's unmerciful and unchristian attitude. In fact, he went into court four days later to ask for a day to be set for Williams' judgement, telling the bench he felt heartfelt satisfaction in the transaction; Place believed this to be nonsense. The case was set for five months ahead, 28 April 1798.

In February Erskine wrote to the Proclamation Society pleading that they show Christian charity and Christian forebearance by accepting as sufficient punishment the time (it would be ten months) which Williams had spent in Newgate. On 27 February Porteus, Wilberforce and fourteen other Committee members met at the Bishop of Durham's London house. They resolved *nem. con.* not to press for a severe sentence; they did not feel justified in asking for leniency, a matter for the Court. Any other course might suggest the offence was trivial.

Erskine threw up his brief. Williams received the minimum sentence of a year's hard labour in the new Middlesex House of Correction at Cold Bath Fields, Clerkenwell. Wilberforce and the Society received a lasting name for unchristian behaviour in persecuting a starveling printer who had been forced by poverty to print a book which he, as a pious man, did not believe in.

This odium derived mainly from a pathetic letter in the Whig *Morning Chronicle* signed by Williams' wife, but actually composed by the Editor; and from a moving account by Erskine, written in 1819 for Howell's *State Trials*. Erskine described how he had thrown up the case after being accosted by a weeping, emaciated woman who proved to be Mrs. Williams. She took him to her hovel where she nursed several children sick with smallpox, and 'the wretched man I had convicted was sewing up little religious tracts which had been his principal employment in trade'.[14]

Wilberforce later came to believe strongly that prosecutions for blasphemy defeated their purpose by advertising a publication; that true religion had nothing to fear from infidel attacks, and might be injured by invoking the secular arm.[15] Moreover the sedition, as it seemed in wartime, which Paine's book nourished was not suppressed by the prosecution. But Erskine's pathetic story of Mrs. Williams, with its implication of cruelty by Wilberforce and his friends, was riddled and ridiculed as 'altogether untrue' by Francis Place in a passage of his autobiography written in 1824 but not published until 1972. Mrs. Williams, said Place, was slovenly and spendthrift but not emaciated; 'the smallpox is an enormous exaggeration'; she did not live in a hovel, and Erskine went to the home of his own volition to persuade Williams to recant. Williams was not a 'wretched man' but a fat and jolly man who liked too much good living for his purse. As for sewing up religious tracts 'this is pure invention,' said Place; 'Williams would sell anything, but these were out of the question,'[16] for he had no connection which might bring him tracts to print or bind, and the profit was too small. Place maintained that Erskine knew all these facts.

Presumably Wilberforce and his friends knew too.*

On 21 December 1798 the House debated the Bill to continue suspension of Habeas Corpus for a further six months. The Opposition, reduced to a handful by the Foxite secession, were powerless to defeat the Second Reading, which received an overwhelming majority, and therefore made their protest by attacking the treatment of prisoners held without trial on suspicion of sedition or high treason, including alleged aiders and abettors of the recent Irish Rebellion.

Many were held in the new Cold Bath Fields (where Mount Pleasant G.P.O. parcels sorting office now stands) which had been designed according to the ideas of John Howard the reformer, who had died in Russia, and approved by Bentham. It included the novelty of single cells to replace the communal incarceration of the old county gaols which Howard had attacked. Later ages would rate solitary confinement inhuman but in 1798 it reflected the latest thinking on penal reform. (By 1829, when the reforming Governor Chesterton took charge, Cold Baths Fields was as bad as any.) The Opposition had a stronger case that unconvicted men should not be punished as if convicts.

The Radicals had dubbed Cold Bath Fields 'the English Bastille' and execrated it as Pitt's instrument of repression. During the debate of 21 December[17] Wilberforce entered the Chamber while John Courtenay, Member for Tamworth, was up. Courtenay had been giving harrowing impressions of sufferings by state prisoners whom he had visited at the prison, and then had described those of a prostitute and of a disobedient boy. Courtenay had a reputation as a humorous speaker who made heavy use of irony and threw insults at respected figures; the House did not take seriously his concern for prisoners, which it regarded as his latest stick for belabouring Pitt.

Courtenay spied Wilberforce, the man whom the House regarded as the friend of gaolbirds. Courtenay thereupon, in a sarcastic, taunting voice, concluded his speech by lamenting that 'an honourable gentleman, celebrated for his humanity, has not visited the prison.' He was sure that his 'vital Christianity' would have provoked his compassion. 'I am certain, however,' he finished with bantering tone, 'that the honourable gentleman will no longer suffer it be said by the unfortunate, "I was in prison and you visited me not".'

Wilberforce was annoyed. He had visited Cold Bath Fields fre-

---

* J. L. and Barbara Hammond, whose account of the case in *The Town Labourer* is severe on Wilberforce, had studied the Place *MSS* in the British Museum, as their references show, but they either missed or chose not to use Place's vivid first hand description of the affair.

quently, long before the arrests for sedition and high treason; it was a pet project. He left the Chamber and retrieved the notes sent him a few days previously by one of the visiting magistrates, the Reverend Dr. Samuel Glasse, Canon of St. Paul's, a man noted for his philanthropy whom Wilberforce had recommended for a bishopric. When he returned, young Sir Francis Burdett was up and Cold Bath Fields again under fire. Two ministerialists followed before Wilberforce caught the Speaker's eye. He had therefore to link his speech to Burdett's but he framed it as an answer to Courtenay and employed the same bantering tone. '. . . The honourable gentleman says the prisoners are starved. But what says a visiting magistrate . . .? With the permission of the House I will read his very words. "I saw their dinners: better I would not wish on my own table. It was roast beef and plum pudding." Aye, Sir, and my friend is a doctor of divinity!' Wilberforce said it reminded him of Parson Adams, the character in the Fielding novel who was astonished, as the stage coach passed a mansion, to hear one passenger say the owner was the best in the world and another that he was the greatest rascal.

Wilberforce maintained that the Opposition had been imposed upon; he then turned seriously to the main subject, whether Habeas Corpus should remain suspended.

Pitt was delighted. Courtenay grumbled about 'religious facetiousness,' but he could appreciate the sarcasm. Later he wrote: 'Mr. Wilberforce . . . is quick and acute in debate; and always prompt to answer and reply. When he is provoked to personality (which seldom happens) he retorts in a poignant and refined vein of satire, peculiarly his own.'[18] Burdett, however, was furious; it was the start of his long enmity against Wilberforce. Wilberforce himself, when next he scanned his soul, became penitent. 'In what a fermentation of spirits was I on the night of answering Courtenay. How jealous of character and greedy of applause. Alas alas, Create in me a clean heart O God and renew a right spirit within me.'[19] Had he foreseen the rod which his misplaced humour had pickled for him, he might have been abashed even more.

Burdett made Cold Bath Fields his cause. The sincerity of the rich baronet who lived in luxury and championed the unenfranchised London mob did not appear to Pitt's friends: they believed that Burdett, Courtenay, Tierney and the *Morning Chronicle* spread lies about the prison. In the spring of 1799 the Government granted a Parliamentary enquiry which exonerated the magistrates and prison officials except on a trivial matter. Burdett remained suspicious and pressed the matter until the Home Office admitted that the prison governor treated men on remand under the Habeas Corpus Suspension Act as if they were convicts – rather in the spirit of Dundas' remark, 'It would not be seriously contended that because a man had been acquitted of high treason, it was a proof he had never been guilty of high treason.'[20] By now Cold Bath Fields had become a symbol to the Radicals. Its single cells, built on Howard's reforming pattern, became the 'dungeon grim' of legend. As for Wilberforce, active sympathizer with Bentham, Romilly and Elizabeth Fry, it became part of the legend that 'the state of the prisons left him cold'.[21]

No one who supported Pitt in these years of wartime crisis can be absolved from the charge of repression. Wilberforce did not see it as repressing the lower orders but preserving the Constitution, for their sake as much as for the higher classes. He was certain Pitt was the only man who could save beleaguered Britain, that Pitt had more disinterested patriotism and a purer mind 'than almost any man not under the influence of Christian principles I ever knew. That he has weaknesses and faults I freely confess, but a want of ardent zeal for the public welfare and for the strictest love of truth are not I believe, as God shall judge me, of the number.'[22] The Opposition, on the other hand, in Wilberforce's view, looked primarily for personal gain.

He backed Pitt in the struggle against those who sought to upset the delicate balance of 'our happy Constitution'. Thus Wilberforce introduced the bill to strengthen the laws preventing workmen combining against their masters, which became the hated Combination Act of 1799 (extended the next year to prevent masters combining against their workmen, though this was virtually a dead letter). He did not regard this as repressing 'the workers': the Combination Acts cannot be seen in terms of 'class struggle' between 'ruling class' and 'working class' without introducing concepts out of historical context. Wilberforce indeed, saw himself as politically on the side of the working men, championing their best interests against those who would use them as pawns. For he and the greater number of his contemporaries at the end of the eighteenth century, including most of the 'inferior classes', accepted with pride the structure of society which they had inherited from earlier generations, and scorned what they knew of foreign systems. It was a structure which rose like a pyramid from the lowest to great ducal landowners and the Sovereign. Each station of life had its place and its own pride and dignity. The orders or ranks were not rigid: families moved up or down, could be ruined or made; the law, trade and the Church were ladders especially, while the universities always had a proportion of sizars or servitors from poor homes.

Among Wilberforce's friends from the lower rungs were Isaac Milner, who had worked as a weaver, William Jay the great Dissenting preacher of Bath, son of a stonecutter, and Sir William Scott (Lord Stowell) and his brother, Lord Chancellor Eldon, whose father had been a coalfactor in Newcastle. Many of the West Riding merchants and mill owners were self-made. Of the younger generation Wilberforce probably chatted in his later years with an under-gardener on his cousin Samuel Smith's estate who became Sir Joseph Paxton, designer of the Crystal Palace.

For Britain to flourish, in Parliament's view, the 'happy Constitution' had to be preserved from those who would wreck it to achieve French victory and their own rise to power. The Gagging Acts and the suspension of Habeas Corpus had blocked them one way; now they pursued their aim another, by encouraging workmen to 'combine' against their masters. Wilberforce saw the Combination Acts as defence of the realm, not economic repression; he was saving the poor from political agitators. Moreover the forcing up of wages would increase the cost of living and thus hurt the poor.

He was not applying economic theory, but reacting to a wartime threat. 'Great political events,' he had written a few years earlier, 'are rarely the offspring of cool deliberate system; they receive their shape and size and color and the date of their existence from a thousand causes which could hardly have been foreseen, and in the production of which various unconnected and jarring parties have combined and assisted.'[23]

It was a tragedy that Wilberforce and Whigs such as Whitbread and Sheridan were indeed 'jarring parties'. With their mutual concern for the wage earners they might together have found a better way, for Whitbread understood more than Wilberforce the harsh new forces at work as England became a great industrial nation. But Whitbread openly wanted French victory, and thus Wilberforce would not take him seriously.

Wilberforce was not a prophet. He was too much a man of his time to realize that the new industrial poor would need the right to combine in trade unions to protect their interests. Nor was he more than a prophet, able to see far ahead to a day when trade unions would attempt to be the dominant element more powerful than Parliament. The Combination Acts, which in fact were seldom used, served as war-time defences against agitation. Ironically, until the repeal of the Combination Laws a quarter of a century later, the early trade unions would shelter behind the Friendly Societies Act brought in by Rose and Wilberforce.

Britain plunged deep into her resources to pay for the war. Wilberforce hovered on the side-lines, frequently called in by Pitt during the Bank crisis.[24] When taxes increased he acted as watchdog for those with lower incomes and large families.

He gave heavily, as he was bound to do 'in my position', to the voluntary Patriotic Contribution, but he disapproved: 'I still wish Pitt would push the measure of a general impost on all property,' he wrote to Muncaster.[25] Pitt introduced an income tax as part of his

Budget of December 1798, provoking a howl from many of the rich and the Foxites. Wilberforce had toyed with the idea of a tax on capital rather than income, a Wealth Tax in fact, and although the Attorney General convinced him it was impracticable, Wilberforce's suggestion shows that he did not hold riches to be sacred.[26]

Like his generation he took for granted the disparities of wealth which had always been known in England and throughout Europe, and believed that men of great estate were necessary to the prosperity of all in the kingdom. He did not want men to set their heart on riches. 'Now remember my dear Mary that a fortune is great or small according to anyone's situation in life,' he wrote to his fatherless cousin Mary Smith before her marriage to John Sargent, the young Vicar of Graffham in Sussex. Wilberforce said that if he lived quietly in the country with Mrs. Wilberforce ('O how I wish I did! and how much more does she!') or was for instance Vicar of Graffham ('O how I wish I were,') he would be affluent with half his present fortune.[27] He would have fewer responsibilities, dependants and charities, less expenses of office as it were. Each station in life had duties; the higher the station the greater the duties. The whole social order of England was an interlocking unity.

This was the ideal. Wilberforce sought to expend his fortune to the glory of God and the benefit of his fellow creatures, but even he did not do so without temptation. 'I honestly declare to you,' he told Mary, 'that I continually find it necessary to guard against that natural love of wealth and grandeur, which prompts us always, when we come to apply our general doctrine to our own case, to claim an *Exception.*'[28] Ambition, vanity, and love of display, these made men greedy, not the desire for domestic comfort. Therefore he welcomed an income tax.

And when, in his old age, his own fortune nearly disappeared he proved that he could practice what he preached.

The Great Hunger of 1799–1800 burdened him, both for the poor's sake and because empty bellies encouraged disaffection.

The harvests of 1798 and 1799 were disastrous and by the early winter of 1799 parts of England approached famine. Friends tried to persuade him that distress among mill workers in the West Riding of his own constituency was not as bad as he made out: he redoubled his enquiries.[29] He hoped the rich throughout the land would give up luxuries to release more food and more money for relief. The House of Commons nominated Wilberforce to the Committee on how to offset the scarcity of grain. He made it 'a strict rule' never to leave its daily sittings 'for any other business whatever'.[30] He found that Adam Smith's persuasive doctrine of *laissez-faire* had prejudiced members against Administration's interfering with the market or with landowners. Wilberforce accepted Adam Smith's general principles yet believed these should not be 'pushed to a vicious extreme'.[31]

Wilberforce now had a new and strong ally in Arthur Young. Since his conversion to active Christian faith through reading *A Practical View*, the great editor of *Annals of Agriculture* had discovered compassion. Previously Young had dismissed the suffering caused to labourers by the Enclosures which he encouraged as an economic necessity. Now he wanted to find ways to prevent distress and to help the agricultural poor recover some of their former prosperity. Wilberforce was already 'truly and deeply (and every hour more and more) interested in the agricultural improvement of the Kingdom',[32] and he consulted Young frequently during the sittings of the Scarcity Committee.

The Committee members took their duties too lightly for Wilberforce. 'Grieved I am to say that the Committee stands adjourned till Friday,' runs a note to Young in February 1800. 'I own *I am shocked at the languor which prevails on this important subject in sensible and feeling men. God forgive them*. I shall endeavour to bring them together to-morrow betimes, and it would be one of my first cares to call for you.' He wanted Young to bring proofs of the efficacy of a scheme whereby the State should provide seed-potatoes for the poor to plant in plots provided by landlords or commoners. He ended with a comment stressing the urgency of the matter: '*My poor rough friends in the West of Yorkshire* are suffering with admirable patience, living on bad barley and oat meal mixed with bean meal and damaged wheat meal when they can get it.'[33] Planting potatoes was Young's particular answer to the food shortage and he convinced Wilberforce.

When the Committee reported[34] at last in March it recommended importing corn all the way from the Mediterranean and America. It talked of rice from India and half-cured herrings from Scandinavia, and urged the rich to try brown bread and Londoners to stop eating new bread. It also advocated the potato scheme, but the landlords disliked the idea of providing land. 'I understand the report of the potato business will be opposed to-day,' Wilberforce scribbled to Young. 'It is really *shocking*, and though used to the *conduct* of country gentlemen on such occasions I find it hard to bear it with due temper and charity.'[35]

A Whig newspaper poked fun at Wilberforce about potatoes. He often complained of Press misrepresentation or misreporting. ('You never saw,' he once wrote a friend in an undated letter, 'such a farrago of unintelligible nonsense as was brought to me under the rather provoking title of Substance of my Speech. I have made it a little better, but really it is even now in a very discreditable state.')[36] He longed for an official transcript. On 7 March 1800 he gave the House

some merriment by reading out what a newspaper alleged he had said
the previous evening: 'Potatoes made men healthy, vigorous and
active; but, what is still more in their favour, they make men tall:
more especially was he led to say so, as being rather under the common
size, and he must lament that his guardians had not fostered him under
that genial vegetable!'[37]

In view of the disastrous potato famines of the next half century it
was perhaps as well that the scheme of Young and Wilberforce did
not catch on very widely.

That summer Arthur Young went on another of his tours. Wilberforce helped by introductions and gave Young liberty to disburse
relief on his account.[38] The book Young wrote about his tour, all the
stronger because of his former callousness to the victims of Enclosures,
backed the Bettering Society's plea that landowners should give back,
for allotments and grazing, some of the land they had enclosed, so
that the poor could feed their families and not depend solely on cash
in wages or relief.

The harvest nearly failed again in 1800 and the price of corn rose
to heights which emptied the pockets of the poor. The Duke of Portland, then Home Secretary, produced a pamphlet[39] which claimed
there was plenty of corn in the country and attacked the idea of setting
a maximum price, which would favour the consumer. The pamphlet
disgusted Wilberforce because the grower generally was the better
off and could bear the loss. He did not himself believe a maximum
price could be imposed effectively but he assured Lord Kenyon, who
held to the contrary, that it would be a 'perfectly just measure'.
Wilberforce added: 'I feel deeply for the poor, and I must say, that it
is trifling with them to announce that there is a sufficiency of food,
unless it be at a price which is within their powers of payment.'[40]

It was the callousness of men like Portland which grieved Wilberforce. His solutions to the problem of hunger might be right or wrong;
he could not rest while his fellow men starved.[41] In November 1800 he
unburdened himself to Montagu at Sandelford Priory in Berkshire,
saying he had reason to believe the poor were spending their all
on bread. 'If so, the argument of the D of P (what a Letter to be
circulated throughout the lower classes with their hungry bellies and
starving infants) that you should not try to reduce prices, but on the
contrary, is inflicting *gratuitous* and *useless* suffering on the bulk of the
Community.'

He scribbled *en galop*, his spirit hot: 'My dear Friend when I look
to the scene Sandelford now presents to my mind's eye, when I see
before me you and your excellent wife and lovely children, when I
reflect on the blessing Providence has shower'd down on us . . .' – a
long, involved ungrammatical sentence spilled over the last page to
the top and bottom of the cover and back to the space left at the letter's

start, submerging the date line. Its drift contrasted the present domestic bliss of Montagues and Wilberforces with the probable ruin of the nation through vice and folly and want of principle. Men starved while others luxuriated; therefore all might be ruined through the coming of revolution. It could be avoided if the rich turned unselfish. 'Alas Alas alas. Great indignation quite overcomes me. But so it is: we cast off the fear of God and we are then left to the fatal effects of our own vicious principles. I must break off. . . .'[42]

And on top of Wilberforce's gloom for Britain lay his gloom about the slaves. The years passed. The slaves whom he had set out, almost gaily, to rescue remained in chains; cargo after human cargo endured the Middle Passage. More slaves had been carried in the seventeen nineties than ever before.

CHAPTER EIGHTEEN

Entr'acte

In the winter of 1796–7 a number of leading planters met in London to discuss how to frustrate Wilberforce. They decided to propose that Parliament should remit the whole question to the Colonial legislatures, ordering that the condition of the slaves be improved so that they bred more children and, as healthier workers, produced more sugar cane. Thus the Slave Trade would ultimately become redundant without upsetting the economy.

Sir William Young, so Wilberforce discovered, explained privately to likely allies that the real object was to avoid a British Abolition Act.[1]

An Amelioration Bill duly became law in 1797 despite Fox, who thundered that it was an indirect attempt to perpetuate the Trade, and Wilberforce, who complained not only that it cancelled the House's solemn pledge to abolish, but that 'the thing is impracticable', since conditions never would improve while the Trade existed.[2] He was right. The House some years later asked the West Indian legislatures what had been done; the answer was 'Nil or worse than Nil',[3] as Wilberforce put it. Even the few islands which had passed an ameliorating law treated it as a dead letter.

Wilberforce always regarded this decision to remit the matter to the Colonies as the Planters' sharpest card, the most grievous single move in their delaying tactics, because the British Parliament thenceforth felt complacent. It threw out Wilberforce's Abolition Bills of 1797 and 1798, and Thornton's attempt to limit slaving geographically, which would have protected 1,200 miles of the West African coast. At least Parliament passed an improved version of Dolben's Slave Regulating or Middle Passage Bill.

Meanwhile the French War muddied the issue. Wilberforce has been charged with hypocrisy for not supporting a Foxite motion (lost by a huge majority) for the removal of British troops from San Domingo, where they fought the blacks: surely he should welcome

blacks carving out a kingdom.[4] But Wilberforce saw the campaign
in the wider strategy of the war, though he had not wanted an invasion
of San Domingo. The Foxite motion aimed to help the French, not the
slaves; and Bonaparte cared nothing for the blacks. He reimposed
slavery and determined to reconquer San Domingo. Meanwhile the
local British Commander, his troops dying by thousands from disease,
evacuated the island on his own initiative after securing the safety of
Jamaica by a treaty with the blacks.

Farther south the British had captured Trinidad from Spain yet the
planters persuaded Pitt and Dundas to issue a Proclamation in November 1797 allowing Jamaica and the Bahamas, despite the war, to export
rum to remaining Spanish colonies, 'and negroes which shall have been
legally imported'. Wilberforce at once pointed out privately to Pitt
that this Proclamation breached the Foreign Slave Bill which had
passed the Commons though it had failed in the Lords: to allow such
trading might prevent the Bill ever becoming law. Wilberforce pressed
the point until Pitt, after much confidential negotiation, withdrew the
Proclamation, confirming Wilberforce's confidence in quiet diplomacy
behind the scenes.

For James Stephen this was not enough. Stephen was now an intimate
friend and fellow-believer. From depth of sorrow at his wife's death
he had discovered, like Eliot before him, the strength and the source of
Wilberforce's sympathy, and they became brothers-in-law too when
Stephen married Sally Clarke as his second wife. In the security of
affection the two men could be uninhibited. Stephen's hot temper
exploded against Wilberforce's refusal to embarrass Pitt publicly: 'I still
clearly think that you have been improperly silent, and that when you
see the government loading the bloody altars of commerce . . . you are
bound by the situation wherein you have placed yourself to cry aloud
against it.'[5] Stephen was sure that Pitt had sold himself body and soul
to the traders and no longer wanted Abolition. He was not alone in
this conviction. Many years later in March 1841 Lord Melbourne's
Cabinet had 'a very agreeable evening' over dinner at Lansdowne
House. There was 'no, or little, business' and they fell to discussing
earlier political figures. Melbourne had a bawdy story about Grafton,
Lord Minto gave his father's recollection of Burke. And then they
dissected Wilberforce. Tom Macaulay defended him; Lord John
Russell retorted he should have abandoned Pitt after Pitt abandoned
Abolition, at which Melbourne pointed out that Pitt had to keep his
Party together to fight a great war. Russell replied that this excused
Pitt but not Wilberforce.[6]

But Wilberforce never believed that Pitt abandoned the Cause. 'I
solemnly declare to *you*,' Wilberforce wrote to a young ally eight years
after Pitt's death, 'my firm conviction that Mr. Pitt was a sincere
friend to the Abolition.'[7] In this letter he ascribed Pitt's failure as an

Abolitionist to 'dilatoriness and procrastination, his great vices', a neat case of the pot calling the kettle black; if Wilberforce's procrastinations were venial, so in a sense were Pitt's: both achieved great things. At the time Wilberforce recognized that Pitt could not devote entire attention to the slave problem in wartime or split his Cabinet over Abolition. James Stephen might give the slaves absolute priority, Wilberforce could not isolate them from the national interest. Stephen chided that he loved Pitt more than Abolition, and Wilberforce acknowledged the danger, but in loving Pitt he loved England. Nor would a British defeat help the slaves. Wilberforce, rightly as it proved, mistrusted French intentions towards the blacks.

Each fresh Parliamentary failure emphasized that Abolition must wait until the Peace,[8] especially as Pitt 'gave him reason to hope'[9] that he would strive to insert a mutual Abolition clause in any peace treaty. To wait was no easy option. When his annual Abolition motion failed by 30 votes in a thin House in 1799 Wilberforce was so scandalized by the debate, he wrote to Muncaster, 'that I cannot think of it or speak of it with patience. It fills me with grief and indignation, and Canning's speech though certainly very clever was far too gay to be in unison or harmony with my feelings. As for Windham! He is intolerable. But I have long remarked in him a strange moral obliquy: and indeed I must say, when men are devoid of Religion, I more and more see that they are not to be relied on.'[10]

There were still ways to help Africa.

On the evening of 12 April 1799 a group of clergy and laymen which had just met at the Castle and Falcon tavern in Aldersgate Street, including John Newton, John Venn and Thomas Scott, invited Wilberforce to become president of a Society they had formed 'for Missions to Africa and the East', afterwards the Church Missionary Society. As far back as 1787 he had tried to help Simeon of Cambridge send Anglican missionaries to the Hindus of Bengal: no one offered, and the East India Company would have refused admission.[11] When the Company's charter came up for renewal in 1793 Wilberforce pushed through the Commons a Resolution authorizing more Chaplains for Europeans and the first State-paid missionaries to the Indians. Hannah More, drinking tea with him at the Grants, felt how 'his warm heart glows at the thought of what extensive good may be done to twenty millions of subjects'.[12] The Lords threw out the clause. He failed again two years later.

On Captain Bligh's return to the South Seas after the Mutiny on the *Bounty*, Wilberforce and Admiral Middleton secured passages for two missionaries to Tahiti, but these withdrew before sailing.[13] Wilberforce subscribed to the new Baptist Missionary Society[14] which sent out Carey as the first English missionary to the East, and was of use in high places to the new-born interdenominational London Missionary Society. Over dinner one July evening of 1797 at Battersea Rise he discussed with Simeon, Grant and Thornton the possibility of a Church of England equivalent, since the Society for the Propagation of the Gospel went almost exclusively to British settlers. The meeting at the Castle and Falcon in April 1799 was partly the result of this discussion.

Wilberforce declined the invitation to be president: none was appointed for the time being. He became one of seven vice-presidents, and lobbied the Archbishop of Canterbury, Dr. Moore, who gave a most guarded response of studied neutrality for public consumption, with private assurances of official blessing once the new Society established itself.[15] It chose West Africa as its field since India could not be entered, and four years after the Castle and Falcon meeting the first missionaries, both German Lutherans, left for Sierra Leone to convert the Susa. Unfortunately one of them, who had married the Venn's governess, turned his cloth and became a slave trader.

All these years the Sierra Leone settlement had limped onward, beset by muddles and misjudgements. Its best work for Africa at this period was the shaping of Governor Zachary Macaulay. He arrived home for the last time in the summer of 1799, married the girl who had waited for him, and eventually settled at Clapham, to become a most necessary member of the widening Clapham circle. Stephen supplied the original mind, fired by passion for the redress of African and West Indian wrongs; Thornton supplied the cool head, decisiveness and patience; Wilberforce, his political skill, Cabinet contacts, and the irrepressible spark of his personality which smoothed awkward corners, reconciled differences, and eased tensions by laughter. Zachary Macaulay, dour, grave, humourless, was their willing drudge, their walking blue-book, who despite being almost blind in one eye could master a long report overnight and keep in his head a vast compendium. Wilberforce as he grew older leaned heavily on Macaulay for facts and figures which in healthier days he would have dug for himself. Macaulay bore it stoically. Wilberforce once wrote: 'I rejoice that there is such a diligent man as yourself. What is more I love you so well that I can truly rejoice you are that man of diligence as well as ability, though you shame me by your efficiency.'[16]

Macaulay founded a merchant house trading to Africa, and (at £400 a year) took over as Sierra Leone secretary. When he found that his Clapham friends planned a monthly journal, the *Christian Observer*, 'to recommend plain serious and practical religion, and to affirm the great evangelical doctrines of our Church without too much encouraging nice theological distinctions',[17] he brought their dream to reality in 1801 as editor. Wilberforce produced a few articles and reviews in the first years ('I am a sad, slow writer')[18] but before very long he would

7

tell Macaulay, 'I assure you it often grieves me . . . that I am not a contributor of anything better than good wishes to the Xn O.'[19]

In September 1799 Wilberforce's doctors urged him to retire for a year.[20] He compromised by cutting the extra Session of Parliament and leaving with Barbara, baby William and baby Barbara for Bath, where he bought a villa and could not resist being a magnet to friends.

John Venn in December was shocked by Wilberforce's physical condition and urged him not to return. 'You are not in state to bear the hurry and fatigue of a winter residence in Town. Do, my dear sir, consider that it is the voice of *Duty* . . . to preserve with care a life invaluable to your children, your wife, your friends, your Country and the Church at large. Your constitution is not robust and you must not endeavour to do what would break down even the stoutest constitution.'[21] Wilberforce ignored the advice and was in his place a week after the opening of Parliament in January 1800.

There was so much to demand his attention at the turn of the century. For instance, the problem of Hannah More's Blagdon controversy, when the Mendip farmers and the local Bishop combined to suppress her. 'Wilberforce persists in thinking you should have gone on with your school in spite of it,' Thornton wrote,[22] and she took the advice in the end. Again, this was the time when Wilberforce with Thomas Erskine, as great an animal lover as lawyer, tried to end the cruel sport of bull baiting; nearly a quarter of a century would pass before success. And he tried to improve Britain's health by urging compulsory inoculation against smallpox: William Cobbett sneered that Wilberforce wanted to compel 'every man to suffer the veins of his child to be impregnated with the disease of a beast'.[23]

The need for a truly national day of rest continued to exercise him. On Sundays the roads thronged with stage coaches, waggons and private chaises, the Thames with pleasure craft. The rich gave great entertainments. Thus a vast number of coachmen, watermen and servants lost their one leisure day nor could attend church.[24] The Bishop of London, with Lord Belgrave, Wilberforce and others drew up a Declaration and formed a Society for the Better Observance of Sunday. Wilberforce begged the Speaker to move his official parties to a weekday. Addington angrily refused, reckoning that this implied they were frivolous, whereas Wilberforce thought of weary hairdressers and coachmen; he too felt angry,[25] but did not show it. Lord Sidmouth (Addington) was astonished when he read the relevant diary entry printed in the *Life*. 'Well,' he remarked to his son-in-law, 'Wilberforce does not speak *of* me as he spoke *to* me.'[26]

Wilberforce would have been gratified at the Victorian Sunday. But his efforts towards it caused him to be abused as a 'Puritanical, hypocritical religionist . . . who made Christianity ridiculous to all sensible, manly, rational and philosophical men.'[27] Bishop Porteus tried to win George III's approval for their Sunday Society. He found him poisoned against it.[28] Indeed, the King harboured suspicions against Wilberforce on all counts, as Lord Essex realized out hunting from Windsor one December day: the King talked about Wilberforce, 'whom he seems to detest as he does all Methodists'.[29]

Suspicion was not the prerogative of the King. 'Pitt has no trust in me in any religious subject,'[30] Wilberforce complained when the Government brought in a Limiting of Toleration Bill, which Pitt intended as a weapon against seditious preachers but Wilberforce realized would hinder religion. According to Thornton the Bishops 'consider Wilberforce as not even half a friend, and conceive of him as not to be trusted, or to be consulted with in such a case. Not at least in the first concoction of a measure, and yet he knows ten times more of what will go down than they do.'[31] The Bill had set all Dissent by the ears, yet only after most strenuous effort could Wilberforce get it withdrawn.

On his forty-first birthday, 24 August 1800, Wilberforce sat in a villa overlooking Bognor Rocks (not yet Bognor Regis) which Cary's Atlas had listed as one of the ten most beautiful prospects in Sussex.

Jotting down on a scrap of paper a penitential review of the past year, he prayed that he might live a life more honourable to God and useful to man, with the glory of God his fixed aim and the love of Christ his habitual motive: 'Oh Lord, purify my soul from all its stains. Warm my heart with the love of thee, animate my sluggish nature and fix my inconstancy, and volatility, that I may not be weary in well-doing, that I may bear about with me a sense of thy presence. . . .'[32]

A few days later his wife, who always felt the heat and was pregnant, became nervous and irritable and lost her appetite. She ran a high temperature. The doctor diagnosed typhoid and soon she was delirious. The Thorntons banished Wilberforce downstairs and took charge:[33] only Thornton could control her. They sent all the children back to Clapham, summoned Milner from Cambridge and Dr. Fraser from Bath and the newly wed Stephens.* Thornton marvelled at Wilberforce's calmness, knowing his mental agony, and encouraged his desire to write round to old friends. 'It has pleased God,' read Montagu at Sandelford, 'to visit my dearest wife with a very dangerous fever. The final issue is not likely to be soon determined; but from the violence of the symptoms and especially the lightheadedness (which is very affecting) at the moment, I am frankly told that I have causes for the utmost

* Stephen, Wilberforce said, treated Sally 'with a tenderness and respect that were never exceeded. Had she been a Venus de Medicis instead of . . . very plain and considerably advanced in life and a widow . . . she could not have been the object I had almost said of a more idolatorous affection.'[34]

apprehension, though not for despair. The thought that my dearest love has made her peace with God is an unspeakable consolation, but for this I own my heart would almost sink within me.'[35]

Five days later on 2 October he could write to Barbara's father, Isaac Spooner: 'I am happy and I hope thankful to be able to tell you that my wife is certainly better though the fever cannot be said yet to have turned or the danger to be over – on this account Dr. Fraser who intended leaving us this morning resolves not to quit us to-day.' She was sleeping a little, 'and is all but quite herself in intellect and mind.'[36] By mid-October Wilberforce was asking Montagu if he could spare any Sandelford game for the convalescent, whereupon partridges rained on Bognor like quails on Sinai.[37]

Barbara bore Elizabeth safely, and another three children in the next seven years. She did not lose one infant, an unusual feat for the early nineteenth century. Nevertheless her nerves and general health never quite recovered from the typhoid of 1800. When therefore on the night of 7 February 1801 Wilberforce went across to the Speaker's house and argued with Addington into the small hours, Barbara was reduced to the utmost alarm, especially as a gentleman had been murdered in a nearby street a few days before.[38] It was at the height of Pitt's crisis with the King over Catholic Emancipation. Wilberforce, after mature reflection, had become 'decidedly favourable' to Union with Ireland, and had wanted admission of Roman Catholics to the united Parliament even before Pitt, his attitude at this time being plainly stated in a letter to Muncaster of 3 December 1798: '*Entre nous* entirely, I am become much more doubtful about the Union with Ireland since I find, that our Govt . . . don't embrace in it the idea of admitting Papists into the Parliament of the united kingdoms. . . . This destroys what was in my mind, the grand presumptive benefit of the union, viz – the enabling you without danger to make the Ro Cathcs such concessions as might make them feel themselves good subjects.'[39]

When the King refused to agree to Emancipation and Pitt resigned and the King secured Speaker Addington's promise to form a ministry, many Pittites were furious that 'the Doctor', whom they expected to heal the rupture between Crown and Minister, had turned supplanter, as they saw it unfairly. They asked Wilberforce as honest broker to convey their views, and these made Addington angry with him. 'But we parted good friends,'[40] and Wilberforce walked back across Palace Yard wistfully, half hoping for office in the new ministry. Sunday restored his sense of proportion.[41]

At first he approved 'Doctor' Addington's government. The war-mongering Cobbett complained in his new *Political Register* that the negotiations for peace were undertaken 'at the suggestion, and in a great degree through the means of Mr. Wilberforce,'[42] a view that was morally though not factually correct. Then Addington failed to include a clause of mutual Abolition in the Treaty of Amiens and resisted Wilberforce's plea for an international convention to achieve it: Wilberforce had already failed to get a mutual friend to holloa like a starling the word *Abolition* 'in the Grand Consul's ear',[43] and was busily lobbying Rufus King, the American minister in London, to use his influence in the same direction.[44] Addington then worsened his reputation with Wilberforce by promising future legislation without immediate suspension of the Trade, thus encouraging traders to increase the export of Africans before the market closed.

'The Doctor' was even more chilling when Canning brought in his motion to stop slaves being put to the fearful task of clearing 'new lands', the virgin soil in Trinidad, which Britain retained under the Treaty. Canning had told Wilberforce in February that some Members who rejected total Abolition would agree to this; they had begun to realize that new lands would cause over-production of sugar. Canning promised Wilberforce to act in whatever way seemed best, 'But I confess, I am inclined to think that the utmost of our chance of doing good at present is, by preventing an enormous increase of evil.'[45] Wilberforce only kept himself from introducing a general motion, which would inevitably be lost, by Canning's promise[46] to bring on his limited one: 'We'll worry the Doctor like a pole-cat.'[47] But in May 1801 'the Doctor' rejected Canning's motion as inopportune, and rubbed salt into the sensitive Wilberforce, conscious of past attempts, when he 'so *strongly* censured Canning and me and indeed Pitt too for having suffered the Slave Trade to the conquered colonies to go on without opposition in the late war.'[48]

Addington shocked him;[49] at the very least Parliament should limit the number of slaves imported to older colonies, to prevent thousands being re-exported to the new. Addington shocked him by allowing British charterers to transport French reinforcements for the reconquest of San Domingo. This was stopped by the renewal of war in 1803 – a war Wilberforce strove to prevent. Bonaparte had broken the spirit of Amiens and was expected to renew his career of conquest, but Britain broke the letter by not handing back Malta to the Knights of St. John, who would let in the French and thus destroy British security in the Mediterranean. Wilberforce seized on the point that Britain was in the wrong. 'Why,' he asked, while the House tried again and again to cough him down, 'Why this Malta in perpetuity for ourselves?' Why this selfishness when their cause proclaimed justice and self-defence?' He persisted, never losing his good humour, and 'made a great impression' according to Creevey: 'It was an inimitable speech for peace and on grounds the most calculated for popular approbation.'[50]

When the war again became a matter of national survival, Wilberforce supported it while watching eagerly for an opportunity to press Abolition. His physical health deteriorated although, as he said quaintly to Earl Grosvenor (the former Belgrave) 'my good spirits prevent my showing it.'[51] Thornton detected the strain beneath the genial exterior. 'Do tell me how you think Wilberforce is,' he asked Marianne in the autumn of 1803. 'I feel anxious about him. Urge him to do less, to talk less, and be less anxious about public affairs. The world has gone on under the same or nearly the same misrule for nearly six thousand years, and we must all send our chief thoughts after that blessed land in which dwelleth righteousness.'[52]

But Wilberforce could not relax in his hope of heaven while men suffered on earth.

CHAPTER NINETEEN

The Fall of Lord Melville

Little Marianne, Henry Thornton's eldest child, played games with Mr. Wilberforce before any grown up. 'He was as restless and volatile as a child himself,' she recalled in old age, 'and during the long and grave discussions that went on between him and my father and others, he was most thankful to refresh himself by throwing a ball or a bunch of flowers at me, or opening the glass door and going off with me for a race on the lawn "to warm his feet". I know one of my first lessons was I must never disturb *Papa* when he was talking or reading, but no such prohibition existed with Mr. Wilberforce. His love for, and enjoyment in, all children was remarkable. . . .'[1]

Wilberforce had never quite grown up. Marianne would hear Milner exclaim when 'Mr. W was flitting after a child, a cat, a flower or a new book', during deliberations, 'Now, Wilberforce, listen, for no power on earth will make me repeat what I am going to say.'[2]

The Wilberforces' elder children were emerging from babyhood as the Abolition campaign mounted towards its climax, and the happiness of the circle at Broomfield formed a secure, delightful base despite Barbara's nerves and fussiness and frequent lassitudes.[3] Clapham neighbours and their children were in and out. The family of William Smith, the Unitarian and Radical whom Wilberforce twitted as 'the first existing Jacobin in the House of Commons',[4] had left the schoolroom, including the future mother of Florence Nightingale. The Macaulays were still in the cradle. But Thorntons, Shores, Grants, and the younger of the Stephens (Sally's stepchildren) were contemporaries, with the Wilberforces rather at the tail end in age.

There were other children in the circle – the black boys, sons of Sierra Leone chiefs whom Zachary Macaulay had brought home by order of the directors for education as leaders and missionaries among their own peoples.

Several had died of the English climate but the remainder were put

to school on the north side of Clapham Common under a Yorkshireman, and the smaller boys of the Clapham friends joined the lessons.
No differences of race or colour interfered. Black boys had been seen
in London as pages, treated as complete inferiors with whom no white
child must mix, but Clapham pioneered racial equality; yet not self-
consciously, for when the boys played at soldiers they gave the role of
bandsmen to their negroes, and since bandsmen in the British Army
flogged defaulters the black boys 'flogged' the white. William Wilberforce Jr. was the most frequent culprit. 'Not one of his schoolfellows,'
recalls Charles Shore, 'was struck at the time by the droll coincidence
of the son receiving such treatment at the hand of a negro just when
and where his father was exerting his strenuous efforts to rescue the
negro from the similar usage of the white.'[5]

Broomfield seemed a rather eccentric home. The unkempt shrubberies displayed their owner's stray genius just as Henry Thornton's
close-mown lawns and trim parterres, or Robert Thornton's magnificent
conservatory of exotic plants reflected theirs.[6] The Wilberforces kept
thirteen or fourteen servants outside and in (seven or eight women and
six men)[7] which was about normal for their rank in life; but Wilberforce tended to enlist domestics who were deserving rather than
efficient, nor would he cast off the useless or infirm until they found
suitable berths. The ill-matched staff ran the master and mistress, the
one hardly noticing and the other lacking gifts of management, and
servants adored Wilberforce, who would sit beside them when they
were ill[8] and turn a blind eye to their shortcomings on duty. Robert
Southey thought the old coachman ought to be on the stage[9] but
Thomas in fact was a cross-grained fellow; once, 'either drunk with
liquor or passion, driving like a madman,' to the great alarm of Barbara's brother. Another day Wilberforce ticked him off, 'which provoked him to explosion. I can truly say I kept my temper completely
but I ought not to have a man of such ungoverned temper.'[10] He meant
to dismiss him. Thomas kept his place.

The whole house attended family prayers twice daily. In the morning
these did not fall particularly early because of the master's getting up
late, 'in which I fear I must (salutis causa) remain incorrigible'.[11]
Everyone knelt against a chair or sofa. Wilberforce knelt at a table in
the centre 'and after a little pause', noted Farington the portrait
painter, 'began to read a prayer, which he did very slowly in a low,
solemnly awful voice. This was followed by 2 other prayers and *the
grace*. It occupied about 10 minutes, and had the best effect as to the
manner of it.'[12] But not when, as one occasion at least, his overloaded
pockets burst in the middle of prayers and he vainly tried to retrieve
their contents from his kneeling position.[13]

Breakfast was a daily magnet for an extraordinary mixture of guests,
bidden or not. The table-talk might unravel some knot in the Abolition

campaign or a grave moral question, or be a 'sort of galvanic stream of vivacity, humour and warm-heartedness'[14] from the host, on an astonishing range of subjects, from portraiture to music, which he loved;[15] while as for literature, James Stephen said 'a man of more varied reading or better taste will seldom be found'.[16]

Stephen's son, James Stephen the younger, was fascinated by the Ariel-like quality of Wilberforce's conversation, 'the same simple-hearted, natural man, talking without effort or preparation or disguise from the overflowing of his mind.' Voice and manner held the audience by continual, unpredictable movement, whether the subject be solemn, or gay: 'He did not dispose of a laughable incident by one terse . . . jest: he rather used it as a toy to be tossed about and played with for a while, and then thrown aside. . . . Being himself amused and interested by everything, whatever he said became amusing or interesting. . . . His presence was as fatal to dullness as to immorality. His mirth was as irresistible as the first laughter of childhood.'[17]

The food, on the other hand was not. Guests fended for themselves in a Yorkshire way. Barbara would see that 'Wilber's' plate had plenty and he was too short-sighted to notice the others; then Dean Milner's stentorian voice (so Marianne Thornton recalls) would be heard 'roaring "There was nothing on earth to eat"'; and desiring the servants to bring some bread and butter, he would add "and bring plenty without limit", while Mr. W. would join in with "Thank you, thank you kindly, Milner, for seeing to these things. Mrs. Wilberforce is not strong enough to meddle much in domestic matters." '[18]

The beautiful Barbara was a poor hostess, being incurably pinch-penny[19] despite their substantial joint income, and though partridges, hares and pheasants might arrive from friends or Muncaster send Lake District venison, this was not always a success: 'The hot weather finished your hospitable intentions. But Amos says this would not have been the case but for the bad packing. The game was *close* sewed up, impervious to air. The venison I believe would have been quite good, but for the neglect of the people at the Inn, who did not send it till the day after its arrival, if it came by the same coach as your letter.' If the parcel had not been delayed in the North, 'and I can ascertain that it was detained in town, I will rate the people if I don't prosecute them.'[20] Most likely he did neither.

To please Barbara, 'Thy Wilber' restricted their dinings out. His energy revived in the embrace of his clinging wife. She grudged his absences at the House. She supported his philanthropies, loved to talk religion, loved her babies. She sorely tried the patiences of his friends. Wilberforce doted on her. The married state is 'incomparably the happiest',[21] he told his cousin Mary Smith on her engagement in 1804.

He had fallen in love and stayed in love, always protective. Even in the rare critical comments in his diary he springs to her defence: 'Sat

7*

up too long, but poor B had a load of grievances and indeed she is to be pitied being very nervous and bearing the load of domestic cares chiefly or solely rather.'[22] He was always ardent too. 'My dearest Love,' begins an undated letter from Clapham when Barbara was perhaps with her parents at Bath and longing to return. He had just heard he might be free to join her, so 'I have resolved to take up the pen though it be Sunday and to send this letter to London, that it may go by the stage and convey to Thee the tender love of Thy Wilber, the wish I feel that you should wait till you hear farther from me. . . .' He instructs her to prepare to 'set sail' but not to 'weigh anchor'. He cannot give particulars, 'I will only state that if you don't soon receive my permission to drive up to me, I hope to drive down to you and stay with you till the beginning of February. . . . You may be assured that I shall admit no needless delay and I shall not be surprised on this day sennight if I am by my love's side, beholding that look of affection with my bodily eyes which is now distinctly visible to my mental.' A long Sunday meditation follows and the letter ends: 'I am most tenderly Thine, *William Wilberforce*. I hope I haven't scribbled so fast as to be illegible. The truth is I did not think of writing above a few lines when I began but I was drawn by my desire to spend a few minutes on the stay with my beloved.'[23]

In May 1803 a deputation of clergy, dissenting ministers, and laymen called at Broomfield to discuss a plan for a society to distribute Bibles. It had originated in the disappointment of a Bala girl wanting a Bible in Welsh, whose minister found that the only edition had long gone out of print. There was in fact an annotated *Family Bible* in Welsh, prepared by the translator of 'Guide Me O Thou Great Jehovah', Peter Williams, but his notes were considered a trifle heretical; besides, the girl wanted a Bible, not a commentary. Her minister raised the problem at a committee meeting of the Religious Tract Society (newly grown out of an idea of Hannah More's supported by Wilberforce) and the pastor of a Baptist chapel near Clapham had exclaimed: 'If for Wales, why not for the Kingdom? Why not for the whole world?' By May, their plans had advanced enough to consult Wilberforce, who long ago had organized distribution of Bibles in a country district and supported the small 'Bible Society' for sailors and soldiers which the Middletons had started during the American War. He listened carefully to this deputation which crossed barriers between church and chapel, and suggested ways to catch the public imagination and the sympathy of the bishops, who could and nearly did crush the idea at birth.[24]

Ten months went by before the founders launched what they christened The British and Foreign Bible Society. On 7 March 1804 they called a public meeting to be held in the great banquet room of the

London Tavern in Leadenhall Street, with its fine Turkey carpet and the culinary turtles swimming below in cellar vats. The summons came in the middle of the uproar over the Government's handling of naval affairs, the beginning of the end for Addington. Wilberforce could not attend but sent round a letter to Granville Sharp, who would be chairman, to express 'my entire approbation of the plan, and my wish to concur in any measures which may tend to the promotion of the great object which is in the view of those gentlemen who so honourably to themselves have come forward on this occasion.'[25]

The meeting nominated Wilberforce to the committee. He accepted 'with great pleasure' but could not attend the first meeting on 12 March since the Cabinet crisis continued; three days later Wilberforce made one of his most effective speeches in the House. Early in April the Baptist neighbour from Battersea chapel, with Charles Grant and another man came to breakfast. Soon afterwards, on a day so unseasonably dark that they sat by candlelight in the late morning, Wilberforce joined the Bible Society founders in a City counting house. At the second general meeting on 2 May his 'attendance and exertions . . . added much to the interest of the day,' commented one of those present. 'He addressed the meeting in a speech of equal animation and judgment. . . . The observations of Mr. Wilberforce produced, as they are accustomed to do, a very sensible effect.'[26]

He took a large part a few years later in the Bible Society's struggles for recognition, survival and expansion. At the time of the founding, however, the political crisis prevented him offering little beyond encouragement. Five days after the meeting of 2 May, Bonaparte proclaimed himself Emperor of the French and Pitt kissed hands as Prime Minister of the United Kingdom.

And ten days after that the West Indian planters met in the same London Tavern where the Bible Society had been founded, to consider a final demand from Wilberforce that they agree to a five-year suspension of the Slave Trade.

The planters rejected the call. Wilberforce immediately waited on the new Prime Minister, who found time to urge a leading planter to reverse the decision, but the planters believed that if ever the Trade were suspended it would not revive.[27] Nevertheless Wilberforce could discern the first split in the anti-Abolitionist ranks. Slavers, and speculators in virgin soil, wanted the Trade for ever; on the other hand, so Wilberforce told Grenville, who was not in the new Cabinet, 'the old Landed Interest in the W. Indies are not against us'.[28] With too small a capital to buy the new lands, they had begun to foresee ruin through Caribbean overproduction should cultivated areas be much farther extended.

Wilberforce was not therefore surprised, when he asked leave of the

House on 30 May to bring in an Abolition Bill, that he got it. The
surprise was his big vote: 124 to 49. A whole batch of the new Irish
Members had been dining together and trooped in to vote for Abolition
after Lord De Blaquiere, an elderly unsavoury jobber with an Irish
peerage from the recent handout of rewards to Unionists, had proposed
Wilberforce's health.[29] Success had rushed suddenly out of the shadows
to raise cautious hopes.

The Abolitionist 'cabinet' drafted a Bill, while Clarkson, who had
returned from his nine years' retirement, applied himself to furnishing
ammunition and the Society for the Abolition of the Slave Trade came
to life again. Wilberforce worked hard to strengthen the case. Thus he
wrote, without introduction, to one of the two American Commissioners
negotiating a commercial treaty in London, the future President James
Monroe, to ask if Monroe could disprove the rumours that individual
states of the Union had revived the Slave Trade after having 'prohibited it for several years'. Whitney's invention of the cotton gin had
stepped up the demand. Monroe replied with such friendly smooth
assurances, which the facts barely warranted, that Wilberforce nearly
jumped into his carriage to call at Old Cumberland Place across the
Park. He wrote instead, praising the United States that 'without having
had so much light thrown on the subject as has been cast on it here,
you have seen enough to induce you to do your utmost to put a stop to
this unjust traffic'.[30] The two men met, and remained friends.

Confident of the Commons Wilberforce dreaded the Lords. On 13
June he ate humble pie to Henry Dundas, now Viscount Melville and
First Lord of the Admiralty, whose doctrine of 'gradual' Abolition
equalled 'Never' to the West Indian lobby. He begged him to revert
to his earlier support of immediate Abolition. 'Will you, my dear
Lord M, excuse my saying, that, having from almost the commencement of my public life, been honoured with your friendly regard . . .
it has long been matter of great pain to me, that in the grand object of
my Parliamentary existence, you should have been the one to oppose
and defeat my wishes. . . .'[31] Although Wilberforce argued that he did
not want to hurt the West Indians' 'feelings' if this could be avoided,
and that the Islands were 'saturated with slaves', Melville remained
impervious.

The Bill passed its Third Reading in the Commons on 27 June 1804.
The Abolitionists hurried back to 4 Palace Yard to celebrate, the
youngest even chirping about 'the final victory of that great cause'.[32]
Wilberforce entered his dining-room late and could not share the
jubilation: prospects in Lords were poor.

Next day the Cabinet told Wilberforce the Bill must wait a year.
He wrote sadly to his old friend Lord Harrowby, now Foreign Secretary: 'Tho' I bore the shock I had to sustain with composure, aided I
own by the consideration that I could not help myself, yet on reflection

I confess I find but too much reason to regret deeply the course which matters are now likely to take.'[33] To prevent matters sinking beneath lordly quicksands, he begged that any necessary hearing of evidence should begin at once, but the sympathetic and affectionate Foreign Secretary could offer only a fresh point of argument: that the establishment of a negro 'empire' in San Domingo had changed the situation drastically, because the more negroes who were imported from now on to the British West Indies, the easier it would be for the independent blacks to foment risings. The planters' own security demanded Abolition. He suggested Wilberforce write a book about it.[34]

That autumn the Wilberforces went to Lyme Regis in Dorset, to a fine view over the bay but 'a house in which chimneys several of 'em smoke in an east wind, which makes sad work for my eyes'.[35] Correspondence pursued him to the seaside: 'Alps on Alps arise,' he would murmur at the piles of letters awaiting answer.

Wilberforce had a quality which a younger friend called 'the elastic rebound of his heart to gladness',[36] and despite discouragements of the summer he could play with the children and fascinate his guests, whereas James Stephen threshed around in frustration. 'I am sorry you are disappointed, my dear S,' Wilberforce wrote, urging him to be not only fervent in spirit, serving the Lord, but patient, 'though to a man of active temper and in such a cause too as ours it is a grievous burden.'[37]

Wilberforce pressed both Pitt and Harrowby to hurry the Order in Council which would stop the Slave Trade to captured Dutch Guiana. He pointed out to Pitt that 'one very powerful and important reason for you to abolish the Guiana Slave Trade by an *act of government* and not by, or in consequence of, a vote of Parliament', is that it would encourage the Dutch to abolish their entire Trade, since the return of their colony at the end of the war could be made dependent on this. The British planters should welcome it too, since cultivation of such rich virgin soil, whether Dutch owned or British, might undercut the older islands.[38]

Pitt continued to dally, immersed in diplomacy and defence affairs, until Wilberforce feared he must raise Guiana in the House, embarrassing the Government. He urged Harrowby on: 'I do not say any more concerning the stopping of the Slave Trade to the conquered colonies because I know you are keeping your eye on that subject when you can get Pitt to attend to it.'[39] The Foreign Secretary at last gave the good news in strict confidence though Wilberforce had already heard it from another Minister, that the Order in Council had come before the Cabinet. He replied: 'I have been so often disappointed, that I rejoice with trembling and shall scarcely dare to be confident till I actually see the Order in the Gazette.' His trembling was justified.[40]

Meanwhile the Abolitionists had secured two important young recruits from very different backgrounds, who had been fellow students at Edinburgh.

Henry Brougham, the future Whig Lord Chancellor, had reached London as a briefless ambitious barrister after founding, with others, the *Edinburgh Review* and writing *Colonial Policy*, a book sympathetic to Abolition, which brought him a blaze of glory and the gratitude and patronage of Wilberforce, who invited him to join the Abolitionist 'cabinet' and even produced a review for the *Edinburgh*. It criticized a work which defended the Slave Trade, though he did not rap the author so roughly as in a private letter to Stephen: 'never surely was there so unconsciable a liar'.[41]

During the Long Vacation Brougham toured Napoleon's Europe disguised as an American. He sent Wilberforce a long paper to prove that the worst subjection of Sicilian vassals was better than 'the greatest freedom known by West Indian negroes';[42] this tuned in with the Abolitionists' starry-eyed belief that once the Trade stopped, the Planters would soon raise their slaves into a kind of feudal vassalage. He wrote enthusiastically from Holland too, that the Dutch had translated his book, were fast moving towards Abolition, and would move even quicker if they might please have their colonies back at once. Wilberforce sent the entire letter to Harrowby. For any other Foreign Secretary he would have copied out extracts, 'but to you in your *personal* capacity, I may be allowed to transmit papers of which you will show such parts to your *political* as it may be proper to lay before it.' He admired Brougham but put little faith in the Dutch; Brougham 'is a very young man, and I greatly fear that with all his cleverness, the Dutch will be too deep for him'.[43]

Brougham was a genuine humanitarian, as became the great-nephew of Robertson the historian, but a thruster. Wilberforce sometimes felt 'a little jealous of Brougham's making our sacred cause of Abolition the ladder by which he climbs into political notoriety and eminence. However, this is a false delicacy. . . .'[44] It did not stifle attempts to further Brougham's career by suggesting him for a diplomatic role or, rather half-heartedly, forwarding to Lord Lowther his request for a (Tory) pocket borough;[45] but it analysed his character neatly.

The other young man was Lord Henry Petty, son of one of the Prime Ministers of Wilberforce's early years in the House, Shelburne, and heir to his bachelor brother, 2nd Marquess of Lansdowne. Petty had gone from Edinburgh to Trinity, Cambridge and into the House as a Foxite, and at a dark moment early in 1805 he offered his help. Lord Harrowby had fallen down the stairs of the Foreign Office on to his head and had been driven by appalling headaches to resign in favour of Lord Mulgrave. In the reshuffle Pitt had brought in Addington, now Viscount Sidmouth, whom he did not want to annoy by pressing

Abolition, and therefore urged Wilberforce to put off renewing his motion. Wilberforce refused, was defeated by seven votes, and next night his dreams were invaded by burning villages in the African interior, by gangs being driven to the coast, by fearful cruelties as the slave ships embarked their human cargoes.[46] And Pitt still had not issued the Order in Council to end the trade to Guiana.

It was at this point that young Lord Henry Petty came forward with an offer to bring Fox and the leading Abolitionists of the Opposition to meet Wilberforce and his friends for a conference of ways and means. 'I was glad to find,' Petty wrote, on 23 March 1805, '. . . that the idea . . . continued to meet with your approbation.' He offered Lansdowne House, 'but it might perhaps be more desirable to have it at your house, or Mr. Fox's,' or that of some other gentleman of resounding importance.[47]

They all met before Easter at Lansdowne House in Berkeley Square, a turning point for Wilberforce. For the first time he demonstrated openly that he might work with Fox, Grey and their friends rather than with Pitt. Yet Wilberforce assured them that Pitt's Order in Council would come very soon, and pretended not to notice Foxite winks and nudges at his simple trust. They deputed him and Bankes to interview Pitt. If Pitt refused to act, Petty should raise the matter in Parliament, which might lead to a Government defeat.[48]

Pitt gave warm assurances. And turned back to the urgent problems of the Napoleonic war on land and sea, especially the depravations of the Rochefort Squadron in the West Indies: British men-of-war could hardly be deflected to enforce an Order in Council against their own merchantmen. Wilberforce pleaded with Pitt. 'Bankes and I are placed in a very unpleasant situation by this delay no less than yourself,' he emphasized, 'and above all the evil is daily increasing.'[49] He reckoned that between twelve and fifteen thousand human beings were enslaved for every year the Guiana trade continued.

Not until September was it abolished, leaving only the neutral American slavers untouched for the present.

Meanwhile, in the spring of 1804 a new political whirlwind had blown in. Wilberforce found himself at the very eye of the storm, and by a single speech may have altered the destiny of Britain.

The Parliamentary Committee of Naval Enquiry set up by Addington had issued its Tenth Report. Wilberforce had been in Downing Street when Pitt, having torn open the Report, showed distress[50] at its finding that Lord Melville, when Treasurer of the Navy many years before, had connived in or at least condoned the malversation of funds by a deputy. Melville had long ago denied this to Pitt.

Melville's appointment as First Lord had pleased Wilberforce because he knew the poor state of naval administration and 'you, of all the public men now on the stage, appeared to me best qualified to fill that important office'.[51] Moreover Pitt had told Melville to depend for professional advice on his own cousin, Wilberforce's great friend Sir Charles Middleton, nearly eighty but experienced in broad naval strategy and detailed administration beyond any man alive. In December 1804 Middleton began officially to reorganize the Navy, but now, after less than a year in office, Melville stood accused by the Tenth Report. As he did not resign despite public disquiet, the Opposition smelt a way to turn out or gravely weaken Pitt. Sam Whitbread tabled a set of Resolutions which, if passed, must lead to Melville's impeachment.

Wilberforce made up his mind slowly.[52] The summer and autumn of 1805 would probably see the climax of the sea war: it was no time for upsets at the Admiralty. Pitt still trusted Melville's word, and the incorruptible Middleton considered his cousin in some ways less a jobber than the rest, only more open: 'in short, where there is no religion there can be no public principle.'[53] Yet his remaining in office would set a damaging precedent. 'Mr. Wilberforce, the Thorntons, Mr. Hawkins Browne and others,' Sir John Sinclair noted, 'took it up as a question not connected with politics but of morality, and not as being connected with the existence of an Administration but merely as an attack upon an individual against whom malversation in office had been proved and reported to the House.'[54]

Whitbread moved his Resolutions in a long, rather feeble speech on 8 April 1805. The debate continued all night. On the ministerial front bench beyond the gangway, just across from Pitt, Wilberforce listened anxiously, having prayed for wisdom to act honestly without fear of man. He hoped Pitt would offer a valid defence of Melville but sensed an uneasy conscience, for Pitt looked upset the whole evening. Fox was as hot as in their fiercest days of rivalry; Canning spoke well for Administration, young Petty well for Opposition. The clamour all over the crowded House 'often amounted to indecency'.[55] Feelings cut right across Party lines and it was impossible to tell which way the vote would go when, at 4.00 a.m. Wilberforce rose and caught the Speaker's eye.

Pitt thereupon caught Wilberforce's eye as if willing him to decide in Melville's favour: Wilberforce had to make a conscious act of mental resistance.[56] Tension rose in the hot Chamber where the chandeliers guttered though several times retrimmed. Members saw Pitt in pain, watching and waiting for Wilberforce to disclose his verdict.

Wilberforce usually tossed a subject around before indicating (not always clearly) which way he would vote. This time he spoke straight to the point: '. . . I must confess that it is impossible for me to leave the House this night without giving my vote in support of the Resolutions.' Pitt sank back in unconcealed agitation. Wilberforce continued:

'. . . Here is a plain, broad fact which no subsequent elucidation can possibly explain away,' that Melville had admitted on oath to tolerating gross dishonesty in a subordinate. 'I really cannot find language sufficiently strong to express my utter detestation of such conduct.'[57]

Robert Plumer Ward the future novelist, then an Under Secretary, wrote to Lord Lowther a few hours later that Wilberforce was 'by far the best speaker . . . during the debate, better even than Fox.'[58] In the opinion of many Wilberforce swayed the waverers – and it needed only a few.

One very brief speech followed from each side, but a third was drowned in cries of 'Question! Question!' The House divided. The tellers approached the Chair, gave the figures – and the division was a tie: 216 ayes, 216 noes. Speaker Abbot turned deathly white. For a prolonged pause the House waited in silence for his casting vote. He gave it against Melville. Bedlam broke loose as Opposition yelled its triumph. Pitt thrust his hat over his eyes to hide the tears.

Wilberforce was attacked afterwards for being Brutus to Pitt's Caesar.[59] He always denied that his speech hastened Pitt's breakdown of health, and in fact their mutual affection ran deeper in the last months of Pitt's life[60] than for long past, a fact which would seem to support Wilberforce's denial. Melville resigned, was impeached and acquitted: his fault was negligence not fraud. He avoided Wilberforce for years until they met accidentally in St. James's Park just near the Treasury Passage. 'For a moment he made as though he knew me not but then his constitutional good nature overcame him and he made up to me: "Oh, is that Wilberforce?" and shook me by the hand most cordially.'[61]

Pitt appointed Sir Charles Middleton as First Lord, to the disgust of Sidmouth who coveted the Admiralty for a supporter, and to the wonder of a public which knew nothing of the vast experience of this 'superannuated Methodist' who became Lord Barham.

And thus, in extreme age yet undiminished vigour, the man who had been like a father to Wilberforce came to the hour for which his entire professional life had been unconscious preparation. He wrote to Wilberforce that he depended on the prayers of his friends, and would do his best in a post that was very arduous and, under present circumstances, hazardous beyond conception.[62] On the very next day he received the news that Villeneuve had dodged past Nelson shadowing Toulon, and had broken through the Straits into the Atlantic.

The far-flung naval campaign which culminated in Trafalgar would hinge on decisions at the Admiralty. These required strategic skill, administrative knowledge, strong nerves and swift judgement: when a despatch, with news which altered the strategic position, arrived late one night and Barham's secretaries left him asleep he was angry, and thought out fresh orders while shaving and sent them off by express. It is doubtful whether Melville or any landsman, or even St. Vincent would have reacted fast enough to the exceptional circumstances of 1805; or found such instant, vital rapport with Nelson when the Commander-in-Chief and the First Lord met briefly at last.

Throughout the Trafalgar campaign Wilberforce gave support, in his place in the Commons and on his knees at home. He shared Hannah More's feelings: 'To know there was *one* efficient statesman who fervently prayed for every measure he engaged in, and who committed the event to the divine superintendence. . . .'[63] At last, in the small hours of a foggy November night, Barham was awoken with the news. 'My lord, we have gained a great victory, but Lord Nelson is dead!' He tore open Collingwood's letter: 'I beg your lordship will allow me to congratulate you on the most complete victory that ever was obtained over an enemy – which I do with a heart flowing with gratitude to the Divine Providence. . . .'[64]

The completeness of the victory, by giving Britain total command of the seas, was to have a very definite effect on Abolition prospects.

The Wilberforces were down in Staffordshire at Yoxall when the stage-coaches rattled through the villages with evergreens for Trafalgar and crêpe for Nelson. Barbara had given birth to Samuel, the future bishop, in September and her recovery was slow. In December they nearly lost little Barbara, six years old. She recovered; but the turn of the year brought Pitt's breakdown in health following Austerlitz and Ulm and the destruction of the Third Coalition.

Pitt was dying of a broken heart: Wilberforce never afterwards doubted that he was killed by the enemy as much as Nelson. On the morning of 23 January 1806 he wrote to George Rose, from Broomfield, that he felt so unsettled 'that I have been near driving to Town again merely because I cannot remain in quiet here but I fear I should have nothing of comfort if I were to go, I will therefore stay here to-day, relying on your being so kind as to let me know if you hear of any change. I own I can scarcely bring myself to conceive the case hopeless, considering our friend's time of life, but physicians are never the first to acknowledge that there is room for hope.'[65]

Had he been certain that he might prepare Pitt for death and the judgement seat of Christ, nothing would have stopped him. But Bishop Pretyman kept the religious ministrations[66] in his own complacent hands, as Wilberforce regarded them, dashing the last hope of a quiet interval with Pitt, for which Wilberforce had wished times without number, when as he put it afterwards to Muncaster, 'he and I might confer freely on the most important of all subjects'.[67] As to the Bishop, 'I never could forgive his never proposing prayer to our poor old friend Pitt . . . till within about six hours before his dissolution,' so Wilberforce wrote to Bankes twenty-five years later.[68]

Even as Wilberforce wrote to Rose on that January day of 1806 Pitt lay dead at Putney Heath. His death, grief though it were to Wilberforce, transformed the Abolition situation.

Wilberforce's signature in 1789 and in 1818

PART THREE

The Arbiter of England
1807–1825

CHAPTER TWENTY

Gleam of Victory

While political leaders manœuvred to form a new Administration, Wilberforce hurried back and forth in an attempt to pay off Pitt's debts by private subscription rather than risk unseemly controversy by asking Parliament.[1]

He tried also to undo the damage done by Henry Lascelles, who without consulting his more experienced colleague tactlessly moved that the Commons attend the funeral as a House. Windham told Wilberforce the attitude of Pitt's opponents towards any form of posthumous public honour, saying he felt 'great softness for his memory, but I cannot concur in anything which is to say that his political life has been beneficial to his country'.[2] Windham would concur in the public payment of his debts, and this was done. In the funeral procession up the aisle of Westminster Abbey, Wilberforce walked as a supporter to Charles Villiers who carried the Banner of the Crest of Pitt.[3]

By then the ministry soon nicknamed All The Talents had emerged, mostly from Pitt's Whig and Tory opponents with Lord Grenville as Premier and Fox Foreign Secretary. Sidmouth insisted on bringing in Lord Ellenborough, who refused the Woolsack and remained Chief Justice. Wilberforce admired Ellenborough's 'vigorous talents and undaunted firmness' and would have welcomed his accession on other terms, but protested to Sidmouth that 'the making of our chief judge a politician seems to be productive of the most pernicious consequences'.[4] Ellenborough promised Wilberforce to keep his judicial and political selves separate, and succeeded, but no Chief Justice has ever entered a Cabinet again.

As for Abolition, the inclusion of three implacable enemies of immediate Abolition, Windham, Sidmouth and Fitzwilliam, might prevent a Government measure but Grenville and Fox quickly showed that their ardour since 1787 had not dimmed. Wilberforce reciprocated: Lord Henry Petty had to stand for re-election on taking office as

Chancellor of the Exchequer, not quite so youthful as Pitt in 1783, and not nearly so successful. Petty contested Pitt's old seat for Cambridge University against the Tory and very young Lord Palmerston whose name meant nothing then. Wilberforce supported Petty. Simeon and Milner were outraged, saying Wilberforce would be accused of changing sides,[5] as indeed he was: nine months later he remarked to Grenville that he had 'exposed myself to censure and misrepresentation not to say calumny in supporting the Government'.[6]

In early March Wilberforce had several conferences with Petty and Fox; and the Prime Minister, whom most men found cold and aloof, received him warmly at Camelford House, the fine mansion at the corner of Park Lane and Oxford Street which had become his when his wife's brother, the wild 2nd Lord Camelford, lost his life in a duel. They all agreed to Wilberforce's intention to put down, once again, a motion for general Abolition.

He was about to cross Palace Yard to the Clerk's office to give his required notice when James Stephen called, bringing a revolutionary idea.[7] Wilberforce listened carefully. He was always ready to change course if a friend showed a better way: it was his biographer-sons who can leave an impression of a master-mind, at whose bidding the others ran messages or looked up details. And now, in the third week of March 1806, Stephen suggested the tactic which led rapidly to final victory. His idea arose from the point reached in the Napoleonic War.

The previous year a long pamphlet, *The War in Disguise*, had created a great stir among politicians, merchants and mercantile lawyers. Anonymously, Stephen had argued with all the authority of his extensive practice in international law of the sea, that a recent legal decision, the *Essex* case, was bad; and that contrary to it a belligerent held the right to search neutrals on the high seas and to condemn cargoes bound for hostile territory. At present enemy colonies actually profited from Britain's involvement in the war: neutral trade with these colonies did not bear the cost of the convoy system which burdened British shipping, so that American bottoms carried enemy sugar to Napoleon's Continent under the guns of the Royal Navy while the British planters could not find markets for their inevitably higher priced product. Stephen's book convinced his readers that Britain had the right to strangle this or any trade carried in neutral ships for the benefit of her enemies. Trafalgar, fought three days after he dated the preface, gave her the power.

At first sight the book had little to do with a barely mentioned Slave Trade, but Stephen designed it consciously as a weapon in the Abolition offensive.[8] He knew that British traders landed slaves in neutral Danish islands for transhipment to enemy colonies, thus buttressing the enemy's economy. If cargoes in neutral bottoms could be condemned, these traders would lose their profit and stop slaving. If slave-grown sugar and rum from enemy islands could likewise be seized the enemy planters would soon cut production and need fewer slaves. Either way the Slave Trade must suffer once the British Ministers acted on Stephen's thesis, which they did not do so until as late as January 1807, when the Cabinet issued the first of the famous two 'Orders in Council' *par excellence* which opposed Napoleon's Berlin Decree.

By March 1806, when Stephen outlined his plan to Wilberforce, his anonymous book had done no more than create a strong feeling that any direct or indirect support of hostile colonies, including the slave-based economies in the Caribbean, gave aid and comfort to His Majesty's enemies. Now, said Stephen to Wilberforce as they talked in 4 Old Palace Yard, we can exploit this feeling, and we have a means to hand. An Act of Parliament is often required to consolidate an Order in Council, such as the Order which Wilberforce's prodding and Stephen's frustrated roars had at last forced from Pitt the previous September, forbidding importation of slaves into conquered Dutch Guiana. The planters in the old islands had approved it because they assumed that colonial conquests would revert to France, Spain or Holland at the peace.

Why not, suggested Stephen, get the new Ministry to bring in a Bill for the Guiana Order? And quietly attach to it all the prohibitions of the oft-defeated 'Foreign Slave Bill': that is, Slaves shall not be imported into captured colonies; no ship trading in slaves to foreign territories shall be fitted out in Britain or British colonies; no British capital or labour shall be used for such slaving. As Windham, Sidmouth and Fitzwilliam had not opposed the Guiana Order in Opposition, they ought not to oppose the Bill in Cabinet; and since it must be a Government measure, being derived from an Order, all ministerialists who were not directly concerned with the West Indies would vote for it as a war measure. Even planters should see it as bolstering their own economy.

Wilberforce added his own point to the discussion: it would be fatal to embark such a Bill 'in the same bottom' as general Abolition; therefore the Ministry must bring in their Bill before he brought in his.

Stephen could put up the brilliant suggestion; he could not approach the Prime Minister or Foreign Secretary. Wilberforce first sounded the Chancellor, and Petty approved. Next he buttonholed Fox on the afternoon of 24 March and understood he would immediately consult Grenville, to whom Wilberforce wrote at length the same evening.[9]

Pitt would have dallied. Fox and Grenville acted at once.[10] Only three days afterwards the Attorney-General, Sir Arthur Pigott, gave notice in the House. All had gone so smoothly that Wilberforce did not bother to listen: he was conversing with another Member and did not realize that anything was amiss until a colleague approached him. Wilberforce then sought out Stephen, who as the lawyer retained by the Law Officers' to draft the Bill had listened beyond the bar of the House, and Stephen asserted that the Attorney-General had given his notice wrong. Pigott was a native of Barbados and had practised in Grenada and perhaps had a subconscious desire to let sleeping slavers lie.

Wilberforce consulted the Order Book, copied out the relevant paragraphs and tried to call urgently on Fox. Fox expected company that evening, so Wilberforce wrote instead: '. . . . But as the Notice now stands, it obviously falls far short of a permanent stoppage of the Trade for supplying foreign colonies (*in general*) with slaves; indeed it is obviously erroneous because it does not respect Dutch Guiana at all. . . . As the matter presses much in time, I trust I need not apologize for begging the favour of you to consider without delay, what is best to be done. . . .'[11]

Fox immediately altered the Order Book and Stephen drafted the Bill, paring it to barest essentials to ensure widest support.[12]

The tactic worked. During April the Foreign Slave Bill went 'quietly on' through thin Houses. As Wilberforce had forecast to Grenville, there was 'little or no opposition in Parliament'.[13] West Indians welcomed a Bill which would cripple their French and Dutch rivals: the only doubter promised not to oppose.[14] Country Members did not bother to come up from their estates for a vote on such an obvious move in the prosecution of the Napoleonic War. Only the Member for Liverpool, the one-handed General Tarleton, fulminated in the House that the Abolitionists were coming in by a side wind. They were in fact keeping very quiet. Wilberforce heard that the Duke of Clarence would oppose in the Lords 'in the warmest manner', and warned Grenville to take care to present the Bill on grounds of national advantage alone, lest a strong opposition form on the 'mistaken idea that it rests on general Abolition principles or is grounded on justice and humanity, an imputation which I am aware would prove fatal to it'.[15] To this harmless dove, wise as a serpent, Grenville agreed heartily, replying that if an anti-Abolition lobby were roused, 'I know that neither reason nor justice will avail much against it.'[16]

The Bill passed its Second Reading in the Commons on 2 May 1806 by 35 votes to 13. The Prime Minister fixed 7 May for the Lords' debate; delay would be very dangerous 'and as it is we may have no little difficulty in carrying it'.[17] Wilberforce itched to listen to the debate but managed to hold to his resolution 'of not showing my *suspicious* face either in the House of Lords or on the avenues to it'.[18] Stephen as the Crown's lawyer could listen while Wilberforce fidgeted in another place.

He had heard that peers would try to defuse the Bill in Committee. If it were to contribute to the grand strategy of Abolition it must go through intact and by a good majority: 'I scarcely need suggest,' wrote Wilberforce to Grenville, 'the advantageous effect on the general measure . . . of the present Bill's being carried through with a high hand.'[19] His fears were unfounded. On 9 May Grenville reported it through Committee, and that he had enough proxies to be sure of the remaining stages. He added: 'How ardently I wish it may be only a prelude to a much more complete and satisfactory measure I need not tell you.'[20]

The Lords voted 43 to 18 for the Bill on 16 May. Wilberforce heard that ships were hurriedly fitting out to beat the operative date, 1 August 1806. He tried to persuade Grenville to bring the date forward and save the human cargoes, but procedural difficulties made this impossible.[21]

With the Foreign Slave Bill about to become law and the first great barrier broken, much depended on the next move. 'We have carried the Foreign Slave Bill, and we are now deliberating whether we shall push the main question,' Wilberforce wrote in his diary on Sunday 18 May. 'O Lord, do thou guide us right, and enable me to maintain a spiritual mind amid all my hurry or worldly business, having my conversation in heaven.'[22]

Stephen drew up a memorandum of *pros* and *cons*: he and Wilberforce wanted to press on. Grenville doubted that a general Bill could be carried so late in the Session. Then Wilberforce offered to stand down. The idea had gained on him that he ought to make the great sacrifice of allowing another the glory for the sake of the cause. On 20 May he spoke to Fox and wrote immediately to Grenville that 'if the measure is to be brought forward at all, it had better be, not by me, but by Mr. Fox. The circumstance of your patronizing the measure in the House of Lords and Mr. Fox in the House of Commons will have, I trust, great weight in neutralizing some who might be active enemies, and in converting into decided friends some who might otherwise be neutral.'[23]

He argued that the Lords should start on any necessary Inquiry above stairs, even if the time were too short for an actual Bill. Apologizing for a long letter he ended: 'May the great Disposer of all events direct to you a right conclusion, and in this and many other instances render your administration a Blessing not only to your own country, but to the whole world. So cordially wishes and let me add, as I know to whom I am writing, prays, your Lordship's obliged and faithful *W. Wilberforce.*'[24]*

* Anstey (*op. cit.*, pp. 377–8) quotes Grenville's reply at length, and notes Samuel Wilberforce's curious comment, 'I think this is dull', on the original (Duke MSS). Anstey suggests that the *Life*'s failure to appreciate Grenville's importance is the origin of the hitherto general lack of appreciation.

The final decision was that Fox should give notice of a Resolution, stating boldly that the Slave Trade was contrary to the principles of justice, humanity and sound policy and that 'this House . . . will, with all practicable expedition, proceed to take effectual measure for abolishing the said trade, in such a manner, and in such a period as may be deemed advisable.'[25] The phrase 'in such a period' would neutralize the advocates of 'gradual' Abolition, who could be out-manœuvred later.

On 5 June, five days before Fox's Resolution, Wilberforce produced a further plan: that he should immediately follow up with an Address to the King that the Crown take the first opportunity 'of negotiating with Foreign Powers with a view to the *General* Abolition of the Slave Trade'.[26] Ever since 1787 Wilberforce had hoped for this, which would stifle the cry of the Traders that other powers would ship the slaves and steal the profit.

He put the idea to Fox on Saturday, 7 June. Fox had already probed for peace with Napoleon and saw no objection or danger. Late on the Monday Wilberforce drafted the Address and sent it to Grenville for approval[27] but on Tuesday, the morning of the debate, sent an amended version because 'I was half asleep last night when I scribbled the Address'.[28]

During the debate Fox made a great speech. Not knowing how near was his end, he said that if during his forty years in Parliament he should have accomplished Abolition and this only, he should think he had done enough and could retire from public life with comfort and the conscious satisfaction that he had done his duty. Though Windham and the young Lord Castlereagh were among those who opposed this attempt to forward a general Abolition by the nations, Fox's Resolution swept through by 114 to 15. Immediately afterwards Wilberforce rose to move the Humble Address to the King. It passed without a division. A fortnight later, on Midsummer Day, Wilberforce listened from the gallery as Grenville carried the Lords. Wilberforce congratulated him. 'May what we have already obtained be the harbinger of our complete success.'[29]

Within days of the Humble Address, Talleyrand in Paris had received a copy from the unsteady hands of Lord Yarmouth, the dreadful Lord Hertford of the future, immortalized by Thackeray as the Marquis of Steyne, who was the fortuitous go-between in the abortive Peace negotiations. It was America, however, not France, which lay foremost in Wilberforce's mind.[30]

Wilberforce had written in his diary after the Commons' vote: 'If it please God to spare the health of Fox and to keep him and Grenville together, I hope we shall see next year the termination of all our labours.'[31] Three days after the Lords' vote William Smith, the true

Foxite of the Clapham friends, blurted out to the Wilberforces that Fox, whom all knew to be in poor health, had dropsy and his life stood in danger. Wilberforce grieved as he thought of their early friendship, their past political duels, and present alliance: of Fox's fidelity to the Abolition cause. He grieved for Fox's soul and longed 'that I might be the instrument of bringing him to the knowledge of Christ!'[32]

If Fox died, the partial Abolition victory of 1806 might not be consummated in 1807. What is more, Grenville had suddenly gone off on a well-meaning tangent. He put to Wilberforce at Camelford House a plan to kill the Slave Trade by high fiscal duties on slaves rather than by outlawing it.

Wilberforce did not commit himself until he had consulted Stephen and then rejected it firmly: 'the Plan is in the highest degree objectionable and . . . would prove in fact altogether ineffectual to its purpose.'[33] Because Sidmouth liked it, Grenville pressed the plan all through the summer. In August Wilberforce said smuggled slaves would be indistinguishable from duty-paid slaves. Nor would fiscal duties stop new ships entering on the Trade. Above all the plan would lower the tone of the campaign by not 'rendering the Slave Trade a crime'.[34]

Grenville seemed ready to drop it if Wilberforce and his friends insisted, yet in September they had to think up further points to convince him. Clarkson suggested that the price of slaves would fall on the African coast; therefore more Africans would be seized to be sold. Babington (now an M.P.) said that the burdened planters would sell their land cheaper, so speculators would keep more to invest in slaves and the demand would actually rise and the Trade thrive. Wilberforce himself foresaw 'a perfect hurricane' of economic distress among the planters until they might force Parliament to rescind the duties.[35] Grenville reluctantly abandoned his plan.*

Wilberforce disappeared to Lyme Regis, where Barbara loved the sea bathing, to play with his children, chase his heavy correspondence and labour at writing a book of Abolitionist propaganda.

Grenville and the dying Fox now plotted a General Election. Fox wanted a Foxite for Yorkshire, which in the Eighty Four had swayed England away from him. The Tory Lascelles' powerful influence and

---

* Grenville's fiscal plan which would have placed a huge financial burden on the planters, is very damaging to Dr. Eric Williams's thesis in *Capitalism and Slavery*, that Abolition was the hurried answer of British statesmen to the economic distress in the West Indies caused by over-production. Another, even more damaging point against Dr. Williams arises from the dates of the Parliamentary Committee on the commercial state of the West India colonies. He claims that it was their Report which opened the eyes of Parliament to the urgent need for Abolition; but this Committee was only set up on 12 March 1807, more than two weeks after the decisive vote on the Second Reading, and did not report until 8 August, more than four months after Abolition had become law. (See R. T. Anstey, *Economic History Review* 1968, 2nd Series, Vol. 21, pp. 307–20, and *English Historical Review* April 1972, pp. 304–332. Also Professor Anstey's book, *op. cit.* p. 386.)

massive funds might win one seat, yet the Ministry did not want to unseat Wilberforce who had supported them. Besides, wrote Grenville to Lord Carlisle about a fortnight before Fox died, 'I do really feel from sentiments of very long and sincere regard for Wilberforce a great anxiety that the first months of my being in office should not be marked by what must be considered so great a discredit to him as his rejection would be.'[36] Thus, a bare month after the shock of Fox's death on 13 September, Wilberforce was further shocked to receive a private warning from the Prime Minister of the impending dissolution of Parliament. He stayed on at Lyme until he heard that he might be opposed. This third shock propelled him rapidly in the direction of Yorkshire, and when passing through Blandford he learned that Walter Fawkes of Farnley (better known now as the patron of J. M. W. Turner) would stand in opposition to Lascelles and himself.[37]

Neither might feel complacent. Both Members had annoyed the clothier co-operatives in the West Riding, who controlled the cottage weavers, by signing the Woollen Report of 1806 which, if adopted, would open the future to mechanized mills owned by big 'merchant clothiers'. Although the sittings of the Select Committee on the Woollen manufacture had coincided with the Foreign Slave Bill, Wilberforce had attended faithfully ('my *ear* open listening to evidence, while my hand and mind are employed in writing'[38]) and had virtually written the Report. His sympathies lay with the cottage industry which ensured an income for its weavers, however low in hard times, whereas a mill might dismiss theirs; yet County and nation needed the new machines. He therefore ensured that the Resolutions in the Woollen Report would not kill domestic weaving, while allowing an expansion of mills.[39] From another Yorkshire industry, on the other hand, Wilberforce had won great acclaim when he led the successful opposition to Petty's proposed tax on iron, which would have crippled Sheffield.[40]

As Wilberforce reached Yorkshire after posting up from Lyme, Lord Muncaster was writing to his neighbour Viscount Lowther: 'What you mention about Wilber making common cause with Lasc. is impossible, for Lasc. some days ago declared he would be neuter as to the other candidates, he should look only to himself. . . . Singular return this, for Wilber's giving him the preference of the Meeting in '96.'[41] Muncaster worried how Wilberforce's purse would stand a poll against Harewood House and against Earl Fitzwilliam, whose vast fortune backed Fawkes.

Wilberforce was swept into a whirlwind of 'speechifying' to tumultuous and mainly friendly crowds.[42] At Sheffield they took his horses out of their traces and dragged him in triumph to the Cutlers' Hall, running over a few careless feet. On the road near Halifax his carriage nearly had an accident with a waggon. In Halifax the mob showed some anger and 'one man threw something which hit me on the forehead, happily not hard', but Leeds had been enthusiastic towards Wilberforce, whereas if Lascelles had dared an entrance to the Cloth Hall the domestic clothiers would have rolled out bales to stop him; 'Beau' Lascelles had treated their witnesses with hauteur and disdain.

Gossip said the Prime Minister had ordered, 'Mr. Wilberforce *must* be supported by the Government interest but not one farthing of money from the Treasury.'[43] Behind the scenes, with ill-concealed distaste, Fitzwilliam obeyed Grenville's order. One agent replied to Fitzwilliam: 'I by no means like Wilberforce – I never did hold him in estimation – nor do I think I shall ever change my opinion of him,' but there could be little doubt that it is 'of infinitely greater consequence', for the County and the Ministry that Wilberforce should be preferred to Lascelles; and if he would give any help to Fawkes they would be invincible. 'Nor shall I be surprised to see the little man's cunning guiding him towards that course.'[44]

On 29 October Muncaster reported happily to Lowther 'that all goes on admirably with our friend Wilber; they have received him at Leeds rapturously. I have just got a letter from him in which he has little doubt of all being in his favour.'[45] Subscriptions came from strangers; Methodists and the Church Evangelicals canvassed hard; Freeholders promised support for Abolition's sake. Several peers and magnates gave their interest because he was a true independent; and this, he assured the Earl of Egremont, was 'the most gratifying kind of popularity'.[46]

He recovered the ground he had lost by dallying at Lyme. By 1 November he knew he would head the poll 'if a poll there should be; but,' he wrote to Lord Grenville, 'I hope there will not be one; for certainly I *whisper* to you in PERFECT CONFIDENCE (what I cannot be as glad of as you, from my personal goodwill to Mr. Lascelles, though I am most scrupulously and *conscientiously* neutral between him and his opponent) that Mr. Fawkes also will be so clearly victorious,' that Lascelles would withdraw.[47] That same 1 November, at Halifax, Wilberforce heard of the withdrawal from Lascelles himself.

The Talents Ministry won the General Election handsomely. Grenville personally was stronger because Sidmouth lost many of his followers while the heirs of Fox did well. Despite Fox's death and the continued opposition within the Cabinet from Sidmouth and Windham, Abolition would be Grenville's first important Bill for the new Parliament. As things turned out, it would also be his last.

Grenville's plan was to reverse the usual procedure and launch Abolition in the Lords at the start of the Session, by a short Bill simply abolishing the Slave Trade and declaring that to engage in it was a misdemeanour. If the Lords insisted on an enquiry, the whole Session lay ahead instead of the tail end which had always allowed them to stalemate measures originating in the Commons. Grenville felt that Wilberforce should raise the subject simultaneously, 'but I should wish *you* to decide for us'. Wilberforce decided the Commons should wait on the Lords.[48]

He hurried straight from Yorkshire to London to be at the Prime Minister's hand. And to rush the completion of the book on the Slave Trade which had been emerging by the usual Wilberforce literary process for six years. It would be entitled, *A Letter to the Freeholders of Yorkshire*. He wanted it out by the opening of Parliament on 15 December. In this, being Wilberforce, he failed. While Grenville's Bill was read a first time in the Lords on 2 January 1807, Wilberforce scribbled away at Broomfield, 'hoping in a few days to finish my work, far too hastily and therefore unsatisfactorily'.[49] He believed a strong book would influence peers and on 15 January begged that the Second Reading be 'a *little* delayed'.[50] But Grenville had already been forced to postpone for a fortnight by a tactic of his opponents.

On 31 January, by that strange forgotten alchemy which could publish a book four days after the author completed his manuscript, the *Letter to Freeholders* reached peers and public. It restated the Abolition argument with vigour and a tender regard for opponents. The *Edinburgh Review* said his 'pamphlet is a written speech; and, with most of the defects, retains many of the beauties which eminently distinguish his oratory.'[51]

The battle in the Lords began quietly four days later with counsel at the bar, and some debate after each counsel's speech. Grenville deflected the Lords from the long trail of summoning witnesses. He moved that it 'be read a second time to-morrow'.

Wilberforce forwarded him news just in from America that Congress had brought in an Abolition Bill, with death the penalty which now was in committee 'without opposition nor was any anticipated'.[52] To James Monroe he wrote of his joy at 'the concurrence of our 2 countries in carrying into execution this great work of Beneficence'.[53] The same thought crossed Thornton's mind on the eve of the great debate in the Lords, as he scribbled to Patty More during a pause in Commons business: 'I hope and trust that tomorrow will be an era for old England and that the Lords will do that in England which the descendants of the Puritans in America are now doing in Congress, for the Trade is surely as ignoble and ungentlemanly as it is unChristian.'[54]

No one could be sure of the Lords. The Traders appeared very low in spirits but the Abolitionists suspected this was dissimulation to breed complacency, and they themselves were afraid of a weak attendance of friendly peers. Grenville wrote round; Wilberforce

Wilberforce in 1801 aged 42, from the pastel by John Russell

Barbara Wilberforce in 1801, aged 24, from the pastel by John Russell

smelt out sick peers who might give proxies, and lazy peers like the Duke of Grafton who would come up only if persuaded that the issue stayed doubtful. Clarkson lobbied Canterbury's chaplain and hoped for a benchful of bishops. The Abolition committee hired 18 Downing Street as a kind of whip's office and met frequently, with or without Wilberforce, to draw up lists of doubtfuls.[55] On the evening of Thursday 5 February Wilberforce went to the gallery of the House of Lords and listened to the entire debate.

Lord Grenville moved the Second Reading in a speech which Wilberforce recalled years later as 'one of the most glorious and affecting effusions of true eloquence that was ever poured forth'.[56] Admittedly he was reminiscing to Grenville, but this was much the contemporary verdict, the more so in that Grenville had no reputation for eloquence. He began, not very convincingly, with the argument that Abolition would save the planters from ruining themselves by overproduction; but even if further imports of slaves, by allowing a vastly increased acreage, should bring them profit, 'is it to be endured that this detestable traffic is to be continued, and such a mass of human misery produced . . . ?'[57] He put the weight of his argument on the justice and humanity of his Bill, rather than on 'sound policy'. His peroration touched Wilberforce deeply, for in Bishop Porteus's words it was the 'most eloquent eulogium upon him I ever heard'.[58] 'I cannot conceive,' said Grenville, 'any consciousness more truly gratifying than must be enjoyed by that person, on finding a measure to which he has devoted his life, carried into effect – a measure so truly benevolent, so admirably conducive to the virtuous prosperity of his country and the welfare of mankind – a measure which will diffuse happiness among millions now in existence, and for which his memory will be blessed by millions yet unborn.'

The Duke of Clarence defended the Trade, while the other royal duke to speak, Wilberforce's young friend Gloucester, commended the Bill. The 16th Earl of Westmorland, famous for his runaway match to Gretna Green with a banker's heiress, prophesied ruin and 'bespattered' Wilberforce.[59] According to the report he did not make his abuse personal: perhaps he glared up at the long nose protruding from the gallery, and since one Westmorland eye was larger than the other the glare could be memorable.

The House sat all night, with Lord Eldon strongly against the Bill and Admiral the Earl of St. Vincent declaring that since Grenville was a man of intelligence a witchdoctor must have laid a spell on him to make him want to do such damage. This raised a laugh but even amongst the Bill's friends few believed Grenville's argument that Abolition would be sound policy, whether economic or political: all regarded it as a quixotic act of national self-sacrifice demanded by humanity and justice.

8

The peers divided at 5 a.m. and astonished themselves – and Wilberforce – by their overwhelming majority for Abolition: 100 to 36, a majority of 64. Next evening the Committee stage passed swiftly, and the bishops of London and Durham and many other peers shook Wilberforce's hand warmly before he and Stephen went back to Camelford House with Grenville.[60]

It was then that Sally Stephen broke her leg, slipping on an icy Clapham lane while going to a dying woman. Despite her nerves and feeble frame she dragged herself back, sent for the doctor and told the groom to ride to Westminster. Stephen hurried home in agitation to find her calm and comfortable. Wilberforce was much upset, but no one could spare time for Sally except the two little Wilberforce girls 'and they cry by her bedside half the day'.[61]

At the Report stage in the Lords, St. Vincent forecast ruin to the Navy and stumped out of the House. On Tuesday 10 February the Bill was read a third time, and introduced in the Commons the same night by the Foreign Secretary and Leader of the House, Viscount Howick, the former Charles Grey. He set the Second Reading for 20 February to allow time for petitions.

Neither Wilberforce nor Grenville felt over-sanguine: 'A terrific list of doubtfuls . . . yet I think we shall carry it too.'[62] On the Sunday, meditating alone, Wilberforce jotted down a prayer that God would turn men's hearts as in the House of Lords, 'and enable me to have a single eye and a simple heart, desiring to please God, to do good to my fellow creatures and to testify my gratitude to my adorable Redeemer.'[63]

Clarkson chose this moment to decide he would like the Chair of Modern History in the University of Cambridge, then a part-time professorship. Wilberforce obligingly solicited the interest of Lord Henry Petty as Member for the University; a proof of great regard for the difficult Clarkson, that Wilberforce should break his rule against asking favours. He assured Petty that Clarkson was 'a man of superior talents and great industry', whom he had known 'many years in his private character and habits as well as in his *peculiar pursuit* (of his indefatigable and zealous perseverance in which I cannot speak too highly). . . .'[64] Clarkson was not elected.

Friday 20 February should have begun the great debate on the Second Reading of the Grenville–Howick Bill for Abolition, but the question came on late and opponents postponed it by arguing unsuccessfully for the hearing of evidence. On the Monday morning Wilberforce wrote hastily to Howick that he had heard they would propose, as an alternative to Abolition, that the Trade should be suspended and enquiry launched into the state of the black population. Wilberforce had tried for Suspension himself in the years unkind to

Abolition, but 'I need not point out to your Lordship that this proposal, made now for the first time by the West Indians, comes with a very bad grace and can be understood as nothing more or less than an expedient for gaining time and defeating us', until the main question could be brought up again 'when our strength may be less formidable than happily it appears to be at this moment'.[65] Howick must have nipped this ploy for it went no farther.

Howick was an elegant though unimaginative speaker and rather hard of manner,[66] but on 23 February 1807 he put the case for Abolition in able terms after starting ill at ease. He did not like Wilberforce and included no graceful allusions. Yet it was a night of compliments. First Fawkes, basking in the glory of being the County colleague of 'that exalted and benevolent individual . . . I rejoice with him on the final and glorious victory he is about to obtain.'[67] Then young Lord Mahon, Stanhope's son, in a maiden speech: he had married Bob Carrington's daughter and so could name Wilberforce as 'an honorable relation . . . whose name will descend to the latest posterity with never fading honour.'[68]

Most of the speeches supported the Bill. Enthusiasm mounted. As one Member sat down six or eight would be on their feet, including young heirs who had entered at the last Election such as Lord Milton, Fitzwilliam's son, as warm for Abolition as his father was warm against. The climax came when the Solicitor-General, Romilly, who loved Wilberforce not only for Abolition but for his interest in penal reform and the poor, swept the House to a pitch of excitement by his peroration. He contrasted Bonaparte and Wilberforce each retiring for their night's rest; Bonaparte in pomp and power at the summit of ambition, yet with sleep tormented by the blood he had spilt, and the oppressions he had committed. And Wilberforce, returning after the vote that night 'into the bosom of his happy and delighted family', to lie down in pure and perfect felicity, conscious of 'having preserved so many millions of his fellow creatures'.[69]

The House rose almost to a man and turned towards Wilberforce in a burst of Parliamentary cheers. Suddenly, above the roar of 'hear, hear,' and quite out of order, three hurrahs echoed and echoed while he sat, head bowed, tears streaming down his face.

A long defence of the Trade and of Slavery itself could not alter the mood of the House. Wilberforce replied briefly to the debate. At nearly 4 a.m. young Earl Percy, Northumberland's heir, began proposing they should immediately prepare to abolish Slavery too. The House rather unfairly scented a red herring and called loudly for the question. Percy sat down.

The House divided: Ayes, 283, Noes, 16, Majority for the Abolition, 267, a surprisingly overwhelming vote.

'No one expected this great question to be carried with so high a hand,' wrote Harrowby's brother, one of the ayes. '. . . No one is more surprised than Wilberforce himself. He attributes it to the immediate interposition of Providence.'[70] The lights still burned at 4 Palace Yard where friends flocked in, including poor William Smith who had lost his seat for Norwich and had listened from the gallery. 'Well, Henry,' cried Wilberforce playfully to Thornton, 'What shall we abolish next?' 'The Lottery, I think!' This reply has been taken as solemn, but Thornton could joke, rather gravely, with Wilberforce; though certainly the lottery was on their list.*

William Smith called out that they should name the sixteen miscreants: he had four already. Wilberforce looked up from the floor, where he was on one knee writing at a table as he often did, and said: 'Never mind the miserable 16, let us think of our glorious 283.'[71]

Congratulatory notes poured in. Wilberforce replied to the Prime Minister: 'You do me far more honour than I deserve. I am only one among many fellowlabourers, and it is no more than justice to yourself to say, that to yourself and to the tone you have taken and the exertions you have made, our success is mainly to be attributed....'[72]

The aged John Newton, near death, rejoiced in the City, and in St. James's Square old Bishop Porteus took down his memoranda book. His spontaneous private sentiments demonstrate the motives and convictions of the Abolitionists: 'Here then after a glorious struggle of eighteen years a final period is at length put in this country to the most execrable and inhuman traffic that ever disgraced the Christian world. And this Act will reflect immortal honour on the British Parliament, the British nation and all the illustrious men who were the principal promoters of it. I am truly thankful for Providence for permitting me to see this great work brought to a conclusion. It has been for upwards of 24 years, long before Mr. Wilberforce brought it into Parliament, the favourite object of my heart; and it will be a source of the purest most genuine satisfaction to fill my mind during the remainder of my life, and above all at the final close of it to have had some share in promoting to the utmost of my power the success of so important and so righteous a measure.'[73]

'Our present utterly unlooked for prosperous circumstances,'[74] enabled Wilberforce to press Howick to insert penalty clauses into the Bill instead of a bare naming of the Trade as a misdemeanour; the British, unlike the Americans, limited the penalty to fines until the uselessness became obvious. Wilberforce regretfully allowed one concession in Committee. To prevent a possible hostile vote Howick deleted from the Bill's Preamble the wounding words 'contrary to

* Since Robert was only 12 years old and Samuel 9 when Thornton died, their story obviously came from W. himself. I find it irresistible to think of him telling it with a chuckle.

justice and *humanity*', leaving only '*sound policy*'. Wilberforce wanted them but told Howick on 9 March: 'I have no *right* to relieve my own feelings at the expense of our great cause.'[75]

A new danger arose. The Government collided with the King over a Bill to allow Roman Catholics to hold commissions in the armed forces outside Ireland where they had won the right already, and although Grenville withdrew the Bill on 15 March the King made impossible demands. If the Ministry fell, the Abolition Bill might fall with it.

The Bill came up for Third Reading on 16 March. Windham pitted his famous eloquence against it to the last, saying that if Parliament abolished the Slave Trade they should abolish Slavery too, and not outlaw the one without the other. Privately he hoped Parliament would outlaw neither. Wilberforce replied that he indeed looked forward to a change in the status of the negroes but 'it was not in our power to heal up both the wounds immediately'.[76] Wilberforce believed with almost everyone in 1807, that Emancipation could come only with the consent of the colonial assemblies, who were adamant. Even the *Edinburgh Review* had called the very idea 'sentimental rant'.[77]

The Bill passed its Third Reading unopposed. Next day Earl Percy moved in a nearly empty House for leave to bring in a Bill for the gradual Abolition of Slavery. Wilberforce opposed it gently, while denying 'ever having disavowed his wish that freedom should ultimately be communicated to the slaves'.[78] He held that slaves must be trained for freedom. He did not say that the noble minded youth's motion could wreck Abolition at the eleventh hour by provoking some very recent friends in the Lords to rat. Percy's motion was counted out.

The Talents Ministry now was almost extinct. On 18 March, the day Wilberforce, Howick and others brought back the Abolition Bill to the Lords with the Commons' slight amendments, Grenville formally refused the King's conditions on the Roman Catholic question. While the King looked for a new, Tory Prime Minister, three Tories who would certainly be in a new Cabinet, Hawkesbury, Castlereagh and Eldon, promised Wilberforce not to frustrate the will of Parliament; but if the Bill did not become law before a new Prime Minister kissed hands, it could conceivably still be shelved.

On the morning of 23 March Wilberforce was horrified to learn that a clerical error of three words had crept into one of the amendments to be laid before the Lords that afternoon. The Lords must correct it, and any Lords amendment could be debated in the Commons. Wilberforce shuttled all morning between Grenville, the Speaker and the legal offices.[79]

That evening the Lords agreed to the Bill, with their own technical amendment, to growls of protest from Westmorland. In the Commons, Howick fended off questions about the Ministry's resignation, and next day, after the customary message from the Lords, the Speaker made 'a particular explanation' that it was the practice of the House to accept without discussion a Lords' amendment if merely a clerical correction. The amendment was agreed to. Thus on 24 March the Bill had passed all its stages. Grenville had already obtained the royal assent to this Bill and two minor ones which thereby became the last Acts of his Administration.

At midday on Wednesday, 25 March 1807, with Grenville and his friends sitting on the Opposition benches although they had not yet delivered up their seals of office, the royal assent was declared by Lord Chancellor Erskine, Lord Auckland and Lord Holland.

The Bill for the Abolition of the Slave Trade became law. The problems of enforcing it began.

CHAPTER TWENTY-ONE

Wilberforce in his Prime

To congratulations from Wyvill Wilberforce replied that his joy was not only for the good to be done by the Abolition Act itself, but because 'the authority which the great principles of justice and humanity have received will be productive of benefit in all shapes and directions'.[1] He was right; his achievement brought him a personal moral authority with public and Parliament above any man living.

Ordinary political manœuvres had to reckon with him. When the displaced Whigs wanted to defeat the new Portland Government, Lord Temple told Lord Howick on 1 April 1807 that the motion must be framed and its mover adapt his speech 'in such a manner as will ensure the support of Wilberforce, Bankes etc. etc. upon whose opinions at this moment much depends',[2] while another ex-minister warned Howick not 'to put them in a state of hostility at this moment'.[3] On the actual day of this debate (its subject is immaterial) Wilberforce had 'a seizure of my old constitutional complaint'[4] and spent it on a sofa at Palace Yard, except for dragging himself across to take the chair at an election scrutiny committee, to prevent the litigants accruing expense. The Whigs lost their motion and grumbled that he had malingered because he did not want to oppose either his recent allies or the Tory Ministers.[5] His bowel complaint was genuine: yet perhaps partly psychological in origin, for he had told Bishop Tomline (formerly Pretyman) that afternoon: 'I should enter the House with a most painful and embarrassing set of conflicting feelings.'[6]

Before Wilberforce could deploy his new authority he was confronted with an unexpected General Election and thrown into a pure Eatanswill situation, the first fight to the finish in Yorkshire since 1784 and the last before Reform.

The Tory Lascelles determined to regain his seat, and although the Whig Fawkes would not stand again because of expense, Fitzwilliam's heir, Viscount Milton, was ready. 'Without prejudice, Lord M is really too young,'[7] considered Wilberforce, and he remained in London, refusing a secret Whig offer of an unopposed return for Hull if he would concede Yorkshire,[8] until convinced that a contest was inevitable, with the Lascelles and Fitzwilliam interests equally set to win.

The comparatively modest Wilberforce fortune had no chance against the immense resources of Harewood House and Wentworth Woodhouse even if a subscription aided him, unless his voice and persuasive presence and unique reputation proved stronger than money bags. By 9 May Lord Milton's mother, Lady Fitzwilliam was alarmed. 'Mr. Wilberforce is received in almost all places with enthusiasm, and appears to carry everything before him.' He had already publicly announced that he would not coalesce with either candidate, Whig or Tory; but, wrote the Countess, 'as I know Mr. Wilberforce is a very artful man I do suspect that he will be ready to help Lascelles instead of Milton'.[9] Her correspondent replied he was perfectly aware of Wilberforce's guile 'and dread its effects'.[10]

At the nomination in the Castle Yard on 13 May the show of hands and roar of voices gave Wilberforce the lead with Lascelles second. Milton demanded a poll, so he told his father the same day,[11] but the official record does not state any demand until candidates and crowd returned one week later on 20 May to the Special County Court, at which Wilberforce made the formal request. At the hustings Wilberforce had a shock – the show of hands and the day's Poll put him second. His friends ascribed it to their failure to organize transport for their voters; but the Miltonites asserted that 'Mr. Wilberforce has ruined his cause by his equivocal conduct',[12] in secretly supporting Lascelles, as they believed, while pretending neutrality.

For the next fortnight Yorkshire gave itself over to the convulsions of a contest. Until the Poll closed at 3 p.m. on the fifteenth day, the three candidates and their committees worked desperately to get Freeholders from near and far, several hundred a day, by coach or barge or packhorse or foot, to cast two votes each at the Castle Yard, not by secret ballot but publicly in a manly way, persuaded by bribery, bullying, honest conviction or drink: even Wilberforce, who had encouraged Lord Belgrave to bring in his no-treating Bill, had to allow his committee to treat,[13] the only occasion perhaps when history can fairly accuse him of humbug, though contemporaries scarcely noticed. The candidates made speeches above the din, bands played, banners waved; the Lascelles banners blazed *No Popery*, to rub in the fact that the Tories had regained power by the King's uncompromising attitude to Roman Catholics. Milton's poetasters exploited the apparent liaison between Abolitionist and slave-owner.* At the end of each polling the High Sheriff announced the day's total and the running total amid cheers and groans.

On the third day Milton led. Wilberforce sent an express for his

---

* Some delightfully scurrilous verses are printed in Furneaux, pp. 266–7.

dearest friends, and Henry Thornton, Robert Grant and James Stephen, with three of his sons, drove up the Great North Road only to stick at Biggleswade because Lord Milton had cannily hired all the post horses between London and York,[14] to bring in his out-voters and stop those of the others, but Wilberforce regained the lead. By 25 May Milton thought he had only a bare hundred votes' edge on Lascelles, though in fact he had more, and wrote: 'I dread the combination between W and L which nobody doubts, it is the only thing that could have hurt us.'[15] Beau Lascelles was cocky now. One of his principal supporters, John Morritt the well-known traveller, who had made Wilberforce's nomination speech, yelled as Milton ascended the hustings on 25 May: 'This is the last dying speech and confession!' The late County Member, Duncombe, hollao'd 'Whoo-up!'[16] That evening Milton scrawled to his father: 'We have had a terrible day; Lascelles has got above me on the whole Poll.'[17]

The Thorntons and the Stephens reached York on 27 May by mail-coach. Henry wrote next day to his ten-year-old daughter, Marianne, that Wilberforce continued to be the winning horse though all the horses were now a little off their speed. He added improvingly: 'I hope that when you are as old as Mr. Wilberforce you will have made many persons so much your friends that they also will be willing to travel a couple of hundred miles for the chance of serving you.' Thornton was well used to rowdy elections from his own experiences in Southwark, where he refused to allow treating, and he now revelled in a 'fine row in the Castle Yard. Lord Milton spoke with spirit but Mr. Wilberforce had the best of the argument'.[18]

Lord Milton gave a different version to his father: 'Wilberforce was very pressed by us to-day after the close of the Poll on the subject of the coalition [with Lascelles]. He was quite out of temper and did not know what to say, and the people were quite against him. He has lost much of his popularity; he is now accused of hypocrisy and duplicity in his conduct during the Election; it is delightful to see that people begin to find him out.'[19]

Against mounting heckling Wilberforce continued to deny coalition; he believed the damaging rumour to be a Whig deceit. But it was easy for his over-enthusiastic Tory supporters to hide from him how they urged Freeholders to vote Wilberforce and Lascelles. Brougham, up in Yorkshire to help Milton, found plenty of evidence and was not surprised on 30 May after Wilberforce renewed his denial from the hustings, to hear a Yorkshireman shout back that he was a liar because 'Your committee canvassed my vote last night for Lascelles.'[20]

Wilberforce did not appear on the hustings again; Milton thought he was 'politically ill'. Thornton knew it was real enough; the usual colitis, no doubt caused by strain. His was not the only illness of the Election: Hannah More in Somerset, who had subscribed more than

8*

she could afford, felt so agitated lest Wilberforce be turned out that her apothecary put her on double doses of opium until the contest ended.[21]

Wilberforce had actually been secure since 23 May: the race now ran for second place. Milton sent for every possible voter from London and the south, pouring out money. He was in despair, certain that Wilberforce's later voters would be turned over to Lascelles as they came in, 'a measure which it will be impossible to stand against . . . though they are certainly as exhausted as we are.'[22] By 1 June Milton discovered that he was catching up.[23] Lascelles had made the fatal mistake of not bothering to bring up London voters, and by the last but one full day of the Poll, 3 June, Milton was jubilant. 'Wilberforce still has not yet made his appearance, he and all his Committee have been *very ill* – Lascelles' friends are said to have the *blue devils*. I fear it will be a fatal disorder.'[24]

And it was. On the late afternoon of 5 June 1807, the High Sheriff of Yorkshire, after taking a maddeningly long two hours to cast up the Poll, announced the figures: William Wilberforce, Esquire: 11,806; the Right Honourable Lord Milton: 11,177; the Honourable Henry Lascelles: 10,989. Mr. Wilberforce and Lord Milton elected Knights of the Shire for Yorkshire.

Wilberforce was much interrupted in his acceptance speech. His reputation for honesty had been damaged by his Tory partisans' efforts under his nose for Lascelles. Within a month, as Brougham predicted, it was largely forgotten. And young Milton became one of Wilberforce's admirers, almost a disciple.

Next day Thornton took cold dinner with Wilberforce at York and endeavoured to set off home. But 'no horses to be had for London, by either Stephen or Grant or me.'[25]

Wilberforce's apparently equivocal conduct in Yorkshire, as some Whigs continued to regard it, did not spoil his position in the House or the country; the five years of the Portland and Perceval ministries, 1807–12, saw the peak of his influence on the men who governed Britain as he struggled to raise the standards of public life.

'The Saints' was a term freely used for the little group he led – Thornton, Bankes, Babington, the Grants, with Stephen who entered the House early in 1808, and others. He scorned the suggestion that they formed a Party, nor did they vote always the same way. The House seldom quite knew which line Wilberforce would take or how he would vote. Members generally heard him with interest and anticipation, but often he left them still guessing at the end. His facility for seeing both sides of an argument, his charitable desire to believe the best and to honour motives, and his unfortunate habit of thinking with his tongue so that the farther he explored the more by-ways, and possibilities, and alternatives opened to his view; all this could make him a confusing speaker. Once when Wilberforce gave the House the benefit of his indecision on a motion by Whitbread (not reported in *Parliamentary Debates*), Whitbread jumped up: 'Mr. Speaker, my Honourable Friend who has just sat down has as usual spoken on *both sides of the Question.*' (Loud laughter.)[26] A Member sneered to Lord Holland that night that Wilberforce 'in short spoke like a Saint, satisfying neither Party by his speech but strengthening Administration by his vote'.[27]

His shrinking from over-positive assertions was also noticeable 'out of doors'. A humorously embroidered account of it appears in a letter to Brougham from the political journalist John Whishaw in 1810: 'I met your friend Wilberforce at Martin's the other day, having never seen this distinguished personage before. He is certainly very lively and agreeable and apparently good tempered, a great courtier (as to general civility) and without any fixed opinions, except on the Slave Trade and the essential doctrines of Christianity. Even on this latter subject I doubt whether he may not occasionally fluctuate between the sub- and supra-lapsarian systems, and whether he has accurately adjusted the degrees of guilt of the Arian and the Pelagian heresies.'[28]

His vacillations increased with age, bedevilled by a habit of taking such copious notes in the Chamber that he sometimes missed the general drift of a debate. His conscience tended to prick him about his vote. 'I wonder,' mused Liverpool to Sidmouth, 'how Wilberforce voted last night.' Liverpool did not know, 'but this I am pretty sure of, that in whatever way he voted he repents of his vote this morning!' And sure enough Wilberforce shortly called (or so Sidmouth relates) to confess doubts about a vote which, he said, had perhaps surprised Sidmouth. 'My dear Wilberforce,' Sidmouth exclaimed, 'I shall never be surprised at any vote you may give,' and proceeded to convince him the other way.[29] The question could not therefore have been Sidmouth's ill-advised attempt to muzzle Dissenters, when Wilberforce's disapproval was clear and decisive.

All who dealt with him and heard him, as distinct from those who knew only printed report, recognized that the indecisiveness sprang from his honesty, his anxiety to do right by the nation and God at every twist of the political road in troublous times. James Stephen's youngest son George was only a boy at this period but he grew up in the world of Westminster, and later heard the ageing Wilberforce frequently; he summed the matter up succinctly long afterwards in his *Anti-Slavery Recollections*: 'Men might doubt about his vote on minor issues, but where the interests of morality, or humanity, or religion were involved, there Wilberforce's perception of what was right appeared intuitive, and his vote was certain: neither rank, nor power, nor eloquence bewildered him for a moment then. All the honours, all the wealth, all the seductions that the world could furnish, would not have tempted him to offend his conscience by even a momentary hesitation; he at once rose above all infirmities of habit, firm as a rock upon the spiritual foundation on which he rested.'[30]

Wilberforce had become in a sense the conscience of England. When Castlereagh sent a challenge to Canning because of facts learned from Lord Camden, and the War Minister and the Foreign Secretary shot at each other on Putney Heath one autumn morning of 1809, men blamed Lord Camden. He thereupon brought the evidence to Wilberforce for an honest opinion which all would accept. Wilberforce cleared him, but warned that 'The most unpleasant reflections arising out of the whole affair are such as impute, to all of you, that you were attending only to each other's personal feelings, and not to the public interests. *I* am aware really that this was not the case, with many of your number, I hope with all. . . .'[31]

A few weeks after the duel Spencer Perceval replaced the dying Duke of Portland as Prime Minister. Sidmouth was not in the Cabinet, though Perceval offered offices to several Sidmouth adherents. The new Ministry looked frail. Sidmouth took an early opportunity of dining with Wilberforce and they sat afterwards from about four in the afternoon, since Wilberforce dined at an old-fashioned early hour, until long after midnight, and for most of next morning. Sidmouth wrote to three of his close supporters long accounts of Wilberforce's views of men and policies, and noted his hopes for a coalition and his desire for Parliamentary reform; his high personal regard for the Tory Perceval, a fellow-Evangelical and Abolitionist, yet his displeasure at some of Perceval's conduct.[32] One correspondent replied that Wilberforce's 'opinion will certainly have considerable weight with many, though there is more of Party feeling respecting him than there is, I think, with regard to any other man who has never been in office'.[33]

During the next two and a half years until Perceval's murder Wilberforce gave discriminating support. The Prime Minister wanted him at his eve of Session dinner but realized it was useless to send an invitation. Wilberforce assured Perceval of regret that they so often differed[34] and the Saints even brought the Ministry to defeat on an important but non-resigning clause of the Regency Bill. 'Wilberforce . . . holds on his honourable course much as heretofore,' wrote Thornton to Hannah More sometime in the Session of 1811. 'His health flags less than might have been expected and his greatness frequently shows forth. The House hears him sometimes ill, and sometimes well but it has become a strange House through the new men, the new topics and a new kind of strife that agitates it.'[35]

The following year when the Liverpool Ministry was in formation after Perceval's death, Wilberforce did his utmost to persuade Canning to swallow his dislike of Castlereagh as Leader of the House and accept the Foreign Office. Canning's long reply of self-justification vexed Wilberforce, who in two immense letters, one of ten sides, 'this long and desultory scrawl', and the other of fourteen attempted to persuade Canning that his personal grounds for not serving with Castlereagh were outweighed by public considerations. He added he was tempted to tear the second letter 'to pieces, because I find I have exhausted all my time, and yet I have argued only one side of the question. Do not however suppose me blind to what is to be said on the other.' He summed up his persuasion succinctly: 'How much should a man be willing to give up for the good of his country?'[36] If Canning had taken the Foreign Office he would have been saved much remorse, and would have led for Britain at the Congress of Vienna.

Canning had sacrificed the public welfare to private feelings. Wilberforce tried to put the public good first, irrespective of personal friendships or political loyalties. He found it impossible to preserve a total detachment from Party if he were to exert any pressure, and his Pittite past inclined him towards the Tories; but when young Lord Milton in 1812 bemoaned the hardship of charting an independent course within his natural Whiggery, Wilberforce revealed a little of what his own independence cost: 'You quite *raze the skin*, you touch me so hard, when you appeal to my own experience and feelings as to the obstructions and difficulties in the way of an *isolated* unconnected man who is trying to do some good in public life, and therefore your lordship would find that I do not so entirely foreswear all Party connection as you may perhaps suppose from my general and unqualified language.' He defined "Party" to Milton as systematic opposition on one side and corruption on the other, with a view to gaining or keeping a place, and believed it went far to extinguish all public spirit and did mischief to the nation's morals, *'the best of all its possessions'*.[37]

He wandered across the pages on this theme. And then, using those quaint images which made his letters sometimes endearingly eccentric, Wilberforce promised to stop, 'for I find as I warm (that as all heated bodies attract substances in the neighbourhood and especially the feathers of quills, paper etc.) that I am strongly tempted to take up another sheet when I should be still hotter; another would *of course* follow, so that there is no knowing where it would end. . . .'

Wilberforce now had a new home. He had been feeling the strain of oscillating between Clapham and Palace Yard yet could not bear to divorce himself from country sights and sounds. Early in 1808 he bought a long lease of a mansion built in the 1750s in Kensington Gore, exactly one mile from Hyde Park Corner yet countrified; the north front faced Hyde Park, then much more rural, with Kensington Gardens beyond, across the busy road to Bath and Exeter, while the south front overlooked one and two-thirds acres of grounds, shaded by fine trees, sloping to market gardens where the museums and squares of South Kensington would one day be built, and away to the Surrey hills.

The Albert Hall covers the site of Gore House – where Admiral Rodney had once lived – and part of its garden; concert-goers who arrive at the main entrance are almost where Wilberforce's guests alighted. The house was stuccoed. He added a dining-room, with books up one wall, for he said every room should have books, and nurseries above. The house was less magnificent than in Early Victorian times when it acquired notoriety as the salon of Lady Blessington and her paramour, Count d'Orsay.[38] In the garden the previous lessee, a government contractor, had been too mean to clear the weeds. Wilberforce made a lawn and shrubberies but never sought to emulate Lord Ennismore's splendid gardens nearby, and if posterity – and a slight prick from his own conscience – questioned whether the benevolent Mr. Wilberforce needed quite such a fine place it was modest beside Ennismore's Kingston House, a 'capital mansion' with a famous art gallery on the highest point between Hyde Park Corner and Windsor. Many County Members might keep less substantial London houses than Wilberforce, but owned one or more country mansions, whereas Gore House was his only home. 'It really will save 5 or 6 hundred pounds per annum,' or so he expected when writing to Mrs. Thornton, adding: 'I don't know how I shall tear myself away from you all, for though I always thought I had felt a good deal about it, I begin now to discover I shall feel still more than I expected.'[39]

All the Wilberforces were immediately happy with Kensington. Wilber occasionally heard the nightingale; he could walk home from Westminster through Green Park and Hyde Park while Barbara rode beside him,[40] or if alone he could comfortably recite the 119th Psalm to himself between Gore House and Hyde Park Corner.[41] The air was excellent for lungs despite closeness to London,[42] though a poor substitute for rural England: 'How you must revel in the rich banquet which I understand your lovely country serves up to you,' he commented in a letter to Huskisson in 1810. 'We are here fond of our villas, as long as the House calls us daily to London and we contrast them with the dust and turmoil and stink of the streets, but they are, to say the truth, but a mimicry of the *real* country.'[43]

Henry Thornton bought the remainder of the lease of 4 Palace Yard, where Wilberforce could still go if engagements prevented return to Kensington. 'Mr. Wilberforce I hope has forgotten that Palace Yard is no longer his,' Thornton wrote dryly to Hannah More, 'for he dines here naturally at any hour except ours. . . .'[44]

At Gore House Wilberforce could see his children more than ever before, growing up in a happy if haphazard home where even the pets might be a little peculiar. 'How can you ask such a Question, will you receive my tame Hare?' wrote Wilberforce to a young expected guest. 'Are you so bad at analogy, and if Love me love my dog is an established axiom, much more Love me Love my Hare holds true in this House, where among some of us Dogs have not their due Estimation.'[45]

'The Wilberforces are all come to town,' wrote Thornton in late autumn 1809, 'all well save a little bilious complaint in Mrs. W and a torn nail on the foot of one of the children and a moderate portion of the accustomed perturbation in the head of the family. He continues to overflow with tenderness and to complain much of want of time to do more than half the benevolent things which he meditated.'[46] When Wilberforce owned two houses nobody quite knew where to run him to earth, but callers flocked to him at Kensington. A great man like ex-Lord Chancellor Erskine could dismount during his morning ride in the Park to discuss preventing cruelty to animals. ('I entirely participate in your feelings and intentions,' Wilberforce said.)[47] Breakfast time invitations were now scattered with such abandon that in Thornton's view Wilberforce 'obstructed his usefulness by not sorting his guests'.[48] After breakfast anyone with a cause or a plea or a problem or an empty pocket might knock at the front door and be placed in his hall or dining-room, until Kensington Gore became a sort of clearing house for British philanthropy and moral reformation, with Wilberforce ready to encourage or advise, or to rebuke, as when the Society for the Suppression of Vice toyed with the idea of using deceit to secure convictions.[49]

Since he lacked time for half the good works in his mind, he liked to be a conducting rail for the charitable sparks of others. 'Factories did not spring up more rapidly in Leeds and Manchester than schemes of benevolence beneath his roof,' declared James Stephen the Younger. Mid-morning presented an astonishing mixture of men and women, with one of his helpers moving around to discover who was begging what. Then an inner door opened and out hurried Wilberforce, a strange little figure with hair still powdered, though the fashion had almost died out, and a sometimes dingy black suit without ornament except for a diamond pin. He would almost skip from group to group, bringing up his eye-glass as he greeted and listened and sympathized. Face and eyes would reflect pity or indignation at some tale of woe, or ardent approval for a new idea. Old friends could detect when the character or the suggestion before him touched his strong sense of the ludicrous, but his laughter never was unkind.[50] And he knew the need for discrimination: 'You can scarcely conceive how much it destroys my influence . . . to come forward under the suspicion of being a common vouchee, or general Hack, ready to lend myself to anyone who comes with a tale of oppression or wretchedness.'[51]

His own charities were legion and it has been reckoned that he was president, vice-president or committee man of no less than sixty-nine societies.[52] In any difficulty they would enlist his aid, especially as probably he had *entrée* to those most likely to solve the problem. Thus the uproar at Cambridge when Simeon and Milner planned a Bible Society Auxiliary, to the rage of the Regius Professor of Divinity and half the Heads of House, produced a flurry of letters from Kensington Gore. Wilberforce regarded the Bible Society as 'one of the most excellent and useful institutions that ever existed'.[53] The situation was saved when he got into his carriage, drove to Piccadilly and called on the Chancellor of the University, none other than his disciple the young Duke of Gloucester. Wilberforce begged him to take the chair at the founding meeting in Cambridge. Gloucester demurred, for it would be a private, not a University function; he sent instead a handsome subscription and strong letter. The opposition collapsed,[54] a victory which helped destroy prejudice as the Bible Society went about diffusing Scripture among the population, and abroad. Wilberforce could tell his friend Earl Grosvenor next year; 'It is gradually clearing away the mist and fog which obscured its earliest rising, and will soon shine with full and unclouded brightness.'[55]

Yet with all Wilberforce's multitude of religious and reforming interests at home, which were helping forward 'the change that has taken place within the last forty years in the general tone of morals,'[56] none counted more with him than the battle for the slaves abroad. This had by no means ended when the Abolition Bill became law.

It was to the Bible Society in London that a missionary in Gorée, the former French settlement in West Africa, described the situation five months after the Abolition Act came into force: 'The fact is, all trade is now at an end, and while the slave masters are pouring out their malediction on Wilberforce, the slaves are at the same time roaring out and wishing the best of blessings to light upon the head of the *Godlike Emancipator*!'[57] This hyperbole did not mask a lie; wherever the British Crown held authority the trading had stopped. But the 'Godlike Emancipator' cherished no illusions about slavers beyond the range of British guns. Moreover the return of Peace would revive the foreign trade unless the nations agreed to Abolition first.

He could turn meanwhile to the second part of his plans for Africa. On the morning of 28 March 1807, three days after the Abolition Act received the Royal Assent, Wilberforce laid a scheme before the Duke of Gloucester who promised his 'attendance and cordial support'. The day passed in summoning the great and good and not so good to a public meeting to form an African Institution, which he described as 'a Society . . . on a very broad Basis, for promoting the Civilization and Improvement of Africa – making discoveries would fall within its scope.'[58]

As long ago as 1791 Thornton had suggested it;[59] Pitt had elaborated it, Wilberforce had talked of meeting 'the obligation under which we lie to repair the wrongs of Africa, in consequence of our having so long and so largely contributed to them'.[60] He secured for his foundation meeting at the Freemasons' Hall near Lincoln's Inn Fields a large number of lawyers, politicians and churchmen. The Duke of Gloucester became the African Institution's very active President at the age of thirty-one.

This prince has been dismissed as 'Silly Billy' by the scorn of his cousins, the King's sons, who hated him for a way of life which contrasted with their own. He was a man of unaffected religion imbibed through Hannah More and Wilberforce. His letters from the Helder campaign, where he had distinguished himself as a very young (because royal) major-general, caused the old Duchess to reply: 'What a happy mother I am, who have as much reason to be proud of my son as a Christian, as I have as a hero!'[61] When he had just succeeded to the dukedom in 1805 she extolled him to Hannah More, adding: 'Religion is not very common amongst young men, yet I am confident that there is much more now than there was when I was young. Mr. Wilberforce is to call upon us in the course of this week, and although I do not see company at present he is so devout a man that everybody must look upon him as an exception. The Duke looks up to seeing him.'[62] And nearly thirty years later when Gloucester died at Bagshot Park in 1834, aged 58, in the presence of his wife (George III's daughter) and Sophia his sister, the chaplain wrote a long account of the final days and the Duke's Last Sacrament, taken fully conscious. 'It was truly delightful to see three persons of the highest rank in life, so entirely forgetting all earthly grandeur and desirous only of throwing themselves at the feet of their Saviour, and pleading His Atonement as the sole ground of their hopes of pardon and acceptance! Oh that we had many such examples of piety and humility amongst the great ones of our land!'[63]

The Duke's Hanoverian face developed a bovine look. He was not particularly bright, and his public speeches were lazily impromptu, though audiences at charity meetings loved them. At the African Institution he laid aside his royalty so that no one need stand, or stay silent until addressed, but hard work and ability won 'more real respect than he loses',[64] Wilberforce said. Wilberforce was chairman. Macaulay was honorary secretary and the committees cut across party lines: The Whigs Grey, Grenville, Brougham and Petty, who succeeded as Marquess of Lansdowne, worked with Stephen and Thornton, while Clarkson was almost a Quaker now and rather radical in politics.

The Institution sought to improve slave life in the West Indies and acted quickly over notorious cruelty, but their primary concern lay with West Africa. They drew up plans which in August 1807

Wilberforce showed to Canning, then Foreign Secretary.*[65] A protectorate centred on Sierra Leone should form an oasis of peace which would encourage education and husbandry, introduce 'industry and the arts of peace' to the interior, and foster the spread of Christianity. These grandiose plans for the opening up of Africa had to wait a generation, for the West Indians feared competition, the Government disliked distraction from the war, and private investors held back: when Wilberforce asserted 'the practicability of actually introducing civilization and its consequences into Africa' (his irony was unconscious) they pointed to Sierra Leone, which had yielded no return on capital.

The Sierra Leone Company had thankfully handed over to the Crown, which left the direction in the hands of the Claphamites. Wilberforce himself added difficulties by recommending, as first royal governor, the son of the senior partner of the Wilberforce firm at Hull, a Methodist, not that he approved the severity with which the man had drummed religion into his children.[67]

Young Thomas Perronet Thompson had much to commend him: a brave naval officer, he was elected to a Queens' College Fellowship which he never took up; instead he transferred into the new rifle regiment. On his return from the Montevideo expedition he dined and slept at the Wilberforces where the talk of an Africa opened to civilization and purged of the Slave Trade so enthused him that he sat up all night to work out how it might be done. Wilberforce promptly offered him the governorship of Sierra Leone if Lord Castlereagh, the Colonial Secretary, would give it.[68]

Thompson soon found the Sierra Leone directors were 'all heart and no head', especially with regard to finance, though Wilberforce he thought, stood out best from 'all the others who profess themselves friends of Africa'.[69] Thompson sailed in June 1808 with high hopes. But he was a man of impetuous judgement and fiery temper. He set Sierra Leone by the ears. Some of his intended reforms were sound, some misconceived, and he ignored his instructions, hurled unsupported accusations at his colleagues and wrote offensive letters to the Colonial Office and Sierra Leone House.

'My dear Sir,' cried Wilberforce when he read them, 'it is with the deepest pain that I sit down to address you, because instead of having to congratulate you on the auspicious commencement of your government I am bound to declare to you (bound by the obligation no less of private friendship than of public duty) that you make me tremble considering myself as deeply implicated in your character and conduct, not so much by any specific step you have taken, as by the temper and

---

* The covering letter to Foreign Secretary Canning contains an example of how a Wilberforce chuckle would obtrude on serious affairs. He had dropped a blot over a word. So he put a note on the blank sheet opposite: 'I must beg Canning to excuse this great Blot to the Secy of State, telling him I am sadly pressed for time and cannot write my letter over again.'[66] (Harewood MSS.)

spirit you appear to have assumed. . . . My dear Sir, you are a young man of bodily health and strength which may I hope long enable you to lead an active life; of superior talent; of an ardent spirit; and of pure and even excellent intentions. Beware of defeating the happy result of all these by any rashness in judgement or conduct, or any intemperance in language. . . .'[70] The gentle Wilberforce could be tough when he chose.

Thompson found the colony so different from the imaginings of the London directors that he conceived an immediate and lasting contempt for them. Had he written more temperately he might have overturned Thornton's belief in his own superior understanding. As it was, Lord Castlereagh recalled him. Wilberforce did all he could to soften his fall but blocked an enquiry, believing it would hurt Thompson more than discredit the Colony, and Thompson went off to the Peninsular War. His subsequent career as soldier in Spain and India, radical politician, newspaper owner, writer, general in the army and designer of a harmonically perfect organ with seventy-two keys to the octave and unplayable, was one of the century's oddest.

Sierra Leone continued on its muddled way, with Wilberforce ever optimistic. Ten years and several uproars (and pamphlet wars) later he could say: 'It is now only in its infancy but it is an infant Hercules, of 10,000 free Negroes, most of whom poor creatures have been rescued from the holds of slave ships, gradually receiving the civilization and comforts, above all the Christian instruction and civil rights of a British community.'[71]

One of Thompson's violent disagreements had a wider implication. H.M.S. *Derwent* had already brought into Sierra Leone a seized cargo of 167 blacks. In conformity with the Abolition Act, and to provide the prize money which the Navy traditionally received from every capture, whether of a 100-gun man-of-war or a slave ship, these had been apprenticed to masters who paid fees for them to Government. Thompson wrote home that apprenticeship was nothing but Slavery in disguise. Wilberforce replied that the apprenticeship clauses had been inserted 'after the whole subject had been considered for years by several of the ablest men that ever lived,' including Pitt. 'In a case abounding with great and . . . almost fatal difficulties,' they produced the least objectionable way of settling rescued slaves.[72]

Wilberforce had relied, as he often did, on the authority of Pitt. Thompson had seen apprenticeship in the raw; his descriptions on return to England may have been a factor in Wilberforce's subsequent horror of it as a help towards Emancipation.

The rescue by H.M.S. *Derwent* produced a further problem. The captured slaver had flown the American flag and claimed that the British Navy had no legal right to confiscate its living cargo.

An awful vision unfolded before the directors of the African Institution, of British slavers evading the will of Parliament by sailing as American, while American slavers evaded Congress by claiming to be British, 'a subterfuge', as Wilberforce put it, 'by which the whole effect of our law may be defeated,' especially as he had learned from counsel that the Admiralty Court might decide in the American's favour for 'the restitution of these wretched men, in which case there is no doubt that they would be sold into perpetual Slavery.'[73] Counsel said the only hope was an appeal to the United States government.

Wilberforce immediately wrote on 8 September 1808 to his friend James Monroe, then living as a private citizen in Virginia, enclosing a letter to the President and begging Monroe (with almost absurd modesty) to 'make my name known to Mr. Jefferson'. To Monroe he pointed out that 'all our hopes of success in our endeavours for the internal benefit of Africa must be grounded on our preventing these infractions of the law'.[74] To the President he emphasized that an enormous British contraband trade could grow up under the protection of the American flag and he begged intervention for the victims, and 'the unknown multitudes whose fate is involved in the decision you may form on this particular case'. He urged an Anglo-American convention to authorize the liberation of cargoes, regardless of which Navy rescued them or which flag the slaver wore.[75] It would be years before such a convention was passed, in the Presidency of James Monroe himself.

The immediate victims were liberated by the verdict in another case. An appeal court upheld in 1809 a ruling that an American slave ship arrested by the Royal Navy must be condemned because engaged in an activity which was illegal under American law. Wilberforce had gone down to Buckinghamshire when he heard this from Macaulay, and was 'ready to leap out of my skin for joy and am in the state of a full-charged bottle of electrical fluid, which wants some conductor to empty itself out. Mrs. W. indeed takes her part in my joy. But I want you or Stephen or Babington or Thornton. You really deserve a statue. But more serious and sober matters for rejoicing remain after the first riotous effervescence has or rather *shall have* fumed away, for this is far from being yet the case. Then and with as much sobriety as I can, I compose myself (You see I am scarcely able to write a regular sentence for the flurry of spirits into which you have thrown me) into a grateful acknowledgment of the goodness of Providence in blessing your endeavour with success.'[76]

Though this legal decision was reversed a few years later, in 1809 it stopped the neutral Stars and Stripes being abused by slavers. Spanish red and yellow then took its place, for the flag of an ally was immune from search at sea. Wilberforce tried to stop this too. He urged Lord Wellesley, going as Ambassador to the Spanish Junta, to spread Abolition propaganda since the Patriots ought to sympathize with all causes of liberty. If they expelled the French 'I am sanguine in my hopes of their consenting to relinquish the Slave Trade and if they should be driven into the New World would carry along with them I trust and there diffuse, a similar disposition'. Wilberforce dangled before Wellesley a fame as the man who laid 'the ground for abolishing the Slave Trade throughout the New World'.[77]

The Spanish belied this optimism. As for the Portuguese, whose government had fled to Brazil, the African Institution asked Canning to forward a communication to de Souza, the ugly little Portuguese ambassador. Canning sent it back. He explained to Wilberforce that de Souza went behind the Foreign Office in commercial affairs and must not be officially encouraged. 'If you can get at him, without my introduction, I will *not* find fault with him for entering into discussion with *you*.'[78] The Spanish and Portuguese continued unmolested except when they attempted to smuggle slaves into a British West Indian colony.

The whole question of right of search had now merged with the wider issue of the British embargo on neutral trade by the 'Orders in Council'. Since these arose from the doctrine propounded in *War in Disguise*, Stephen defended them in the great debate of January 1808, but 'Wilberforce lags behind his brother-in-law and hesitates and trembles'.[79] When the Orders led to the War of 1812 the thought of fighting America was 'so peculiarly and preeminently shocking that I am quite sickened'.[80] These Orders in Council split the Abolitionists: despite contrasting morals and politics, Brougham the woman-chasing Whig and Stephen the Evangelical Tory had worked happily together until Brougham came to fame by his attack on the Orders. Then they were not on speaking terms for two years.

They all united, however, to suppress illegal slave trading by British subjects, which Parliament made a felony punishable by transportation to Botany Bay. Brougham brought the subject before the House in June 1810 in the first of his great Parliamentary orations, he piloted the Bill in 1811, and rightly took the credit.

CHAPTER TWENTY-TWO

Two Problems of Liberty

Samuel Roberts, prosperous from a Sheffield plate and silver business, spent time and fortune in philanthropy and writing: Wilberforce joked that one of Roberts's singularities was a conviction that he wrote 'not only very good prose but also very creditable poetry'.[1] The two men were barely acquainted when in June 1811 Roberts secured an appointment to discuss some Constituency matter. Wilberforce never turned up. On leaving Gore House Roberts met a Yorkshire neighbour who told him that Wilberforce frequently behaved like that to constituents; worse, he would deceive them by promising support which he did not give. Roberts wrote to Wilberforce that inconsiderateness was unChristian; he must be attempting more than his time and energy allowed and should do something about it.

The letter[2] won Wilberforce's affection: as he reminded Roberts six years later, 'It was a letter from you telling me of my faults, which first established and I believe immovably, in my mind, the persuasion and feeling of your being my real friend'.[3]

Wilberforce was relieved to discover that the Yorkshire neighbour was only a tiresome fellow called Watson, who always believed himself in the right and was cross because Wilberforce saw differently over the Bawtry and Selby Road Bill.[4] But Roberts's thrust went home.[5] Wilberforce wondered whether Yorkshire had begun to be too much. He was ageing: even in 1807 Thornton had thought him 'thin and old beyond his years, but still he is a horse well capable of work'.[6] He once said he had never felt entirely well since Dr. Warren had put him on opium twenty-three years before;[7] and although, as the young Bristol banker, John Harford, said on their first meeting a few months later, 'he was serene, cheerful and happy, and at the age of fifty-two had the gaiety and the spirits of a young man of twenty,'[8] Wilberforce bent under the burden of his numerous campaigns from Freetown to Demerara, from Newgate to Bible House, and the vast

230

correspondence which chased and choked him. Even on holiday at the seaside this held him at the low drudgery of quill driving when he longed 'to walk abroad with Cowper and Milton'[9] or take the children on an expedition.

'In the hurry of finishing and making up my last letter,' runs a typical apology that very summer of 1811 to Lord Sidmouth, 'when the carriage was at the door and I was detaining a party, I omitted one very important particular. . . .'[10] Letters piled 'until they form a mass that is absolutely terrific'.[11] He made matters worse: 'One of my faults is being seduced into making too free both with my friends' time and my own when I either talk or write to them.'[12] It was no use. 'You will, I know, suggest to yourself an excuse for me if I return you a short and hurried reply,' he began to a Yorkshire friend, 'and you see that, knowing my own proneness to garrulity when engaged in a friendly tête-à-tête, I have taken against it the precaution of a small sheet of paper being resolved not to encroach on a second. . . .' But of course he did take a second, and went on to eight sides.[13] Writing was a compulsion to Wilberforce. 'It is my standing counsel to all my young friends,' he commented, 'never to be sparing of pen and ink, or to trust to a verbal communication what may be conveyed on paper.'[14]

If he resigned Yorkshire for some small borough his Constituency correspondence would dry to a trickle, nor would he need to attend the House and its committees so incessantly; the rapid progress of the Industrial Revolution caused a stream of private and public Bills which had increased the Yorkshire work enormously in the twenty-seven years since his first election. The question seemed urgent, that first Regency summer of 1811, because George III was expected to die and the demise of the Crown must bring on a General Election. The crisis passed, and Wilberforce proceeded to make up his mind slowly in the usual way. He consulted close friends, who offered contradictory advice; he wrote himself long memoranda; he prayed, 'O Lord, give me wisdom to guide me rightly.'[15]

The factor, other than health, which grew dominant was his emphatic desire to give more time to the six children, especially the older boys, since he did not expect an old age. According to Henry Thornton's eldest daughter they were 'clever amusing restless little creatures, kept in very little order, though they had a large retinue of governesses and tutors, and friends who acted half as governesses and tutors'.[16] When William was ten and the Thorntons hired a lecturer with an electrical machine, he paid no attention yet got half the answers right, 'playing a thousand monkey tricks the whole time, spinning cup and ball, holding a flower by the stalk by curling down his upper lip. . . .'[17] In a tableau, as the Pope to Tom Macaulay's Bonaparte, he forgot his lines.

Wilberforce was an indulgent Papa who loved to read aloud in their summer holidays and even play cricket, though a fast ball from William damaged his foot. Most men of the upper class, whether religious or not, kept well away from their smaller offspring or else subscribed to the doctrine that children should be Seen and not Heard. In the House of Commons Wilberforce might rue 'the bustle and turmoil . . . the vulgar and harsh contentions',[18] but never the noise of the children playing and laughing and scrapping round his desk on a rainy day. A friend was with him at Kensington Gore as he hunted for a vital despatch until he looked vexed. At that moment came a din from the nursery above. The friend thought: 'Now, for once, Wilberforce's temper will give way.' But he turned, a seraphic smile on his face, all flurry forgotten. 'What a blessing,' he exclaimed, 'to have these dear children! Only think what a relief, amidst other hurries, to hear their voices and know they are well.'[19] On the other hand, when they kept up an almost incessant din in a small house he confessed it a little wearing, and his relief at getting away for a quiet walk, or reading and talking after they had been put to bed.[20]

For education he placed the boys at small private establishments because, like most of the Evangelicals, he regarded a Public School as a hot-bed of vice. He liked to broaden their minds in the holidays, sharing his love of literature and poetry and the wonders of nature. Charles Shore noticed that they naturally took boyish advantage of their father's playfulness: 'On a visit . . . I observed him during a considerable time walking round the lawn followed by three of these striplings. Whilst he selected each in his turn as his companion, the other two amused themselves with practical jokes of which he was the victim. Repeatedly brought to bay, and remonstrating with his persecutors, each of whom in turn profited by his instructive converse, he passed much of his time fruitlessly on the defensive.'[21] Above all, Wilberforce liked to watch their progress in religion, 'the grand concern of life'.[22] He desired from the bottom of his heart that they should not wait, as he had, until their mid-twenties before discovering the wonder of Christ's friendship. He did not expect or even welcome any sudden conversion but looked for signs of what he called 'the great change', as each began to allow Christ to work on his character.

He held that parents 'should labour to render religion as congenial as possible'[23] but, again like most Evangelicals of the day, he could not leave their souls alone: 'just as a gardener walks up again and again to examine his fruit trees,' he wrote to nine-year-old Samuel, 'and see if his peaches are set, if they are swelling and becoming larger, finally if they are becoming ripe and rosy. I would willingly walk barefoot from this place to Sandgate to see a clear proof of the *great change* being begun in my dear Saml at the end of the journey.'[24]

When rumours leaked out that Wilberforce contemplated resigning Yorkshire it was said his real worry was defeat, that if Lascelles tried again, Wilberforce would be thrown out for his behaviour in the 1807 Election.

He denied fear of defeat. And he was right, for the powerful Wentworth Woodhouse interest was now friendly while Brougham wrote to him: 'I hope there is no truth in Lascelles standing for Yorkshire. Commend me as a canvasser, *brawler* etc.'[25] Lord Liverpool went to the country in the autumn of 1812. Earl Grey (the former Howick) wanted to ditch Wilberforce for not supporting the Whigs who had given him Abolition, even if he did not support Liverpool either, but Brougham disagreed, and pointed out that Wilberforce's national popularity could be exploited: 'The Ministry being against Wilberforce is sufficient reason for supporting him. You say *he* is a bad one. What then? Lascelles is worse. And by supporting W. you both beat the government and gain, independent of W. and his Parliamentary friends, a great following in the country.'[26]

Wilberforce had settled to resign. He dithered to the last, hardly bearing to drop Yorkshire, yet early in September he began to write long letters to justify his decision.[27] Lascelles took his place unopposed. One of the Holland House set heard that Lord Harewood would produce a rotten borough in exchange: 'If so, how are the godly fallen!'[28] But Wilberforce had another berth. Barbara's first cousin, rich young Lord Calthorpe who was a Wilberforce disciple,[29] brought him in for one of the two seats for the tiny two-seat borough of Bramber in Sussex. The 36 electors were the burgage holders paying scot or lot; Calthorpe owned 20 burgages and could bring in whom he liked.

Wilberforce had qualms that as a known Parliamentary reformer (if a poor one in Radical eyes) he should sink to a rotten borough: at the next Election he wrote a most involved letter to Calthorpe going over all the ground.[30] But he had already concluded, before ever he thought of giving up Yorkshire, that the entire system was rotten; that many seats with big and apparently popular electorates were really carried by money 'aided by a little rioting',[31] and that bribery and treating were more important objects of reform than Corfe Castle or Old Sarum – or Bramber. Grey himself, the arch-reformer, manipulated elections by money. While the system existed Wilberforce would work within it, rather than throttling his usefulness by Quixotic protest.

It has been said that family life in the nation received distinct encouragement by his resignation of Yorkshire to devote more time to the children. Physically, it came just in time. Already he had chest trouble in addition to his tendency to colitis, and within a year or two he developed a curvature of the spine. One shoulder began to slope; his head fell forward, a little more each year until it rested on his chest unless lifted by conscious movement: he would have looked grotesque were it not for the charm of his face and the smile which hovered about his mouth.

He was obliged to wear 'a steel girdle cased in leather and an additional part to support the arms. . . . It must be handled carefully, the steel being so elastic as to be easily broken.'[32] He took a spare one ('wrapped up for decency's sake in a towel') wherever he stayed; the fact that he lived in a steel frame for his last fifteen or eighteen years might have remained unknown had he not left behind at Lord Calthorpe's Suffolk home, Ampton Hall, the more comfortable of the two. 'How gracious is God,' Wilberforce remarked in the letter asking for its return, 'in giving us such mitigations and helps for our infirmities.'[33]

After 1812 Wilberforce went down to the House less. Unless sick he always attended the big debates, entering on the arm of some younger Member to guide him to his seat. He followed every twist and turn of the main speeches, not only with cheers and groans but muttered comments grave and gay, as he rejected arguments or punctured pomposities. His amusing asides could convulse his neighbour and he acquired the reputation of the 'noisiest' Member.[34]

The House regarded him with a mixture of profound respect and tolerant amusement: almost a mascot. Because movement was painful to eyes and limbs Wilberforce would arrive in his place with pockets stuffed with pens and paper and a portable inkstand, and his hat with books. At dull parts he wrote letters 'out of my hat' and when the debate grew interesting he jotted down notes in thick black ink, because he could not read pencil. He applied his quill to the bottle so vigorously once that it splashed the nankeen (buff silk) trousers of Sir Thomas Baring, whereat Wilberforce cut capers of agitation until the debate dissolved in delighted laughter and Baring left to change.[35]

Wilberforce spoke less than formerly and his voice was sometimes weak and a trifle shrill.[36] On great occasions, especially when he knew his own mind without hesitation, he could still captivate the House. Two such occurred in 1813, one being his speech in favour of Roman Catholic Emancipation on 9 March 1813.

Wilberforce's attitude had been indecisive since 1800, when he had waited to approve Pitt's plan for Union until he knew it included the right of Catholics to sit at Westminster. The intransigence of George III and the fall of Pitt having killed this clause he swung back, reckoning that the times were not propitious for relief. He held that Roman religion was in error, and opposed the grant to Maynooth College for the training of priests and would have welcomed Ireland's conversion to Protestantism;[37] but he held an even lower opinion of 'political'

Protestants, men who had no religion yet belaboured the Roman Catholics for political ends. He was alarmed at a report (erroneous) that a Privy Councillorship was to be conferred on Patrick Duigenan,[38] a rabid anti-Romanist: Duigenan's antique bob-wig and Connemara stockings might make him a figure of fun in the House but his ideas were obnoxious to Wilberforce, for whom religion was too sacred to be a political toy.

Wilberforce began to mistrust the system whereby the Catholic community, which in England was still numerically small, had to be represented by Protestants. This requirement was not merely unjust, it actually increased Catholic influence, for Catholics would become less vocal once they had representatives of their own faith. He refused to look on Roman Catholics as sinister in themselves, as much of the public did and many of his close friends, though not Henry Thornton. Grattan in May 1808 moved eloquently that the petition of the Catholics be received, and Canning supported him rather facetiously and Windham bitterly opposed. Wilberforce spoke next. Lady Holland, listening from the ladies gallery high up, told Lord Grey: 'Wilberforce all parties agreed to laugh at. When W. implored good words on behalf of the Catholics, he and Sir John Hippisley were coughed down.'[39] Wilberforce recorded in his diary that he remained undecided whether to admit Catholics to Parliament.[40]

But by 6 March 1813 he knew his mind at last. As Thomas Barnes, then a young reporter, wrote: 'he has at length broke the chain of his scruples, and . . . with a warmth of language and manner quite his own, unequivocally recommended the abolition of penal statutes in matters of religion.'[41]

Wilberforce also enthralled the House in 1813 with the cause of Christian missions in India.

At the renewal of the East India Company's Charter in 1793 he had failed to open India except to a few more Anglican chaplains for Europeans. The failure had been offset a little by the missionary zeal of the chaplains secured by Charles Simeon, but Baptists, including the great Carey, who tried in the next decade to bring Indians the Christian gospel had to reside in the Danish enclave of Serampore.

Lord Wellesley when governor-general helped Carey by giving him a professorship at Fort William college. Soon after Wellesley's return to England early in 1806 Wilberforce enlisted him for a campaign to insert a toleration clause in the Charter at its next renewal. 'You will know,' he wrote on 14 April 1806, 'how deeply I feel on the subject, when I frankly confess to your Lordship that next to the Slave Trade, I have long thought our making no effort to introduce the blessings of religious and moral improvement among our subjects in the East, the greatest of our *national* crimes.'[42] He arranged for Wellesley to 'spur on the Archbishop to the task'.*

Wilberforce soaked himself in information about the cruelties which at that time disfigured Hinduism. He would read out at the dinner table a list of women who had died recently by committing *suttee* on their husband's funeral pyre.[43] He knew something about the tyrannies of caste, and the Juggernaut car and other fearful religious customs. He knew little of the mystic and philosophical elements of Hinduism, for this was a period when such lay largely submerged. Yet even if he had known, his fervent conviction that Jesus Christ had come as Saviour for all mankind must urge him to open the way for ambassadors of Christ: not in arrogance but in honesty and love.

The culprits, to his eyes, were less the proconsuls in the East than the Court of Directors in Leadenhall Street who had proved their determination to keep the door 'close locked and barred against all that might disturb the profound moral darkness of these vast regions',[44] since they feared that evangelization would provoke further disturbances like the Vellore mutiny. He had as advisers Charles Grant, who was a director himself, and Teignmouth, the former governor-general. In 1812 he tried with modest success to rouse the Church of England and also led a deputation to Perceval; as an Evangelical the Prime Minister showed sympathy but was murdered before he could take action. Wilberforce repeated the process on Perceval's successor, Liverpool, suggesting cannily that godliness and national policy sang here in unison, since a Protestant India would be less open to French blandishment;[45] it occurred to no one that India could avoid a European overlord.

Liverpool came up with a plan for a bishop of Calcutta and three archdeacons, with their clergy, for the entire East Indies from Baluchistan to the South Pacific. The new East India Company Charter would also permit the activity of missionaries ordained or lay, whether of the Established Church or Dissenters.

Tom Babington wanted to attack this plan because he feared that a stiff Churchman like Liverpool would choose a bishop who was hostile to missionaries. Wilberforce shared this fear, and rightly, but 'I do not think it proper under all . . . circumstances of the case to oppose it publicly.'[46] The friends of the Court of Directors, however, planned to

---

* The vain and glorious Wellesley could not dazzle Wilberforce, the friend of his youth, who teased him a little when conveying Canterbury's desire to call and to receive a call: '. . . This I suppose between mere rank and file would imply "I wish you would knock at my door at Lambeth". I am not master of *manners* enough to adjust the ceremonial between an Archbishop and a Marquess, though at this very moment I do recollect Burke in his work on the French Revolution does settle the priority so decidedly as to authorize one to desire you to give the Archbishop a call. Indeed were I not thus fortified by Authority, you have made me so entirely forget you are a great man by seeming to forget it yourself in all our intercourse . . .' (British Museum, Wellesley Papers).

oppose it publicly enough, and hoped to expunge the missionary clause from the Charter.

During the Parliamentary committees on every aspect of Indian affairs Wilberforce busied himself securing witnesses and ensuring the presence of sympathetic Members and peers. Ex-Lord Chancellor Erskine having expressed himself in favour, Wilberforce dashed off a note imploring his presence: 'Really, we have too many in both Houses who seem to think our dominions safer under Brahma and Vishnu, than under that of the Almighty – But to say the truth it is, I believe, the result of ignorance in the greater part. The fact however is that we sadly want in the Committee of the H. of Lords, friends to the diffusion in India of Christianity and its attendant blessings among our Asiatic subjects. Surely your Lordship will not fail us in such an emergency. . . . The Committee meets again to-morrow so we have not a moment to lose.'[47]

Meanwhile he fanned a great campaign for public petitions. 'My dear Sir, excuse my asking,' he added to a letter on another subject to a Scot in Edinburgh, 'are you, and the (blessed be God) *many* others who have at heart the diffusion of the light and happiness of Christianity all asleep?'[48] Edinburgh had sent no petition as yet. In the end, the weight of petitions surprised the Government and was a proof of the growth of religious feeling in the twenty years since the last renewal of the Charter.

As the debates crept nearer the vital clause, Wilberforce knew he had no secure majority. He summoned support regardless of political disagreements, and three days before the question came before the House he accosted Samuel Whitbread, with due apology for the liberty, warning him that the Anglo-Indians were using every means to oppose, 'and I see symptoms of shrinking in some whom I deemed our friends'.[49] He begged Whitbread to come up from the country since the Government would be swayed more by Parliamentary strength than by the crowd out of doors.

At last, on 22 June 1813, when the Commons had been wearied night after night by the debates on every aspect of Indian diplomacy, commerce and finance, Wilberforce rose in a full House. Thomas Barnes in the press gallery described the scene: 'He spoke three hours, but nobody seemed fatigued: all indeed were pleased, some with the ingenious artifices of his manner, but most with the glowing language of his heart. Much as I differed from him in opinion, it was impossible not to be delighted with his eloquence. . . . He never speaks without exciting a wish that he would say more.'[50]

The House of Commons with its quick reaction against cant or sermonizing listened enraptured as Wilberforce almost turned the Chamber into a church and his place into a pulpit as he stood, all physical weakness of lung or spine forgotten, taking them through the horrors which the evidence had thrown up, and their remedy. 'That remedy, Sir, is Christianity, which I justly call the appropriate remedy; for Christianity then assumes her true character . . . when she takes under her protection those poor degraded beings on whom philosophy looks down with disdain or perhaps with contemptuous condescension. On the very first promulgation of Christianity it was declared by its great Author as "Glad tidings to the poor", and, ever faithful to her character, Christianity still delights to instruct the ignorant, to succour the needy, to comfort the sorrowful, to visit the forsaken.' Wilberforce said that were he not conscious of this he would not 'have had the heart to persevere in dragging you through the long and painful procession of humiliating statements to which you have been lately listening'.

There were passages when the speech seemed almost a Parliamentary version of 'From Greenland's Icy Mountains'. The hymn had been published the year before by a Shropshire clergyman, though Reginald Heber had no idea that in a few years he would be sent to 'India's coral strand', as the second Bishop of Calcutta after Lord Liverpool's man had died.

Wilberforce rebutted the charge that he advocated compulsory conversion to Christianity. 'Compulsion and Christianity! Why, the very terms are at variance with each other – the ideas are incompatible. In the language of Inspiration itself, Christianity has been called the "law of liberty". Her service in the excellent formularies of our Church has been truly denominated "perfect freedom"; and *they*, let me add, will most advance her cause who contend for it in her own spirit and character.' He was not asking Parliament should organize or ordain evangelism; he was asking for mere toleration, 'that we should not substantially and in effect prevent others engaging in it'.[51]

The House of Commons responded, the Lords did not object, and the East India Company Charter of 1813 guaranteed liberty to the propagation of the Christian faith. If Wilberforce's vision of all India turning to Christ was not fulfilled; if missions became mixed to some extent with the attitudes of the *raj* and were slow to foster Indian leadership in the Churches, yet an unbiased historical verdict must honour the enormous good done from that time onwards by the long roll of Christian missionaries. Parliament had opened a fast-locked door and it was Wilberforce who had turned the key, in a speech which Lord Erskine said 'deserves a place in the library of every man of letters, even if he were an atheist'.[52]

CHAPTER TWENTY-THREE

Lost Opportunity, 1814

'My dear Lord E., Surely your well known voice will be heard to-morrow in the Cause of Humanity?' wrote Wilberforce to Erskine on 25 March 1814. 'As for the money, what is given or withheld by one who is able to serve the cause so much more than by his purse, is not worth a thought. But do my dear Lord for the sake of the credit of our country abroad as well as at home. Do come and treat the subject in connection with those serious topics which you know so well how to introduce. . . .'[1]

The Cause this time was a relief fund for starving north Germans whose land had been ravaged by the final stages of the war. Wilberforce wrote round wherever eloquence might be found and was vexed when Grenville and Lansdowne refused. Wilberforce put it down to Party feeling: 'How disgraceful and unprincipled, though they are not aware of it.'[2]

The great meeting at the Freemasons' Hall was badly managed: a strange fear of showing off stopped Wilberforce drawing up a sensible list of speakers, and then the Duke of York, in the chair, ordained 'no speeches'. 'The Duke of York made a poor figure literally as well as figuratively,' noted Thornton. 'Sussex did much better. The names of the Committee being read out, that of Wilberforce produced the finest burst of applause I have ever heard.' Barbara burst into tears. A dull secretary read out a huddle of resolutions and the feast of oratory would have been bare had not thanks been proposed to the royal chairman by a Cabinet Minister, 'and Mr. Wilberforce seconded it in the silver tones of a seraph'.[3]

Madame de Staël heard them, the brilliant French writer, mistress of Talleyrand and of many others. She had already met Wilberforce by her special request at a dinner party arranged by the Duke of Gloucester, to which Wilberforce went with groans because he feared the effect equally on his vanity and his digestion. Madame de Staël was charmed. She said afterwards she had always heard that Wilberforce was the most religious, but now found he was the wittiest man in England.[4] She persuaded him to dine with her and a party of his own choosing but he deplored the damage of these decorous junketings to his soul, however much he prayed before entering the room; they made his mind race the next morning and prevented concentration. His doctor thought he ate too little, but even a little over-eating upset his constitution. 'I *must* not feel overloaded after dinner. Lord, even in this little matter,' he prayed as he wrote his diary, 'I know from sad experience my own weakness. O strengthen me and enable me to live more strictly and take care to be "watching unto prayer", to be filled with the Spirit, etc.'[5]

Whatever his private wrestlings he had won a firm ally in Madame de Staël who would give considerable aid to the Abolition cause when she returned to Paris. As for the German Relief meeting she put it in her book on the French Revolution, describing Wilberforce as the best-loved and mostly highly considered man in all England.

The war now neared its supposed climax. About half past four on the afternoon of Tuesday, 5 April 1814, Wilberforce was walking down Piccadilly, perhaps worrying about eleven-year-old Robert just back from school, who said he got nothing to eat except 'hot shoe and cold shoe', when J. C. Villiers stopped him excitedly with the news that the Allies were marching into Paris. A few days later he read in the evening paper that Napoleon had abdicated. 'O for the Abolition of the Slave Trade, generally. Could I but talk French I'd go to Paris immediately. How nobly the Emperor Alexr has behaved, I'm delighted Paris spared.'[6]

Tsar Alexander, in his mid-thirties, was now the great man in Europe. He was known to be sympathetic to liberal and humane causes and, indeed, to Evangelical religion having undergone, so Wilberforce was assured, a spiritual experience which seems to have been genuine enough, even if it faded somewhat in later years when his liberalism faded too. Wilberforce decided to write him a pamphlet-size private letter setting out the Abolition case and the need for an international convention which, under the Tsar's chairmanship, should abolish the Slave Trade everywhere.

Wilberforce began at once. The following Sunday, having a touch of trouble on his lungs, he did not go to church but worked at it 'as in God's sight'.[7] All through the next weeks with their incessant excitements and interruptions he toiled away. 'I kept growling and correcting, and correcting and growling as Ancient Pistol eat the Leek,' he told John Harford, 'and only going on because I had begun and that the time already spent on the work would be wasted if I should not finish it, yet it is now a very wretched business. . . .'[8]

The Tsar's sister, the Grand Duchess of Oldenburg, had already

The Wilberforces in the Library at Battersea Rise about 1824, from the pen and ink sketch by Marianne Thornton

Wilberforce in the Last Year of his Life,
detail from the engraving by S. Cousins of the watercolour by George Richmond

taken the entire Pulteney's Hotel in Piccadilly with its bow-fronted windows which looked on to Green Park and the red brick of Buckingham House beyond. At a dinner party there in April the Duke of Clarence boasted that the Regent was about to send a message advocating renewal of the Slave Trade. Wilberforce, when he heard of this, guessed that Clarence had said it to tease the Duke of Gloucester, who at the Duchess's dinner had argued hotly, knowing that his cousin lied: the Regent had already said he favoured Abolition.[9]

On April 28 Wilberforce went to the Duke of Gloucester's in Piccadilly (afterwards Palmerston's house, and later the Cavalry Club) for a meeting of the West India committee of the African Institution, including Grey, Grenville and Lansdowne, Thornton and Stephen. They decided to concentrate on International Abolition and to put aside their agitation to stop up the holes in the British Abolition laws.[10] If all European nations acted together no black would ever again endure the Middle Passage. On 3 May, therefore, Wilberforce moved an Address to the Regent praying him to instruct his Ministers to use the gathering of the Powers in Paris to effect Abolition. The motion, as Wilberforce scribbled to Grenville immediately, 'passed not merely unanimously but with zealous and triumphant unanimity,'[11] for the West India and the merchant lobbies which had opposed him all the way to 1807 had no desire to see other nations profit from a Trade forbidden themselves. The Foreign Office circulated the Address round European capitals.

The best hope lay in the peace negotiations with the restored Bourbon Government dominated by Talleyrand. If the French outlawed their Slave Trade so that it was not revived, Spain and Portugal would be shamed and pushed into honouring tentative promises; and here the Abolitionists realized that Britain held a trump card, the captured French colonies. These should not be returned unless France abolished the Trade, as Castlereagh, the Foreign Secretary who was now plenipotentiary in France, was expected to insist. Wilberforce knew him as 'one of our most determined opponents previously to the Abolition, though I really believe fairly co-operating with us ever since',[12] and if Castlereagh had not much feeling for the blacks, he knew that Britain's mercantile interests now coincided with those of 'Wilberforce and co.', as he called them.

Wilberforce again wondered whether to cross to France but his lack of French, and a sense that his own strength lay in the House, dissuaded him. He wrote instead to Talleyrand, and approved the African Institution's decision to send the French-speaking Macaulay as an encyclopaedia of Abolition information, who left London on 21 May with Wilberforce's instructions to promote a French Bible Society as well.[13]

Three days later a rumour that the French would recover their colonies without being required to abolish, sent Wilberforce hurrying

9

to the Chancellor of the Exchequer, his fellow-Evangelical (though a solemn, stodgy one) Nicholas Vansittart. Wilberforce proposed another Address to the Throne, to pray that the colonies be yielded on no other terms. Vansittart warned him this would be resisted by the Ministry. Wilberforce argued to no avail,[14] and since any public display of dissent would harden the French,[15] he sadly yielded. The next week was so busy with charities (the solicitor of the society for destitute Lascar seamen had run off with the funds) that he was sleepy in sermon time that Sunday, and his dreams ranged to Paris, wondering why Macaulay had not written.

On 31 May Wilberforce had the 'mortification' to learn that Macaulay had failed in both his missions and was on his way home. Wilberforce told Lady Olivia Sparrow that he did 'not despair of succeeding even within the short compass of my little span'[16] of achieving both undertakings, but he waited anxiously for details, while June came in with an unseasonable north-east wind and a warm 'mizzly rain', and Lizzie and little Henry were miserable with measles.

Lord Sidmouth, the Home Secretary, had sent round a note asking him to call, and on the morning of 3 June Wilberforce heard official details of the French treaty. He poured it out ungrammatically in his diary: 'France to receive back all her colonies . . . and to abolish in 5 years!!! Alas! Alas! How can we hope she will in 5 years with so many additional motives to cling to the Trade give it up in 5 years. My spirits are quite lowered by it, yet let us do what we can and trust to God's blessing on our labours.'[17] They must pin their hopes on the Tsar.

On Sunday Wilberforce managed to clear his mind for worship, but thoughts of the disaster to international Abolition rushed in on Monday 'and grieved me deeply'.[18] He sat through a committee at Suffolk Street on the condition of liberated negroes but his mind stayed far away, appalled by a traffic of fresh slaves out of Africa, by five more years of misery and blood.

That evening Castlereagh returned in triumph to a packed House of Commons after his long absence as Britain's plenipotentiary. As he entered from behind the Speaker's Chair and Members saw the peace treaty under his arm, the House rose in thunderous cheers, loosing the pent-up feelings of victory after twenty-one years of war. Only Wilberforce sat, silent in his place, head bowed.[19] Had his first consideration been popularity, as Hazlitt charged[20] who never knew him personally, he would not have spoiled that moment.

After Castlereagh had moved that the treaty do lie upon the Table, Wilberforce rose to explain his attitude, which he said was no less patriotic. 'But . . . I cannot but conceive that I behold in his hand the death-warrant of a multitude of innocent victims, men, women, and children. . . . When I consider the miseries we are about to renew, is it possible to regard them without the deepest emotions of sorrow?' He supposed that only the most imperious and almost irresistible necessity had caused the noble lord to sign such a treaty. 'For my own part I frankly declare no considerations could have induced me to consent to it.' He confessed his extreme regret that after so long a fight, when he thought he was 'nearly in possession of the great object of my life . . . when the cup is at my lips it is rudely dashed from them, for a term of years at least, if not for ever.'[21] He sat down, almost in tears.

At Camelford House next day Grenville, Grey, and the Duke of Gloucester too, disgusted him by treating it as a glorious opportunity to needle the Tory ministers.[22] The same evening after dinner at Thornton's the newly returned Macaulay read out Talleyrand's answer to Wilberforce, translating as he went. 'All flummery,' was Wilberforce's verdict, though he could not help smiling at the wily excuse that if England had taken nearly twenty years to abolish, why should she grudge France five.[23]

The Allied sovereigns had now arrived with Blücher and Metternich. Tsar Alexander was at Pulteney's Hotel, a mere two miles from Kensington Gore, having refused St. James's Palace. All hopes centred on him; the laborious letter had been finished, translated and despatched. Walking back next afternoon through Green Park from the founding of the Kensington, Chelsea and Fulham Bible Society Auxiliary Wilberforce saw the excited crowd to which the Tsar had waved and bowed from the balcony whereas the Regent had not dared pass through it for fear of being hissed.[24]

All London was in fête and Wilberforce took Dean Milner and the newly-married John Harford to view the illuminations. After admiring the fairy lamps decking Carlton House he insisted, to Harford's dismay, on alighting from the carriage in the middle of a shoving, good-humoured mob to get a better view. 'Mr. Wilberforce was much amused,' records Harford, 'and appeared little aware of the difficulty I had in guiding and protecting him, for we several times narrowly escaped being run over, and in one place got jostled amongst a set of pickpockets.'[25] They regained the carriage, were back at Kensington Gore by eleven, where 'Harford found a note instead of his wife',[26] she having been summoned to a relative's deathbed.

On the Saturday afternoon during a family dinner party Wilberforce was handed a command to wait on the Emperor of Russia next day,[27] a most exalted honour for a private commoner in the world of 1814. He rose specially early that Sunday morning to pray, and went to the Lock Chapel at Hyde Park Corner incongruous in court dress, with sword, leaving before the end of the sermon to walk the short distance farther to Pulteney's Hotel. The Tsar was not yet back from the Greek Church. Escorted at last into the presence, Wilberforce was about to kneel and kiss the imperial hand when the tall handsome Alexander seized Wilberforce's and shook it warmly. They were soon deep in Abolition talk, apparently in English. Wilberforce spoke of his fear that the French never would abolish in five years. The Tsar 'replied heartily, we must make 'em, and then corrected himself, we must keep 'em to it. He afterwards said when I was expressing my concern, "What could be done when your own Ambassador gave way?" '[28]

What was to be done perplexed Wilberforce, especially when this ambassador, Castlereagh, summoned him next morning, only to fob him off on the Prime Minister the other side of Downing Street, having been called away to the sovereigns. Lord Liverpool told Wilberforce that the French were strongly against Abolition and felt their colonies would not be ready for it when returned. Moreover they 'resented our dictating to them, believing that all our pleas of having abolished ourselves or urging them to abolish on grounds of Religion, Justice, Humanity were all moonshine, mere hypocrisy'.[29]

With this swimming round his head Wilberforce went to a committee meeting of the African Institution.[30] Lord Liverpool seems to have touched Wilberforce's chord of respect for authority, for when Romilly urged a great public meeting of the friends of Abolition to consider petitioning Parliament, or the Regent, to amend the treaty, Wilberforce ('who is always afraid of giving offence to ministers,' Romilly noted[31]) objected that the resolutions might be too violent, and that anyway nobody would come – they were all gaping at Blücher and the allied sovereigns. He was overruled by Gloucester, Grey, Lansdowne, Erskine and most of the others.

His fears were unjustified. With only four days' notice the Abolitionists packed out the great room at the Freemasons' Tavern with peers (mostly Whig) and M.P.s, with lawyers, clergy, and gentry from the shires, many of whom had come up to London for the peace celebrations and the sovereigns, until every chair was taken and men thronged the aisle. The meeting had begun when Wilberforce arrived, leaning on John Harford's arm, with head sunk on breast. A lane quickly opened and he heard cheering. 'Have you caught what is going on?' he whispered as they walked towards the platform. Harford replied: 'They seem to me to be all cheering you.' Wilberforce emerged on the platform. The room burst into loud applause which continued for some minutes before Lord Grey could resume his elegant, classically cold oration.[32]

Wilberforce then rose and it was difficult to believe that the frail little man who had been led up the aisle was the speaker who now entranced and enthused the audience until it resolved to petition Parliament, and to call for petitions from throughout the kingdom, that the treaty should be amended. To convince the Tory Ministry that this was no Whig ploy to embarrass them, the Freemasons' Tavern meeting resolved that their own petition should be presented by Wilberforce 'the father of our great cause'.[33]

In the ten days before the vital debate in both Houses, and in the weeks following, a deluge of 806 petitions descended on Westminster, with over a quarter of a million signatures from the British Isles' small population of some fourteen million.[34] Castlereagh admitted that it was the voice of the nation, that hardly a village had not met and petitioned on the subject. It was a display of national conscience, for few of the signatories knew much about economic policy, which would have been inconceivable thirty years earlier at the time of Wilberforce's Conversion, and was in itself an unconscious tribute to the deep change in attitudes to moral questions which he himself had done so much to bring about.

Wilberforce drew up the Address to the Regent for amendment of the treaty, to move after he had presented the Freemasons' Tavern petition, in terms as uncontroversial as possible, because 'the whole efficiency of the measure appeared to me to depend on the Address passing unanimously'.[35] Thus he did not insert a clause fettering the Crown's right to dispose of French colonies, knowing Ministers would oppose it, and at the opposite end of the political spectrum he took particular pains to secure the co-operation of Whitbread, the unabashed Bonapartist.[36]

He meant to prepare his speech carefully, but what with taking the chair at a public meeting for Blücher, and having Clarkson to dinner whom the Tsar had received with a group of Quakers, he had not worked on it by the day of the debate, 27 June. A summons to Downing Street for discussions with the Prime Minister and the Foreign and Colonial Secretaries – a quick call on Gloucester – further talk with Babington, who had long been a kind of Parliamentary Private Secretary to Wilberforce – not a quarter of an hour's quiet before entering the Chamber; and no outline of a speech in his head.[37]

When he knew his mind as plainly as now, Wilberforce was at his best speaking extempore. He soon had the House with him as he urged that the obnoxious clause be rescinded, and completely quiet as he reached his peroration: 'When the heads of all those now living are laid low, and the facts which now excite such powerful feelings are related by the pen of the cold, impartial historian; when it is seen that an opportunity like the present has been lost, that the first act of the restored King of France was the restoration of a trade in slavery and blood, what will be the estimate formed of the exertions which this country has employed, of the effect which they have produced upon a people under such weighty obligations? Surely no very high opinion will be indulged either of British influence or of French gratitude.'[38]

Whitbread, who thought the French had nothing to be grateful for in being given Louis in exchange for Napoleon, 'growled and others

showed disinclination'.[39] Lord Holland, the slave-owning Whig abolitionist who listened to the debate from under the gallery, hoping it
would embarrass the Tory Administration, thought that 'Wilberforce
is trimming and shabby in the extreme but many good men and all
neutral men go with him. Romilly made the best speech ever made by
him. . . . It had a surprising effect. To me, who am perhaps too peaceable a man, it appeared in point of judgement, not of justice, too bitterly
sarcastic on Wilberforce and the compliers with Government. It cut
them to the quick. . . .'[40] Despite those schismatic roarings from
fellow-Abolitionists, the Address passed without a division. It passed
the Lords also, and from then onwards it was politically impossible for
Castlereagh to do other than work on the French to abandon the
Trade.

The scene now shifted from Westminster to Paris, and to Vienna
where the Congress would shortly gather: the Abolitionsts wanted
the Congress of Vienna to outlaw the Slave Trade and declare it piracy.
For the next months the leading actors in the drama were Castlereagh
in Vienna, doggedly attempting to carry out the will of the nation;
the Duke of Wellington, now British Ambassador in Paris and strongly
Abolitionist; and Thomas Clarkson. Wilberforce had tried to dissuade
Clarkson from going to Vienna, fearing that Castlereagh would thereby
feel he was not being trusted; if he succeeded he would resent sharing
the credit, if he failed he would 'allege *you did not leave the whole to me*'.[41]
Clarkson then wanted to try Paris. Wilberforce ordered him to keep
away from his revolutionary friends and not to publish anything in his
own name, an interdict which Clarkson 'felt to be very heavy indeed'.[42]
But Wellington received Clarkson so warmly that he considered himself loosed from the interdict, and for the rest of that summer did much
for the Abolition cause in Paris, thus disproving Wilberforce's prejudice: it derived from Clarkson's Radical reputation in government
circles, and his vanity: Clarkson always felt underrated whereas Wilberforce genuinely considered himself overrated.

Wilberforce kept up the pressure, corresponding privately with
Wellington, and publicly with Talleyrand 'to chase away that base
and detestable suspicion which I hear is so common in France, that
we are acting from mercenary or malicious motives, not withstanding
all we talk about Justice and Humanity'.[43] It is a suspicion still held in
different parts of the modern world, though not by any who have
faced the evidence.

He prodded Lord Liverpool too, offering the idea that the French
be bribed with the gift of a British-owned island. Liverpool agreed in
principle but feared that one island might not look enough and, he
asked Wellington, 'Where are we to stop? Mr. Wilberforce and his
friends evidently think that the Abolition of the Slave Trade is not only
worth one island but that it is worth anything and everything.'[44] After

infinite pain and difficulty Wellington extracted some concessions from the French during the winter of 1814–15.

The whole situation changed on Napoleon's return from Elba. He included among his decrees the total Abolition of the French Slave Trade, on 29 March 1815, hoping to win favour from British public opinion. When the Bourbons returned after Waterloo they did not dare rescind the decree. 'Whatever your opinions may be in other respects of Napoleon,' wrote Lady Holland when imploring Wilberforce's help in easing the conditions of exile in St. Helena, 'you cannot forget that he was the only individual in authority who abolished the Slave Trade without delay or limitation.'[45]

French Abolition was soon a dead letter. Even before the British had entirely evacuated Gorée 'one of our officers . . . witnessed the embarkation of 200 slaves on board a French vessel,'[46] and evidence of evasion trickled in from Senegal and elsewhere and the ports of France as slave ships fitted out.

CHAPTER TWENTY-FOUR

The Black King

Once when all the Wilberforces paid a week's visit to Broomfield, Henry Thornton wrote to Hannah More: 'I feel much pleasure in thinking that I had with me my old chum. We shall go down the hill together differing a little, but not much and preserving all our affection and good humour.'[1] Neither of the two doubted that Henry, though never robust, would survive his chum. In the late autumn of 1814, however, Henry fell seriously ill with tuberculosis ('consumption') and moved to the better air of Kensington Gore while the Wilberforces borrowed Barham Court, Teston, from Baroness Barham, the late First Lord's daughter.

Wilberforce had forebodings when he left Gore House after seeing Henry on 13 January 1815 to return to Kent, though still hoping for recovery. A few days later a note came that Thornton might not last the night. Wilberforce hired a post chaise, got as far as Palace Yard and heard that his dearest friend was dead.

Next morning at Kensington Gore Wilberforce saw the body, laid out but not coffined. 'I stood for some time looking upon his poor emaciated frame; I cannot say countenance for that was no more. I should not have known him so ghastly was the face, so discoloured, so meagre. I was shocked at first, but Reflection corrected my erroneous impression. I said to myself what was said by the angel to one of our Saviour's faithful female attendants, *He* is not here, *He* is gone to Paradise. . . .' The faithful nurse who had led him into the death room began to weep. 'I observed to her, *This* is not our friend. This is but the earthly garment which he has thrown off. The man himself, the vital spirit has already begun to be clothed with immortality.'[2]

'Poor Wilberforce,' added Hannah More when comforting the widow, 'he has lost a great part of himself – his right hand in all great and useful measures. Heavily indeed will he go down to the House of Commons without his own familiar friend.'[3]

Mrs. Henry Thornton clung to Wilberforce. Thornton wisely had not named him as guardian to the nine children but instead a childless couple, young Robert Inglis, afterwards baronet and M.P., and his wife.* Within a few months Marianne herself lay dying of tuberculosis at Brighton. The Wilberforces came down, and he remained sanguine but, as Mary Inglis said, 'His feelings are so much carried away by the impulse of the moment.'[4] The disease moved remorselessly as Marianne well knew. To Wilberforce she said: 'God is gently leading me to that blessed place which he has provided for those that love him,' and to her eldest daughter, then seventeen, she spoke of 'that warm and steady and uninterrupted affection' between her Henry and Mr. Wilberforce. 'He is the tenderest wisest friend that he ever possessed, that you can ever have, and I should not leave you in peace if I did not think that he would be consulted on every occasion.'[5]

The deaths of the Thorntons were the first of several shadows which fell across Wilberforce in the first years of the Peace. There were more deaths, including that of his sister Sally Stephen, after a very short illness, which sent James Stephen into paroxysms of grief.[6]

Barbara nearly lost her father, old Isaac Spooner, the same month. One afternoon Wilberforce was called out of the Chamber by young William who though nearly eighteen burst into tears and said he had found his mother sobbing over a letter: Grandfather lay in a coma at Bath and might be dead already. If she might go to him at once she would pay half her fare. Wilberforce would have none of that, and sent William riding back with money for three fares. Within an hour or two Barbara, William and Robert were on the stage-coach spanking down the Great West Road.[7] Isaac Spooner recovered to live another two years.

The death of Sally drew Stephen even closer to Wilberforce: he bought a house in Kensington Gore and it was at this time that he extracted a promise that Wilberforce should be buried in Stoke Newington churchyard beside Stephen and Stephen's wives and mother: a promise which Wilberforce intended to be honoured; Westminster Abbey never entered his mind.

But if the brothers-in-law were closer personally, Stephen already was lost as a Parliamentary colleague, having resigned his seat in 1815 in protest at the Government's refusal to support a Registry of Slaves Bill. This Bill would bind colonial legislatures to register all slaves kept in each island, which had been done in Trinidad (where order in council was sufficient) since 1812. Once the exact number of slaves lay on record no planter could add to his gangs from blacks smuggled in by slavers defying the Abolition laws; thus a Register would stifle smuggling, force owners to treat their slaves properly, thus preparing

---

* Inglis was an inflexible Tory. Brougham called him 'the bigoted baronet'. The Inglises proved very successful and affectionate foster-parents.

9*

them to become a 'free peasantry'. The Registry Bill was Stephen's pet project. In the debate of 1815 it was blocked by the Tory Ministry, which he supported consistently in general politics; he carried out a threat made the previous year, and resigned despite Wilberforce's pleas and arguments.

In the spring of 1816 Wilberforce himself launched a further bid for the Registry Bill, now 'my chief Parliamentary object',[8] as he wrote to John Harford, who with his wife was travelling on the Continent to further his knowledge of the arts.* The planters indignantly denied that large numbers of slaves had been imported illegally, and certainly not to Jamaica. Wilberforce's information pointed the other way, even for Jamaica, which at first he had believed to be clear; he admitted that most of the slaves were smuggled from Cuba and the Spanish Main, not direct from Africa.

He wrote vast private letters, despite his bad eyesight, to Lord Bathurst the Colonial Secretary (Apsley, the friend of his youth) with much underlining and double-underlining, to prove that slaves poured in.[9] Bathurst begged delay to see whether the colonial legislatures would pass Registry Bills themselves, a course which Wilberforce dreaded in view of their previous failure to take effective steps to protect the slaves, whatever laws went on statute books. Lord Castlereagh pressed this course also, and so did the Whigs, so that on the evening of 22 May 1816 'it was by the united and strong pressure of Sir Samuel Romilly, Brougham and Horner',[10] that Wilberforce was reluctantly led to give up the intention of giving the Bill a First Reading as an opportunity for general discussion.

Then came the news of a slave revolt in Barbados, which was instantly ascribed to the Registry Bill having raised hopes of immediate Emancipation: 'Mr. Wilberforce and his adherents . . . have created a volcano,' wrote Langford Lovell Hodge, the Codrington agent in the island. '. . . Indeed I believe these calamities will be to them sources of real pleasure.'[11] The rising was suppressed quickly but led to violent attacks on Wilberforce, in and out of the House, especially by two widely distributed pamphlets written by Joseph Marryatt, father of Captain Marryatt the novelist. He was M.P. for Sandwich and agent for the island of Grenada. Wilberforce privately called the second a very scurrilous pamphlet abounding in the grossest misstatements which might better be termed lies.[12] He grieved at the charge of doing mischief and exciting insurrection, for it was to avoid stirring up the slaves that he had deliberately abstained from crying out their miseries by public agitation at home.

* The phrase comes in a long letter of 9 July 1816 (in Duke MSS) which is a curiosity. To save Harford paying heavy postage Wilberforce first filled eight sides or 2 quarto sheets folded, in black ink. Instead of a third sheet he wrote in *red* ink between the lines of the entire first four sides! Harford (a Quaker turned Anglican) acted as Wilberforce's link with the restored Pope Pius VII.

Wilberforce believed slave-owners themselves were victims of an evil system,[13] especially those not living in the islands but sitting in the House beside him or opposite; thus he laid himself open to a charge, which was never expressed in his lifetime, that he put the well-being of planters before that of slaves. Wilberforce was entrammelled in his own humanity: he always believed the best of any one unless forced to the contrary; even then the actual sight of the offender would generate kindly feelings of mitigation.[14] A Quaker said of him that 'he looked on his fellow men through a happy medium. . . . He was no backbiter with his tongue.'[15]

A little venom might have been in order when the Registry Bill was debated at last in the summer of 1816, in the shadow of the Barbados insurrection.[16] Venom could not, however, have saved the Bill, and Wilberforce feared such might provoke the planters to worse repressions: they held the whip.

The campaign for Registration was further complicated by the current negotiations with Portugal and Spain for Abolition of their Slave Trades. Portugal, in return for financial aid from Britain, had abolished the Trade north of the Equator in 1815, but since the chief Portuguese traffic ran direct between Angola and Brazil the concession was almost worthless except as a token of what might be extracted if Britain persisted. With Spain the diplomacy had reached a point so delicate that a display of dissension in the Commons might harden the Spanish: this was why the Tory Foreign Secretary joined the Whigs Brougham, Romilly and Horner in urging Wilberforce to postpone the First Reading of his Bill.

The slow diplomatic campaign by Castlereagh and his ambassadors had already achieved more than the Congress of Vienna's toothless Declaration against the Slave Trade, which was all that had emerged from the high hopes of the Tsar's London visit. Wilberforce could not be one of the principals in the negotiation. He could only keep the diplomats to the pitch or strengthen their hands by stirring up Parliamentary oratory at appropriate moments. Thus on 3 July 1817 he wrote to Lord Grenville: 'When I consider how many lives, and still more how much greater an amount of happiness is in question, I cannot but hope you will excuse my imploring your aid if you can give it.'[17]

He could also feed them with dry facts ferreted by Macaulay, which took on life and horror under the pen of Wilberforce. His letters to Castlereagh, who in turn kept him informed at each stage, are almost all lost but some must have been like one he wrote to Grenville about the 'unrestrained great and continually increasing Spanish Slave Trade, or Trade under the Spanish flag'.[18] The well-armed vessels were not designed for human cargoes 'and as they are crammed full as ever they can hold, the miseries of the poor creatures are extremely aggravated'.

In one ship 340 blacks out of a cargo of 540 died on a shortish voyage.[19] Furthermore in areas near Sierra Leone where the African Institution had encouraged peaceful commerce and started schools, the chiefs had turned to their slaving again.

Castlereagh at last bought, in effect, a treaty from Spain in September 1817, abolishing the Trade north of the Line at once, and in three years to the South.* This Spanish treaty allowed British cruisers to search suspected vessels for slaves. Without that, as Wilberforce said, 'the Abolition might become a mere name'.[20] He deplored the stipulation that slaves must actually be on board before a ship could be seized, however much the Navy might suspect that she sailed to pick up human cargo, but Stephen, as the leading maritime lawyer, told him that the clause must stand.

Problems concerning rights of search entangled the Powers whenever they discussed the need to outlaw the Slave Trade and name it piracy, which would be the quickest way to make the Vienna Declaration effective. Such matters appeared regularly on the agenda of the congresses and ambassadors' meetings which were a feature of the post-war world: an Abolitionist lobby always appeared too, either Clarkson or William Allen the Quaker. Wilberforce did not travel abroad. Thus for all his correspondence and activity the details[21] are of little moment to the story of 'the work I have undertaken of redressing, if it may be, the grievances of the most oppressed class of the human species'.[22]

One enterprise brought him much hope and disappointment.

Henry Christophe, a black of remarkable talent and courage, born in slavery, had seized power in Haiti (or Hayti as it was then spelt) after the death of Dessalines. Christophe's writ ran only in the northern half of what had been French Sante Dominque, for a rival held the south, but since 1811, first as President and then as 'King Henry I' he had been creating a black-ruled country which should recover the prosperity and civilization of the former French colony. Whites had been removed by death or flight, slavery was abolished. He had reacted against all things French (except for admiring Napoleon as a man) and he had turned in 1815 to England for help – and to Wilberforce.

Wilberforce responded with enthusiasm. He took the most sanguine view of King Henry's genuine desire for the people's welfare, even to the extent of believing at first that every black in Hayti could read. Wilberforce received letters of elevated sentiment and a request for teachers. Then in August 1815 he had a black visitor from Boston,

---

* During the Commons' Committee on the Spanish Treaty Wilberforce records that 'Sir Oswald Mosley opposed most invidiously on the grounds of money and helping Spain against her colonies.' (MS Diary, 9 Feb. 1818). He was the great-great-grandfather of the twentieth-century Sir Oswald Mosley.

Massachusetts, one Mr. Prince Sanders who taught writing, arithmetic and geometry and wanted to go to Sierra Leone. When Wilberforce talked of Hayti, Sanders decided to go there instead, despite it being pointed out that he could not speak French. So Wilberforce sent him off carrying a recommendation to King Henry Christophe and a supply of vaccine virus 'properly prepared and secured',[23] with instructions on how to vaccinate the Haytians: if Wilberforce was after their souls and minds he did not forget their bodies.

Within six months Sanders was back, glowing with the King's graciousness and bearing letters and a verbal message: 'Tell the friends of coloured men all you have seen and heard in Hayti, and return with the professors I have been asking for.'[24] Wilberforce and Macaulay had already begun searching.

Prospects were cheerful but they must all act cautiously; enemies at home were 'eager to avail themselves of every possible ground for assailing our principles and motives',[25] as Wilberforce reminded Stephen when urging him not to write injudiciously to the 'Duke of Lemonade' (he meant the Comte de Limonade, the King's Secretary of State; it was Marmalade who had a dukedom, he was commander-in-chief and they both wore magnificent uniforms). Wilberforce kept as quiet as he could about the whole affair except to close sympathizers like Grenville: 'I have seen such proofs of the terror of Black Improvement among even the better kinds of West Indians . . . that every degree of opposition may be anticipated.'[26] Planters and agents who opposed instruction of their own slaves would do their utmost to nullify the Hayti project, because its success would be evidence that Emancipation did not lead to anarchy, that negroes were not intellectually inferior because of their colour or race. Wilberforce even urged King Henry to educate the women.

Macaulay went to Edinburgh to enlist 'professors' of classics, mathematics and surgery, not forgetting three rustic ploughmen to teach the plough, hitherto unknown in Hayti. Withdrawals and illnesses dogged him until the first party left in August 1816, at King Henry's expense. 'Oh what a business we had at last in getting off our people to Hayti,' wrote Wilberforce to Babington. 'We could not have effected the thing at all but through Macaulay.'[27] A parcel of Bibles went too. Wilberforce had intended to send specially prepared New Testaments in French and English in parallel columns, bound in Russian leather to discourage mildew and white ants, but the Bible Society slipped up and these were still not ready when another teacher left in November 1817. By that time, King Henry was reputed to have shot the Comte de Limonade at a public dinner but Wilberforce did not believe it, and he was right: Limonade was alive and sent a liberal donation to the Bible Society by the King's express command.[28]

Clarkson was active. King Henry appointed him Haytian agent in

Paris and entrusted him with a letter to hand to the Tsar at the Congress of Aix-la-Chapelle. Clarkson worked with Wilberforce happily and in January 1819, after return from the Continent, wrote him a long letter of consultation about a proposed treaty between Hayti and France.[29]

King Henry had shown remarkable powers in codifying the law, organizing education and instilling self-respect in his subjects; 'a very extraordinary man,' was Wilberforce's verdict, who was doing great good by lifting up a much injured race in Hayti, 'whence a still farther prospect opens,' or what might be done through black leaders elsewhere.[30] The Haytian experiment coincides with a shift in Wilberforce's thought towards a West Indian Emancipation earlier than he had believed possible, provided it came without violence.

But the sands were running out for King Henry. The streak of megalomania became more pronounced, he grew to be a tyrant rather than a strict father to his people; he was also increasingly libertine. In August 1820 epilepsy and a stroke incapacitated him, and since the autocrat refused to abdicate yet could not rule, the Duke of Marmalade led a rebellion. King Henry threw off his nominal Catholicism and Wilberforce's Bible teaching, and reverted to *voodoo*. His royal guard deserted and he shot himself in October 1820, and the state slipped back into anarchy. Wilberforce, however, maintained his belief in the King's genuineness. Though his system had been too rigid 'the word tyrant is unfairly applied to anyone who, possessing no more original advantages than Christophe and having been placed in such circumstances, is animated by as generous a wish for the improvement of his people as ever actuated a human bosom'.[31]

Eighteen months later followed a sad little footnote when King Henry's widow and daughters landed in England and sought out the Clarksons, who consulted Wilberforce. He replied to Mrs. Clarkson: 'I am persuaded for the benefit of the ladies it is much to be desired that you should accompany them to town. I must say that the idea of taking them to the Extremity of Scotland seems to me a very strange plan....'[32] On a snowy Easter Monday in early April 1822 Mrs. Clarkson brought the jet-black Madame Christophe and her daughters to the Wilberforces.[33] 'Dinner just going on the table,' Wilberforce scribbled to his cousin Mary Sargent when franking Barbara's letter to her, 'with an ex-Queen and 2 Ex-Princesses with others of inferior note for guests. . . .'[34] The evening passed in music, partly in talk, and the former royal family left, eventually to settle in Italy.

CHAPTER TWENTY-FIVE

Wage Slaves and William

'I have reason to believe,' wrote Wilberforce on 21 March 1817, 'both from what I have heard and read in print, that it is the plan, deliberately formed and acted upon by our West Indian opponents to run down myself and Mr. Stephen and Mr. Macaulay as their most forward opponents.'[1] One of their accusations stuck to Wilberforce long after its origin was forgotten, and still is mentioned in books or essays as if a proven fact: that he loved the black slaves yet did nothing for the white 'wage slaves' of Britain.

Wilberforce knew and repudiated the libel. He nearly broke his rule not to publish answers to personal attacks,[2] not that he minded losing reputation but because this false idea might damage the cause; and early in 1817, a time of economic distress and popular unrest, he suggested to Clarkson that it might be wider to postpone a move they had in mind for the slaves. 'My own notion is that considering the circumstances of the country it will be more politic not to bring forward any measure, at least early in the Session. Our so doing would subject us to the imputation, which has been sometimes most falsely cast upon us, of having our minds so filled with African and West Indian griev-ances, that we are insensible to the suffering of our own countrymen and our grand object should be to take off the false impression which has been made on the public mind.'[3]

The shadow of distress and unrest lay heavy on post-war Britain. Wilberforce in all good faith had helped to cause it by advocating the Corn Laws in 1815, by which no foreign corn should be imported until the price of home grown had risen to a certain figure; he wished the figure to be rather lower than Parliament decided, but even a much lower figure would not prevent the hunger, which few had foreseen. Like many others who accepted the Malthus theories of economics, Wilberforce believed he was helping the nation and especially the poor, whatever their temporary hardship, by resisting Free Trade and advocating Protection for British agriculture, as the only way to stop prices permanently rising. 'I wish you could see Mr. Wilberforce's speech,' wrote the poet Wordsworth to a friend, 'it is word for word what I had said by our fireside before,' and Wordsworth exclaimed to his sister that the Free Traders had talked a great deal of pernicious nonsense, and that nothing was more deplorable than the errors of the Mob.[4]

Wilberforce had not intended to speak on the question. He knew the mob hated the prospect of Corn Laws, yet he had reached his conclusion honestly. During his private devotions on the morning of the debate he saw he would be a coward not to make his position plain. Furthermore, in supporting the Government by voice as well as vote he might bargain a more favourable attitude to the Registry Bill.

The mob showed an ugly mood. Even Wilberforce feared for his windows and the safety of his wife after he had come out for the Corn Laws, and agreed to have a guard squad of four soldiers and a sergeant in the house for a few days; they were Scots, and obediently attended family prayers.[5] Pitt might have been amused.

The Corn Laws, the rising unemployment as soldiers and sailors were thrown off by the state, the ending of lucrative wartime contracts before overseas markets could be opened – all helped create misery for the common man while the rich displayed the dandified Regency extravagance which Wilberforce deplored. He grieved and marvelled that instead of the prosperity and glory which men had expected to follow victory, Britain suffered class strife and 'this ruinous decay which is now wasting the vitals of the country'.[6]

In the prevailing climate of economic thought, Wilberforce could not understand the roots of the trouble any better than his contemporaries. Nor did he probably fully realize the extent of the hardship caused by the quickening pace of the Industrial Revolution. Barbara prevented him travelling far; his days of personal investigation were over, he depended too much on information from others, yet was impatient with the tedium of newspapers being read aloud because of their small print. His view of industrial labour was dominated by memory of Boulton and Watt's iron works many years before, where he had watched strong men glorying in their craftsmanship at forge and steam engine. When he knew of suffering he sought to relieve it, as in his Parliamentary support of the Robert Peels, father and son, in their efforts for factory children. He had helped found a Society for the Relief of the Manufacturing Poor, and when two Manchester men wanted help in exposing 'cruel usage of poor children in cotton spinning', it was to Wilberforce they turned.[7]

But he supposed political agitators were the prime cause of unrest. He trusted the Liverpool Cabinet whose reaction of fear and repression has not won the approval of history. Harrowby and Sidmouth were personal friends whom he knew as mild and kindly men seeking the country's welfare; Castlereagh was his courteous ally in the fight against the foreign Slave Trade. Eldon, the Lord Chancellor so hated by the Radicals, 'is a man for whom I feel real regard. He once used to be a good deal at my house. . . . I believe him to be utterly incapable of the conduct imputed to him.'[8]

On the other hand he had a deep distrust of the Radicals, especially 'that worst of varlets, Cobbett',[9] whose activities he assumed were 'dictated by a wish to produce discontent and confusion'.[10] The dislike was mutual. Neither could acknowledge the passionate sincerity of the other. They never met in person, only through the spoken or printed word.* Cobbett had begun as a hack of Windham and even after turning to the side of the people he kept many of Windham's prejudices. Cobbett hated Wilberforce's desire to abolish bear baiting, had hated him for advocating inoculation against smallpox and for the campaign to encourage the growing of potatoes, two of Wilberforce's schemes for the welfare of the working classes. Cobbett was on firmer ground attacking the refusal of the Liberator to support the Norwegians in their desire for liberation in 1814, when the Allies blockaded them into surrender to Sweden: it was not one of Wilberforce's better decisions. 'Norway question a most distressing one,' he noted in his diary; after nine days' agonizing he concluded that the promise made to Sweden in wartime must be honoured, against the wishes of the Norwegians, 'but the idea of starving these poor people is shocking.'[11]

Cobbett persisted in a belief, probably acquired from Windham, in the virtue of West Indian Slavery: 'I believe our own laws for the treatment of slaves are . . . mild. . . . A *few* lashes; no *effusion of blood*; no contusion even; the number of lashes fixed; even the *degree of force* fixed.'[12] Wilberforce could have well retorted in a phrase of Wellington's: 'If you believe that, you will believe anything.' It was partly in defence of Slavery that Cobbett would write his most famous attack on Wilberforce some years ahead, remembered still when its invalidating context is forgotten.

Wilberforce's strongest ground of mistrust lay in the extreme Radicals' hatred of Christianity. They did not simply attack the defects of contemporary religion, which Wilberforce himself assailed in his gentler way: 'they conceive that they may safely avow,' as he wrote to Lord Milton, 'the most unqualified hostility to every species of religion as in itself a delusion, and as being at war with the morality and happiness of mankind.'[13] Since Wilberforce considered the State the guardian of the people's welfare he was bound to support its efforts to suppress blasphemous publications. He did not advocate the prosecuting of men for holding opinions, however pernicious, for that 'is to act on the

---

* The Hammonds' idea that Wilberforce could not reconcile his conscience to reading Cobbett is nonsense. He considered him 'a very able and influential teacher' (see Jay, *Autobiography*, p. 309) and subscribed to his paper.

principles of the Inquisition'.[14] They should be punished when they circulated 'injurious and corrupting matter, which if suffered to pass unrestrained, will vitiate by degrees the whole community'.[15]

He was not against atheists as individuals. Richard Carlile, the impassioned 'infidel' whose efforts and imprisonments did more than anyone's to secure freedom of the Press, was visited in Dorchester gaol by a kindly stranger whose face he did not recognize. After some conversation the stranger spoke of religion and Carlile demurred; he had made up his mind long ago. The stranger took out a pocket Bible. Carlile said: 'I wish to have nothing to do with that book; and you cannot wonder at this, for if that book be true, I am damned for ever!' 'No, no, Mr. Carlile,' cried the stranger, 'according to that book, there is hope for all who will seek for mercy and forgiveness; for it assures us that God hath no pleasure in the death of him that dieth.' They talked further, without visible effect on Carlile, who was astonished to discover accidentally after his release, when listening to a sermon by Jay, the Dissenting minister in Bath, that the stranger had been Wilberforce, who had recounted the conversation to Jay. Perhaps the prison visit formed a link in the chain of events which led Carlile at last to 'declare myself a convert to the truth as it is in the Gospel of Jesus Christ', though the theological views of this ex-freethinker turned a sort of Christian were decidedly odd.[16]

Wilberforce opposed Radical teaching against religion because he saw that the moral condition of the people mattered most; if material and mental progress became the only criteria the nation would lose its spirit. Thus Wilberforce showed interest in Robert Owen's socialist theories for the workers' well-being at his New Lanark mill, and had him read a paper about them after dinner at Kensington Gore which sent everyone to sleep except Barbara and her woman companion.[17] But when Owen in the most public manner declared war on religion Wilberforce sided with Owen's Quaker partner at New Lanark, William Allen, and spoke and voted against referring Owen's theories to a Commons' Committee;[18] any other course would have been inconsistent. Owen acknowledged this,[19] but the early twentieth-century Fabian writers shook their heads sadly that Wilberforce should oppose a reformer merely because he excluded religion.* These Fabians who wrote at the end of an age of social progress which was based, thanks partly to Wilberforce, on Christian ethical standards and principles, failed to foresee what happens when a nation rejects religion. A century or so later men know about the crushing of freedom of thought in atheist Soviet Russia; of the endurance of religion under persecution; and of the Russian Christians, whether intellectuals and writers or obscure citizens, who uphold the liberty of the human spirit. Wilberforce's principle is vindicated.

* E.g. the Hammonds in *The Town Labourer*, p. 236.

He recognized the flaw in the Radical outlook. The agitators, and their poets and essayists, were in effect spreading to the working classes the doctrines of the Enlightenment which put man in the centre of his world and drove God to the edges, or abolished him. Wilberforce cared as truly as Cobbett or Shelley or Hazlitt, though such men refused to believe this. He opposed them because their doctrine must fail the very people whom they intended to help, but he encouraged Christian social reformers such as James Montgomery of Sheffield and Michael Sadler of Leeds, son of his own political agent in Yorkshire.[20] Throughout the heated debates in the era of post-war unrest Wilberforce continued to reckon himself as politically on the side of the poor.

One answer to Radical teaching, for Wilberforce, was to promote the education of the poor, 'educating our people up to our newspapers, if I may use the expression: by which they may be less likely to become the dupes of designing and factious men.'[21] Another was to encourage the increase of devoted clergymen who would promote 'true honest practical Christianity'.[22] He saw the role of clergy as that of reconcilers, harmonizers and quieters:[23] he would not have liked radical parsons who preached political revolt, even against glaring injustice, for revolt bred distress and confusion for the common man. Wilberforce's eye was on the happiness of families rather than on the creation of a distant better order through civil strife; the French Revolution had been proof enough of the misery such might cause, and he was too near to appreciate its lasting contributions to liberty.

He did not like idle clergy. The small group of determined infidel Radicals, concentrated mainly in London, did less harm, in Wilberforce's eyes, than clergy scattered across the land who neglected their flocks, set a bad example to the gentry and brought the name of Christ into disrepute. His ideal was a parson like Francis Cunningham of Pakefield near Lowestoft, whom Wilberforce found 'quite delightful' when they took a seaside house there for the autumn of 1816. In three years Cunningham and his wife, the sister of Elizabeth Fry, had got to know every parishioner, had strengthened education and fostered public worship, so that before the herring fishing fleet sailed for their annual ten weeks' expedition, when Wilberforce went to the special service, 'The whole was a very impressive scene. I saw the tears in and falling from the eyes of faces so rough as you would have supposed unused to the melting mood.'[24]

'Yet such is the man,' he pointed out to Earl Bathurst, 'who in many of our dioceses . . . would be frowned upon, calumniated and as far as possible thwarted and opposed,' because stigmatized by the epithet Evangelical or Calvinist. The next parish was neglected by an absentee rector and a curate who spent all his weekdays at a neighbouring boys' school, yet an offer to supply a working curate was spurned by the absentee rector, 'a very vicious bad man' who had the favour of a powerful bishop. How different England would be, suggested Wilberforce, if every parish had a man like Francis Cunningham or his brother John, a Clapham curate who now had the living of Harrow on the Hill (and stayed there fifty years).[25]

Wilberforce urged the justice and wisdom of encouraging Evangelicals. Believing that much of the prejudice sprang from ignorance he urged the Prime Minister to taste their sermons, or send his wife. Lord Liverpool vaguely promised, chatting with Wilberforce behind the Throne in the House of Lords, to attend to their claims yet did nothing. Except for Henry Ryder, Lord Harrowby's brother who was made Bishop of Gloucester in 1815, no avowed Evangelical received an English diocese until 1827 when Wilberforce's cousin Charles Sumner, to whom George IV had taken a fancy, was translated to Winchester by direct intervention of the King.* As for lesser preferments in the gift of the Crown or of the Lord Chancellor, Wilberforce saw them go to 'notorious and bitter opponents of the Bible Society' which Liverpool professed to support.[26]

The British and Foreign Bible Society was another of Wilberforce's recipes for England's happiness, the only religious organization uniting Churchmen and Dissenters. Wilberforce publicly applauded when Roman Catholics began one too.[27]

The Bible Society in its home distributions encouraged Christianity among 'the lower orders', and literacy too, as the young Lord John Russell, the future Prime Minister, pointed out in Parliament.[28] It affected the nobility and gentry also since county auxiliaries often enlisted as their active vice-presidents any local grandees of good repute even if, hitherto, of lukewarm faith. Wilberforce regarded the auxiliaries as a means for spreading vital religion because the county families, whether titled or only landed, were moulders of manners and morals in their districts whether for bad or for good; they had an influence comparable to that of television in a later age. Thus the spread of the Bible Society in the first quarter of the nineteenth century, against much opposition, helped to change the tone of English life.†

Wilberforce refused invitations to speak for county auxiliaries unless he had an obvious connection. Staying in Francis and Richenda Cunningham's parish of Pakefield in 1816 he broke his rule, and thus made a close friend of a man who would become an eminent Quaker, Joseph John Gurney of Earlham near Norwich, then aged twenty-eight. Gurney was Richenda Cunningham's brother. More important, he was brother of Elizabeth Fry and of Hannah Buxton, whose husband, the brewer

---

* He had been consecrated Bishop of Llandaff the previous year. Neither Porteus of London (d. 1808) nor Barrington of Durham (d. 1826) considered themselves Evangelicals.

† It is interesting that in the last quarter of the twentieth century, now that most 'foreign' countries have their own Bible Societies, the BFBS is again concentrating primarily on its 'British' role.

Thomas Fowell Buxton, thirty years in age and six foot four in height, had not yet entered Parliament.

Gurney drove over to Pakefield to beg Wilberforce address the Norwich Bible Society's annual meeting. 'Wilberforce very pleasant and interesting,'[29] he recorded in his diary. Wilberforce was charmed by this rather solemn Friend and agreed to speak, provided Gurney would accommodate in his capacious mansion of Earlham the entire Wilberforce party: Barbara, six children ranging from eighteen to six, two clergymen tutors, the private secretary, lady's maid, valet and possibly a nursemaid or two. Gurney and his wife already had a houseful coming for the meeting, including the Buxtons and both Cunningham brothers with their wives and children, but 'what house would not prove elastic in order to receive the abolisher of the Slave Trade?'

'A vast party in the house,' Gurney scrawled in his diary in his untidy handwriting. 'Never I think can society have been much more pleasant and I hope it has also been profitable. The Bible Society on the fifth day was *favored* and passed off delightfully – Wilberforce's speaking most interesting – about 60 at dinner at Earlham. The next morning dear Bris left us after affecting an lively supplication. . . . Since that we have been almost entirely occupied by the Wilberfs – his mind is indeed rich and varied and elevated. It is equally pleasant and instructive to enjoy his company.' They stayed a week, and in after years Gurney fondly recalled Wilberforce's 'rapid movements . . . the illumination of his expressive countenance, and the nimble finger with which he used to seize on every little object that happened to adorn or diversify his path. Much less can we forget his vivacious wit – so playful, yet so harmless – the glow of his affection – the urbanity of his manners – the wondrous celerity with which he was ever wont to turn from one bright thought to another. Above all, his friends will never cease to remember that peculiar sunshine which he threw over a company by the influence of a mind perpetually turned to *love* and *praise*. . . . As he walked about the house he was generally humming the tune of a hymn or psalm as if he could not contain his pleasurable feelings of thankfulness and devotion.'

Gurney enjoyed their walks through the Earlham gardens and fields, listening to anecdotes and information and wisdom as the Wilberforce mind hopped like a bird from branch to branch. Yet it was not a monologue. Wilberforce was too inquisitive, too good mannered for that. The timing of his day, however, was not exactly convenient: late down, and at his sparkling best about midnight in the Parliamentary tradition. Gurney was gravely amused at Wilberforce's habit of allowing the morning to glide away in the joys of conversation, until the hour for catching the post loomed upon him, whereupon a sudden explosion of letter writing while friends and relations hunted for missing papers

and the household willingly endured convulsions of inconvenience to
serve this adorable little man, whose selfishness was entirely unconscious and totally forgiven.

Fowell Buxton, at the time of this Earlham visit, was busy in his
ponderous way with schemes to relieve the near-starvation which the
bad times had brought to Spitalfields, the weaving village on the
eastern edge of the City of London. This philanthropy, and Buxton's
interest in penal reform, laid the foundation of Wilberforce's affection
for his eventual successor. Elizabeth Fry and her husband, a banker,
were not at Earlham. Wilberforce must have known of her pioneering
work to relieve the miseries of women prisoners in Newgate which
she had begun the previous year, because he had never dropped his
long-standing concern with prison conditions, and indeed had caught
a cold that same winter visiting Bury St. Edmunds gaol (he spelt it
goal[30]) when staying with Barbara's cousin Lord Calthorpe, the
patron of Bramber, 'dear faithful Calthe'.

It was not for another sixteen months that the Buxtons brought
Elizabeth Fry and her husband to dinner at Kensington Gore on a
February evening. The previous day the Wilberforces had attended a
large dinner at Stephen's to honour, by eloquence, prayer and what
must have been somewhat sad feasting, the birthday of poor Sally,
dead two years.[31] They now had a thoroughly Gurney evening. Accom-
panying Hannah Buxton and Elizabeth Fry were their spinster sister
Priscilla and a brother-in-law, Sam Hoare. 'Very interesting talk
indeed,' Wilberforce recorded.[32] His mind was full of slave affairs,
because three days earlier Lord Castlereagh had sought to impress
upon him the wisdom of postponing Emancipation until the entire
Atlantic Slave Trade had been abolished[33] – it was not abolished until
about 1860. But Wilberforce listened rapt as Elizabeth Fry in her
distinctive Quaker dress described the sufferings and sorrows of
women prisoners in Newgate. After the ladies withdrew, Buxton told
him as they drank their port 'many most interesting facts respecting
convicts', especially the damage done to boys cooped up with lusty
men; this problem of sodomy in prisons had engaged Wilberforce's
attention several years earlier.

Wilberforce wanted to see Elizabeth Fry's work. Next morning,
after a naval officer had been to breakfast about a Sailors' Association,
and Wilberforce had called at his oculist, he took Barbara and two
young women guests to Newgate. He was profoundly impressed by
the order and quiet that Mrs. Fry had produced among the female
prisoners whose savage behaviour had once been a by-word. She had
helped them by her school and her comforts and, as he specially
approved, by teaching them to help themselves. The cold damp of
early February in the prison seemed a little less grim because of
Elizabeth Fry. He then talked with five boys under sentence of death,

forced to spend their last days 'with the refuse of society'. He discussed matters with the governor, Brown, and Cotton the chaplain, but noted in this connection 'the place from its construction bad'. [34]

During the following week Mrs. Fry called with Mrs. Steinkopff, wife of the Lutheran pastor in London for whom Wilberforce had raised a fund when Napoleon's campaign in North Germany had ruined them. Mrs. Fry wanted him to secure pardons for two women about to be hanged for forgery, who were of the group whose characters had been changed by the Classes, for the Home Secretary had refused. Wilberforce was powerless. During the night before their execution he lay awake, 'thinking of slaves' wretched suffering and partly of 2 poor women to be hanged this day – within 2 or 3 hours. Alas. How Bloody are our Laws.' [35] Mrs. Fry was to attend them to the scaffold. He wrote her a note: 'I think I need not assure you that I had not forgotten you this morning. In truth, having been awake very early this morning, and lying in peace and comfort and safety the very different situation of the poor women impressed itself strongly on my mind. I shall be glad, and Mrs. W. also I assure you, to hear your bodily health has not suffered from your mental anxiety and I will try to get a sight of you when I can to hear your account and remarks on the effects of the events of the last 4 days, both on the poor objects themselves and their prison companions.' [36]

He naturally supported Romilly's efforts to humanize the English criminal code ('the abominable system of punishments, and I fear of trials also,' Wilberforce had called it) [37] and Henry Bennet's demand for enquiry into the evils of transportation. Correspondence with Samuel Marsden had made Wilberforce aware of the cruelties perpetrated at Botany Bay and he exchanged hot words with Castlereagh, who claimed little was wrong. [38] Romilly, Bennet and Wilberforce campaigned together also against the Game Laws, and for the 'climbing boys', the children sweeps who were forced up twisting chimneys of town houses. [39] Flogging in the army had long been another 'object of my abomination', though he accepted sadly the current conviction that 'sailors must be scourgeable'. [40]

When Romilly killed himself in November 1818, deranged by grief at his wife's death, Wilberforce stepped into the breach and promised to present the Quaker petitions, organized by Joseph John Gurney, that capital punishment should be imposed only for the most serious crimes. Wilberforce wished he were young enough to take on the whole question of reform, but turning sixty, with the West Indian slaves and the Abolition of the foreign Slave Trade still needing his chief energy, he hoped, rightly, that his friend Sir James Mackintosh would make it his own mission.

He went down to the House with the petitions, his mind full of the subject, intending to put together a speech while sitting through the previous question. The House, however, was very noisy and Wilberforce could not concentrate. When the Speaker called him 'it appeared to me that everybody was in haste to get to dinner'. He decided to say a very few words extempore. 'But when I had begun,' he told Gurney, 'I found a very attentive and contrary to my expectation, a very sympathising audience so that if I could have collected myself sufficiently I would have gone somewhat into the *rationale* of the subject. But like a general whose troops were scattered abroad on the plain, I could not at once call them into order. So that I was fain merely to pour forth what was uppermost and this happened to interest my own feelings deeply, and when that is the case we often interest the feelings of others.'[41]

A typical Wilberforce effort, with a typical Wilberforce reaction: he sat down ashamed of his performance, and felt surprised and pleased to be thanked warmly. Greville the diarist said the speech 'reminded one of the better days of the House of Commons'.[42]

Wilberforce wanted reform, not revolution. With most of the House he had believed during the early months of 1817 that revolution lay only a hairbreadth away. He hated Sidmouth's system of employing spies such as the notorious Oliver, and he claimed to be the first to object to it.[43] Yet he accepted the evidence of plots and conspiracies, some of which in fact were provoked by the spies themselves.

He knew only too well about hunger in the land. He held that happier times would come if only the Constitution be preserved, by temporary repression if necessary, since preservation of the rule of law was more important than the personal liberty of a few agitators. This attitude cut across Party boundaries; a majority among the educated of England, though hardly of posterity, were in agreement that the Liverpool Government acted rightly in suspending Habeas Corpus in March 1817. But Brougham, Mackintosh, Romilly and Burdett emphatically disagreed.

Wilberforce did not reach his conservative position in this by automatic reaction, like Sidmouth. It was the puzzled decision of a man attempting as usual to see both sides of the question in the sight of God, not the 'moral equivocation' which Hazlitt called it in his *Spirit of the Age*. In one debate on the Suspension of Habeas Corpus his struggle to be fair and judicious became painful to watch, as cheers from one side of the House suggested to him unfairness to the other, then cheers from that side swung him back again, until to an observer in the gallery his speech became a shuttlecock.[44] No one could predict his vote. It went to Government.

In another debate on the Suspension, an attack on Wilberforce led to a memorable incident. Francis Burdett said with heavy sarcasm that he was 'astonished at the concurrence in this measure of an honourable *and religious* gentleman who lays claim to a superior piety. . . .' Burdett, mocking and taunting, used again and again the phrase 'honourable and religious', which provoked cries of *Order! Order!* from all parts of the House, for only 'honourable and learned', for lawyers, and 'honourable and gallant', for service officers, were in order.

Wilberforce, who had not intended to speak, caught the Speaker's eye and began, ominously, to suggest that the Member for Westminster was 'greatly mistaken if he thought that the sarcasm he had used did not rather injure himself than others – it was not those who talked loudest and longest about their love and admiration of the Constitution that were the most sincere in their professions.'[45] He then poured out what Brougham, who supported Burdett's politics in this but not his behaviour, described as a 'strain of sarcasm which none who heard it can ever forget'.[46] Burdett sat on the tier immediately behind Wilberforce, who spoke from the Opposition benches. To some of the Tories Burdett's head, held high, his back stiff with anger, actually appeared slightly above little Wilberforce as he stood. But when Wilberforce turned and spoke directly at Burdett, amid cheers, Acland thought it was 'like a giant dangling a dwarf'.[47]

A Whig whispered to Romilly that it outmatched Pitt himself, the great master of sarcasm. Romilly replied: 'It is the most striking thing I almost ever heard. But I look upon it as a more singular proof of Wilberforce's virtue than of his genius, for who but he was ever possessed of such a formidable weapon, and never used it!'[48]

With Habeas Corpus suspended, Cobbett fled abroad. Describing to 'Orator' Hunt the pleasures of America he wrote: 'Think of it. A hundred brace of woodcocks a day. Think of *that*! And never to see the hang-dog face of a tax-gatherer. Think of *that*! No Alien Acts here. No long-sworded and whiskered captains. No Judges escorted from town to town and sitting under a guard of dragoons. No packed juries of tenants. No crosses. No Bolton Fletchers. No hangings and rippings up. No Castleses and Olivers. No Stewarts and Perries. No Cannings, Liverpools, Castlereaghs, Eldons, Ellenboroughs or Sidmouths. No squeaking Wynnes. No Wilberforces. Think of *that*! No Wilberforces!'[49]

The glorious harvest of 1817 put an end to hunger and agitation. Before the next round of popular unrest and repression Wilberforce suffered a family trouble.

In the spring of 1817 Wilberforce became alarmed by the shiftless character of his eldest son William, nearly nineteen and being educated at home by a young Oxford clergyman, Matthew Rolleston, whom Wilberforce much admired. William had no intellectual interests or curiosity. He was idle and self indulgent, yet 'very kind and attentive' to his father. He had his father's mercurial temperament and a dangerous slice of his charm, but as the diary was told, 'I fear he has no energy of character or solid principle of action.' Wilberforce began consulting friends and relatives. Dean Milner, who took 'truly kindly interest in Wm', Lord Calthorpe, William Spooner and Rolleston himself 'all most decided for his going from home. Hence 'tis needful, if only to prevent its being said we ruined him by keeping him here. . . . Present plan is to wait in hope of Wm's getting into Oriel by some unexpected vacancy.'[50] Oriel was not Rolleston's college but he may have recommended it, and Wilberforce had been impressed by a conversation, sitting on the top of the Oxford coach in March 1815, with a young tutor of Oriel, Edward Hawkins the future provost, who had just escaped from Paris as Napoleon entered after the return from Elba.

As late as June 1817 Wilberforce still had hope of Oriel College, Oxford, but no vacancy came, and at Michaelmas William entered the much larger Trinity College, Cambridge, which Wilberforce chose in preference to his own St. John's, possibly because the Sumner cousins had done well there. A more expected choice would have been Queens', but Milner was old now and in poor health. William in his first term tried to behave worthy of his name, though his father saw the idleness of his own undergraduate days repeated.[51]

For the holidays of 1818 Wilberforce fulfilled a long-standing promise to introduce the family to the beloved Lake District. First he asked Southey to look for a house in Keswick, then changed his mind, and a stream of letters descended on Dorothy and William Wordsworth,[52] who found two small houses side by side at the bottom of their own hill at Rydal beyond Ambleside. Bringing five of their seven house servants to be bedded out on villagers, the Wilberforces made a tribal migration rather than a family move: their party numbered no less than nineteen plus horses.

The servants came first – the old cook grumbled that the first floor of Kensington Gore would swallow both houses. A few days later Dorothy Wordsworth heard that the family had arrived. She found them at dinner, except for Wilberforce and the two youngest still on the road, and all talking at once and brimming with delight at the rooms and gardens. Even Mrs. Wilberforce, whom Dorothy later thought rather whining and a little sanctimonious, charmed her at first, while the two girls, Barbara (19) and Lizzie (17) looked lively, animated, modest and unaffected, 'in short just what well-educated girls ought to be'. Wilberforce's carriage drove up and 'all ran to meet him'. Dorothy had not seen him for nearly twenty-five years and she felt much affected at his feeble body but soon discovered he was stronger than he looked, and he even walked up Skiddaw, though possibly not to the top, and got wet. For all his weakness of lung, bowel, spine and eye, and the opium pills, Wilberforce had a remarkable capacity for walking until almost the end of his life.

Dorothy Wordsworth, after being a close neighbour for six weeks, decided that 'There never lived on earth, I am sure, a man of sweeter temper than Mr. Wilberforce. He is made up of benevolence and loving-kindness, and though shattered in constitution and feeble in body he is as lively and animated as in the days of his youth.'[53]

Southey called, and marvelled at the 'pell-mell, topsy-turvy and chaotic confusion' of the Wilberforce apartments, in which the wife sat like Patience on a monument while her husband 'frisks about as if every vein in his body were filled with quicksilver'.[54] They returned the call and Southey was highly amused: 'such a *straggling* visitor – he was longer *going, going, going* than a bad bale of goods at an auction; and even when he began to go, he brought to at the bookcase on the stair-case, and again in the parlour, to the utter despair of his wife, who resigns herself with comical composure to all his comicalities.'[55]

The older boys did great walks on the fells,[56] and then Robert and Samuel returned to their schools. And William to Trinity. His second year began satisfactorily except for some extravagance, until January 1819 when Wilberforce discovered that William had bought a second horse, for a high price, at a time when his father was already retrench-ing because of the bad times.[57] Nor was William reading hard enough, if at all. Wilberforce had a dread of idle young men who wasted their college years, and William was too weak a character to withstand the influence of undergraduates who took a sneaking pleasure in tripping up the eldest son of Mr. Wilberforce. 'O that my poor dear Wm might be led by thy Grace O God,' he wrote in his diary on the night of Sunday 10 January 1819.[58] He saw no sign in William of 'the great change'.

Two months later he was appalled to hear that William had told lies; had been convivially and beastly drunk on a Sunday night although his friend Blundell's body lay in the next set of rooms awaiting burial; and despite having written on Blundell's death 'as if affected by it and half penitent!!!!!!'[59] Next day Wilberforce wrote to Henry Venn, the late John Venn's son, who though only two years older than William was a Fellow of Queens', to ask for a candid report: 'I already know so much that you can scarcely tell me anything, I am very strongly inclined to remove him instantly from College.'[60] In his diary Wilberforce poured out his grief: 'O my poor Willm. How strange he can make so miserable those who love him best and whom really he loves. His soft nature makes him the sport of his companions, and the wicked and idle naturally attach themselves like dust and cleave like burrs. I go to pray for him. Alas, could I love my Saviour more and serve him God would hear my prayer and turn his heart. . . .'[61] It was fear of William becom-ing an idle profligate, rather than as punishment for any wrongdoing, which inclined Wilberforce to take him away.

Venn replied that suspending William would be best since he would

not read. Wilberforce decided not to let him come home for the present
though it tore at his heart: 'Alas my poor Willm! How sad to be compelled to banish my eldest son.'[62] Confiscating his new horse and stopping his allowance he placed William temporarily with John Cunningham
at Harrow, hoping to return him to Trinity the following year.

William took it well. The affection between father and son grew
deeper. Whereas Zachary Macaulay, a year or two later, was furious
with his brilliant, industrious Tom for failing in Mathematics, Wilberforce showered love with his discipline, and after good reports let
William come on a visit to the rich Evangelical Lady Olivia Sparrow
near Huntingdon 'to show him that I was pleased with him'.[63]

William did not return to Trinity. He was put to reading for the
Bar in the care of John Owen, the secretary of the Bible Society, and
promptly fell in love with the Owen's penniless daughter, Mary, a
very handsome girl in Wilberforce's estimation. They married early
the next year.

On 16 August 1819 Wilberforce worked in London, mainly on
Sierra Leone business, while in Manchester a peaceful meeting of
some 50,000 people in St. Peter's Fields, to be addressed by 'Orator'
Hunt, was broken up on the orders of a nervous Lancashire magistracy
with the unintentional loss of eleven lives and several hundred wounded.
Before the news reached London Wilberforce left on a round of country
house visits in Warwickshire and Worcestershire, and though he had
newspaper accounts read to him of 'the late melancholy transactions at
Manchester', and the widespread outcry in the nation, he felt he had
gathered no authentic version when Lord Milton wrote inviting him
to a Yorkshire County Meeting called to condemn the Lancashire
magistrates – an invitation which Milton would not have sent had
Wilberforce been the unbending Tory of later legend. Wilberforce
wrote back deploring that no official account had been published, since
false statements must prejudice the minds of men. He would give no
opinion, and would 'endeavour to keep my own mind unprejudiced'[64]
until he knew the facts, though certainly not approving a meeting
merely for recrimination.

Like all England he deplored the loss of life at 'Peterloo'. His chief
reaction was regret at an event which gave opportunity to 'those wicked
men who are endeavouring to destroy all that is valuable among us',
to exploit the 'humanity and generous feelings of our countrymen'.[65]
Had he attended Milton's protest meeting side by side with Fitzwilliam, whom Sidmouth dismissed from his lord-lieutenancy for so
doing, the sensation would have been tremendous, a total reversal of
his famous ride to York at the time of Pitt's Gagging Bill at 1795.
But the danger to the Constitution lay uppermost in his mind as he
thought of Peterloo. He did not call on the Government to hurry on

with Reform, but instead approved the Six Acts which were passed to limit further public meetings and the spread of sedition and blasphemy; his speech in the Peterloo debate caused Francis Place the Radical to dub Wilberforce 'an ugly epitome of the devil'.[66]

It was because Wilberforce was recognized as an independent and not a Tory that the Radicals tried hard to win him. When they failed they called in question the sincerity of his political independence. 'He reaps the credit of independence without the obloquy,' claimed Hazlitt in the famous newspaper essay reprinted in his *The Spirit of the Age*. 'Mr. Wilberforce,' he wrote with heavy sarcasm, contrasting him with the rigid Tory Eldon, 'is not a party man. . . . He has all the air of the most perfect independence, and gains a character for impartiality and candour, when he is only striking a balance between the *éclat* of differing from a Minister on some vantage ground, and the risk or odium that may attend it.'[67] Hazlitt's claim that Wilberforce acted from mixed motives, desiring to do right yet to be well thought of by the Crown and the Church, could not be accepted by anyone who knew Wilberforce personally or has studied the actual record. But posterity eventually accepted it as a true portrait, seeing him as Hazlitt's 'specimen of moral equivocation' who 'preaches vital Christianity to untutored savages, and tolerates its worst abuses in civilized states'.

Hazlitt gives his case away when he asks: 'What have the *Saints* to do with freedom or reform of any kind?' Wilberforce, with others of 'the Saints', would vote for Parliamentary reform in the future as in the past, but he rejected the Radical version. Not being a political prophet he did not see that the hierarchical form of constitution, which he regarded as the bulwark of British liberty for the lowest in the land, need not last for ever. Yet the moral sanction he gave to those who defended it did much to enable the constitutional development of Britain to continue gradually and peacefully with a minimum of violence.

Whether or not his political judgement was at fault it never sprang as Hazlitt asserted, from the humbug of 'fluctuating time-serving principle', but from deeply held conviction. An unpublished diary entry* demonstrates this, from the period just before the post-war suspension of Habeas Corpus. Lord Milton, whom Wilberforce had once regarded almost as a fellow-independent, had sat with him on the Secret Committee examining subversive activities; and Milton had agreed to its Report recommending Suspension, or so Wilberforce understood. Entering the Chamber after dinner at Babington's when Milton was up, he was therefore astonished to hear him attacking the Report. Milton's opinions were in fact sincere but Wilberforce did not believe it and was shocked, feeling misled and betrayed. He would have tried to speak but 'I felt myself so stupid and heavy from a good dinner that my powers for immediate action greatly dulled and still more

* Original punctuation retained as an example.

called to mind that Govt. would not help me about my Slaves etc and also I felt so indignant what I might have said I know not but I must now say that I never remember so treacherous a proceeding in any man of any principle. It shows how party spirit can blind a man and something may proceed from the habit of laying down the law. I never remember so unfair a proceeding Alas Alas. Yet I believe Ld Milton though he must be a violent party man, to be a good man, at least as good as is consistent with being so run away with by party feelings.'[68]

CHAPTER TWENTY-SIX

Queen Caroline

On 6 June 1820, almost six months after George IV's Accession, Queen Caroline returned from exile to claim her rights as Consort. Amid the cheers of the populace she drove across Westminster Bridge beside Alderman Matthew Wood, the moderately radical former Lord Mayor; it was his generosity to the debt-ridden Duke of Kent which had made possible Princess Victoria's birth on English soil.

Queen Caroline took up residence at Wood's house. The squabble between the new King and his separated Queen took a fresh twist, since Parliament was about to investigate the Queen's conduct as a preliminary to the Divorce Bill demanded by the King; the evidence had been brought down in the famous 'Green Bag'. Wilberforce like many others dreaded the damage that would be done to the nation: the Liverpool Ministry and the King had been wildly unpopular since Peterloo and 'the Mob' now had a figurehead whom they cast in the rôle of injured wife. Should she be voted guilty by the Lords, and divorced, the fury of the people might overturn the Throne. Wilberforce did not feel censorious towards a royal couple who were victims: 'We marry our Kings and Queens contrary to the laws of God and nature.'[1] He privately believed in Queen Caroline's adultery abroad, probably on information from Brougham, her Attorney-General, whose own confidential investigation had led him to try to stop her return, though now she was back he took her side.

Behind the scenes Brougham and Denman, her Solicitor-General, negotiated with the Ministry for a compromise which should avoid a divorce yet make the Queen 'go away at any rate'. The negotiations stuck at the apparently trivial question of the State Prayers. The King refused to allow the customary petition for the Consort, and the Queen refused to abandon her right to a place in the Liturgy, saying that to do so would be admission of guilt.

On the day after the Queen's return Wilberforce moved the adjournment of the 'Green Bag' debate, wishing to allow the parties time to reach a settlement. The thirty-four-year-old radical Whig, John Cam Hobhouse, Byron's friend, who had entered the House for West-minster that year, described the scene caustically in his diary:* Brougham defended himself, 'Tierney spoke next and gave Brougham a sly rap – then got up Wilberforce and proposed an adjournment of the question till Friday upon pure motives of charity to spare the public *the horrid and disgusting details* of the King's green bag and of the green bag which the Queen might bring against the King. Buxton seconded the motion – it caught like wild fire. Stuart Wortley and county gentleman after county gentleman rose to support the proposi-tion. Canning went under the gallery to speak to the Duke of Welling-ton who was there. Huskisson was sent to Lord Liverpool . . . Castlereagh was obliged in a sulky fit to consent to an adjournment. In any other times ministers would resign on such an occasion.'[2] Having nearly brought down the Government Wilberforce went home to Kensington Gore and to bed by 2 a.m. The mob were breaking windows of the King's courtiers and he heard that soldiers in the Guards verged on mutiny.

According to Hobhouse the idea of moving the adjournment had been put to Wilberforce by Buxton, as intermediary for General Sir Robert Wilson, the Queen's supporter, but nothing of this appears in Wilber-force's own diary. Next morning, 8 June, he wrote a letter and sent it by William to Carlton House: William and Mary were then living at Kensington Gore. The letter suggested that in view of the ferment the King should graciously accede to the Queen's demand for her rightful mention in the State Prayers of the Liturgy. Wilberforce received no answer.†

Life was a little distracted at Gore House because William had painful ear-ache, while his father pondered how to resolve the State crisis. Liverpool would resign if the Commons forced the question of the Liturgy against the King's wishes, and Wilberforce believed that the King would refuse to send for the Whigs and then the Army would mutiny: on 16 June the Third Guards were ordered out of London because the officers could not guarantee the loyalty of the men.

On 17 June Brougham called. He seems to have brought the con-fidential papers of his negotiations with the Ministers. Wilberforce read them carefully. He then decided to bring in a Motion for an Address to the Queen, for he thought he had found a basis for compromise. 'It was this,' he told his second son Robert, then in his last term at school. '*Her* Legal Advisers in their conference with the King's Ministers had sug-

---

* The entire episode of Queen Caroline is omitted from the published extracts (6 vols. 1911) and must be studied in MSS (British Museum).

† See *Life*, V, p. 56. This letter is not in the Royal Archives. Wilberforce's Manuscript diary for 8 June 1820 shows: 'I wrote to – and sent Wm with my letter. . . . Wm went to deliver a letter from me.' Wilberforce did not usually put blanks when he scrawled names into his diary.

gested that they pressed the restoration of her name to the Liturgy for the recognition of her rights and vindication of her character, and they added that if it could not be granted in substance, an equivalent might be found for it, for instance the recommendation of the Queen to any Court on the Continent. Well then said I, surely the Address of the H. of Commons,' assuring her formally that her giving up this only remaining point of dispute was not an admission of guilt, 'would be at least as good an equivalent as presenting at a foreign state. In truth it would have been a much better, and Mr. Brougham felt so. . . .'[3] Indeed, Wilberforce believed afterwards that Brougham had virtually suggested the idea that if the House humbly begged instead of the Crown demanding, the Queen would drop the point about the Liturgy and go away. What Wilberforce could not know was that the Queen was furious with Brougham for having tried to stop her coming to England.[4]

Friends in and out of the House approved and on 20 June Wilberforce gave notice that he would move a Humble Address to the Queen. He did not reveal the contents. Alderman Wood, M.P., guessed them. The Opposition seemed more than ever disposed to make the Queen a Party issue.

Wilberforce returned home to find two Spooner relatives, who had been to dinner, and he chatted a while. As he went up to bed 'I heard a knocking at the kitchen stairs door and Charles the footman's voice, "Sir, a letter from the Queen".'[5] It was in the writing of a lady-in-waiting at the dictation, Wilberforce decided, of Alderman Wood, and was signed in a very girlish hand: 'Caroline, Queen of England, Tusday [*sic*] the 20th Juin. 1820, Portman Street No. 22.' 'The Queen,' it ran, 'has heard with the greatest surprise and regret that such a religious and worthy character as Mr. Wilberforce should have given notice in the House of Commons this evening of his intention to move an Address to Her Majesty; the substance of which she is informed, is to renounce that most important right, of being restored to the Liturgy.

'A right which is so justly due to Her Majesty's conscience and her honour, against the foul accusations and slanderous attacks on her character.

'Her Majesty assures Mr. Wilberforce that she *never will abandon this point* – as her honour is dearer to her than her life; therefore trusts Mr. Wilberforce will take this into his serious consideration and not propose such a motion in the House. . . .'[6]

When he showed this letter next day to his seconder, Stuart-Wortley, they decided to change the motion slightly and postpone it by a day for the Queen to reconsider, and for Wilberforce to sound opinion. His decision went against the advice of all his other friends, some of whom pressed him to make his motion a defence of the Ministry. He saw, however, that all depended on his remaining

10

independent if an Inquiry into the Queen's conduct were to be avoided. The decision also annoyed the House, which (by Hobhouse's description) was 'as full as it could hold in expectation of Wilberforce's motion. . . . Wilberforce called by Speaker – did not appear – at last he came and said he begged to put off his motion until next day – something had occurred – he would not tell what. There was a cry of No No – but the House finally consented. . . . All business at a stand.'[7]

That evening Wilberforce had no time to go out to dinner and ate from a canister in the Speaker's room, talking with Charles Wynne of the Home Office (Cobbett's 'squeaking Wynne') and Stuart-Wortley, young Acland, Bankes and 'worthy Buxton'. He walked home through the June evening, calling at Stephen's. Here Brougham brought him a second letter from the Queen,[8] unsigned and composed by Brougham himself, in which she (or he) acknowledged Wilberforce's good intentions and her respect for Parliament and left the question more open. In the discussion at Stephen's, Brougham made a promise: he would press the Queen to give a definite pledge that when the Address was presented she would agree to her name being dropped from the Liturgy. But even as Wilberforce had been walking home from Westminster, Alderman Wood in a hackney carriage had been telling Burdett and Hobhouse of the Queen's anger with Brougham's propositions. She had sent him a note by Denman 'in very stormy language'. The equally angry Wood believed Brougham was double crossing the Queen. Hobhouse commented: 'in short, Brougham seems a most consummate scoundrel.'[9]

Whether or not Brougham had even shown the Queen the second, milder letter he had drafted for her, or had any authority to pledge her word to accept the omission of her name from the Liturgy, Wilberforce took him at his word and remained firm. There was no need for Canning to make a point of seeing him next day 'from fear', as Canning noted in his diary, 'of his vacillations.'[10]

The terms of the motion were polished by Sir Thomas Acland, the young West Country squire who was a warm disciple.* Wilberforce gave himself no quiet to prepare his speech, 'but God in whom I trusted graciously blessed me'.[11] That evening of 22 June 1820 the Chamber filled until Members could find no seats. – it was said that 560 Members were present. Greville the diarist could 'never remember to have seen the public curiosity so excited as on Wilberforce's motion.'[12] Charles Shore, Teignmouth's son, watched from the Gallery as Wilberforce spoke from the Opposition front bench.[13] 'It was an interesting spectacle to see the feeble and half-blind veteran led to

---

* Acland once received a letter (3 July 1818) which ended, scrawled along the top, with a Wilberforce apology for any errors as it was not read through: 'Forgive, and mend *your own* handwriting as well as mine.' (*Acland MSS*). It was Acland whose tree planting beautified the barren slopes of Dunkery Beacon. In a long life he was a pioneer of rural education.

his seat. And when he rose, accredited umpire and mediator in a great national dispute, he spoke well and worthy of the occasion.'[14] Wilberforce spoke with confidence – born of having received Brougham's written secret pledge, probably in a note passed in the Chamber, that the Queen had indeed promised to agree. The debate became noisy, with Burdett violent and bitter but very able; yet the uproar counted for less than Wilberforce's moral authority. At 5 a.m. the House gave a resounding *aye* by 391 to 124. He was deputed to present the Address.

Barbara and the younger children had left London for the summer holiday at Weymouth. Wilberforce spent a flea-bitten night in lodgings in Downing Street. (After the first night he ever spent there he wrote of being troubled by a flea, 'O how little a thing can trouble me, swagger as I may.'[15]) On Midsummer Day he went to Lord Calthorpe's house in Grosvenor Square, put on full court dress, and with Stuart-Wortley, Bankes and Acland drove to 22 Portman Place. A mob outside which cheered the Queen and forced passers-by to raise their hats had alarmed Barningham, Wilberforce's ex-secretary and hanger-on, who begged his master to creep in by the back door, not risk his life. The crowd had swollen in expectation of the deputation, and included several gentlemen on horseback. As Wilberforce alighted he heard boos and hisses and chants of 'Dr. Cant-well! Dr. Cant-well!' – a new nickname.

The Queen, flanked by Brougham and Denman in wig and gown, received the deputation upstairs. The slatternly odiferous Caroline looked stern and haughty as Wilberforce read the Address with its request that she graciously agree to the omission of her name from the Liturgy.

With dignity, she refused. Brougham stepped briefly on to the balcony. Apparently he gave a pre-arranged signal, for the M.P.s heard howling against themselves and the King which was frightening in intensity. Brougham escorted them downstairs and took pains for their safety until the coachman had driven them away.[16] That evening Stuart-Wortley read to the House the Queen's answer, 'with Wilberforce for prompter – they boggled and looked foolish.'[17]

Wilberforce had been invited to Battersea Rise for the weekend by the Inglises and his 'dear Marianne', Thornton's daughter, now twenty-three. Fearful for the Throne itself, and wounded by Brougham's apparent double-cross he arrived at Clapham, recalls Marianne, 'very low and dispirited . . .; when stepping out of the library window before dinner he caught sight of a gorgeous moss-rose that grew up the wall, and seeing how it transfixed him I gathered it. Oh the beauty of it. Oh the goodness of God in giving us such alleviations in this hard world. The bell rang for dinner, there was a large assemblage of notables to meet him, but there was no getting him to go in while he stood worshipping his flower, and when he had lavished all other endearments and admiration he ended with, "And Oh how unlike the Queen's countenance".'[18]

Brougham speedily managed to convince him that the Queen had taken matters into her own hands. Wilberforce therefore never revealed the secret pledge, for which Brougham was profoundly grateful. Yet Brougham did not disclose that he and Denman, when she asked how to answer the imminent deputation, had refused an opinion; they knew the crowd would be furious if she gave way, and they feared she would cast the odium on them. In the Brougham Papers is a witty doggerel in his own hand which further implies that he did not play fair with Wilberforce:

> Let spies and picklocks now no more assail
> The Queen, or join to fabricate a tale,
> Since even W——ce the Saint declares,
> She is not in a *state*, to need our *prayers*,
> But really 'tis a most alarming thing,
> To think they all are wanted for the K——g.[19]

The failure of Wilberforce's mediation led to the long drawn out process known as 'The Trial of Queen Caroline', when Brougham's brilliant defence made him the most famous lawyer in England, whereas Wilberforce, by refusing to reveal the secret pledge or Brougham's original suggestion exposed himself to the public's conviction that he had thought up the scheme himself, a sanctimonious meddler, a toady of the King. Cobbett published a virulent tract in the form of an open letter to Wilberforce, who drove to Dolby's shop in Wardour Street to get a copy: 'very clever, but very mischievous and full of falsehoods'.[20] He was used to having his conduct misrepresented and his views misconstrued, especially by Cobbett, but this hurt. Simeon of Cambridge might write congratulations, 'I am longing and panting that others may feel . . . the obligation which the whole land, and the Government especially owes you for your conduct in Parliament,'[21] and Macaulay might say how Wilberforce had raised his reputation yet higher, as indeed he had in the House.[22] But as he wandered in his lonely garden at Gore House, where the weeping willow looked lovely, he knew that his interference in the Queen's business had made the populace cross.

'What a lesson it is to a man,' he mused, 'not to set his heart on low popularity when after 40 years disinterested public service, I'm believed by the Bulk to be a Hypocritical* Rascal. O what a comfort it is to have to fly for refuge to a God of unchangeable truth and love.'[23] A few days later, again in the garden, he meditated on the Twenty-Third Psalm. He wrote his thoughts to Barbara and added: 'I long,

---

* 'Hypocritical' is Bowdlerized in *Life* V, p. 68, followed by Furneaux, to '*perfect*'!

if it might be the will of God, yet to do something more for his Glory and for the credit of my Christian professions.'[24]

Wilberforce continued to hope for mediation. He thought the King should go down to the Lords and publicly sacrifice his personal feelings to the need for national peace, by asking Parliament to drop judicial proceedings and make a just settlement with the Queen: 'I think I could write him a speech which without an abatement of dignity would get him out of the scrape, and all the rest of us also, and would make him universally popular with all but the absolute Radicals – avowed enemies of God and man.'[25] He abandoned the idea because it might bring Liverpool down.[26]

Before leaving for Weymouth to join 'the group that my fancy draws of you all on the sands'[27] he was invited to call on the Duchess of Kent. He makes no mention in his diary but described to Hannah More how the year-old Princess Victoria, on the floor, made him her toy as he stood chatting with her mother.[28] It was their only recorded meeting, the future Queen playing with the man who would so strongly influence her age. At Weymouth his eyes suffered from the glare and the wind. On the morning of 7 August his secretary, opening *The Times*, astonished him by reading a *Letter to William Wilberforce* by Lord John Russell, who the next year would move a famous motion on Parliamentary Reform for which Wilberforce voted. The open letter called Wilberforce the only man in Britain who could arbitrate, and urged his intervention to stop 'The Queen's Trial' from beginning. Cobbett, in his next *Political Register* sneered at 'the proud Whig crawling to the obsolete Saint'.[29]

Wilberforce feared that the intervention of a leading member of the Opposition might checkmate any further move by himself as an independent, yet he returned for a few days to London and concocted with Stephen another unsuccessful scheme. The Queen's Trial began. He was heartily relieved in November, at Bath, when the arrival of the stage-coach covered with ribbons announced her 'Acquittal'. 'What a mess have Ministers and the Queen's advisers and the House of Lords altogether made of this sad business,' he wrote to Bankes.[30]

The following July the Queen was barred from entering Westminister Abbey for the Coronation. It fell to the young Thorntons' foster-father, Inglis, dressed in absurd mediæval costume, to shut the door in her face. The crowd had now turned against her, and a fortnight later in August 1821 Queen Caroline died.

By then Wilberforce had left Gore House. His finances no longer could support it. The Markington Estate in Yorkshire yielded little when he would not put up rents, and he had made an unfortunate land investment at Wick Wick in Gloucestershire, managed by his brother-in-law Richard Spooner, a Worcestershire banker who later crashed.

On buying the land Wilberforce reduced the rents and then Spooner put unwarrantable confidence in an attorney named Mills, and 'I have been a great sufferer'.[31] Wilberforce still financed William; Robert was about to go up to Oriel, the small Oxford college selected originally for William, and now chosen firmly for Robert in preference to Trinity College, Cambridge, whose numerous, mostly rich and too frequently idle undergraduates had ruined William. Oriel was embarking on its golden age and Robert already had shown intellectual prowess. Wilberforce did not wish to keep his sons on too narrow an allowance, nor to restrict philanthropy.

He sold 'K. Gore' to Mr. Mortlock who kept a china shop in Oxford Street. Maria Edgeworth the novelist, who had often stayed with the Wilberforces' neighbour Lady Elizabeth Whitbread (Whitbread's widow, Grey's sister, and possessor of the best cook in London outside the royal family) heard a story that Mortlock on completion of the sale, guessing that the money alone made Wilberforce sell a house which suited him so well, begged him in vain to accept back the title deeds as 'testimony of esteem due to your public character and talents'.[32]

Maria Edgeworth met Wilberforce again not long after, at Lord Carrington's Wycombe Abbey, and was entranced by the liveliness of his conversation, his political anecdotes, his '*indulgent* and benevolent temper', especially towards political opponents. She had feared she would be too bad for him. 'No such thing. He made no pretension to superior sanctity or strictness – never led or turned the conversation that way – never made any side blows or probings and in the course of an hour I was quite at ease with him.'[33]

He took a lease of Marden Park at Godstone in Surrey, fifteen miles down the Brighton road from Westminster Bridge, and six miles beyond Croydon. Hatsell, the celebrated clerk of the House of Commons, had lived there once.

Wilberforce was rising sixty-two and subject to weak lungs, and apparently to colitis and the unrecognized morphine poisoning which the doctors had pumped into him by thirty years of their opium pills. Alexander the oculist probably put an opiate into his eye drops too. Illness kept Wilberforce from the House for much of the spring session of 1821.

His clerical brother-in-law, William Spooner, wrote to Lord Calthorpe on 17 May 1821: 'I do not hear without pain the reports from various quarters of the very ill look of Mr. Wilberforce. He is very generally thought to be greatly aged of late; and much less adequate to Parliamentary fatigues. My sister has kept him at Bath as long as she could; she returns to London with many uneasy apprehensions and her fears are extremely in accordance with the remarks of various friends who have seen him lately.' Echoing no doubt his sister's feelings, Spooner discussed how to preserve him for his family, now at impressionable ages. 'Perhaps he *ought* to leave Parliament; and I almost question if, by employing his then greater leisure in writing, he might not do more essential service to Society than by now retaining his seat. . . . I *especially* dislike the thought of his engaging to Parliamentary life, with his family distant twenty miles or more. He is now no longer young enough to return even occasionally to the bachelor state; and to be left to the management and remembrance of such a servant as he has, and is *likely* to have about him; or to any other than female care, assiduously alive to his health and comfort.'[34]

Wilberforce would not resign his seat. He agreed that he must nominate an associate who could complete the long haul, still so far uphill, of his Parliamentary load for the Blacks. Brougham expected the position.[35] Wilberforce wanted a man of firm Christian faith. In contrast to 1780, when scarcely one man of strong religious and humanitarian conviction sat in the House of Commons, Wilberforce had many disciples. He might choose Acland, a man of gaiety of heart and buoyant spirits[36] or even the Earl of Rocksavage who perhaps may symbolize the change coming over England: his father, the first Marquess of Cholmondeley, was a Regency rake whereas the son, Rocksavage, was a reflection, if rather a feeble pale reflection, of Wilberforce.[37] (He also bred spaniels, 'one of the greatest beauties' being promised to Samuel, aged 12.)[38] He had his eye, however, on Fowell Buxton, now in his mid-thirties; and on the night of 23 May 1821 Wilberforce heard Buxton make a mighty speech supporting Mackintosh in his Bill for humanizing the criminal law.

Next day Wilberforce wrote Buxton a long letter proposing another 'Holy Alliance', not of emperors and kings but of two M.P.s who would campaign to win for the slaves the status of a free peasantry; 'and if I should be unable to commence the War (certainly not to be declared in this Session) and still more, if commenced, I should (as certainly would, I fear be the case) be unable to finish it, you would kindly continue to prosecute it. Your assurance to this effect would give me the greatest pleasure, pleasure is a bad term, let me rather say peace and consolation; for alas my friend I feel but too deeply how little I have been duly assiduous and faithful in employing the talents committed to my stewardship. . . . Both my head and heart are quite full to overflowing, but besides that my eyes are tired, the time which by snatches I have seized amid continual interruptions for penning this hasty scrawl all gone and I must conclude.'[39]

The next seven months brought a great sorrow. The Wilberforces' move into proper country had been partly for the health of their elder daughter, the cheerful pretty Barbara, who evidently had 'consumption'. By the autumn of 1821 she was sinking. They took her to Bath, then back to London in early December, to Stephen's house in Kensington

Gore for the best medical opinion. After a brief rally she relapsed and on Christmas Day Wilberforce walked about London after church looking for another medicine. 'Oh, my dear Friend,' wrote Wilberforce to Calthorpe, 'it is in such seasons as these that the value of the promises of the Word of God are ascertained both by the dying and the attendant relatives.'[40] Though Wilberforce could have wished to find her a little more joyful at the prospect of Heaven he was assured, by her composure and faith, that she was at peace with God. With breaking yet obedient hearts the parents watched her die on 30 December 1821.

'The assured persuasion of Barbara's happiness has taken away the sting of death,'[41] Wilberforce wrote, but the blow shook his remaining strength. In March 1822 'My very dear Robert will be perhaps surprised to hear I am confined by a new malady, the Gout.'[42]

CHAPTER TWENTY-SEVEN

'Unable to Finish it'

Samuel, still a schoolboy, rode through the gates of Marden Park from Croydon on 13 August 1822 with an alarming rumour that Castlereagh (Marquess of Londonderry) had committed suicide. Wilberforce could not credit it: Castlereagh's coolness and self-possession made suicide most unlikely. Wilberforce was already in a disturbed state because Barbara's rheumatics gave her strange fancies at night that an intruder lurked in her room; now he could scarcely finish a letter to Bathurst on Slave business.[1]

The suicide brought back Canning to the Foreign Office, and Wilberforce plunged into correspondence. In place of the distantly polite, generally co-operative Castlereagh had arrived one of the closest political friends of any long standing, for a warm relationship. It would end in deep disappointment.

Canning loaned him all foreign Slave Trade confidential papers as they came in, and Wilberforce tended to lock them up safely and forget their existence. He asked 'if I may show the substance of the papers to Mr. Stephen and to Macaulay,' since almost all his own information now came through them, though he alone could command the attention of the Foreign Secretary. But Canning restricted him to word of mouth.[2] Like their mutual hero Pitt, he treated Wilberforce as if he were a privy councillor, so that when Cabinet Ministers were scattered to their estates Wilberforce knew the latest relevant news before them.

The next year Canning became a neighbour. Wilberforce gave up Marden, and moved, with 'all my books, pamphlets, papers, the accumulated stores of a whole life'[3] to Brompton Grove, the present Brompton Road. His new lease, Grove House, stood just where the short side-turn now leads to Ovington Square, and it had an extra large room which a former resident had built to entertain the Prince Regent.[4] Canning lived at Gloucester Lodge where the old Duchess had died, beyond Brompton village: it is commemorated in the name of Gloucester

10*

Road. Canning's route to and from Westminster led past Grove House and sometimes they travelled together, though if Wilberforce's nose smelt weather that might give him a cold, he was liable to retreat indoors.

His letters to Canning included a long plea that 'you, and indeed Government itself . . . will endeavour to obtain . . . complete Toleration' for the Waldenses, the Protestants of North Italy with their long history which runs back centuries before the Reformation. Canning replied: 'I have sent your Waldenses . . . to the Duke of Wellington and to Mr. Hill, our minister at Turin.'[5] Wilberforce later begged Canning to secure Protestant Toleration in the newly independent South American nations. Canning replied that he had already thought of it.[6]

Canning in fact had thought of most things which Wilberforce wrote about. With utmost consideration Canning consulted him over the negotiations to end the foreign Slave Trade, yet the long file of their correspondence, now in the Harewood House manuscripts, made little difference. He had entered office as the Congress of Verona began (Friend Allen thumbed a lift off the Duke of Wellington, Britain's chief plenipotentiary) and the Liverpool Government were already sincere in their efforts to stop the Trade, whereas Tsar Alexander's liberalism cooled fast.

Each move at this time gave an appearance of success without its substance. Thus Wilberforce wished Abolition to be a precondition of recognition for the new Empire of Brazil. Soon he could congratulate Canning on his promptitude and decision in using Independence 'for suppressing the Slave Trade'.[7] But the Trade went on, and Wilberforce called the Portuguese 'the most perverse and obstinate of all nations'.[8] It continued decades longer than Wilberforce. Again, Britain and America signed a treaty acknowledging the Slave Trade as piracy and allowing a mutual right of search. Parliament ratified it immediately and Wilberforce rejoiced;[9] but the Senate refused to ratify. The point was not gained for ten years after Wilberforce's death.

At Verona the British delegation failed completely to win a practical end to the Slave Trade, and came home with nothing to the point except another denunciation in general terms. Wilberforce suffered extreme mortification and determined to show his displeasure. When the Verona despatches were to be voted on in April 1823 Wilberforce told Canning he would stay at home.[10] Canning replied with a Private and Most Confidential complaint that Wilberforce had not allowed for 'the difficulties of my situation. But surely, surely in that case, I have the stronger claim upon your *justice*. I am upon my trial *today*. Come and *hear* me! I should rather that you should "hear and vote" than that you should stay away,'[11] and leave the world guessing. Wilberforce the aged remained a political force.

Wilberforce's handwriting in 1818 from a letter dated 21 February to Joseph John Gurney. 'Emancipation . . . has ever been . . . both yᵉ real and the declared Object of all yᵉ friends of yᵉ African Race . . .'

He responded to Canning's appeal, heard his vindication, and at four in the morning went home without voting. Canning thus received a more public snub than if he had allowed Wilberforce to miss the debate.

Canning had already dismayed and disappointed him by a turn-about on Emancipation, the Abolition of Slavery itself, the last great issue of Wilberforce's career.

Emancipation had always been the ultimate aim, postponed to win the more urgent Abolition. Thus in 1794 when he had reason to believe the West Indian lobby might co-operate in Abolition if they thought it would preclude Emancipation, he wrote to Clarkson: 'This is a compromise to which so far as I am concerned I should not be indisposed.'[12] Emancipation would follow naturally, this was the conviction; but, to their deep regret, Wilberforce and his colleagues had miscalculated. Abolition of the British Slave Trade in 1807 had not begun that improvement in physical and moral treatment which, by barely perceptible progression, would make the slaves ready for the status of free peasantry. With a few honourable exceptions the plantations remained deserts of human misery despite a number of laws passed by Colonial legislatures at the behest of Westminster. Even on well-run plantations the slaves lacked legal security against sale to pay an owner's debts; nor could a slave testify in court against a white.

Apparently valid objections had blocked Wilberforce whenever he wanted to quicken the pace, as in 1818 when Castlereagh warned him that Emancipation must wait upon total Abolition of the foreign Slave Trade. '*Should* greatly like to lay a foundation for the Emancipation of the poor slaves,' and after that would gladly retire, he had told Stephen in 1820, 'I am quite sick of the wear and tear of the House of Commons and the envy malice and all uncharitableness. Oh may I be permitted to dwell in a calmer region.'[13] Failure to help the slaves oppressed him. On a wet April day (in 1818) when he had been sleepy and muddled in the House and then found that he had forgotten his opium pills and a cold was coming on, he moaned in his diary:* 'I feel more and more convinced of the decay of my own faculties both bodily and mental and I must try to husband the little that remains. Alas Alas how grieved I am, that I have not brought forward the state of W. Indian slaves.'[14] Next day he was to speak about them at the anniversary meeting of the African Institution and propose motions, but mislaid his notes and arrived 'extremely distressed . . . I never so much discredited myself in any public meeting to my recollection as to-day. Was it not my state of mind bad angry and irritated more than contrite and humble Lord mercy mercy I am wretched and miserable and poor and blind and naked. O supply all my wants and give me all needful supplies of Grace and Strength.'[15]

His sense of guilt grew until he believed that but for the all-atoning blood of Jesus Christ he would be condemned everlastingly for this failure to rescue the slaves from bondage.[16] He even wished that he had called the bluff in 1792 when, in effect, he had been offered gradual Emancipation if he would abandon the fight for immediate Abolition. Wilberforce had thought then that Dundas's scheme must be a sham unless the Trade be extinguished first, as was expected in a year or two of 1792, not fifteen.

Early in 1823 Wilberforce, Stephen, Macaulay, Buxton, Clarkson and others determined to delay no longer. Clarkson the skilled and

---

* Original punctuation (or lack of it) retained as an example.

tireless propagandist fanned public opinion until it surged in sympathy towards the slaves. On 31 January a great meeting founded the Anti-Slavery Society with the Duke of Gloucester as the president whose emotional speeches were cheered to the echo. The new Society's full title was '. . . for the Mitigation and Gradual Abolition of Slavery throughout the British Dominions'. The founders did not yet believe that a simple Parliamentary vote could effect it. They were dominated by fear that if the Blacks were not made ready, the immediate chaos would create irresistible planter demands for Slavery's reimposition.

Both Clarkson and Wilberforce produced tracts to support the new Society's aim: Wilberforce managed with uncharacteristic speed to pen a fifty-six page *Appeal to the Religion, Justice and Humanity of the Inhabitants of the British Empire in Behalf of the Negro Slaves in the West Indies*. He attacked the theory that negroes were degraded because of their colour or race: 'the language of insult,' he called it. They were degraded by Slavery itself, and he described the free Blacks in Hayti and Sierra Leone who had proved themselves true men, not the brute beasts which some planters believed negroes to be. He did not denounce planters as a class. They too were victims both of a system, and of their own absurd belief that Emancipation must mean ruin. He called on all men to help the slaves, by urging better treatment, by diffusing the light of Christianity, and especially by giving them firm hope until, before too long, they could enjoy the legal status or condition 'of free British labourers'.

His argument, like all Wilberforce writings, would have been better spoken. His pen had lost the incisiveness of *A Practical View*. The pamphlet of 1823 lacked clarity and form. Its quality lay in its sincerity, and when the stage-coaches carried it the length and breadth of the kingdom, it proved a powerful opening bombardment to the campaign.

In March 1823 Wilberforce made one of his increasingly rare descents on the House to present a petition from the Quakers, praying Parliament to abolish Slavery.

Presentation of petitions normally provided a general introductory debate before the substantive motion which would follow in a few weeks. But this one misfired. Not wanting to speak his pamphlet over again Wilberforce said little in his opening speech, intending to be more copious in his reply. He did not realize that Canning, in his desire not to rock the West Indies at a time when he was being midwife to the new South American nations, had turned against him politically, though not personally. Cunningly the Foreign Secretary warned the pro-Slavery party to stay silent. Nothing was said against Wilberforce. Therefore none of his friends liked to speak and 'There was no debate at all'.[17] Wilberforce was confounded: almost he thought that the God whose aid he had sought silently, as always before rising to speak, had deserted him. 'I chiefly blame myself now,' he told Brougham next day, 'for not having been *strong* enough to impel us and the warmer West Indians to enter into a contest, and yet I can truly say I feel unaffectedly for the West Indians, their incomes for some times past worse than those of any English landholders and being as they conceive attacked on all hands.'[18]

The campaign had begun without clear strategy. He sought out Brougham to ask him 'by what specific measures we ought to prepare for the universal Emancipation of the W. Indian slaves'. Wilberforce not only wanted to improve conditions but to give the slaves hope. It was hopelessness that remained their worst misery; every free man however poor, however hard his life, had hope. One idea which Wilberforce put forward would allow them to buy their freedom 'by driblets', through letting them earn wages, first on one day, then on two or three in a week.[19] Yet, as he said in the abortive debate, 'We have no right to pay our debt to the West Indians from African pockets.'[*][20] He had already toyed with the idea of Britain buying the slaves' freedom by a Treasury grant, for to any early nineteenth-century gentleman of England it was unthinkable that property, lawfully held, should simply be confiscated; nor should Britain penalize the West Indians for enjoying the fruits of Britain's own crime, the Slave Trade.

The big debate followed in May when Buxton, with Wilberforce sitting beside him, moved 'That the State of Slavery is repugnant to the principles of the British Constitution and of the Christian Religion; and that it ought to be gradually abolished . . .', as fast as was consistent with the wellbeing of the parties concerned. Overawed by the solemnity of his task, and a little too conscious that he was not making a speech of public protest but seeking to sway a critical and divided House, Buxton's apparent lack of urgency did not satisfy Wilberforce who, indeed, felt it necessary in his own speech to emphasize: 'We ought not to prolong their Slavery an hour longer than is absolutely necessary.'[21]

Canning outgeneralled him again. Canning persuaded the House that the right course was for the Crown to order Colonial governments to undertake detailed measures of amelioration, without making any clear promise of Emancipation. He did it so cleverly that even Wilberforce and Buxton thought they had made progress and withdrew their motion. Lord Bathurst as Colonial Secretary sent out a circular despatch within days; the islands at least accepted it more seriously than previous directives from London.

The West Indian lobby launched their counter-attack. In August 1823 William Cobbett joined them with a violent defence of Slavery. In his *Weekly Register* Cobbett frequently shaped his own chief

---

* Not, as recorded in *Hansard* (VII, 624–30) 'Never forgetting that we have no right to pay British debts with African freedom.' Nor, as alleged by Charles Ellis in the next debate: 'We had no right to pay a debt of African humanity with West Indian property.'

article in the form of an Open Letter to a public figure or body; he had addressed three to Wilberforce over the past twenty years. The issue of 30 August began: '*Wilberforce*, I have you before me in a canting pamphlet . . .,' the recent *Appeal . . . in behalf of the Negro Slaves*. Much of Cobbett's Open Letter concerned the grievous state of cotton factory labourers and especially the trial of Andrew Ryding for attacking one Horrocks, M.P., a factory owner, with a cleaver. The rest of it weighed into Wilberforce in Cobbett's graphic, cantankerous style. He called Wilberforce's *Appeal* 'a great deal of canting trash; a great deal of lying; a great deal of that cool impudent falsehood for which the Quakers are famed. . . . There is no man who knows anything at all of the real situation of the Blacks, who will not declare you to be totally ignorant of the subject on which you are writing, or to be a most consummate hypocrite.'

Wilberforce's plea that the slaves should be raised to the (legal) condition of free British labourers was debased deftly by Cobbett who implied that the word 'condition' meant, 'make them as well off'. He proceeded to contrast the wretched physical condition of the Lancashire mill hands with what he believed to be the state of the Blacks: 'You seem to have a great affection for the fat and lazy and laughing and singing and dancing negroes . . .,'[22] whereas Cobbett cared for the downtrodden, pinched white 'wage slaves'.

Cobbett then laid a charge which, as former editor of the *Parliamentary History* he must have known to be a 'cool impudent falsehood' of breathtaking size. 'Never have you done one single act in favour of the labourers of this country.'[23]

There followed a famous passage which has echoed down the years. Taking as cue the fact that Hatchards of Piccadilly published Wilberforce's pamphlet and shutting his eyes to any Slavery beyond the pampered domestics of the chief ports or plantation houses, Cobbett thundered: 'You make your appeal in Piccadilly, London, amongst those who are wallowing in luxuries, proceeding from the labour of the people. You should have gone to the gravel-pits, and made your appeal to the wretched creatures with bits of sacks round their shoulders, and with hay-bands round their legs; You should have gone to the road side, and made your appeal to the emaciated, half-dead things who are there cracking stones to make the roads as level as a die for the tax-eaters to ride on. What an insult it is, and what an unfeeling, what a cold-blooded hypocrite must he be that can send it forth; what an insult to call upon people under the name of free British labourers; to appeal to them in behalf of Black slaves, when these free British labourers; these poor, mocked, degraded wretches, would be happy to lick the dishes and bowls, out of which the Black slaves have breakfasted, dined, or supped.'[24]

Small wonder that John Gladstone of Liverpool, the future Prime

Minister's father, who owned slaves (and treated them well) saluted Cobbett as a powerful and intelligent advocate for the planters.[25]

Wilberforce stayed unrepentant. Four years later, warmly encouraging a friend who was battling for the 'climbing boys' of Britain he added that he was 'a little scandalized at your calling their case an evil not less grievous . . . than that of the Negro slaves. This shows what I have often remarked, that even those who are best informed on the subject . . . have frequently a very inadequate idea of its real enormity; for this does not so much consist in extraordinary instances of cruelty as in the habitual immorality and degradation and often grinding sufferings of the poor victims of this wicked system . . . the systematic misery of their situation.'[26]

Wilberforce did not believe in the sincerity of the Colonial governments, which he once called 'the most vicious part of our whole system',[27] nor in their judgement. Thus he and his colleagues who had long pleaded that slaves should not be driven to work with the whip, even if malefactors must still be whipped, were grateful that Bathurst's despatch specifically abolished the practice. But they were concerned to hear of no explanation being given that the withdrawal of this symbol of Slavery did not imply imminent Emancipation. Wilberforce dreaded hopes falsely raised, leading to frustration and violence, which would be an excuse for further repression.

Early in October 1823, down at Barmouth in North Wales with his family (Samuel was on the point of going to Oriel) he received newspaper accounts of the reception of Bathurst's Despatch in the Caribbean. He wrote to Canning warning him not to believe without independent corroboration the glowing reports from the Colonial governments. If they would 'set themselves in earnest to the work of reformation', none could do it better, 'But after all I have witnessed of their conduct, it is really not uncandid of me to feel a rooted distrust of their professions in this instance.'[28] He was shocked to receive Canning's reply, from the Foreign Office, dated 11 October 1823: 'My dear Wilberforce, Your letter could not have arrived more inopportunely . . . for at nearly the same moment arrived account of an Insurrection of Negroes at Demerara which was very formidable in appearance and was not quelled when the account came away. The cry was immediate unqualified freedom. I am sure you do not doubt my sincerity as to the good of the Blacks: but I confess I am not prepared to sacrifice all my white fellow countrymen to that object.'[29]

Wilberforce commented to Macaulay on reading the letter: 'I fear Canning is becoming more our enemy than formerly.'[30]

The Demerara rising in fact advanced the Anti-Slavery cause because it led to the death in prison of a Methodist missionary named Smith after court martial on the charge of fomenting the insurrection. Smith became the Anti-Slavery martyr,[31] and in championing the Smith case Wilberforce would make his last appearance in Parliament.

During the winter of 1823–4, back in London, he suffered from colds on the chest. He pressed Canning about the Slaves and took active interest in three schemes for Britain: the creation of the National Gallery,[32] the establishment of Trustee Savings Banks,[33] and the founding of what became the Royal Society for the Prevention of Cruelty to Animals.[34] On 16 March 1824 he spoke in the House in the context of the Demerara rising, imploring speedy steps towards Emancipation now that hope had been roused by Parliament itself.

He overtaxed his strength but a few days later went down for a foreign affairs debate and returned to Brompton Grove so amused by Canning's wit and comedy when destroying a weak speech by Lord John Russell that he collapsed in helpless laughter.[35] Whether this contributed or not, he collapsed physically the same night and lay for a month with pneumonia, surrounded by adoring members of his family. He passed the crisis, began to mend, and endured Barbara's fussing with good-humoured patience. 'Your dear mother,' he wrote to thirteen-year-old Henry at school, 'so strenuously resisted my taking up my pen that I began to be afraid I should lose the faculty of writing. Indeed my life has been to a great degree of the animalised kind – eating drinking airing napping being its *daily business*. . . . Of course my Henry knows me and my habits too well not to be aware that I am not to be taken in this account as speaking with *very* great accuracy and also that my serious occupations have not been discontinued.'[36]

On 1 June the Smith case brought Wilberforce to the House of Commons. Brougham would thunder against the Government; Wilberforce would be back from the brink of the grave, perhaps for his last speech. The godly crammed the galleries – for an absurd anti-climax: the benches showed almost empty because Members were scattered around the roofs of St. James's gaping at one Graham and his intrepid wife as they ascended in a balloon. Brougham and Mackintosh duly thundered. The House was counted out.[37]

In the resumed Smith debate ten days later Wilberforce made a short speech, imploring the Ministry not to depend on Colonial governments to alleviate Slavery, his last appeal to the House of Commons.

On Midsummer Day 1824 he was led to his seat on the platform at Freemason's Hall for the first anniversary meeting of the Anti-Slavery Society. Macaulay's Tom, who had just won a Fellowship at Trinity and was reading for the Bar, carried the audience to the heights by a speech which foreshadowed his *Essays, History,* Speeches and even the *Lays of Ancient Rome.* Throughout Tom's speech the platform could hear ejaculations from Wilberforce, 'Capital!' 'Wonderful,' and when

Tom left the rostrum amid thunderous applause, Stephen and Wilberforce each seized a hand and pumped it up and down for joy while the Duke of Gloucester could scarcely restrain his tears.

Wilberforce's own speech made a graceful classical allusion to 'the young Alexander' who would take the aged father's place in the battle. His own words were heard with great emotion, as he stood there so small and bowed, the voice weak yet still musical, and the face lit by that wonderful smile. He ended with a reference to the veterans: 'We have been engaged in many a long and arduous contest, and we also have had to contend with calumny and falsehood. But we are more than repaid, by the success that has already attended our efforts, and by the anticipations which we may derive from what we have witnessed this very day, when, if our sun be setting, we see that other luminaries are arising to shine with far greater lustre and more efficient strength.'[38]

The following day Wilberforce had an attack of his old bowel trouble. Barbara and he were due to stay at Iver in Buckinghamshire with pious, stodgy, old Admiral Lord Gambier. The illness worsened on the road and when they arrived 'about 5 o'clock, whether from exhaustion or what else I know not, I was so overpowered by sleep that I could only be put to bed, as I was with my clothes on and it was not until I woke at about 4 o'clock next morning that I found I had my clothes on and that a part of them could be put off.'[39]

Although soon able to trouble Canning again for Emancipation, Wilberforce came under pressure from Barbara to resign his seat before the next Session. His doctor, the brilliant, fashionable William Chambers, who had a Wilberforcian addiction to note writing, added the warning: attend the House in congenial weather only, or risk another and fatal attack on the lungs.[40] Wilberforce had decided already not to stand for another Parliament, and therefore he postponed a decision because Lord Liverpool might dissolve a year before time.

Barbara certainly hoped Lord Liverpool would kill that Parliament: She 'considered my husband's life in danger from its continuance', and hailed with gladness 'every report of its fate drawing nigh'. Acquaintances who had not seen Wilberforce in private might doubt the need for resignation, 'for many are disposed I fear to work him to death without due mercy misled by his cheerful spirit.'[41] In February 1825, when early Dissolution looked less likely, Wilberforce capitulated.

His old friend Sir John Sinclair of Ulbster, the agriculturalist, thought he should go to the Lords. Knowing that nothing would induce Wilberforce to leave a coronet on young William's unsteady head, Sinclair suggested an ingenious solution: the peerage patent should specify a remainder 'to the Heirs *born after the date of the grant*'.[42] A life peerage in fact though not in name. But Wilberforce wanted no title; he was a House of Commons' man. Nor did he consider himself deserving of honour. His thought was well expressed to James Montgomery, that he found himself 'much more humiliated by the consciousness of opportunities of usefulness not duly improved, than exulting in any success which may have crowned his efforts'.[43]

To the veteran Abolitionist William Smith (who now had a five-year-old granddaughter named Florence Nightingale) he wrote: 'I cannot leave the House of Commons without mixed emotions which I will not attempt to describe. . . . I rejoice to think that really I am not wanted. We never before were so strong in the House of Commons since the early days when Pitt and Fox were our advocates, and we have a support from popular opinion now which we then wanted.'[44]

Buxton decidedly disagreed with Wilberforce's sense of being not wanted. 'The Carthaginians,' he wrote back, 'put upon Hannibal's tomb, "We vehemently desired him in the day of battle," which exactly describes my feelings.'[45]

Epilogue: 1825–1833

CHAPTER TWENTY-EIGHT

The Path to the Abbey

'They have been several times to look at a place called Highwood in the parish of Hendon, "with equal valour" as Gibbon said "but unequal success", for the first time when Mamma saw it she thought it pretty, the next time it was a gloomy day, and she and Papa thought it vile and detestable, voted there was not a tree in the visinage. They went again a fine day, Mamma thought it a very pretty place and Papa thought it tolerable but they both seemed to think it prettier than Stanmore which they had since seen. Furthermore Papa is of the opinion that there are not trees at Stanmore!!!'[1]

Thus Robert wrote to Samuel in February 1825. The Wilberforces were living at Uxbridge while house hunting, in a hutch of a place, so small that guests and half the servants slept in the inn a mile away. The household remained overloaded with lame, impotent or half blind servants, including Barningham the ex-secretary (too blind himself) and his wife who had nursed poor Barbara at her deathbed; and old Knowles the butler they wished would give notice; and Mrs. Knowles, now too crippled to cook. But Marianne Thornton 'would willingly sit in despair of getting one's plate changed at dinner and hear a chorus of bells all day which nobody answers, for the sake of seeing Mr. Wilberforce in his element'.[2]

He bought the Highwood Hill estate, a fairly large house with farm and cottages and 140 acres, though its need of repair kept them from moving in until the spring of 1826. It lay in the north Middlesex countryside by the hamlet of Mill Hill, only two and a half miles along a pleasant lane from the Whetstone turnpike on the Great North Road, with its frequent stage-coaches to bring friends and relatives. Sir Stamford Raffles, the former governor of Java, whom Wilberforce much admired, bought the neighbouring property but died within a few months of arrival.

Hardly had the Wilberforces settled in when William, Mary and the surviving grandson (the second boy died an infant) and Lockett the nurse, joined the parental roof. William had tried hard as a law pupil. His father invited Lord Stowell (Eldon's brother) to introduce him on his call to the Bar,[3] and invited Brougham, as leader of the Northern Circuit which William planned to join, to cleanse the Mess of an indecent toast which Wilberforce wished no child of his to utter.[4] Then William, his doctor, and Babington's son George decided that William would never make a barrister.

His performance at the Anti-Slavery Society's second annual meeting in April 1825 suggests otherwise. Wilberforce, forbidden to attend, sent him to reply to the motion of thanks and tribute on the lamented retirement. Standing before the crowded hall, with the royal duke beside him, William promptly burst into tears, at which old James Stephen collapsed in grief, Dan Sykes wept so much that he retired to hide behind the platform, and sobs rent the body of the hall. William then delivered a creditable speech, possibly written by Robert.[5]

Headaches and a liver complaint indicated an outdoor livelihood for William. He would farm his father's fields, and he met a Major Close who persuaded him (and Wilberforce) that a dairy farm and retail business at St. John's Wood, a few miles south on the edge of London, would do nicely in partnership; William need only ride over twice a week. Wilberforce complied with William's 'earnest wish to purchase it', although telling Calthorpe that 'my finances are in a sad plight and I must carefully scrutinize my accounts and endeavour to lessen my expenditure'.[6] A year later the dairy business required further investment. Wilberforce had settled small portions on each of his sons. William invested his share in the St. John's Wood milk trade, and his father felt it was best on the whole to let him risk 'his own fortune'. The business was at least innocent; William angrily rejected hints that perhaps it was a little degrading. An eldest son's portion did not prove enough. Still trusting Major Close the once-rich Wilberforce borrowed £6,000 from his cousin Samuel Smith of Woodhall. William himself apparently borrowed secretly from a moneylender, as well as openly from the Thornton family bank.[7]

If William's character and career brought grief, the three other sons rejoiced their father. He had no need to tell them as he told William, to be in earnest. The prayers he poured out for all his sons seemed answered in the younger. At the time of Queen Caroline's affair he told Robert at Oxford: 'But I wish you from my heart not to become a Politician. I hope you will act on a far higher level and where the path blessed by God is clearer as well as more peaceable.'[8] Nor did he wish them to associate with the lordly and extravagantly wealthy such as he went with in his youth; he kept them away from the great houses, a little to their resentment.

In 1823 Robert won a Double First at Oxford and delighted his father by deciding on Holy Orders.* Samuel followed him to Oriel and won a First in Classics in 1826. Samuel had his father's impulsive, gay, warm-hearted nature and his hot temper too, though less well schooled, and his delicate constitution. Robert outwardly seemed a plodder, his manner masking his brilliant mind. Marianne Thornton called him dull Robert who ought to be labelled Spooner,† while Sir James Stephen, in a diary entry for 13 May 1845 writes: 'Honest Robert, a little dull and gauche was pleasantly kind and courteous.'[9] By the adjective 'honest' Stephen probably refers to Robert being no seeker after popularity, no compromiser with the ways of the world. As for Henry, Wilberforce confessed himself 'a little nervous' whether to send him to Oriel, 'and have been chiefly I think influenced by the consideration that Sam will be there one or two terms after your going into residence and that *perhaps* Robert will be a Fellow.'[10]

Robert indeed became a Fellow and Tutor of Oriel. 'My dear Mr. Tutor, for in that character you present yourself to me in the epistolary view, though in the negative relation; i.e. a Tutor of Oriel is too busy to write letters. Perhaps also to read them. Yet nature claims her rights and your affectionate old father begs you will some day, when your tutorial gown is on the peg and yourself in an un-academical simplicity (before you put on your clothes, say, when you get up or after unrobing and going to bed) direct your mind's eye towards this place and resolve to gladden the hearts of its inmates by visiting them on paper when you cannot do it in person. My appetite for a letter from you is more grieving because your pupil Henry is so incorrigibly idle, that he never writes except when he wants his quarterage. . . .'[11] Henry sent a letter home. Wilberforce replied that 'not all the pains that may be required for deciphering its hieroglyphics . . . can render it unacceptable,' but begged him not to write so small.[12]

Henry developed intellectually until he too won a First, and Wilber-force (in Southey's earlier charming phrase) frisked about with pardon-able pride, saying he must be the only man in England who was the father of three First Class men, and one of them a Double First.

Oriel friends who were to be famous in the annals of the Oxford Movement came to stay at Highwood. Wilberforce delighted in the appearance of John Keble's *The Christian Year*, which echoed three of his own great loves, nature, poetry and the goodness of God. He kept a copy in his pocket. He would have been less pleased with Keble's rigid disapproval of Dissenters, and rebuked Samuel for displaying similar antagonism.[13]

---

* David Newsome's *A Parting of Friends*, 1966, describes the Wilberforce sons at Oxford in admirable detail, and their relationship with their father. Space forbids more than a passing reference here to the subject so thoroughly explored by Dr. Newsome. See also *Lord Bishop: the Life of Samuel Wilberforce* by S. Meacham (1970).

† Mr. C. E. Wrangham, Robert's direct descendant, considers that Robert 'would have been quite beyond Marianne Thornton's comprehension'.

Richard Hurrell Froude, then an Oriel Tutor, he thought 'a very out of way but very intelligent and extraordinary man'.[14] Edward Hawkins, the only one of the brilliant Oriel group who did not become a Tractarian, he already knew. Of John Henry Newman, Wilberforce wrote to his youngest: 'It gives me no little pleasure my dear boy to reflect that you enjoy the society of so excellent a man as Mr. Newman. Indeed your preference of him and his preference of you, have long been a subject with me of no little pleasure, and I will add gratitude.'[15] Like that other future Cardinal, Manning, Newman came from an Evangelical home.

The mutual preference of Newman and Henry would be one of the formative factors in the early Oxford Movement, many elements of which would have dismayed Wilberforce, who had watched closely over his sons' spiritual growth. Though inevitably they saw more of their mother with her unfortunate blend of daily complaining and pious prattle, he prayed with them, talked with them and throughout school-days and college sent long letters of encouragement and teaching, rebuke and guidance, which they treasured all their lives. Their shift from Evangelical theology was slow enough to be disguised from an adored and adoring father: Samuel, indeed, always maintained that he only ripened the fruit on his father's tree.

Wilberforce certainly loved their pastoral zeal and disciplined lives, and accepted with some amusement that 'my three Oxonians are strong friends to High Church and King doctrines,'[16] but listened with concern when Robert preached a sermon which implied that no one baptized in infancy needed to be born again. Wilberforce did not live to see his sons move into new paths widely different from his own. When he died he could not have known of Newman's recent crisis of soul while in southern Europe, which eventually affected them until, one by one except Samuel, they joined Newman in the Roman Catholic Church; and Keble's Assize Sermon, which is generally regarded as the public start of the Oxford Movement, was preached only a fort-night before Wilberforce's death, and the first *Tract for The Times* came out two months after.

Wilberforce would have approved the Tractarians' earnestness, and long before they were born he had reached their '*deep* and *established* conviction of the blessings we derive from our Church establishment,'[17] as had also his dear friend and fellow-Evangelical Charles Simeon of Cambridge. He would not have approved all their thought, and as for the mental fisticuffs which Tractarian practices provoked, on both sides, these would surely have summoned a characteristic 'Alas! Alas!' He practised a brotherhood which was more than a century ahead of his times.

One great love, to the end, was evangelism, helping friends to begin or to strengthen their inward walk with Christ, regardless (unlike the early Tractarians) of the outer form of their religious allegiance. When he found that an elderly invalid fellow-lodger at Bath had been given his *A Practical View*, he sought by kindness and conversation 'to press on him the most important doctrines of true Christianity and of showing where the case is really so that he may embrace those doctrines and still continue a good Roman Catholic.'[18] On the other hand when William Smith, Wilberforce's old friend and fellow Abolitionist, was going down to his constituency to take the chair 'in what is termed an Unitarian Meeting', Wilberforce was 'quite grieved' to hear it, that Smith still rejected the divinity and lordship of Christ. 'I had indulged a hope that he was rather retiring from his Unitarian opinions and this proof to the contrary has given me real pain.'[19] For this meant to Wilberforce that Smith denied himself 'the tenderness of the Great Shepherd of the sheep'.[20]

The surviving daughter, Lizzy, drew very close to her father after the elder sister's death. Lizzy had her troubles. He had to rebuke her for bickering with her mother. 'Granting that there may be faults both sides I cannot forget a saying common among men, It is the second blow that makes a battle.'[21] He urged her to reflect on the great obligation she owed her Saviour, and in gratitude take up this cross.

In the spring of 1827, when Samuel had just become engaged to his cousin Emily Sargent, Lizzy fluttered the nest by falling in love with a West Indian slave-owner, and a debt-ridden one at that. Robert weighed in with ponderous arguments, the family was torn between love for Lizzy and loyalty to the wider issue, until she decided on her own that she would be wrong to ask William Wilberforce to have a slave-owning son-in-law. 'Lizzy has really behaved nobly about the whole affair,'[22] Robert told Samuel on 12 May 1827 and their father wrote to him a few days later, 'Dear Eliz . . . it is very gratifying to me to see that she does not appear to feel much, apparently no distress from what has passed.'[23] Four years later she married an impecunious curate.

Wilberforce continued his concern for the Blacks. He kept up a wide correspondence, growing more verbose with age. He warned Buxton frequently of 'the utter hopelessness of any honest co-operation from the Colonial assemblies'.[24] He reminded him of the importance of vindicating Sierra Leone 'and urging the absolute duty of endeavouring to compensate Africa for the long course of injuries by which we tormented depraved and barbarised her – O that Pitt were alive – I have heard him expatiate on this head with becoming feeling. I beg you will let off upon it with a *smart* fire.'[25] He reminded him too that the utter Abolition of the continuing Slave Trade should be 'your prime and grand object':[26] to Wilberforce this still remained the crime most grievous.

He supported Macaulay during his persecution by those who traduced his motives, and lent him £10,000 when his business failed because of it.[27] He shared, with discrimination, Clarkson's enthusiasm for the Liberia experiment, and he encouraged a scheme by which the British Government would purchase all West Indian slave women and children to set them free. He remained a realist: Whatever the cruelty and crime, he reminded old William Smith, it was absurd to expect the slave owners themselves to hurry the Emancipation which they believed spelt ruin.[28]

When Canning died in 1827 Wilberforce hoped the Whigs or a coalition might come in, and Brougham hold high office: 'May it please God,' he wrote to him, 'to bless you both in council and in action and to render you the instrument of delivering such a mass of human beings from a worse than Egyptian bondage and enabling them to exchange their present misery and degradation for the rights and enjoyments of a free and a civilised community. . . .'[29] The Whigs and Brougham had to wait another three years.

For Wilberforce, politics now lay out of the focus of his worsening sight. Those still fighting for his various causes could feel his sympathy and the strength of his prayers. 'We want our dear friend Wm. Wilberforce young again!' wrote Joseph Gurney, reporting the hanging of six youths aged 18 to 25. 'It is a detestable system.'[30] But Peel was now Home Secretary and had the humanizing of the criminal law among his objectives.

At Highwood Hill the Wilberforce household retained its charming eccentricity. While Barningham played on the organ or sang, the family would drift down one by one for prayers, joining in the singing. Wilberforce himself would hurry in, his clothes shabby and awry since he never bothered to look in a glass which he could not see clearly. Flowers might be tucked in three or four buttonholes.

Family prayers got into full swing, 'Lizzy calling out "Don't go near dear Mamma, she sings so dreadfully out of tune, dear" and William, "Don't look at Papa, he does make such dreadful faces." So he does, waving his arms about, and occasionally pulling the leaves off the geraniums and smelling them, singing out louder and louder in a tone of hilarity: "Trust Him, praise Him, trust Him, praise Him ever more." Sometimes he exclaims "Astonishing! How very affecting! Only think of Abraham, a fine old man, just a kind of man one should naturally pull off one's hat to, with long grey hairs, and looking like an old aloe – but you don't know what an aloe is perhaps: it's a tree – no a plant which flowers . . ." and he wanders off into a dissertation about plants and flowers.'[31]

Charles Shore, Teignmouth's son, watched Wilberforce wander around on a summer morning entirely unconscious that the floral display in his buttonholes wilted in the heat. And he saw him once, when on a visit to their own parish church, suddenly discover a pressed flower in a hymn book, and remain on his feet gazing lovingly at it while the people, who had sat down at the end of the hymn, goggled at this strange little man.[32]

Highwood Hill with its flower beds in summer and its walks all the year round was not conducive to concentration. 'When did I last write to you?' he began a letter to Harford one November day. 'I *really*, honestly and *utterly* forget.'[33] But it was most conducive to contemplation. Wilberforce looked upon this happy place where he had chosen to finish his course, and the 'measure of comfortable health that I enjoy,' as yet another proof that 'goodness and mercy have followed me all the days of my life'.[34]

During their spring and summer 'ramble' in 1827 the Wilberforces and Lizzy were staying with Henry Ryder, now Bishop of Lichfield and Coventry, an increasingly industrialized diocese which he treated as a mission field, when Wilberforce suddenly decided to revisit Yorkshire. His intention brought a flood of invitations ('such as Lord Milton's, Archbishop of York etc.'[35]) and the family enjoyed a quietly triumphal tour, even staying at Wentworth Woodhouse. For August they found lodgings at Scarborough. Samuel was in Switzerland with a young clergyman, 'a man of superior talents as well as piety,[36] named Lyte' – the future author of one of the world's most famous hymns, 'Abide with me'. Robert and Henry came up to Scarborough.

Sydney Smith, whose writings in the *Edinburgh Review* had often attacked the 'patient Christians of Clapham', wrote to Lady Holland: 'Little Wilberforce is here, and we are great friends. He looks like a little spirit running about without a body, or in a kind of undress with only half a body.'[37] Marianne Thornton had the same impression not long before: 'He looks very very thin . . . but really he is almost a proof already of the immortality of the soul – for I never saw him in such spirits – or appear so keenly alive upon all subjects.'[38]

Troubles, however, now gathered. Back in 1825 when Wilberforce had first looked at Highwood, he found it too far from the parish church of Hendon for his own comfort or the welfare of the farmers and cottagers of Mill Hill. He planned with Sir Stamford Raffles to build a church. He approached the Vicar of Hendon, Mr. Williams, and could tell Raffles 'he appears well disposed', indeed 'really desirous'[39] for a chapel-of-ease. Although suspicious of Evangelicals the Vicar seemed at first willing to allow Wilberforce and Raffles the kind of minister they valued.

Guided by James Stephen the younger, Wilberforce after Raffles' death began to build the church under the Act which allowed a founder the right to appoint the incumbent. Williams thereupon changed sides and declared war. Late in 1829 he wrote and circulated far and wide a pamphlet in which Wilberforce read that he was 'prosecuting by the grossest falsehood a scheme for my own and my family's pecuniary gain under the pretended motive of promoting the spiritual interests of my poor neighbours.'[40] Williams also believed that Wilberforce was disloyal to the Established Church, a Dissenter in disguise.

He knew Williams to be an unprincipled, violent man, deeply in debt and loathed in the parish,[41] moreover, as Wilberforce told his head gardener, Edwell, a lifetime of attacks on his public self left him little affected by any on his private self.[42] But in an almost absurd humility he feared lest some of his friends should believe them. He wrote out a statement and circulated it to prepare them, he told Lady Olivia Sparrow, 'for any rumour you might hear of my being dis- covered at seventy and upwards to be a liar a covetous rogue and a hypocrite'.[43] Brougham, in his reply, doubted any friend could be found rash or silly enough to look at Williams' charges, and thus open an opportunity for rebuttal. 'Indeed I hardly suppose it could be necessary to vindicate you even among strangers – who only know you by reputation.'[44]

The church edifice continued to rise. Sam's father-in-law, John Sargent, discovered accidentally that it pressed 'somewhat heavily' on Wilberforce's funds, and wrote round to Calthorpe[45] and a few others who promptly showered Wilberforce with substantial donations which he accepted with gratitude and admiration, proudly showing the list as proof simply of their attachment to the spread of the Gospel and the welfare of poor cottagers.

His funds were soon pressed far more heavily and disastrously. William's dairy business ran into difficulties. The first hint, in March 1830, came from a backer who withdrew, warning the Wilberforces that Major Close the managing partner was a rogue, which they refused to believe. The business went rapidly downhill, and Wilber- force found 'all this sad turmoil'[46] very wearing, at a time when he had hoped that retirement would bring him peace. Major Close departed, and 'circumstances of a very suspicious nature have since come into view'.[47] William did a little better and remained sanguine, and hid from his father the full extent of his liabilities until creditors foreclosed and obliged him to ask Wilberforce for very substantial aid. It was a time of severe agricultural depression and the flow of rents from Wilberforce's Yorkshire land, already lower than they should be, had dried to a trickle since he refused to press his tenants. He had even reduced the rents of his Highwood estate by as much as thirty or forty per cent.[48] His brother-in-law Richard Spooner, whose bank was in difficulties, and his cousins, Abel and Samuel Smith spent much time in consultation to lessen William's ruin. Several friends wanted to club together to pay off the son's debts, more than £50,000, as a tribute to the father's long self-sacrificing public service. Wilberforce refused. Lord Fitzwilliam, his old antagonist, approached an intermediary with an offer to pay the entire sum himself, an action greatly to his credit even if the money was a trifle to the vast Fitzwilliam fortune. The intermediary declined on the spot, knowing Wilberforce's determination to retain his independence to the end.[49]

By late 1830 Wilberforce decided that he and Barbara must leave Highwood, a large house run extravagantly by an ill-managed household, 'so as to be able to allow to' the children 'so much as to enable them to live in comfort'.[50] Samuel offered them a cottage, which proved impracticable. They accepted summer rooms in his rectory: he had been given the living of Brightstone in the Isle of Wight by Bishop Sumner of Winchester. Samuel knew what a difficult guest his mother would be, what a sacrifice his wife, Emily, must make. Robert hoped to give the parents a roof for the rest of the year, for he had decided to seek a country living having fallen in love with Agnes Wrangham, and after marriage must lose his Oriel Fellowship.* Each spring and summer the parents would want to make the usual 'ramble' between their friends, and of course must take the waters at Bath. Wilberforce accepted his sons' offers, paying them board and lodging.

William, his wife and children went to Italy, partly for the cheap living and partly to avoid a possible lawsuit, presumably from the moneylender, which eventually was settled somehow. Wilberforce paid off William's debts, and ate into remaining capital, selling his birthplace and some land near Hull and Beverley, to buy annuities for all the old servants and his charity pensioners, so that these would not be dependent on William after his death. And far from cutting William off, Wilberforce saved and pinched for the remainder of his life to provide a fresh start. William was grateful for his father's 'kindness to me,' and Barbara said 'his affection for his father is exceedingly great'.[51] William stayed hopelessly self-justifying. He would angrily deny any suggestion that he had 'engaged in a speculation unfitting to my station which proved so ruinous to my father's fortune as to compel him to break up his establishment'.[52]

On 11 January 1831 Lizzy's marriage to her impecunious curate, J. James, brought a last and happy gathering to Highwood. The parents left in early April. Wilberforce let the house, mainly furnished, to a Dr. Fritton, and worried a little lest Edwell the gardener be rude to him and make him cross and he would damage the books.[53] Wilberforce was touched by the kindness of friends and the children. 'I own however that it is *some* trial to me to be compelled to quit my garden and still more my books and more than this have no residence to which I can ask an old friend to take a dinner or a bed with me. Even our great Apostle thought the having no certain dwelling place not

---

* He was able to keep it, though married, until 1833.

unworthy of being classed (with others doubtless of a far higher value) in the catalogue of his sufferings.'[54]

Brougham was now Lord Chancellor in Grey's Ministry. One day during judicial business in the House of Lords he leaned across to the aged James Stephen, soon to retire as Master in Chancery, and asked him about Wilberforce's losses. Brougham expressed deep concern and a determination to help by finding livings for the sons. He promptly offered East Farleigh in Kent which Robert, after some high Tory distaste for a Whig Lord Chancellor's patronage, accepted for his father's sake. 'How handsomely,' exclaimed Wilberforce, 'Brougham has behaved to me,' especially when he also produced, with Lord Milton's warm acquiescence, the Yorkshire living of Rawmarsh near Wentworth Woodhouse for Lizzy's husband. He even tried to find a prebend for Samuel.[55]

Lord Brougham spoiled it slightly. A few days after announcing these presentations he sent his secretary to Stephen's house, where Wilberforce had just finished his solitary dinner and was 'on the point of lying down to take my siesta', to ask him to write round his Cambridge friends asking them to vote for Palmerston in the General Election.[56]

'In truth I have entirely done with politics,' Wilberforce replied to Brougham on 28 April 1831.[57] He could not read a newspaper. Joseph his amanuensis had insisted on staying at half salary, though eventually agreeing to go to Stephen when Wilberforce cut down yet further,[58] but the tedium of being read the news was often too much. His general sympathy at this time of crisis lay with Reform, partly because 'it is my decided opinion that if Lord John Russell's Bill should pass without any great alteration it will D.V. produce a House of Commons far more favourable than that we now have, to the cause of West Indian reform'.[59]

Only Slavery and the Slave Trade could excite him to 'internal heat', as he expressed it to Buxton. When unable to attend the Anti-Slavery Society's 1831 meeting he sent his best wishes and fervent prayers. 'Our Motto must continue to be *perseverance*. And ultimately I trust the Almighty will crown our efforts with success.'[60] A year later he urged Buxton not to allow another delaying enquiry which the West India lobby demanded.[61] The Anti-Slavery cause now split between the cautious, led by ancients such as Macaulay and Stephen, 'our worthy efficient, indefatigable old labourer or warrior shall I term him';[62] and the impatients, led by Stephen's youngest son George. Wilberforce and Stephen senior shook their heads sadly and feared the youngsters would ruin the cause which, in fact, they hustled to its triumph.

Stephen now lay dying at his country house in the Chilterns. 'Our poor friend is a very great sufferer,' Wilberforce told Macaulay in

August 1832. 'Entre nous, his spirits are greatly affected.'[63] The Wilberforces persuaded him to try Bath. He died there in October. Wilberforce, whose imminent decease had been expected again and again since 1788, lived on.

Stephen's death was the second great sorrow of 1832. Lizzy had caught a chest infection. Her husband brought her and their infant down from their bleak Yorkshire winter to the Isle of Wight, to a house at Ryde taken for the winter by the John Sargents, who received her there on 3 February.[64] She continued to decline and her parents (who perhaps had been staying with Spooners in Warwickshire) came south. At Oxford Wilberforce wanted to call on Provost Hawkins. Newman when looking through old letters in 1860 scribbled at the bottom of a Wilberforce note: 'This is a letter of *the* Wilberforce, so well known. The last time I saw him must have been in 1832, at which date, I think, he passed through Oxford on his way to the Isle of Wight where his married daughter was dying. I think S. Wood and I on that occasion supported him on each side, so infirm was he, from the Star down to (I suppose) Oriel.'[65]

Lizzy died soon after her parents reached her. 'My poor son-in-law and his little infant are indeed much to be pitied,' Wilberforce wrote to Lord Carrington. 'But I am cheered by the strong persuasion that my dear Elizabeth has gone to a better world. She retained her faculties to the last and was perfectly resigned and calm, being quite aware of her situation.'[66]

On 1 January 1833 Wilberforce wrote a letter in a rather unsteady hand at Robert's vicarage in East Farleigh, only a mile from Barham Court where, so long ago, he had discussed with the Middletons their insistence that he should take up the cause of Africa. The Admiral's grandson, one of Wilberforce's most devoted disciples, now lived there.

The letter, to Samuel Roberts in Sheffield, ended: 'I must not lay down my pen without informing you at length after all our disappointments, I am confidently looking forward to the fulfilment of our long offered prayers for the oppressed and much injured sons and daughters of Africa.' He had been looking at the printed evidence of a Commons Committee on the subject and considered it irresistible; every fair-minded man must agree 'that the danger of refusing or even of delaying the Emancipation of the Slaves is far greater than that which is to be apprehended from granting – ' He broke off in mid sentence as his man entered to say the letter must go at once to the post office.[67]

Wilberforce saw as a wonderful providence the probability that he would live long enough to see the slaves set free. And he reflected in wonder too at the providence which had led him in his last years to

II

live at East Farleigh and Brightstone. Far from whining at his losses he found more cause for praise than ever. 'Surely,' he wrote to Lady Olivia Sparrow on 6 February 1833, 'none ought more habitually to feel and to adopt the Psalmist's language Goodness and mercy have followed me all my days. And now have not my dear Mrs. W. and myself great cause for thankfulness, in being moored in our latter days in the peaceful haven which we enjoy (after all my homes during my long and stormy voyage in the seas of politics) under the roofs of our sons in Kent and the Isle of Wight: relieved from all the worry of family cares,' and watching the domestic happiness and pastoral zeal of those most dear to them. He himself would never have thought it wise to give up his only residence, 'But it is really, I am speaking unaffectedly, that our heavy loss has led to a solid and great increase of our enjoyments.'[68] To Mrs. Buxton he said he could not complain of loss of fortune when it led to so happy an asylum for his old age.[69] The two sons and their wives were devoted in their attentions, regardless of Barbara's difficult ways.

Wilberforce loved to hear his sons preach. Sermons made him sleepy, but he found a way. Charles Shore watched fascinated, during Sunday morning service, as Wilberforce climbed up on his front pew as Sam began to preach, and leaned over the pulpit and gazed through his eye-glass from a few inches away. He beamed approval and nodded his head and gestured with his hands, and even rose on tip-toe, 'quite unaware that every eye of the rustic congregation was fixed upon him'.[70]

During the spring of 1833 a wave of popular agitation pushed Anti-Slavery forward. Wilberforce signed the local petition and insisted on attending Maidstone's public meeting and even made a short speech, his last. He sent private encouragement to Buxton, though 'my mind is in such a state of bustle and confusion that I scarcely know what I am writing'.[71] On the night that Buxton moved for immediate Emancipation someone at the East Farleigh dinner table casually mentioned that the debate must now be starting. Wilberforce sprang from his chair and in a voice loud enough to startle, cried 'Hear, hear, hear'.[72]

He had been weakened by a bout of influenza that winter, and his chest still gave trouble when he and Barbara moved to Sam's in late April. In mid-May, therefore, they went to Bath for the waters. Henry joined them. One week later the new Colonial Secretary, Lord Stanley, introduced the Government's resolutions for ending Slavery. Wilberforce heard from Macaulay: 'Last night its death blow was struck. Stanley's allusion to you was quite overpowering and electrified the House.'[73]

To Wilberforce it was far away in the dimness of his fading sight, but vivid to his imagination. He objected especially to Stanley's

Apprenticeship proposal, whereby the emancipated slaves would work for nothing for a number of years. 'Get rid of the Apprenticeship system,' he wrote to Buxton on 11 June.[74] Buxton came under severe pressure in the House, as old William Smith described, to whom Wilberforce replied on 25 June: 'I cannot bear remaining silent when you touch on a string which vibrates in my inmost soul. . . . Do go to Buxton and say from me all that is affectionate. Future ages will justly regard the work as a grand national victory over wickedness and cruelty.'[75] He added after the signature: 'You will be sorry to hear I am seriously ill. But thank God suffering very little pain.'

That very day his knees and thighs had swelled, and what Henry called 'a protusion a posteriori' grew worse and stopped him taking exercise.

On 11 July Joseph Gurney passed through Bath unexpectedly and found him suffering from a bilious attack and lying on a sofa with his feet in flannel. Wilberforce received him with delight and affection and when Gurney, as a ministering Friend, dilated to him on the glories of Heaven, 'the illuminated expression of his furrowed countenance, with his clasped and uplifted hands, were indicative of profound devotion and holy joy.' Wilberforce told Gurney that his favourite text now was the word of St. Paul, 'Be careful for nothing; but in everything by prayer and supplication with thanksgiving let your requests be made known unto God. And the peace of God, which passeth all understanding, shall keep your hearts and minds through Christ Jesus.' As for himself, he said, he had nothing to add but the plea of the publican in the parable, 'God be merciful to me, a sinner.' Gurney never forgot the emphasis with which Wilberforce defined the word *mercy*: 'Kindness to those who deserve punishment.'[76]

His Bath doctor suggested he stop taking the waters, consult Dr. Chambers while passing through London and then return to East Farleigh. The fear was of a lingering illness ('gangrene of the lung') and not of imminent death.[77]

On 15 July Mrs. Wilberforce sent a note to Jay, the Dissenting preacher, to come and say good-bye. Jay was shocked by the physical deterioration of his old friend but they chatted freely. Wilberforce said: 'I see much in the state of the world and church which I deplore, yet I am not among the croakers. I think real religion is spreading; and, I am persuaded, will increasingly spread, till the earth is filled with the knowledge of the Lord, as the waters cover the sea.'[78] His optimism was not unjustified. Religion certainly was spreading. Wilberforce would disclaim the credit, but the essentials of his beliefs and of his conscience formed the foundation of the British character for the next two generations at least. He was a proof that a man may change his times, though he cannot do it alone.

Then he seized Jay's hand and thanked him for keeping 'to the common, plain and important truths in which all Christians are nearly agreed. And I hope you will never leave the good old way. God bless you.'

The Wilberforces reached London with Henry on 19 July and stayed at the house of cousin Lucy Smith, 44 Cadogan Place off Sloane Street.[79] Parliament still sat, to dispose of the Abolition of Slavery Bill. The Commons were debating the Second Reading.

Dr. Chambers considered Wilberforce less ill than was feared and hoped to get him into the country after a short rest. Each morning Wilberforce took the air in a wheelchair for ten minutes before family prayers and breakfast at ten, and then received friends on a sofa in a back room while Barbara fussed complainingly, keeping some of them out and shooing others away when he began to tire. On 25 July young William Ewart Gladstone, M.P. 'went to breakfast with old Mr. Wilberforce – heard him pray with his family. Blessing and honour are upon his head.'[80] Gladstone then went down to the House to speak and vote on the planter side.

Wilberforce remained alert and full of talk about things in heaven and things on earth. He seemed to be getting better. Late on Friday, 26 July he heard that the Abolition of Slavery had passed its Third Reading in the Commons. Passage through the Lords being not in doubt, Slavery as a legal state was to all intents dead – at a price. 'Thank God,' said Wilberforce 'that I have lived to witness a day in which England is willing to give twenty millions sterling for the Abolition of Slavery.'[81] Tom Macaulay, fresh from the House, saw how he 'excelled in the success which we obtained . . . as much as the youngest and most ardent partisan could have done.'[82]

Macaulay found him lively and cheerful. On the Saturday he suddenly tired, though when his mind worked it was tranquil and contented. On the Sunday he suffered fainting fits and sank rapidly.

Late that night he stirred, and Barbara and Henry heard him murmur, with apparent reference to his body, 'I am in a very distressed state.' 'Yes,' said Henry, 'but you have your feet on the Rock.' The old humility asserted itself. 'I do not venture to speak so positively. But I hope I have.'[83]

At 3 a.m. on Monday morning, 29 July 1833, he knew.

Within hours of the announcement of Wilberforce's death two letters signed by the Duke of Gloucester, the Lord Chancellor and as many peers and Members of the House of Commons as could be reached hurriedly, asked the family to permit burial in Westminster Abbey.[84] On Saturday, 3 August[85] while thousands of Londoners wore mourning, Wilberforce's coffin entered the Abbey. Two royal dukes, the Lord Chancellor, the Speaker and four peers supported the Pall. Members of both Houses walked in the procession.

'The attendance was very great,' recorded a Member in his diary that night. 'The funeral itself with the exception of the Choir of the Abbey perfectly plain. The noblest and most fitting testimony to the estimation of the man.'[86]

References and Notes

The first name of a MSS source refers to the list of MSS Authorities, e.g.
Bod. = Bodleian Library, Duke = Duke University Library, BM = British
Museum (British Library) manuscript room. Details will be found in the
Select Bibliography for the following which are indicated in the References
by capital letters:

C: *Correspondence of William Wilberforce*, ed. by R. I. and S. Wilberforce.
DNB: *Dictionary of National Biography.*
H: Harford, John, *Recollections of William Wilberforce.*
HMC: Historical Manuscript Commission *Reports.*
L: *Life of William Wilberforce*, by R. I. and S. Wilberforce.
PH: *Parliamentary History.*
PP: *Private Papers of William Wilberforce*, ed. by A. M. Wilberforce.
PR: *Parliamentary Register.*

Preface

1. Trinity MSS, to Hannah M., 15 Aug. 1833.
2. Refs. for the W. quotation, and the Carrington story below, are given at
   the appropriate places in the text, Chapters 2 and 12.
3. Davis, D. Brion, *Slavery in an Age of Revolution*, p. 461n.

1 Two Guineas a Vote

1. Samuel W., 'Fragments of his Father's Conversation' (hereafter cited as
   'Fragments') Bod. e. 11, 122.
2. Quoted Namier, L, *The Structure of Politics at the Accession of George III*
   (1957 e.d.) p. 342.
3. H, pp. 207, 218.
4. 'Fragments,' f. 123.
5. 'Fragments,' f. 124.
6. For Kingsman Baskett etc., see Sands, *A History of Pocklington School*,
   pp. 52, 64–7.

7. Quoted from Wrangham MSS in Furneaux, *William Wilberforce*, pp. 8–9.
8. 'Fragments,' f. 125.
9. *Ib.*, f. 126.
10. Biddulph MSS, Robert Smith to Abel Smith, 9 Dec. 1774.
11. 'Fragments,' f. 126.
12. For W's Matric., Tutor, etc., see Scott, R. F., *Admissions* IV, p. 143.
13. St. John's, Cantab. MSS, Examination Book.
14. *Ib.*
15. 'Fragments,' f. 128.
16. W's chest measurement etc. is deduced from a suit preserved at Wilberforce House, Hull.
17. H, p. 201.
18. Bod. d.15. 22, E. Christian to W. [1792].
19. Lincolnshire Papers, W's account with Smith, Payne and Smith's Bank, 1786.
20. Wyvill MSS (ref. code is ZFW), 7.2.59.11., W. to Wyvill, 25 July 1787.
21. Farington, J., *Diaries*, V, p. 194.
22. St. John's, Cantab., MSS, Examination Book.
23. 'Fragments,' f. 134.
24. Noel-Edwards MSS, Gerard Edwards to Lady Jane E., 7 Nov. 1779.
25. Quoted, K. J. A. Allinson (ed.), *Victoria County History of Yorkshire: East Riding*, Vol. I (1969), p. 193.
26. St. Quentin's and other replies to W's canvass quoted below are in Wilberforce House, Hull, MSS (hereafter cited as Hull MSS).
27. Hull MSS, Unknown (signature missing) to W., 22 Sept. 1780.

2 Man About Town

1. PP, pp. 49–50.
2. PR III, p. 350.
3. Duke MSS, Croker Papers, Croker's Carrington Memo. This is a report in Croker's hand, written very small, of an interview given him while preparing his *Quarterly Review* article on the *Life*. No name appears but internal evidence points only to Carrington.
4. PH XXII cc. 800ff.
5. 'Fragments,' f. 129.
6. *Memorials of Brooks's* (1907), p. 30. (MS Election Book for 1783 is missing); White's MS Membership Book.
7. H, p. 205, L I, pp. 18–19.
8. Brougham, *Statesmen*, I, p. 269.
9. H.M.C., *Carlisle*, 15th Report, Pt VI, 1897, p. 602.
10. Croker's Carrington Memo. as above. Carrington names the bachelor as Henry Halford (formerly Vaughan) the doctor, whom she married. But he was much too young at this time.
11. Trinity MSS, O. 152, f. 318. Lord Macaulay's MS Journal, 16 May 1850.
12. Roberts MSS, W. to S. Roberts, 2 Apr. 1817.
13. Boodles MS Club Book.
14. 'Fragments,' f. 41.

15. See H.M.C. *Carlisle*, op. cit., p. 555.
16. Duke MSS, W. Papers, Pitt to W., N.D.
17. 'Fragments,' ff. 31–2.
18. Stanhope MSS 731 (11), W. to Eliot, 28 Sep. 1785.
19. *Ib.*
20. Headlam, C., *The Letters of Lady Harriot Eliot*, p. 60.
21. Bod. d.13.183, G. Edwards to W., 5 Dec. 1782.
22. BM Add MSS 5883.
23. L I, p. 149; L III, p. 62.
24. Croker-Carrington Memo. as above.

3 *'Bravo Little Wilberforce!'*

1. Lauriston House details were supplied by Merton Borough Librarian.
2. Duke MSS, W. Papers, Pitt to W. [N.D.].
3. PP, p. 60.
4. (and next quote) Boston MSS, W. to Lord St. John, 30 July 1782, (filed under 'to anon.').
5. Thornton MSS 7674, 1. L. 1. Marianne Sykes to Mrs. Sykes, [N.D.] 1790. She was recalling W. in 1782.
6. Stanhope MSS 731 (11), W. to Eliot 15 Oct. 1782.
7. Hartley MSS, Berkshire R.O., D.EHy. 017.3, W. to David Hartley, 1782.
8. Duke MSS W. Papers, Pitt to W., 6 Aug. 1782.
9. L I, p. 25.
10. HMC *Fortescue* VI, letter 4120.
11. L I, p. 27.
12. L I, p. 28.
13. Erhman, John *The Younger Pitt: The Years of Acclaim*, p. 108.
14. Headlam, C., *The Letters of Lady Harriot Eliot*, pp. 70, 76.
15. Coupland, *Wilberforce*, pp. 24–5.
16. Duke MSS, W. Papers, Arden to W., 24 Aug. 1783.
17. Harrowby MSS, VIII 197, W. to D. Ryder, 18 Sep. 1795.
18. H, pp. 146–7.
19. L I, pp. 35–45; H, pp. 147–50.
20. PH XXIII c. 1248.
21. L I, p. 48.
22. PP, pp. 60–1.
23. See PH XXIV cc. 406, 705, 977.
24. Huntington MSS, Macaulay Papers, W. to Macaulay, 8 July 1826.
25. H, p. 203.
26. 'Fragments,' f. 129.
27. C. J. Wilson MSS, W. Mason to Christopher Alderson, 5 March 1784.
28. The Address to the Throne is printed in *York Chronicle*, 26 March 1784.
29. L I, p. 52.
30. For the County Meeting and speeches etc.: see *York Chronicle*, 26 March 1784, Wyvill, *Political Papers*, II, pp. 349–51, and L I, pp. 53–6.
31. Pottle and Scott, *Private Papers of Boswell*, XVI, pp. 45–6; and Bod. b.1.18, Samuel W's note of W's conversation at Brighton, 30 Sep. 1831.

Professor Pottle (letter to the author, 16 Feb. 1972) does not consider this a characteristic Boswell remark, and it is preserved only in W's reminiscences to Samuel W. forty-seven years later. At the time, Dundas described to W. Boswell's enthusiasm, but without a direct quote.

32. Stirling, A.M.W., *Annals* II, pp. 189–90 (based on Spencer Stanhope MSS).
33. *Ib.*
34. For cost of Hull Election see Lincolnshire Papers, W's account with Smith, Payne and Smith's Bank.
35. Bod. d.13.201, Hawke to W., 29 March 1784.
36. Bod. d.13.254, Fauconberg to W., 30 Mar. 1784.
37. For Yorkshire Association, see Christie, *Wilkes, Wyvill and Reform*, pp. 202–3.
38. Wyvill MSS, 7.2.59.1, W. to Wyvill Thursday [i.e. 8 April 1784].
39. Stanhope MSS 731 (11), W. to Eliot [N.D.].

4 *Unexpected Horizons*

1. BM Add MSS 37843 f. 239, Windham Papers, C. J. Fox to Windham, 17 April 1805.
2. Fitzwilliam MSS (Northants), Daniel Sykes to Fitzwilliam, 16 April 1784.
3. Greville, Charles, *Memoirs* ed. H. B. Wheatley (1884 ed.), IV, pp. 103–4.
4. Barnes, T., *Parliamentary Portraits*, 1815, p. 72. See also Brougham: *Statesmen* I, p. 272.
5. See W's complaints PH 34: cc. 109–11, 155, 166–7. He was an early advocate for an official transcript.
6. Farington, *Diaries* V, p. 195.
7. HMC *Rutland*, VI, p. 125; Erhman, *The Younger Pitt: The Years of Acclaim*, p. 230.
8. PH, 24: c. 100, 16 June 1784.
9. HMC *Rutland*, III, p. 112.
10. L I, p. 185.
11. Bod. d.13 f, Arden to W., 11 Sep. 1784.
12. For details of the tour to France, and the W-Milner conversations, see L I, chapter IV; H, pp. 206–11.
13. PP, p. 9.
14. 'Fragments,' f. 131.
15. H, p. 206.
16. BM Add MSS 35127 f. 449, Young Papers, W. to Arthur Young, 15 Aug. 1797.
17. Teignmouth, Lord, *Reminiscences of Many Years*, I, p. 62.
18. PP, p. 9.
19. Duke MSS, W. Papers, H. More to W., [N.D.] 1793.
20. For Doddridge's importance to W. see, e.g., Bod. d.16 f. 168, W. to Robert W., 22 Feb. 1822: 'I happened to meet with it by a striking instance of Providential arrangement at a very critical period of my life and it was I trust of singular benefit to me.'
21. St. John's, Cantab. MSS, W. to Sir Edward Parry, 25 June 1829.
22. PH, 25: c. 462.

23. PRO, 30.8. 189. f. 192, Chatham Papers, W. to Pitt, 2 Aug. 1785.
24. PH, 25: c. 651.
25. Osborn MSS, Yale, W. to – Clapham, 14 May 1785.
26. PRO 30.8.189, f. 152, Chatham Papers, W. to Pitt, 2 Aug. 1785.
27. For W's irritation with his mother see H, p. 209 (not referring to this incident specifically).
28. H, p. 208.
29. 'Fragments,' f. 132.
30. Ib.
31. Stanhope MSS 731(11), W. to Eliot, 28 Sep. 1785.
32. W. to – O'Hara, 27 June 1795, quoted anonymously, L I, p. 107.
33. 'Fragments,' f. 132.
34. Headlam, C., *The Letters of Lady Harriott Eliot*, p. 116.
35. Pitt's letter is printed PP, p. 13 and Furneaux, *William Wilberforce*, pp. 48–9.
36. L I, p. 90.
37. For the visit to Newton, see L I, pp. 96–7 and H, pp. 208, 210.
38. C I, p. 56.
39. 'Fragments,' f. 133.
40. Bod. d.15.151, W. to Sally W., 16 April 1786.

5 Between Two Worlds

1. HMC *Rutland* III, p. 286; see also p. 369.
2. Bod. b.1.16–17, Samuel W's note of W's conversation at Brighton on 30 Sep. 1831. The version quoted in L V, pp. 340–1 turns Pitt's statement to W. into a request for advice rather than for confirmation. Whether W's small part in the Hastings case justifies Coupland's giving such a long disquisition on India (Furneaux follows the same path), is a matter for debate.
3. Hey's letter is printed in Stirling, A.M.W, *Annals*, II, pp. 250–1.
4. For W's Bill see Radzinowicz, I, L., *A History of English Criminal Law*, pp. 476–7; for background of popular view of hanging and dissection, see Hay, D., and Linebaugh, P., *Albion's Fatal Tree*, pp. 65–107; for W's verdict on Loughborough's opposition: Sidmouth MSS 152 Bos 32.1, W. to Sidmouth, 5 Feb. 1816.
5. Wyvill MSS 7.2.59, W. to Wyvill, 25 July 1787.
6. Wyvill MSS 7.2.54, Duncombe to Wyvill, 29 June 1786.
7. Ib. 7.2.54, Stanhope to Wyvill, 8 July 1786.
8. Ib. 7.2.59, W. to Wyvill, 30 July, Wyvill to W., 10 Aug., W. to Wyvill, 17 Aug. 1786.
9. 30 July as above.
10. For W's attitude to theatres in 1786 etc. see 'Fragments,' ff. 28–30.
11. L I, p. 119.
12. W. to Wyvill, 30 July as above.
13. 'Fragments,' f. 133; and H, p. 45.
14. Huntington MSS, Montagu Papers, W. to Matthew Montagu, 10 Aug. 1788.

15. Duke MSS, W. Papers, W. to John Harford, 8 Sep. 1812.

16. L I, p. 310.

17. Names of tenants from his East Riding Rent Rolls 1791–2, Lincolnshire Papers. I may have missed a documentary reference to W. lowering Yorkshire rents, and rely on tradition in the family. For W's lowering rents at Wick Wick, Glos., and Highwood, Middx., see Ch. 28.

18. Wyvill MSS 7.2.54, W. to Wyvill, 30 July 1786.

19. Hull MSS, W. to Henry W., 30 Jan. 1829.

20. L I, p. 198.

21. Bod. d.16.160, W. to Elizabeth W., 25 June 1821.

22. Bod. c.4.15–16, paper dated 30 Nov., 16 Dec. 1786.

23. Lincolnshire Papers, W. to Lord Carrington, 17 Aug. 1829.

24. *Hunter Archeo. Soc.* VIII, p. 59, W. to Jas. Walker, 1 Apr. 1789.

25. Wyvill MSS 7.2.59, W. to Wyvill, 30 July, Wyvill to W., 10 Aug. 1786.

26. Church Missionary Society MSS, Venn Papers, Catherine King (afterwards Mrs. John Venn) to George King, 1 Nov. 1786. The advowson of Drypool church was part of Robert W's marriage settlement. W. presented Henry Venn (son of above Venns) to the living, 1826, and passed it, probably by gift, to Simeon Trustees *c.* 1830. *Victoria County History of Yorkshire: East Riding*, Vol. I, ed. K. J. Allinson, 1969, p. 298.

6 *The Cause of the Slaves*

1. *Spencer Papers* IV, p. 4 and *Markham Papers*, p. 50 (Naval Records Society). For Barham generally, see *Barham Papers* (Naval Records Society) not DNB. Other details from author's own research in unpublished Barham Papers in possession of Lord Gainsborough.

2. Porteus MS, Maidstone.

3. See Ramsay's *Essay*: pp. 113, 118, 173, 157, 281–90.

4. See Ramsay's *Inquiry*: pp. 33, 39.

5. L IV, p. 306 (W. to Stephen, 15 Jan. 1817).

6. C I, p. x.

7. Speech to Bible Society 1819, Owen, *History of the British and Foreign Bible Society*, III, p. 482n.

8. Ignatius La Trobe, *Letters to My Children*, 1851, p. 3. Benjamin La T. died 29 Nov. 1786.

9. W. wrote to E. H. Locker 23 Oct. 1820 *re* the 2 vols., that 'though so far accurate in that nothing is said in them which is not true, and more what is not *intended* to be so, yet by no means conveys a just conception of all that deserves commemoration in the history of that great cause until the period of our obtaining our grand parliamentary victory in 1807 . . .' W. specially singles out the gap during Clarkson's retirement and goes on: 'Nevertheless I know not any other connected account . . .' (Huntington MSS, Locker Papers.)

10. La Trobe, p. 22.

11. W's reply to Middleton is paraphrased in La Trobe, p. 22 (shorter version of La Trobe was used for L I, pp. 142–6).

12. La Trobe, p. 23.

13. L I, p. 147.
14. La Trobe, p. 23.
15. *Ib.*
16. Stanhope MSS 731 (12), W. to Tomline (Pretyman), 15 May 1806. For the code see Burke's *Works* (Little, Brown ed.) VI, pp. 262–89. A MS copy is in BM Add MSS 37890. 3–12, Windham Papers.
17. Wyvill MSS 7.2.59. W. to Wyvill, 21 May 1787.
18. Palace Yard details from Archives Dept., Westminster City Libraries.
19. Bod. d.20, f. 44, Barbara W's recollections.
20. Pierpont Morgan Lib. MSS, W. to Lord Lothian 15 Feb. [?1787].
21. Duke MSS, W. Papers, W. to Macaulay, 6 Aug. 1811.
22. Trinity MSS, Macaulay to Selina M. 2 Jan. 1839.
23. PH XXVIII: c. 48, W's speech of 12 May 1789.
24. Clarkson I, pp. 251–5.
25. Boswell's MS Diary entry for Tues. 13 March 1787, kindly furnished by Professor Pottle of Yale. (The only mention of Clarkson in the Diary. A few days between 1 March and 20 December 1787 are missing but it is unlikely the dinner would have gone unrecorded.) Now that the date of the party can be fixed so early in the spring, the open air conversation under 'Wilberforce Oak' cannot be placed before the dinner as in L I, p. 157.
26. Baring, H., *Diary of William Windham*, p. 108.
27. BM Add MSS 212554, Fair Minute Book II, f. 35.
28. Porteus MS (Lambeth) 2103.4.
29. L I, p. 151. The traditional date is kindly supplied by Mr. C. E. Wrangham. Furneaux, p. 72 uses this date but wrongly puts the Langton dinner as coming afterwards.
30. Bod. b.1.15, Samuel W's note of W's conversation on 27 Sep. 1831.
31. H, p. 139.

7 Remaking England

1. For Proclamations *re* Virtue and Vice, see *Handlist of Proclamations 1714–1810*, Bibliotheca Lindesiana, 1913.
2. Porteus MS (Lambeth) 2103.8. Middleton came with W. to the interview.
3. Furneaux, R., *William Wilberforce*, p. 57.
4. BM State Paper Room, B.S. 68.45 (100).
5. Radzinowicz, L., *A History of English Criminal Law*, III, p. 490.
6. Dolben MSS D(F)45, Dolben to his son (J. E. Dolben) 9 July 1787. For details of London and Middlesex magistrates' action, see *A Narrative of Proceedings Tending Towards a National Reformation*, by a County Magistrate (i.e. S. Glasse) 1787.
7. Horace Walpole's MS Journal in possession of Lord Waldegrave.
8. HMC 15th Report App. VII, *Ailesbury Journal*, p. 286.
9. *Ib.*
10. Wyvill MSS 7.2.59.11, W. to Wyvill, 25 July 1787.
11. Duke MSS, W. Papers, Manchester to W., 18 Sep. 1787.
12. Baring, H., *Diary of William Windham*, 1866, p. 121.

13. Fitzwilliam (Wentworth Woodhouse) MSS E 234.14, 15, Fitzwilliam to Rev. H. Zouch, ND [Aug.] and 11 Sep. 1787.
14. Quoted from *The Poor Man's Plea in relation to all the Proclamations* . . . (1698) in Radzinowicz II, p. 15.
15. Harrowby MSS VIII, 194, W. to D. Ryder, 27 Sep. 1787.
16. Sidmouth MSS 2.4B.1C, W. to H. Addington, 23 Aug. 1787.
17. Chatterton, Lady, *Memorials of Lord Gambier*, I, p. 165.
18. Porteus MS (Lambeth) 2103.33 (entry for 11 March 1791).
19. Sidmouth MSS 2.4B.1C, Bishop Hungerford of Hereford to Addington, 27 Sep. 1786.
20. *Ib.*, Addington to his father, 26 Sep. 1786.
21. *Ib*, Pretyman to Addington, Thursday [ND] Sep. 1786.
22. Bod. d.13.181, Eliot to W., 30 Aug. 1797.
23. Durham County R.O MSS D.He.28, Sept. 1798, W. to Harriot Eliot.
24. BM MSS Loan 57. XI, 1179, Bathurst Papers, W. to Bathurst, 3 Sep. 1816.
25. Stanhope MSS 731(11), W. to Eliot, 6 Aug. 1792.
26. Kenyon MSS, W. to Sir L. Kenyon, 29 Feb. 1788.
27. Huntington MSS, Montagu Papers, W. to M. Montagu [ND] 1790.
28. This was to Walter Spencer Stanhope. Stirling, *Annals* II, pp. 256–7.
29. 'Fragments,' ff. 43–4.
30. Duke MSS, Croker Papers; Croker's Carrington Memo.
31. Lincolnshire Papers, W. to Lord Carrington, 17 Aug. 1829.
32. Bod. d.15.153, W. to Muncaster [ND].
33. Melville, Lewis, *William Cobbett*, I, p. 158 (quoting BM Add MSS 37853.38).
34. Westminster MSS, W. to Earl Grosvenor, 15 Oct. 1802.
35. Huntington MSS, Montagu Papers, W. to M. Montagu [ND] 1790.
36. 'Fragments,' ff. 143–4.
37. See PP, pp. 73–4, and G. M. Trevelyan, *Grey of the Reform Bill*, p. 51n, where Trevelyan suggests that Pitt would have proceeded to Parliamentary reform.
38. *The Rolliad*, edition of 1790 (i.e. 4th Edition, Part II), pp. 118–19.
39. L I, p. 149 – the capitalizing is shown in the facsimile reproduced as end paper of L IV.

8 *No Doubt of Our Success*

1. Wyvill MSS 7.2.59, W. to Wyvill, 25 July 1787.
2. Bod. c.1.63, W. to Sam W., 12 Oct. 1823.
3. Lincolnshire Papers, Accounts with Smith, Payne and Smith. These also show the income from the East Riding properties only (£1051.7.6 in 1791). On 16 April 1784 Rev. Richard Sykes told Fitzwilliam that W. had inherited from father and uncle a total of £2000 p.a. in land, of which two-thirds went as jointures to his mother and sister; that W. had inherited £25,000 cash, of which he had already spent half on the two Hull Elections, £8000 in 1780, £5000 in 1784. Fitzwilliam (Wentworth Woodhouse) MSS. Figures should be multiplied by at least ten for modern equivalents.

4. Wyvill MSS, 7.2.59, W. to Wyvill, 25 July 1787.

5. *Ib.* 7.2.56, Wyvill to W., 31 July 1787 (copy).

6. Sidmouth MSS, 2.4B.1C, W. to Addington, 23, 30 July, 1787.

7. HMC, *Fortescue* I, p. 280.

8. Information from my friend Canon R. O. C. King ('four generations removed from Slavery') of Kingston, Jamaica.

9. Sidmouth MSS as above.

10. Boston MSS, W. to J. J. Gurney, 21 Feb. 1818.

11. BM Add MSS 34427.13, Auckland Papers, W. to W. Eden, 7 Dec. 1787.

12. *Ib.* 20 Oct. 1787, Auckland, Lord, *Journal and Correspondence of William Lord Auckland*, I, p. 239 (letter missing from Add. MSS).

13. *Ib.*

14. Clements Lib. MSS, Michigan Univ., Pitt to W., 22 Sep. 1787. See Erhman, J., *The Younger Pitt: The Years of Acclaim*, pp. 520–36 for the crisis.

15. BM Add MSS 34427.121, Auckland Papers. For a modern study, see Basil Davidson, *Black Mother*, 1961.

16. *Ib.* f. 13, W. to Eden, 7 Dec. 1787.

17. *Ib.*

18. L I, p. 157.

19. Bod. d.17.6, Eden to W., 6 Jan. 1788.

20. Auckland I, p. 304.

21. BM Add MSS 34427.366, Auckland Papers, W. to Eden, 5 Jan. 1788.

22. *Ib.* f. 403, W. to Eden, 18 Jan. 1788.

23. See Bod. d.13.334, Lafayette to W., 25 Feb. 1788.

24. Bible House MSS, J. Wesley to G. Sharp, 11 Oct. 1787.

25. Rhodes House MSS, Ramsay to W., 27 Dec. 1787.

26. Nat. Lib. Scotland MSS 3943.250 to W. Robertson, 25 Jan. 1788. W's thanks for infm is 20 Feb. 1788. For the Jesuit experiment in Paraguay, see Philip Caraman, *The Lost Paradise*, 1975.

27. Stanhope, G., and Gooch, G. P., *Life of 3rd Earl Stanhope*, p. 72 (MS missing from Stanhope Papers).

28. Duke MSS, Easthope Papers, Fuller Letter Book, Fuller to Jamaica Cttee of Corr., 30 Jan. 1788.

29. *Hunter Archeo. Soc.* VIII, p. 52, W. to James Walker, 15 Jan. 1788. (The W. letters are *verbatim* and are the best examples in print of his abbreviations, punctuation, etc.)

30. Duke MSS as above, Fuller Jamaica Cttee, 6 Feb. 1788.

31. *Ib.*

32. Kenyon MSS, Kenyon's diary.

33. Porteus MS (Lambeth) 2103.8.

34. L I, p.167 for W's illness.

35. Kenyon MSS, W. to Kenyon, 29 Feb. 1788.

36. H, p. 90.

37. L I, p. 169.

38. Fitzwilliam (Wentworth Woodhouse) MSS F.34.160, J. Beckett to Fitzwilliam, 24 Mar. 1788.

39. Wyvill MSS 7.2.59, Smith to Wyvill, 27 Mar. 1788. (Smith misdates Warren's taking over the case.)

40. Duke MSS, Croker Papers, Croker's Carrington Memo.
41. On opium in 18th-century medicine, see Hayter, Alethea, *Opium and the Romantic Imagination*, 1968. Dr. Oliver Ransford in *The Slave Trade*, 1971, pp. 188–9 misunderstands, and equates W's opium with a weakness like drunkenness.
42. Quoted in Hayter.
43. Bod. d.15.32, Milner to W., 16 Nov. 1793.
44. Bod. d.13.274, Harrowby, to W., 11 Oct. 1804; Harrowby MSS XII, 193, W. to H., 15 Oct. 1804.
45. Furneaux, R., *William Wilberforce*, p. 141 quoting Wrangham MSS.
46. Hull MS Diary, 3 April, 1 Mar. 1818. This dose means 12 grains, twice as much as Furneaux (p. 79) suggests as W's greatest dose.
47. Coleridge, *Letters* (ed. Grigg) IV, pp. 674–5, quoted Hayter, *op. cit.*, p. 26.
48. Levesley MS, from which also the following quotes. No folio numbering.
49. Sidmouth MSS, W. to Addington, 13 May 1788.
50. To Lady O. Sparrow, 7 Oct. 1814. Copy among Hull MSS. Original missing from BM Eg. MSS 1964, presumably mislaid before the letters given to BM.
51. Dolben MSS D(F)42., 5 June 1788.
52. MS copy in Wyvill MSS, 7.2.59.36.
53. Fitzwilliam (Wentworth Woodhouse) MSS, F.34.147, Lord Downe to Fitzwilliam, 26 Aug. 1788.
54. Stanhope MSS 731(13), W. to Pitt, 3 Oct. [1788].
55. Wyvill MSS 7.2.59.24 (copy), Wyvill to W., 4 Oct. 1788.
56. Farington, J., *Diaries* VII, p. 284.

9 *The Commons Turns Aside*

1. Bod. c.3.35, Milner to W., N.D. but 1793.
2. *Codrington Corr.*, letter 55103.
3. Kenyon MSS, W. to Kenyon, 12 Feb. 1788.
4. L I, p. 206; *Journal of John Wesley*, ed. Nehemiah Curnock, VII, p. 471.
5. Grey of Howick MSS, W. to Grey, 17 May [1789].
6. See Granville Sharp's warning of 1790 recalled in his letter to W., 11 Dec. 1796, Bod. c. 3.22.
7. Bod. c.4.46.
8. L I, p. 219 quotes Burke differently. It should be remembered that in the absence of Official Reports, various versions circulated of any important speech. Coupland, and Furneaux, blur this fact by the curious use of the term 'Hansard'. W's speech is PH XXVIII, cc. 41–67; debate, cc. 67–101.
9. Dolben MSS, D(F) 44, Dolben to J. Dolben, 3 July 1789.
10. Boston MSS, W. to Abbé de la Jeard, 17 July 1789.
11. Based mainly on Barbara W's MS 'Recollections', Bod. d.20.
12. L I, pp. 239–40, 246–7, Roberts, *Memoirs of Mrs Hannah More*, IV, pp. 173ff.
13. Duke MSS, W. Papers, H. More to W. [Sep. 1789].
14. Kenyon MSS, Kenyon's Diary, 19, 31 Aug., 2 Sep. 1789; L I, p. 237.
15. Huntington MSS, Montagu Papers, W. to M. Montagu, 12 Oct. 1789.

16. *Ib.*
17. Selincourt, E. de, and Shaver, C. L., *Letters of William and Dorothy Wordsworth*, I, pp. 25–6.
18. Sidmouth MSS, W. to Addington N.D., probably 1789, possibly 1790 or 1791. MS wrongly marked '1797' by Pellew.
19. Bod. d.16.80, W. to Muncaster, 12 March 1811.
20. St. John's Cantab. MSS, W. to John Campbell, 25 July 1814; for the stratagem of 1790 see PH XXVIII cc. 307-15.
21. Duke MSS, Smith Papers, W. to W. Smith, 5 May 1832.
22. *Ib.*
23. Commons' Committee 1790–1: only about 200 pages survive of printed evidence in *Parl. Reports*, 2nd series, XXIX, XXX, XXXIV. Collated evidence *against* the Trade is in *Digest of the Evidence . . .* publ. by J. Phillips, 1791.
24. PH XXVIII, cc. 712–13.

10 *I Shall Never Relinquish Their Cause*

1. Wyvill Papers, 7.2.59. 25, W. to Wyvill, 16 Oct. 1788.
2. L I, p. 276; Bod. d.15.48, W. Mason to W., 20 Dec. 1793.
3. Fitzwilliam (Wentworth Woodhouse) MSS, F.34.168, J. Beckett to Fitzwilliam, 24 March 1788.
4. Huntington MSS, Montagu Papers, W. to M. Montagu, April 1789.
5. Stanhope MSS, 731 (12), W. to Pretyman, 30 June 1796.
6. BM Add MSS 35128 f 239, Young Papers, W. to Arthur Young, 3 July 1800.
7. *Ib.* 20 July 1799. *Ib.* f. 122.
8. BM Add MSS 37308 f. 228, Wellesley Papers, W. to Mornington, 20 April 1799.
9. Rylands MSS, W. to Muncaster, 24 Aug. 1798.
10. *Ib.* [Nov. or Dec.] 1798.
11. Bod. d.15.58, Gisborne to W., 11 Jan. 1798.
12. Teignmouth, Lord, *Recollections* I, p. 253.
13. Wyvill MSS 106.19, W. to Wyvill, 23 Feb. 1796.
14. Wyvill MSS 59.25, W. to Wyvill, 16 Oct. 1788.
15. Stanhope MSS 731(12), W. to Bishop Tomline (Pretyman), 8 April 1805.
16. Sidmouth MSS, 2.4B.1C, W. to Addington, 23 July 1787.
17. *Hunter Archeo. Soc.*, VIII, p. 63.
18. *Ib.* p. 61; *Senator* II, pp. 78–9.
19. Spencer-Bernard MSS OE5.2., Lord Hawke to W., 10 June 1790; W. to Scrope Bernard, 16 June; Bernard to W., 1 July 1790. For another case, see Hay and Linebaugh, *Albion's Fatal Tree*, p. 46.
20. Bod. d.15. ff. 44, 46, W. Burgh to W., 29 April, 18 May 1795. A similar case is in Kenyon MSS, 28 Aug. 1790.
21. For the Register Bill see Wyvill, *Political Papers*, IV, 29; Wyvill MSS 7.2.66, Mason to Wyvill, 27 Feb. 1787; *ib.* 59, W. to Wyvill, 8 Feb., 21 May 1787.

22. Wyvill MSS, 7.2.59, W. to Wyvill, 8 Feb. 1787.
23. *Ib.* W. to Wyvill, 9 Aug. 1788.
24. Duke MSS, Wilberforce Papers, Wyvill to W., 11 Nov. 1789.
25. *Ib.*
26. Wyvill MSS 74.8, W. to Wyvill, 24 Nov. 1789.
27. Fitzwilliam (Northants) MSS, W. Hammond to Fitzwilliam, 15 June 1790.
28. L I, p. 271.
29. Thornton MSS, 7674. J.R. Thornton's Diary.
30. Stanhope MSS, 731 (12), W. to Pretyman, 27 July 1799.
31. See *Abstract of the Evidence . . . before a Select Committee . . . 1790 and 1791 . . .* printed by Jas. Phillips, London 1791. 155 pp. Captain Wilson's remark is p. 50.
32. Marianne Sykes' letters to her mother from Yoxall (including the comments on W's mother's feelings) and Carnarvon are in Thornton MSS 7674. I.L.I., various dates, 1790.
33. Bod. c. 4.18 (scrap marked Yoxall Lodge 10 Oct. 1790).
34. Lincolnshire Papers.
35. Huntington MSS, Montague Papers, W. to Montagu, 19 Sep. 1790.
36. Thornton MSS as above, Marianne Sykes to Mrs. Sykes, N.D.
37. *Ib.* 2 Oct. 1790.
38. Currie MSS, Cur. 49, W. to Jas. Currie, 11 Nov. 1790.
39. PRO 30.8.189. f. 151, Chatham Papers, W. to Pitt, 10 Nov. 1790.
40. *Senator* I, p. 90.
41. *Senator* II, p. 363. (8 April 1791.)
42. *Codrington Corr.* p. 36.
43. Duke MSS, Easthope Papers, Stephen Fuller Letter Book, S. Fuller to Cttee of Corr. 5 July 1791.
44. *Hunter Archeo. Soc.*, VIII, p. 57.
45. Wesley's letter (24 Feb. 1791) is in *Letters of John Wesley* ed. John Telford, VIII, pp 265–6.
46. L I, 298.
47. For the debate see *Senator* II, pp. 548–636. (The *Senator* series was published contemporaneously with the debates it reported during its comparatively short life. It is certainly more authentic than Cobbett's PH, and in the opinion of Mr. John Erhman is the most reliable record.)
48. Dolben MSS D(F) 59.

11 *Serving Africa*

1. Lloyd-Baker MSS, W. to Sharp, 25 Jan., Sharp to W., 6 Feb. 1790, W. to Sharp, N.D. [1790].
2. Hallett, R., *The Penetration of Africa*, I, p. 214.
3. For Sierra Leone generally see Fyfe, *A History of Sierra Leone*.
4. Stanhope MSS, 731 (11), W. to Eliot, 2 Aug. 1791.
5. See *Banks Correspondence*, p. 869 (the MSS are in Dept. of Botany, British Museum, Natural Hist.).
6. See Fyfe, *op. cit.*, pp. 32–3.

7. BM Add MSS 41262A f. 5, Clarkson Papers, W. to J. Clarkson, 8 Aug. 1791.
8. *Ib.* f. 27, 28 Dec. 1791.
9. *Ib.* f. 125, 7 July 1792.
10. Duke MSS, Croker Papers, Croker's Carrington Memo.
11. U.C.L. MSS, Brougham Papers, W. to Brougham, 16 Sep. 1809.
12. Fyfe, *op. cit.*, p. 57.
13. Bowood MSS, W. to Lansdowne, 17 July 1821.
14. BM Grenville MSS (not calendared at time of research), W. to Grenville, 20 Sep. 1806.
15. BM Add MSS 41262A f. 82, W. to J. Clarkson, 27 April 1792.
16. *Ib.*
17. Selincourt, E. de, and Shaver, C. L., *Letters of William and Dorothy Wordsworth*, I, p. 54.
18. Lewis-Walpole Lib. MSS, Farmington, Conn., W. to – Cookson (brother of William C.) 30 Dec. 1791.
19. *Ib.*
20. *Ib.*
21. A letter from W. thanking for a petition from Cambridge, is in Boston MSS (to anon., 8 Feb. 1792).
22. *Senator* IV, p. 349.
23. Debate of 2 April 1792: *Senator* IV (W's speech at p. 505). See also Windham's speech, pp. 249–50.
24. Burke, *Correspondence*, VII, 1968, p. 123.
25. Bowood MSS.
26. Wyvill MSS, 74.23, Wyvill to W., 7 April 1792.
27. BM Add MSS 41262A f. 82, Clarkson Papers, W. to J. Clarkson, 27 April 1792.
28. PH XXIX: cc. 1176–7.
29. Burke, VII, pp. 123–4.
30. *Codrington Correspondence*, p. 37.
31. See *The Trial of Captain John Kimber*, Bristol, 1792, and L I, pp. 357–8.
32. Wyvill MSS 74.23, W. to Wyvill, April 1792.

12 *The Coming of War*

1. See Groves, J. W., *Old Clapham*, p. 52 and Pym, D., *Battersea Rise*, *passim*.
2. Boston MSS, W. to W. Hayley, 25 Aug. 1807.
3. Bod. d.15.188, W. to H. More, 19 June 1793; Stanhope MSS 731 (11), W. to Eliot, 31 July 1793.
4. Church Missionary Society MSS, Venn papers, Venn to H. Venn [1793] and see Venn Papers c. 21 for tour to Bath, and Hennell, *John Venn and the Clapham Sect*, pp. 184–6.
5. Stanhope MSS, 731 (12), W. to Pretyman, 21 June 1804.
6. Thornton MSS 7674.I.R, Thornton's Diary, 14 Jan. and N.D. 1795.
7. Church Missionary Society MSS, Venn Papers, W. to Henry Venn Jr., 6 June 1829.

8. Wyvill MSS, 7.2.59, W. to Wyvill, 21 May 1787.

9. Stanhope MSS, 731 (11), W. to Eliot, 20 July 1792.

10. Huntington MSS, Montagu Papers, W. to Montagu, 25 July [1789].

11. Petworth House MSS, 55, W. to Lord Egremont, 15 Oct. 1796.

12. Huntington MSS, Montagu Papers, W. to Montagu, 21 Sep. 1799.

13. Bod. b.1.17, Samuel W's note of W's conversation on 30 Sep. 1831; and L I, pp. 360–1, V, p. 339.

14. Infm from Prof. Pottle. Incident was 31 July 1792. Boswell's Journal is blank 11 April–17 Aug. 1792.

15. Stanhope MSS, 731 (11), W. to Eliot, 20 July 1792.

16. Chatterton, Lady, *Memorials of Lord Gambier*, I, p. 200.

17. Duke MSS, W. Papers, H. More to W., N.D. [?1795].

18. Quoted Jay, W., *Autobiography*, pp. 312–13, from *Cambridge Intelligence*, *circa* 1794; the newspaper is not indexed and of such small print that the present writer abandoned his search for the source.

19. Duke MSS, W. Papers, H. More to W., 10 July [1794].

20. Waldegrave MSS, Duchess of Gloucester to H. More, 4 July 1794.

21. Waldegrave MSS, H. More to Princess Sophia, 11 Sep. 1807.

22. Waldegrave MSS, Duchess of Gloucester to H. More, 18 May 1795.

23. Porteus MS (Lambeth) 2103.51 (6 April 1792).

24. BM Add MSS 41263. f. 189, Clarkson Papers, W. to T. Clarkson, 11 March 1820.

25. Wyvill MSS, 7.2.82.2., W. to Wyvill, 14 Feb. 1793.

26. Bod. d.15.173, W. to anon, 6 Nov. 1792.

27. Cf. *Quarterly Review*, Vol. 62, p. 26 (Croker's anon. review).

28. Wyvill MSS as above, 14 Feb. 1793 (postscript).

29. PH XXX c. 79.

30. Wyvill MSS as above, 14 Feb. 1793.

31. Currie MSS, 920 Cur. 52, W. to Jas. Currie, 13 Aug. 1793.

32. Wyvill MSS as above, 14 Feb. 1793.

33. PH XXX c. 779.

34. Wyvill MSS, 7.2.82.10, W. to Wyvill, 30 July 1793.

35. See PP, pp. 74–5.

36. PH XXX cc. 514–30; Wyvill MSS, 7.2.82.5, W. to Wyvill, 26 Feb. 1793.

37. PH XXX c. 659.

38. Aspinall, A., *Corr. of George Prince of Wales 1770–1812*, II, p. 349.

39. Currie MSS, 920. Cur. 52, W. to J. Currie, 13 April 1793. For a similar false rumour, see HMC. *Ailesbury* 15th Report, App VII, p. 265.

40. Chatterton, Lady, *Memorials of Lord Gambier* I, p. 210. Carhampton's joke is not recorded in the printed debates but see L II, p. 25 quoting W's Diary for 15 May 1793: 'Lord Carhampton abusing me as a madman.'

41. Duke MSS, Easthope Papers, Fuller Letter Book, S. Fuller to Jamaica Cttee of Corr., 5 June 1793; see PH XXX cc. 947–9.

42. Thornton MSS, 7674. L I, Thornton to Macaulay [Feb. 1794].

43. Duke MSS as above, S. Fuller to Jamaica Cttee, 4 March 1794.

44. Duke MSS, W. Papers, Dundas to W., 25 Sep. 1793.

45. Bod. d.17.74, *ib*, 7 March 1794.

46. Chatterton, *op. cit.*, I, p. 241.

47. BM Grenville MSS, Grenville to W., 4 April 1794 (copy).

48. Duke MSS, as above, S. Fuller to Jamaica Cttee, 4 April 1794.
49. Bod. d.15.37, Stephen to W., 20 Sep. 1794.

13 *The Independent*

1. Wyvill MSS, 7.2.82.12, W. to Wyvill, 9 Nov. 1793.
2. Currie MSS, 920 Cur. 53, W. to Currie, 21 Jan. 1794.
3. *Ib.*
4. *Ib.*
5. Bod. d.15.192, W. to Muncaster, 30 June 1794.
6. L II, pp. 63–8.
7. Stanhope MSS, 731 (11), W. to Eliot, 22 Dec. 1794.
8. Harewood MSS, Canning to Mrs. Leigh, 4 Jan. 1795.
9. Fitzwilliam (Wentworth Woodhouse) MSS, F.31.36, Portland to Fitz-william, 7 Jan. 1795.
10. Aspinall, A., *Later Letters of George III*, II, Letter 1185.
11. As above, Portland to Fitzwilliam, 7 Jan. 1795.
12. *Ib.*
13. L II, p. 72.
14. Duke MSS, Easthope Papers, Fuller Letter book, Fuller to Jamaica Cttee, 31 March 1795.
15. Farington, J., *Diaries*, I, p. 85.
16. Sir George Beaumont's comment is in an unpublished typescript at Windsor of further Farington Diary entries.
17. PRO.30. c. 189.156, Chatham Papers, W. to Pitt, 6 Sep. 1794.
18. Roberts MSS, W. to S. Roberts, 21 March 1817.
19. Stanhope MSS, 731 (13), W. to Pitt, 12 July, 29 Aug. 1798.
20. L II, p. 71.
21. BM Add MSS 41085.16, Melville Papers, W. to Dundas [1795].
22. Roberts MSS, W. to S. Roberts, 2 April 1817 (misdating the incident to 1796).
23. L II, pp. 85–6. See also Camden MSS, Kent R.O., Mornington to Camden, 24 April 1795, reporting Fitzwilliam as universally condemned: 'Wilber-force particularly and even Bankes' were of opinion that he stood con-victed on his own evidence.
24. BM Add MSS 41085.16, Melville Papers, Dundas to W. (draft) N.D. (Saty night 11 o'clock) but by context clearly April or May 1795.
25. L II, pp. 89–90, PH XXXII cc. 1–36.
26. Camden MSS, W. to Camden, 18 June 1795.
27. Currie MSS, 920 Cur. 54, W. to Jas. Currie, 10 June 1795.
28. Sidmouth MSS, Hawkesbury to Addington, 27 Aug. 1796. The Latin is a quote from Samuel Parr's *Praefetio ad Bellendum de Statu*, p. xli. (I owe this identification to Mr. C. E. Wrangham.)
29. Baring, H., *Diary of William Windham*, p. 336.
30. Aspinall, A., *op. cit.* (George III), II, p. 416n.
31. *Senator* XIII, pp. 166–7, 10 Nov. 1795.
32. *Senator* XVI, p. 194, 2 Nov. 1796; and see PH XXXIV, c.155.
33. Bod. d.13.77, Bankes to R. I. and S. Wilberforce, 13 Sep. 1834.

34. *Senator* XIII, p. 205.
35. Huntington MSS, Macaulay Papers, W. to Macaulay, 8 July 1826.
36. L II, p. 114.
37. *Senator* XIII, p. 205, 12 Nov. 1795.
38. *Proceedings and Speeches at the Meeting 17 November 1795 . . . to petition Parliament against Lord Grenville's and Mr. Pitt's Treason and Sedition Bills.* Norwich (1795) p. 19. I owe the reference to Mr. Charles Jewson.
39. Wyvill MSS 7.2.82.7, W. to Wyvill, 19 March 1793; *ib.* 106.13, 23 Nov. 1794; *ib.* 7.2.106.19, 23 Feb. 1796. The offending letter is printed in Wyvill, *Political Papers*, IV, p. 41.
40. *Senator* XIII, p. 506, 27 Nov. 1795.
41. For the foray to York, see L II, pp. 124–30.
42. Travel details kindly supplied by Mr. C. E. Wrangham.
43. Wyvill MSS 7.2.106.16, W. to Wyvill, 5 Dec. 1795.
44. Stirling, A. M. W., *Annals* II, p. 263.
45. *Senator* XIV, p. 665, 4 Dec. 1795.

14 *Prisoners and the Poor*

1. Bod. d.15.9 (C I, pp. 64–5) 8 Dec. [1786] and PP, pp. 16–17, Pitt to W., 23 Sep. 1786.
2. PP p. 21 (mis-dated), Pitt to W., 28 June 1788.
3. BM Add MSS 33542.8, Bentham Papers, W. to Bentham, 27 Jan. 1795; *Ib.* f. 57, 17 April 1795.
4. *Ib.* f. 151, 2 Mar. 1796; *ib.* f. 163, 22 Mar. 1796.
5. UCL MSS, Bentham Papers, Bentham to W., 2 April 1796 (draft).
6. BM Add MSS 33542.278, Bentham to W., 6 Sep. 1796 (draft).
7. *Ib.* f. 300, W. to Bentham, 26 Oct. 1796.
8. *Ib.* f. 304, W. to Bentham, 28 Oct. 1796; *ib.* f. 308, Nov. 1796.
9. L II, pp. 171–2.
10. BM Add MSS 33544. 75, Bentham Papers, Bentham to W., 31 May 1803 (draft).
11. *Ib.* f. 80, 1 June 1803.
12. *Ib.* f. 461, W. to Bentham, 9 May 1810.
13. St. Bart's Archives, Ha 1.15, MS Minutes of Meetings of Board of Governors, pp. 66, 455, 466, 574; L II, p. 180.
14. Harford MSS, W. to Hannah More, 13 Aug. 1810, for infm of anon. benefactor.
15. Heasman, K., *Evangelicals in Action*, p. 200.
16. Huntington MSS, Macaulay Papers, W. to Macaulay, 7 July [1826].
17. L I, pp. 252, 255.
18. Bod. d.15.214, W. to W. Hey, 9 Feb. 1798 *re* Atkinson of Leeds.
19. Harford MSS, W. to H. More, 13 Aug. 1810.
20. L II, pp. 304–7.
21. Thornton MSS, 7674. L.2, Thornton to H. More, 26 Oct. 1798.
22. Petworth House MSS, 55, W. to Lord Egremont, 15 Oct. 1796; see L II, p. 304.

23. Bod. d.17.103, Sinclair to W., 30 Jan. 1800. The questionnaire is printed L III, pp. 414–16.
24. Baker, J., *Sir Thomas Bernard*, p. 13.
25. See the annual volumes of Reports, e.g. origin: V, p. 3; cotton mills: IV app. pp. 1–22; 'In pauperism as in slavery . . .' V, p. 24. These volumes are a mine of information. A set may be studied in the Library of the Royal Institution.
26. See PR 3rd Series XVII, c. 448 (6 April 1802).
27. Managers' Minutes (MS in R.I. archives) I, p. 126. See also Farington, *Diaries*, III, p. 285 and L III, p. 186.
28. Farington Diary, 21 July 1806 (reporting W's conversation) TS copy at Windsor.
29. See Halsbury's *Statutes*, 3rd Ed. (1972) XV, pp. 255–6.
30. *Senator* XIV, p. 845, 17 Dec. 1795.
31. *Ib.* XV, p. 1197, 3 March 1796.
32. Bod. d.15.138 (printed C I, p. 122), Bentham to W., 8 March 1796.
33. Melville MSS, SRO GD 51.1.435, W. to Lord Melville, 13 June 1804.
34. Wyvill MSS, 7.2.106.19, W. to Wyvill, 23 Feb. 1796.
35. Rhodes House MSS, c. 106.9, quoted W. to Buxton, 28 April 1828.
36. L II, p. 142. For debate, see PR XLIV cc. 292–324. (List of majority: c. 324.) For list of minority, PH XXXII cc. 901–2. W's speech is in *Senator* XV, p. 1258.
37. Stanhope MSS 731(12), W. to Pretyman, 30 June 1796.
38. L II, p. 147.
39. Bod. d.15.5, Stephen to W., 24 June 1796.
40. Fitzwilliam (Wentworth Woodhouse) MSS F.34.204, R. Sinclair to Fitzwilliam [N.D.]. This also describes the scene at the hustings.

15 *The Heart of the Matter*

1. St. John's, Cantab MSS, W. to Sir Edward Parry, 25 June 1829, a covering letter with a gift of his book, *A Practical View* . . .; A similar point made when sending it to Fanny Burney, Mme d'Arblay in 1820: see her *Diary and Letters* V, pp. 384–5.
2. Stephen, *Essays.*, pp. 500–1.
3. Huntington MSS, Montagu Papers, W. to Montagu, 14 Oct. 1800.
4. BM Add MSS 35649.121, Hardwicke Papers, W. to Lord Hardwicke, Feb. 1811.
5. BM Add MSS 35128.122, Young Papers, W. to Arthur Young, 20 July 1799.
6. Letter to Lieut. (aftwds Cmdr) G. Reynolds, R.N., 15 Mar. 1806, in possession of his descendant, the Rev. J. S. Reynolds.
7. BM Add MSS 35127.442, Young Papers, W. to Arthur Young, 8 Sep. 1797; 'Fragments,' f. 52.
8. Massachusetts Hist. Soc. MSS, W. to —Walker Esq., Trinity Coll., Cantab, 31 Dec. 1817.
9. L II, p. 199.
10. Duke MSS, W. Papers, W. to Bishop Porteus, 14 March 1797.

11. L II, p. 199.
12. Bod. d.17.82, Rev. R. Cecil to W., 6 April 1797.
13. Thornton MSS, 7674, L I, Thornton to Macaulay, 22 May 1797.
14. For a digest of the argument, see Furneaux, R., *William Wilberforce*, Ch. XII.
15. *Practical View*, pp. 405–6.
16. *Practical View*, p. 375.
17. Bod. d.16.235, W. to Robert W., 3 June [1826].
18. Thornton MSS, 7674 1.L.2, H. Thornton to H. More, 21 Oct. 1798; L II, p. 208.
19. Grimshawe, T. S., *Memoirs of Rev. Legh Richmond*, pp. 28–9.
20. Young, A., *Autobiography*, p. 288.
21. BM Add MSS. 35127.438, Young Papers, W. to A. Young, 15 Aug. 1797.
22. Bathurst MSS 82.77, W. to Lord Apsley, 10 Aug. 1792.
23. Young Papers as above, f. 439, W. to A. Young, 15 Aug. 1797.
24. 'Fragments,' f. 81.
25. Young Papers as above 35128.122, W. to A. Young, 20 July 1799.
26. Bathurst Papers, as above W. to Apsley, 10 Aug. 1792.
27. Bod. c.4.16, W's Diary, 13 Jan. 1789.
28. Bod. d.16.114, W. to Babington, 29 June 1820 (a letter about Queen Caroline).
29. Bod. d.15.160–5, W. to Mary Bird, 24 Oct. 1789. For evidence of this letter's suppression, see David Newsome's review of Ford K. Brown's *Fathers of the Victorians*, in *Historical Journal* vi, 1963.
30. Bod. d.16.196, W. to Robert W., 5 Sep. 1823.
31. BM Add MSS 35131.128, Young Papers, W. to A. Young, 21 July 1811.
32. Hull MSS, W. to Henry W., 3 Nov. 1818.
33. Bod. c. 3.255, 'Miss A. Sullivan to Mrs. Huber, about 1815' (copy).
34. Southey, R., *Life and Corr.*, IV, p. 317.
35. *Harford Annals*, p. 101, W. to John Harford, 26 May 1814.
36. BM Add MSS 38191.280, Liverpool Papers, W. to Liverpool, 30 Sep. 1821.
37. Bathurst MSS, Vol. 11.1179, W. to Bathurst, 3 Sep. 1816.
38. Bod. d.6.47, W. to H. More, 15 Jan. 1806.
39. Bod. d.16.135, W. to Stephen, 29 Sep. 1820. (Omitted from the badly garbled printed version, C II, p. 441.)
40. Bod. d.16.212, W. to Mary Bird, 27 Dec. 1827.
41. Sidmouth MSS, W. to Addington, 9 Nov. 1799.
42. Kinghorn MSS, Joseph Kinghorn to David Kinghorn, 27 June 1797.
43. *Ib.* to *ib.*, 25 July 1797.
44. *Ib.* to *ib.* 22 Aug. 1797.
45. Hull MS, Diary.
46. Jay, W., *Autobiography*, p. 302.
47. See W's long letter to James Walker 20 Jan. 1790 printed *verbatim* in *Hunter Archeo. Soc.* VIII, p. 57.
48. For the Repeal debate of 1790 see L I, pp. 258–60.
49. *Senator* XVIII, p. 1651.
50. *Ib.* XVII, p. 615.
51. C I, p. 93.

52. Bod. c.3.244, N.D. [13 Aug. 1792].
53. Mrs. Wesley's thanks, 20 Aug. 1792, is Bod. d.15.24.
54. BM Add MSS 41085.10, 14, 18, Melville Papers, W. to Dundas, 24 Jan., 26 March, 26 Oct. 1798.

16 *Barbara*

1. Thornton MSS, 7674 L10, Marianne Sykes to Joseph Sykes, N.D.
2. Knutsford, Lady, *Zachary Macaulay*, p. 204.
3. Thornton MSS, 7674.L.1, Mrs. H. Thornton to Mrs. Robert T., 19 Sep. 1796.
4. Calthorpe MSS, W. to Lord Calthorpe, Dec. 1821.
5. Duke MSS, Croker Papers, Croker's Carrington Memo.
6. Thornton MSS, 7674.1.N, f. 501, Marianne T's MS Recollections.
7. The Calthorpe, Croker and Thornton MSS lead me to the view, as against Furneaux, p. 161, that Babington mentioned Barbara *before* 13 April.
8. Thornton MSS, 7674.L.4.150, Infm. on Goughs and Spooners kindly furnished by City Librarian, Birmingham.
9. As above, Marianne's Recollections, ff. 503–4.
10. Duke MSS, W. Papers, H. More to W., 25 April 1797.
11. Knutsford, *op. cit.*, p. 244.
12. Stanhope MSS, 731(11), W. to Pitt N.D. [17 April 1797]. *Re* Burke see L II, pp. 211–12.
13. For the engagement, see Furneaux, *William Wilberforce*, pp. 162–3, with charming quotes from W's secret journal in Wrangham MSS.
14. Huntington MSS, Montagu Papers, W. to Montagu, N.D.
15. Duke MSS, W. Papers, H. More to W., Sunday [29 April 1797].
16. Extracts from two letters in Thornton MSS, 7674 L.1., Thornton to Mrs. T., May 1797.
17. L II, p. 217.
18. PRO 30.8.189, also ff. 166, 169, 170, Chatham Papers, W. to Pitt [May 1797].
19. Huntington MSS, Montagu Papers, W. to Montagu, N.D. [June 1797].
20. Bod. d.20.33, Barbara's MS Reminiscences.
21. Chatterton, Lady, *Memorials of Lord Gambier*, I, p. 324.
22. W. to Montagu as above.
23. Stanhope MSS, 731(11), W. to Eliot, N.D. [1797].
24. Stanhope MSS, 731 (12), W. to Pretyman, 10 June 1797.
25. Rylands MSS, W. to Muncaster N.D. [1797].
26. Boston MSS, W. to John Clarkson, 5 Sep. 1797.
27. Stanhope MSS, 731 (11), W. to Eliot, 17 Aug. 1797.
28. *Ib.*
29. Duke MSS, W. Papers, H. More to W., 26 Sep. [1797].
30. Huntington MSS, Montagu Papers, W. to Montagu N.D. [1797].
31. The move into Broomfield was not until 19 May 1798.
32. Bod. d.6.8, W. to Muncaster, 4 July 1803.
33. Duke MSS, Smith Papers, W. to W. Smith, 20 July 1798.
34. Bod. d.17.88, Addington to W., 24 July 1798.

35. Duke MSS, W. Papers, W. to T. Harrison, 22 Oct. 1814.
36. Rylands MSS, W. to Muncaster, 13 Nov. 1798.
37. Calthorpe MSS, W. to Lord Calthorpe, Dec. 1821.
38. Duke MSS, Croker Papers, Croker's Carriñgton Memo.

17 *Britain at Bay*

1. L II, p. 280.
2. Rylands MSS, W. to Muncaster, 24 Aug. 1798.
3. Duke MSS, W. Papers, Pitt to W., 30 May 1798. (Printed *verbatim* L II, pp. 281–2.)
4. Fitzwilliam (Northants) MSS, F. Laurence to Fitzwilliam, 26 Nov. 1797, referring to W's reply on Laurence's speech on the Address 10 Nov., see *Senator* XIX, p. 117. For Burke's sentiment see L II, p. 72 (Laurence was Burke's literary executor).
5. Stanhope MSS, 731 (12), W. to Pitt, N.D. [17 April 1797].
6. Letters to Grimston are in E. Riding R.O.
7. Arundel Castle MSS, W. to Duke of Norfolk N.D. (marked 'March 16–97').
8. Stanhope MSS 731 (12), W. to Pitt, marginal note on copy of letter from W. Riding magistrates to W., 5 Dec. 1796.
9. BM Add MSS 41085.10, Melville Papers, W. to Dundas, N.D.; see also PRO HO 50.418.45, letters of W. to Secy. of State enclosing letters of 3rd parties *re* recruiting.
10. L II, p. 287.
11. Porteus MS (Lambeth), 2103.54 (under date 12 March 1793).
12. For the Williams case: L II, pp. 251, 279; *Autobiography of Francis Place* (ed. Thale, 1972), pp. 159–72; Hammond, *The Town Labourer, 1760–1832*, p. 235; Radzinowicz, *A History of English Criminal Law*, III, p. 171.
13. L II, p. 251.
14. See Howell, T. J. (ed.), *State Trials*, XXVI, pp. 653–720.
15. Quoted in Jay, W., *Autobiography*, p. 316.
16. Place, *op. cit.*
17. PH XXIV cc. 111–125, espec. 115, 122–3. Report of W's speech is collated with version in L II, p. 321. For Glasse as philanthropist, see Bettering Society's *Reports*, Vol. I, Report III, pp. 60–65, and Vol. II, p. 93. Also DNB.
18. Courtenay, *Characteristic Sketches*, p. 33.
19. L II, p. 323.
20. PH XXIV c. 116.
21. A comment by M. W. Patterson in his *Sir Francis Burdett*, 2 vols., 1931, repeated by Eric Williams.
22. Duke MSS, Smith Papers, W. to W. Smith, 20 Feb. 1798 (printed L II, pp. 267–71).
23. Currie MSS, Liverpool R.O., 920 Cur. 51, W. to Jas. Currie, 29 July 1793.
24. L II, pp. 244–5, 250.
25. Rylands MSS, W. to Muncaster, N.D. (prob. early 1798).
26. *Ib.*

27. Wilberforce MSS, W. Sussex R.O. 27, W. to Mary Smith, 20 Aug. 1804.
28. *Ib.*
29. L II, pp. 385–6.
30. BM Add MSS 35128.286, Young Papers, W. to A. Young, N.D.
31. Huntingdon MSS, Montagu Papers, W. to Montagu, 6 Nov. 1800.
32. W. to Young as above.
33. BM Add MSS 35128.187, Young Papers, W. to Young, 'February 1800'.
34. PH XXXIV cc. 1544–8 (*re* Young's evidence, see c. 1498).
35. W. to Young, f. 286 as above.
36. Duke MSS, W. Papers, W. to Thomas Harrison N.D. (probably *circa* 1819 and thus not referring to a Parliamentary debate but a public meeting. However, it makes the point).
37. PH XXIV c. 1550. As early as 21 March 1793 he had told Wyvill he had long wanted official transcripts (Wyvill MSS 7.2.82.8).
38. BM Add MSS 35128.239, W. to Young, 3 July 1800. (The Wilberforce–Young letters are not bound in proper sequence.) See Inglis, *Poverty and the Industrial Revolution*, pp. 87–9.
39. *Letter to the Lord Lieutenant of the County of Oxford*, 29 Sep. 1800; part of pamphlet, *The Whole Proceedings and Resolutions of the Freeholders of Middlesex*, 1800.
40. Kenyon MSS (printed HMC *Kenyon*, p. 55), W. to Lord Kenyon, 9 Jan. 1801.
41. Osborn MSS, W. to Mrs. Nugent, 2 Jan. 1801.
42. Huntington MSS, Montagu Papers, W. to Montagu, 6 Nov. 1800.

18 *Entr'acte*

1. BM Grenville MSS, W. to Grenville, 31 Jan. 1807.
2. Debate is PH XXXIII cc. 251–94, but for W's speech see *Senator* XVII, p. 1145.
3. W. to Grenville, as above. The papers were laid before the House in May 1804.
4. Gratus, J., *The Great White Lie*, p. 98.
5. This oft-quoted letter is in L II, p. 265. Gratus, pp. 97–8 misreads the relationship between the two men, and ignores what W. had already achieved by negotiation on the point.
6. BM Add MSS 56563.166, Broughton Papers, Hobhouse (Broughton) Diary, 31 March 1841.
7. Duke MSS, W. Papers, W. to Thomas Harrison (secretary of Africa Association), 22 Oct. 1814.
8. See W's speech in debate of 4 Nov. 1801. PR, 3rd Series, XVI c. 146.
9. BM Grenville MSS, W. to Grenville, 5 June 1806.
10. Rylands MSS, W. to Muncaster, 13 March 1799.
11. Carus, W., *Charles Simeon*, p. 79; H. C. G. Moule, *Charles Simeon*, pp. 87–9.
12. Chatterton, Lady, *Memorials of Lord Gambier*, I, p. 218.
13. Wood, A. Skevington, *Thomas Haweis*, p. 179 (see p. 203 for W. and LMS).

14. Subscription to BMS: Hennell, *John Venn and the Clapham Sect*, p. 227.

15. Hole, C., *The Early History of the Church Missionary Society*, pp. 45, 58; Hennell, p. 239.

16. Huntington MSS, Macaulay Papers, W. to Macaulay, 23 July [1826].

17. Preface to *Christian Observer*, vol. III.

18. Bod. d.16.30, W. to Stephen, 20 Sep. 1804.

19. Bod. d.16.85, W. to Macaulay, 11 Dec. [1812].

20. Sidmouth MSS, W. to Addington, 14 Sep. 1799.

21. Duke MSS, W. Papers, J. Venn to W., 11 Dec. 1799.

22. Thornton MSS, 7674. c. 2, H. Thornton to H. More, Dec. 1800.

23. *Cobbett's Weekly Political Register*, III, p. 96.

24. For Sunday working, see Porteus MS (Lambeth) 2103.96.

25. See L II, p. 272.

26. Sidmouth MSS, written on a scrap of paper in hand of Pellew, his son-in-law and biographer.

27. Thornton MSS, 7674 L.1, quoted by H. Thornton to Patty More, 14 April 1794.

28. Porteus MS (Lambeth) f. 96, and Bod. c.3.40, Porteus to W., 31 March 1798.

29. Aspinall, A., *Letters of George Prince of Wales 1770–1812*, V, p. 160n.

30. L II, p. 360.

31. Thornton MSS, 7674 L.2, H. Thornton to H. More, 13 March 1800.

32. Bod. c. 4.23.

33. Thornton MSS, 7674 L.2, H. Thornton to H. More, N.D. [Aug. 1800].

34. Roberts MSS, W. to S. Roberts, 6 Oct. 1832.

35. Huntington MSS, Montagu Papers, W. to Montagu, 27 Sep. 1800.

36. St. John's, Cantab. MSS, W. to Isaac Spooner, 2 Oct. 1800.

37. Huntington MSS, Montagu Papers, W. to Montagu, 14, 28 Oct. 1800.

38. 'Fragments,' ff. 139–40.

39. Rylands MSS, W. to Muncaster, 3 Dec. 1798; see also BM Add MSS, 37308.229, Wellesley Papers, W. to Mornington, 10 April 1799. 'Fragments' records his reflections in old age on the subject.

40. 'Fragments,' f. 140.

41. L III, p. 3.

42. *Cobbett's Weekly Political Register*, II, p. 411; Melville, *William Cobbett*, I, p. 154.

43. L II, p. 369.

44. See Anstey, R., *The Atlantic Slave Trade and British Abolition 1760–1810*, p. 325. The W.–King Corr. MSS are at New York Hist. Soc.

45. Harewood MSS, Canning to W., 5 Feb. 1802.

46. PRO 30.29.8.2, reported by Canning to Lord G. Leverson-Gower, 16 March 1802.

47. Bagot, J., *George Canning and his Friends*, I, p. 188.

48. Harrowby MSS, XII, 194, W. to Harrowby, 24 Oct. 1804.

49. Stanhope MSS, 731 (13) W. to Pitt, 29 May 1802; L II, p. 85.

50. Creevey MSS, Creevey to Jas. Currie (copy).

51. Westminster MSS, W. to Earl Grosvenor, 15 Oct. 1802.

52. Thornton MSS, 7674 L.3, Thornton to Mrs. T., 9 Sep. 1803.

19 *The Fall of Lord Melville*

1. Thornton MSS, 7674.1.N. ff. 500–1, Marianne Thornton's Recollections.
2. *Ib.* f. 592.
3. Barbara's nerves, etc.: deduced from frequent references in Marianne T. and others, and Hull MS Diary.
4. Duke MSS, Smith Papers, W. to W. Smith, 15 July 1802.
5. Teignmouth, Lord, *Reminiscences of Many Years*, I, pp. 2–3; C. Fyfe's *History of Sierra Leone* has many details about the later careers of the S.L. boys.
6. Groves, J. W., *Old Clapham*, p. 75; Burgess, J. H. M., *The Chronicles of Clapham*, p. 63; Marianne Thornton, as above, ff. 592–3.
7. Farington, J., *Diaries*, III, p. 285.
8. L III, p. 112.
9. Southey, *Life* IV, pp. 316–17.
10. Hull MS Diary, 4 May, 13 June 1818.
11. Bod. d.3.19, W. to T. Gisborne, 21 Jan. 1803.
12. Farington, *op. cit.*, III, p. 285.
13. Teignmouth, *op. cit.*, I, pp. 244–5.
14. Stephen, J., Jr., *Essays*, p. 480.
15. Farington, *op. cit.*, III, pp. 285ff for a good description of W's table talk.
16. Stephen, J., *Memoirs*, p. 110.
17. Stephen, J., Jr., *Essays*, pp. 480–1. The last quoted sentence, 'His mirth . . . childhood,' is in the original shorter essay, *Edinburgh Review*, April 1838, but is omitted from the volume of collected essays.
18. Marianne Thornton as above, f. 593.
19. *Ib.* (Others bear out her pinchpenny housekeeping.)
20. Rylands MSS, W. to Muncaster, 24 Aug. 1798 (see also 3 Dec. 1798).
21. Wilberforce MSS 27, West Sussex RO, W. to Mary Smith, 24 Aug. 1804.
22. Hull MS Diary, 15 Dec. 1819.
23. Bod. d.6.6, W. to Mrs. W., N.D.
24. L III, p. 91; Owen, J., *History of the British and Foreign Bible Society*, I pp. 17–18; *re* Welsh *Family Bible*, see DNB, art. Peter Williams 1722–96. The girl's minister, Thomas Charles of Bala, co-founder of BFBS, is believed to have been one of the instigators of Williams's expulsion from the Welsh Calvinistic Connexion, for heresy in his notes. The *Family Bible* nevertheless became immensely popular.
25. Bible House MSS, W. to Granville Sharp (presumed; no addressee mentioned) 7 March 1804.
26. Owen, I, p. 61.
27. Duke MSS, W. Papers, Pitt to W., N.D. (printed L III, p. 167).
28. BM Grenville MSS, W. to Grenville, 26 June 1804.
29. L III, p. 168. For De Blaquiere's character, see *Complete Peerage*, IV, p. 108, note (f.). DNB (II, pp. 667–8) is kinder.
30. Monroe MSS, New York P.L., W. to Monroe, 6, 7 June 1804.
31. Melville MSS., Scottish R.O., G.D. 51.1.435, W. to Melville, 13 June 1804.
32. Remark by Brougham. News, *Henry Brougham to 1830*, p. 27.

33. Harrowby MSS, XII.182, W. to Harrowby, 28 June 1804.

34. Bod. d.17.131, Harrowby to W., 25 Sep. 1804.

35. Bod. d.16.40, W. to Stephen, 20 Dec. 1804.

36. Stephen, J., *Essays*, p. 478.

37. Bod. d.16.32, W. to Stephen, 2 Oct. 1804.

38. PRO 189.176, W. to Pitt, N.D.

39. Harrowby MSS XII.198, W. to Harrowby, 1 Nov. 1804.

40. *Ib.* 200, W. to Harrowby, 9 Nov. 1804.

41. Bod. d.16.32, W. to Stephen, 2 Oct. 1804.

42. Brougham's Sicily paper is in Duke MSS, W. Papers.

43. Harrowby MSS, XII.184, W. to Harrowby, 25 Sep. 1804.

44. *Ib.* f. 193, W. to Harrowby, 15 Oct. 1804.

45. Duke MSS, W. Papers, W. to Pitt, 25 Oct. 1805; H.M.C. *Lonsdale*, 13th Report, App VII, pp. 182–3.

46. L III, p. 213.

47. Michigan Univ. MSS, Lacnite-Lansdowne Papers, Lord H. Petty to W., 23 March 1805.

48. L III, pp. 216–17.

49. PRO 30.8.189.178, W. to Pitt, 1 June [1805].

50. L III, p. 218.

51. Melville MSS, Scottish R.O. GD 51.1.435, W. to Melville, 13 June 1804.

52. L III, p. 222.

53. *Barham Papers* (Naval Records Society) II, pp. 215–16.

54. MS Memorandum by Sir John Sinclair in Thurso MSS, Sinclair of Ulbster Papers.

55. *Ib.*

56. L III, p. 221.

57. *Parl. Deb.* III, cc. 517–19.

58. Lowther MSS, R. Plumer Ward to Lord Lowther, 9 April 1805.

59. Bod. d.13.361, Sir John Legard to W., 10 Dec. 1806. This letter is quoted *in toto* by Furneaux, pp. 235–6, and in part (garbled) L III, pp. 222–3.

60. L III, pp. 236–9.

61. Bod. b.1.18, Samuel W's note of W's conversation in May 1832. A slightly different version, L III, p. 230.

62. Barham and prayers of friends: C II, pp. 32–3.

63. H. More to Alexander Knox, 10 May 1806, MS in possession of late Dr. M. Jones who showed it to me in 1954.

64. Gainsborough MSS: Note by Sir John Deas Thompson, Barham's secretary. Collingwood's letter is in Royal Archives, Windsor.

65. BM Add MSS 42772.297, Rose Papers, W. to George Rose, 23 Jan. 1806.

66. Farington, J., *Diaries, III*, pp. 290–1, reports W. saying that when the Bishop tried to speak to Pitt on his deathbed about spiritual matters, he was rebuffed, whether by Pitt or the doctors is not plain.

67. L III, p. 245.

68. Bod. d.16.258, W. to Bankes (at whose house the Bishop had died) 19 Nov. 1825. W. adds: 'still – I cannot hear without emotion of the death of a man with whom we associated on such friendly terms in early life.'

1. E.g., see BM Add MSS 42772.297 and 309, W. to George Rose; and to Wellesley, *ib.* 37309.81; and to Windham, *ib.* 37883.10.
2. Clements Lib MSS, Michigan Univ., Windham to W., 4 March 1806.
3. Farington, J., *Diaries*, IV, p. 151.
4. Sidmouth MSS, W. to Sidmouth, 7 Feb. 1806.
5. Furneaux, R., *William Wilberforce*, p. 245, quoting Wrangham MSS.
6. BM Grenville MSS (as all references to the W.–Grenville correspondence below), W. to Grenville, 1 Nov. 1806.
7. W. to Grenville, 24 March 1806.
8. Stephen's object in writing *War in Disguise*: L III, p. 234; and David Newsome, *Historical Journal* VI (1963), p. 303. See Anstey, R., *English Historical Review*, April 1972, pp. 317–18, and his *The Atlantic Slave Trade and British Abolition*, pp. 350–6. I am grateful to Professor Anstey for his personal elucidation and discussion of this point.
9. W. to Grenville dated 24 March 1806.
10. Grenville to W., 25 March 1806 (copy).
11. Clements Lib. MSS, Michigan Univ., Fox Papers, W. to Fox, 27 March 1806.
12. W. to Grenville, [2 May] 1806.
13. *Ib.* 24 March 1806.
14. *Ib.* 23 April 1806. The doubter was G. Rose.
15. *Ib.*
16. Grenville to W., 25 April 1806 (copy).
17. Grenville to W., 5 May 1806 (copy).
18. W. to Grenville, 8 May 1806.
19. *Ib.*
20. Grenville to W., 9 May 1806 (copy).
21. W. to Grenville, 9 July 1806; G. to W., 10 July (copy); W. to G., 11 July.
22. L III, p. 261.
23. W. to Grenville, 20 May 1806.
24. *Ib.*
25. Fox's Resolution: *Parl. Deb.* VII c. 585 (10 June 1806).
26. W. to Grenville, 5 June 1806.
27. *Ib.*, 9 June 1806.
28. *Ib.*, 'Tues. Morning'.
29. W. to Grenville, 25 June 1806.
30. Monroe MSS, New York P.L, W. to James Monroe, 21 Aug. 1806.
31. L III, p. 263; Diary, 10 June 1806 (misprinted 10 April).
32. L III, p. 268.
33. W. to Grenville, 2 June 1806.
34. Duke MSS, Smith Papers, W. to W. Smith, 18 Aug. 1806.
35. Objections of Clarkson, Babington and W. are described in W. to W. Smith, 5 Sep. 1806, *ib.*
36. BM Grenville MSS, Grenville to Lord Carlisle, 28 Aug. 1806 (copy).
37. L III, pp. 274–5.
38. BM Add MSS 37309.112, Wellesley Papers, W. to Lord Wellesley, 22 April 1806.

39. L III, pp. 265, 267; Farington, *Diaries*, III, p. 292.

40. L III, p. 264.

41. Lowther MSS, Lord Muncaster to Lord Lowther, 29 Oct. 1806.

42. For the election campaign, see L III, pp. 275–84.

43. Fitzwilliam (Wentworth Woodhouse) MSS E.209, Joseph Armytage to Fitzwilliam, 25 Oct. 1806.

44. *Ib.*, Robert Sinclair to Fitzwilliam, 22 Oct. 1806.

45. Lowther MSS, Muncaster to Lowther, 29 Oct. 1806.

46. Petworth House MSS, West Sussex R.O, W. to Lord Egremont, 25 Nov. 1806.

47. W. to Grenville, 1 Nov. 1806.

48. Bod. d.13.220, Grenville to W., 5 Nov. 1806.

49. W. to Grenville, 30 Dec. 1806.

50. W. to Grenville, 15 Jan. 1807.

51. *Edinburgh Review*, X, p. 199.

52. W. to Grenville, 4 Feb. 1807.

53. Monroe MSS, New York P.L, W. to James Monroe, 10 Feb. 1807.

54. Thornton MSS, 7674.L.3, Thornton to Patty More, 4 Feb. 1807.

55. For the whipping activities, see W. to Grenville, 29 Nov. 1806, 31 Jan., 7 Feb. 1807; BM Add MSS 21256, Abolition Cttee Fair Minute Book, 10, 11, 13 Feb. 1807; Thornton MSS 7674.L.3, Mrs. Thornton to H. More, 10 Feb. 1807.

56. W. to Grenville, 21 Dec. 1814.

57. *Parl. Deb.* VIII, cc. 657–664.

58. Porteus MS (Lambeth) 2104.91.

59. L III, p. 294: *Parl. Deb. ib.* c. 667.

60. L III, pp. 294–5.

61. Thornton MSS, 7674.L.3, Mrs. Thornton to Patty More, N.D. [Feb. 1807 from context].

62. L III, p. 295.

63. *Ib.*

64. Bowood MSS, W. to Lord Henry Petty, 19 Feb. 1807.

65. Grey of Howick MSS, W. to Lord Howick, 23 Feb. 1807.

66. H p. 182.

67. *Parl. Deb.* VIII c. 967.

68. *Ib.* c. 969.

69. *Ib.* c. 978.

70. Richard Ryder M.P., quoted Anstey, R., *The Atlantic Slave Trade and British Abolition 1760–1810*, p. 399 and n.

71. L III, p. 298.

72. W. to Grenville, 25 Feb. 1807.

73. Porteus MS (Lambeth) 2104.91.

74. W. to Grenville, 25 Feb. 1807.

75. Grey of Howick MSS, W. to Howick, 9 March 1807, replying to Howick's letter of 8 March, Bod. d.13.275 printed L III, p. 300.

76. *Parl. Deb.* IX cc. 136, 139, *re* Colonial Assemblies, W. had even believed at one time that they could block Abolition, let alone Emancipation. He wrote to Harrowby on 24 Oct. 1804: 'Remember, our grand practical difficulty in Abolition is that the Colonial legislatures will not concur and

that without their concurrence we can do nothing.' (Harrowby MSS, XII, 194).

77. *Edinburgh Review*, IV, p. 407 (1804).
78. *Parl. Deb.*, IX c. 142.
79. See L III, pp. 301–4.

21 *Wilberforce in his Prime*

1. Wyvill MSS, 7.2.192, W. to Wyvill, 3 March 1807.
2. Grey of Howick MSS, Box 8, File 8 (2), Temple to Howick, 1 April 1807.
3. *Ib*, Box 21, file 17, Thomas Grenville to Howick, 26 March 1807.
4. Stanhope MSS 731 (12), W. to Tomline (Pretyman), 9 April 1807.
5. Fitzwilliam (Wentworth Woodhouse) MSS, Milton to Fitzwilliam, 2 June 1807.
6. Stanhope MSS (731 (12) as above.
7. BM Add MSS 45130A. 40, W. to T. Acklon, 4 May [1807].
8. Fitzwilliam (W.W.) MSS, R. Sykes to Fitzwilliam (endorsed 5 May 1807).
9. Fitzwilliam (Northants) MSS, Lady Fitzwilliam to C. M. Wentworth, 9 May 1807.
10. *Ib.*, Wentworth to Lady F., 11 May 1807.
11. Fitzwilliam (W.W.) MSS, M. to Lord F., 13 May 1807.
12. *Ib.*, John Lowe to Fitzwilliam, 20 May 1807.
13. Thornton MSS, 7674.I.L.4, Thornton to Macaulay, 31 May 1807.
14. *Ib.*, Thornton to Macaulay N.D. [1807].
15. Fitzwilliam (W.W.) MSS, Milton to Fitzwilliam, 25 May 1807.
16. From an anon. Whig account pasted into a commonplace book in Harewood MSS.
17. Fitzwilliam (W.W.) MSS, Milton to Fitzwilliam, 25 May 1807.
18. Thornton MSS as above, 28 May 1807.
19. Fitzwilliam (W.W.) MSS, Milton to Fitzwilliam, 28 May 1807.
20. BM Add MSS 52178.7, Holland Papers, Brougham to John Allen, [5 June 1807].
21. Bod. c.3.89, H. More to W. [15 June 1807].
22. Fitzwilliam (W.W.) MSS, Milton to Fitzwilliam, 30 May 1807.
23. *Ib.*, 1 June.
24. *Ib.*, 3 June.
25. Thornton MSS as above, Thornton to Mrs. T., 10 June 1807.
26. *John Bull* IV, p. 292.
27. BM Add MSS 52193.231, Holland Papers, R. Sharp to Lord Holland, 6 July 1807. And see *Quarterly Review* 1838, pp. 279–80.
28. UCL MSS, Brougham Papers, John Wishaw to H. Brougham [1810].
29. Pellew, G., *Life and Correspondence of Addington*, I, p. 50.
30. Stephen, G., *Anti-Slavery Recollections*, p. 80.
31. Camden MSS, Kent R.O. U 840 c. 89.5.1, W. to Camden, 27 Dec. 1809.
32. Sidmouth MSS, Sidmouth to C. Bragge-Bathurst, 29 Dec. 1809.
33. Sidmouth MSS, Lord de Dunsterville to Sidmouth, 3 Jan. 1810.
34. David Holland MSS, Perceval Papers, W. to Perceval, 28 April 1810.

12

35. Thornton MSS, 7674.L.5.6, Thornton to H. More, N.D. 1811.
36. Harewood MSS, W. to Canning, 30 July, 19 Aug. 1812.
37. Fitzwilliam (Northants) MSS, Box 149, W. to Milton, 21 Nov. 1812.
38. For Kensington Gore, etc. see Faulkner, Thomas, *History of Kensington* (1820), pp. 618–19; Chancellor, E. B., *Knightsbridge and Belgravia* (1909), pp. 195–7; *Survey of London*, Vol. XXXVIII (1975), pp. 12–13.
39. Thornton MSS 7674, I.H.2.
40. Hull MS Diary, 11 Feb. 1814.
41. *Ib.*, 12 Dec. 1814.
42. BM Eg MSS 1964, 68, W. to Lady Olivia Sparrow, 12 Aug. 1817.
43. BM Add MSS 39948.25, Huskisson Papers, W. to W. Huskisson, 4 July 1810.
44. Thornton MSS, 7674.L.5.93, Thornton to H. More, 29 May 1812.
45. Osborn MSS, Yale, W. to Marianne Francis, 28 March [1815].
46. Thornton MSS, 7674.L.4.115, Thornton to H. More, 30 Nov. 1809.
47. Buchan MSS, W. to Lord Erskine, 3 May 1813 and 21 June [1808?]
48. Thornton MSS, 7674.L.5.24, Thornton to Mrs. T., 8 Jan. 1812.
49. H.M.C. *Dartmouth*, 15th Report, pp. 288–9. (Original W. MSS in Stafford R.O.)
50. Stephen, J., *Essays*, pp. 498–500.
51. Nat. Lib. Scotland 1755, W. to James Grahame, 14 May 1809.
52. Brown, Ford K., *Fathers of the Victorians*, p. 357.
53. Westminster MSS, W. to Earl Grosvenor, 14 Nov. 1812.
54. On Cambridge Bible Society see L III, pp. 561–2 and Winstanley, D. A., *Early Victorian Cambridge* (1940).
55. Westminster MSS, W. to Earl Grosvenor, 8 Dec. 1812.
56. 'Fragments,' f. 95.
57. Bible Society MSS, E. G. Hill to Secy., BFBS., 31 May 1808.
58. BM Grenville MSS, W. to Lord Grenville, 28 March 1807.
59. Bod. d.15.19, Thornton to W., 17 Nov. 1791.
60. BM Grenville MSS, W. to Grenville, 8 July [1817].
61. Waldegrave MSS, Duchess of Gloucester to Prince William Frederick, 25 Sep. 1799.
62. *Ib.*, Duchess to H. More, 10 Sep. 1805.
63. *Ib.*, Chaplain's name does not appear.
64. Duke MSS., W. Papers, W. to Thomas Harrison, 5 Aug. 1813.
65. Harewood MSS, W. to Canning, 17 Aug. 1807 (11 foolscap pp in clerkly hand).
66. *Ib.*
67. Hull MS Diary, 17 Feb. 1814, *re* Thomas Thompson and his younger son Charles.
68. Johnson, L. G., *General T. Perronet Thompson*, p. 26.
69. *Ib.*, p. 29.
70. Hull Univ. Library MSS, Thompson Papers, W. to T. P. Thompson, 19 Oct. 1808. See the other letters in this file. Also Johnson, *passim* and Fyfe, C., *A History of Sierra Leone*, pp. 105–10.
71. Huntington MSS, Locker Papers, W. to E. H. Locker, 23 Oct. 1820.
72. W. to Thompson, 19 Oct. 1808, as above.
73. New York P.L. MSS, Monroe Papers, W. to James Monroe, 8 Sep. 1808.

74. *Ib.*
75. *Ib.*, W. to President Jefferson, 5 Sep. 1808.
76. Bod. d.6.66, W. to Macaulay, 19 Oct. 1809.
77. BM Add MSS 37309.287, Wellesley Papers, W. to Lord Wellesley, 7 June 1809.
78. Copy in Harewood MSS.
79. Thornton MSS, 7674.L.4.74, Mrs. Thornton to H. More, [Jan.] 1808.
80. U.C.L. MSS, Brougham Papers, W. to Brougham, 7 Aug. 1812.

22 *Two Problems of Liberty*

1. Bod. c.3.190, W. to Sam W., 23 Nov. 1832.
2. L III, pp. 519–20.
3. Roberts MSS, W. to S. Roberts, 21 March 1817.
4. *Ib.* 29 July 1811.
5. For influence of Roberts on decision to resign, see *ib.*, W. to Roberts, 10 Dec. 1824.
6. Thornton MSS, 7674 L.4.56, Thornton to H. More, 22 Sep. 1807.
7. The remark *re* never feeling well was made to Harford.
8. H, p. 8.
9. Bod. d.16.63, W. to Sally Stephen, 21 July 1808.
10. Sidmouth MSS, 152 M, Box 32.3, W. to Sidmouth, 22 Aug. 1811.
11. BM Add MSS 35131.541, Young Papers, W. to A. Young, 27 Oct. 1813.
12. Roberts MSS, W. to S. Roberts [1817].
13. Bod. d.6.76, W. to R. Creyke, 9 Jan. 1811.
14. Church Missionary Society MSS, Venn Papers, W. to Henry Venn, 29 June 1822.
15. L IV, p. 54.
16. Thornton MSS, 7674 1.N., Marianne T's Recollections, f. 504.
17. *Ib.* L.4.70, Mrs. Thornton to H. More, 29 Jan. 1808.
18. BM Eg MSS 1964. 17, W. to Lady Olivia Sparrow, 24 Jan. 1817.
19. Cutting from *Christian Keepsake* pasted above W. autograph signature torn from a letter to Dr. W. Thackeray, Duke MSS, W. Papers. A somewhat similar story is in L IV, p. 208.
20. Furneaux, R., *William Wilberforce*, p. 294.
21. Teignmouth, Lord, *Reminiscences of Many Years* I, p. 250.
22. St. John's, Cantab. MSS, W. to Rev. Mr. Joyce, 29 Oct. 1805.
23. Hull MS Diary, 17 Feb. 1814.
24. Bod. d.9.87 ff, W. to Sam W., 13 Sep. 1814.
25. Bod. d.15.80, Brougham to W. [1812].
26. Grey of Howick MSS, Brougham to Earl Grey, 17 Sep. 1812.
27. *e.g.* Brougham, Lord, *Life and Times* II, pp. 43 ff. (MS in UCL, Brougham Papers).
28. UCL MSS, Brougham Papers, John Allen to Brougham, 29 Sep. 1812.
29. The one personal reference to 3rd Lord Calthorpe quoted in *Complete Peerage* is so out of character, as revealed in the correspondence with W., that it is probably a case of mistaken identity.
30. Calthorpe MSS, W. to Calthorpe, 15 Feb. 1820.

31. W. to Major Cartwright, 18 March 1809. Seen by the late Prof. Aspinall, but no provenance given in his notes.
32. Calthorpe MSS, W. to Calthorpe, 23 Oct. 1823.
33. *Ib.*
34. Teignmouth, *op. cit.*, I, p. 245.
35. *Ib.*
36. Sir Egerton Brydges in *Gentleman's Magazine*, June 1825, p. 502 (refers to period 1812–18).
37. L III, pp. 361–3.
38. *Ib.*, p. 361.
39. BM Add MSS 51549.64, Holland Papers, Lady Holland to Grey, 27 May 1808.
40. L III, p. 362.
41. Barnes, T., *Parliamentary Sketches*, p. 71.
42. BM Add MSS 37309.108, Wellesley Papers, W. to Wellesley, 14 April 1806.
43. Farington, J., *Diaries*, VII, p. 190.
44. Copy in Harford MSS, W. to H. More, 25 March 1813.
45. BM Add MSS 38191, Liverpool Papers, W. to Liverpool, 30 June 1812.
46. Harford MSS, W. to J. Harford, 8 April 1813.
47. Buchan MSS, W. to Lord Erskine, 5 Feb. 1813.
48. Scottish R.O. G D 50.235.11, W. to John Campbell, 19 March 1813.
49. Whitbread MSS, Bedford R.O. W.1.5116, W. to Whitbread, 19 June 1813.
50. Barnes, p. 72.
51. There were in fact two speeches by W.: 22 June 1813, *Parl. Deb.* XXVI, cc. 831–72, and 1 July 1813 (answering objections) *ib.* cc. 1051–79. As *Parl. Deb.* reprints from the version corrected by W. and published by J. Hatchard, the speeches are much more accurately *verbatim* than the summaries usually given in the printed records of debates.
52. Bod. d.13.190, Erskine to W. [1813].

23 *Lost Opportunity, 1814*

1. Buchan MSS, W. to Erskine, 25 March 1814.
2. Hull MS Diary 25 March 1814. German relief had long been a W. charity. He wrote to Perceval about it 15 July 1810 (David Holland MSS).
3. Thornton MSS, 7674.L.6.5, Thornton to H. More, 29 March 1814. See Hull MS Diary, 26 March 1814.
4. L IV, p. 167; H, p. 67.
5. Hull MS Diary, 1 March 1814.
6. For all information in this paragraph, see Hull MS Diary 9–10 April 1814 (dating becomes muddled as W. made entries for this week twice).
7. Hull MS Diary, 1 May, 17 April 1814. For Tsar's evangelical conversion, see Palmer, *Alexander I*, p. 253 and other references.
8. Duke MSS, W. Papers, W. to J. Harford, 26 July 1814.
9. Hull MS Diary, 12 April 1814.
10. *Ib.* 28 April 1814.
11. BM Grenville MSS, W. to Grenville, 3 May 1814.

12. Bod. d.15.86, W. to T. Clarkson, 4 Aug. 1814 (copy).
13. BM Eg. MSS 1964.10, W. to Lady O. Sparrow, 31 Mary 1814.
14. Hull MS Diary, 24 May 1814, W. once said if everyone were like Vansittart, later Lord Bexley, the world would be a better place but a very dull one. ('Fragments'.)
15. Duke MSS, W. Papers, W. to Harford, 26 May 1814.
16. To Lady O. Sparrow as above.
17. Hull MS Diary, 3 June 1814. See also W. to Grenville N.D. and G's reply, 5 June 1814 (copy) in BM Grenville MSS.
18. Hull MS Diary, 5 June 1814.
19. H, p. 51 (L copies from Harford's MS).
20. Hazlitt, W., *Spirit of the Age*, pp. 331–4.
21. *Parl. Deb.* XXVII cc. 1078–1084.
22. Hull MS Diary, 7 June 1814.
23. *Ib.*, and Knutsford, Lady, *Zachary Macaulay*, p. 314.
24. Hull MS Diary, 7 June 1814.
25. H, p. 58.
26. Hull MS Diary, 8 June 1814.
27. H, p. 54.
28. H, p. 55; Hull MS Diary, 12 June 1814.
29. *Ib.* 13 June 1814.
30. *Ib.* (13 June).
31. See News, C, *Henry Brougham to 1830*, pp. 137–8.
32. H, p. 57.
33. L IV, p. 193.
34. News, *op. cit.*, p. 138; Gurwood, John, *Wellington's Supp. Despatches*, IX, p. 174; Castlereagh, *Memoir and Correspondence*, X, p. 73.
35. BM Grenville MSS, W. to Grenville, 21 Dec. 1814.
36. Whitbread MSS, Bedford R.O. W.1.4161, W. to Whitbread, 20 June 1814.
37. Hull MS Diary, 20–27 June 1814.
38. *Parl. Deb.* XXVIII cc. 268–78, see espec. c. 275.
39. Hull MS Diary, 27 June 1814.
40. BM Add MSS, 52172.87, Holland Papers, Holland to John Allen, 30 June 1814.
41. Bod. d.15.86, W. to Clarkson, 9 Aug. 1814 (copy).
42. Shaver, C. L., Moorman, M., and Hill, A. G., *Letters of William and Dorothy Wordsworth*, II, p. 156.
43. BM Grenville MSS, W. to Grenville, 21 Dec. 1814. Letters to Wellington and Liverpool are printed in *Wellington's Supp. Despatches* IX.
44. *Op. cit.* p. 226.
45. Bod. d.13.290, Lady Holland to W., N.D.
46. BM Grenville MSS, W. to Grenville, 2 July 1817.

24 The Black King

1. Thornton MSS, 7674.L.4.100, Thornton to H. More, 14 Aug. 1809.
2. Melville MSS, Scottish R.O. gd 26.13, W. to Lady Leven and Melville (T's sister), 18 Jan. 1815.

3. Thornton MSS, 7674.L.10, H. More to Mrs. Thornton, N.D. [Jan. 1814].
4. *Ib.*, L.6, Mrs. R. Inglis (Inglis became 2nd Bart. in 1820) to Miss M. Thornton, 30 Sep. 1815.
5. *Ib.* L.6.161, quoted in Miss M. Thornton to W., conveying message from her mother.
6. Wilberforce MSS, West Sussex R.O., Wilb. 27, W. to Mrs. Sargent, 23 Oct. 1816.
7. Hull MS Diary, 30 May 1816.
8. Duke MSS, W. Papers, W. to J. Harford, 9 July 1816.
9. W's letters to Bathurst are in BM Loan 57, Bathurst Papers and printed in HMC *Bathurst* (1923) where the double-underlined sentences are printed in capitals.
10. BM Grenville MSS, W. to Grenville, 23 May 1816.
11. *Codrington Corr.* pp. 57–8.
12. Duke MSS, W. Papers, W. to Harford, 9 July 1816.
13. BM Loan 57.1153, Bathurst Papers, W. to Bathurst, 1 July 1816.
14. Teignmouth, Lord, *Reminiscences of Many Years*, I, p. 248.
15. Gurney, J. J., *Familiar Sketch*, p. 11.
16. For a caustic account of the Registry Bill debate, see Gratus, J., *The Great White Lie*, pp. 156–8.
17. BM Grenville MSS, W. to Grenville, 3 July 1817 (postscript to 2 July).
18. W. to Grenville, 2 July 1817 as above.
19. *Ib.*
20. *Ib.*
21. For negotiations with Portugal, see Bethell, L., *The Abolition of the Brazilian Slave Trade*, ch. 1; with Spain, see Corwin, A., *Spain and the Abolition of Slavery in Cuba*, ch. 2.
22. BM Eg. MSS 1964.51, W. to Lady Olivia Sparrow, 24 Jan. 1817.
23. BM Grenville MSS, W. to Grenville, 30 March 1816.
24. *Ib.*
25. Bod. d.16.42, W. to Stephen, 4 Nov. 1815.
26. BM Grenville MSS, W. to Grenville, 21, 30 March 1816.
27. Bod. d.16.101, W. to Babington, 15 Aug. 1816.
28. See file of W. letters in Bible Society MSS: the long letter to Lord Teignmouth is printed in C I.
29. Cornell Univ. MSS, Clarkson to W., 15 Jan. 1819.
30. Nat. Lib. Scotland MSS, W. to Robert Paul, 31 Aug. 1817.
31. Bod. d.16.151, W. to Stephen, 11 Dec. 1820.
32. BM Add MSS 41266.215, Clarkson Papers, W. to Mrs. Clarkson, 11 March 1822.
33. Hull MS Diary, 8 April 1822. Furneaux (pp. 398–9), who seems to imply that W. refused to receive the Haitians, is perhaps misled by a printed source.
34. Wilberforce MSS, West Sussex R.O., W. to Mrs. Sargent, 8 April 1822.

25 *Wage Slaves and William*

1. Roberts MSS, W. to S. Roberts, 21 March 1817.

2. *Ib.* 'I believe I have not been sufficiently active in vindicating my character'; and see Jay, *Autobiography*, p. 312.

3. Boston MSS, W. to T. Clarkson, 13 June 1817.

4. Shaver, C. L., Moorman, M., and Hill, A. G., *Letters of William and Dorothy Wordsworth*, II, p. 219.

5. L IV, pp. 244–6.

6. BM Add MSS 35133.183, Young Papers, W. to Arthur Young, 29 Jan. [1816].

7. Hull MS Diary, 20 Jan. 1818.

8. Quote on Eldon actually concerns the quarrel with Canning which led to Eldon's dismissal. Rhodes House MSS, c. 106.11, W. to Buxton, 12 March 1827.

9. Ashwell, A. R., *Life of Samuel Wilberforce* (1880), I, p. 18.

10. Bod. c.1.77, W. to Samuel W., 5 Nov. 1823. W. did not underestimate Cobbett's skill and influence as a political teacher.

11. Hull MS Diary, 4, 13 May 1814.

12. *Cobbett's Weekly Political Register*, vol. XIX (1811), c. 1514.

13. Fitzwilliam (Northants) MSS, Box 99, W. to Lord Milton, 27 Sep. 1819.

14. Roberts MSS, W. to S. Roberts, 24 Dec. 1819.

15. *Ib.*

16. See Jay, *op. cit.*, p. 314, and Calder Marshall, A. R., *Lewd, Blasphemous and Obscene* (1973), pp. 118–19.

17. L IV, pp. 90–1.

18. Hull MS Diary, 16 Dec. 1819.

19. L V, p. 46.

20. A letter from W. to James Montgomery is in Osborn MSS and another in St. John's, Cantab. MSS, and several favourable references to him in W's letters to Roberts. The Sadler Papers are mostly lost, but DNB refers to the friendship. For Hazlitt, see end of chapter.

21. Roberts MSS, W. to S. Roberts, 13 July 1820. He used this phrase also in a letter to Chalmers, the Scottish church reformer. The same answer to Radical teaching is found in James Mill the Utilitarian.

22. W. to Liverpool, 30 Sep. 1820, see below, note 26.

23. BM Loan 57, Vol. 11.1179, Bathurst Papers, W. to Lord Bathurst, 3 Sep. 1816.

24. BM Add MSS 35133.375, Young Papers, W. to Arthur Young, 23 Sep. 1816.

25. W. to Bathurst, as above.

26. BM Add MSS 38191.274 and 280, W. to Lord Liverpool, 16 and 30 Sep. 1816, two very long letters on discrimination against Calvinist clergy, while pointing out he is not a Calvinist himself.

27. R.C. Bible Society was est. 1813; see Ward, Bernard, *The Eve of Catholic Emancipation* (1911) II, p. 197, quoting a letter of Lord Clifford to the Vicar Apostolic, 7 Aug. 1815: 'Mr. Wilberforce . . . triumphantly refuted our calumniators in the House of Commons when he understood we were engaged in publishing the Bible ourselves.'

28. See Lord John Russell's speech April 1822. *Substance of the speeches of Lord John Russell . . . on Reform . . .* (1822), p. 41.

29. Joseph Gurney, MS Diary, Sep. 1816 (the dating is rather erratic and in

Quaker form). The sources for W's visit to Earlham are this Diary and Gurney, *Familiar Sketch*, pp. 7–10 (six children in Diary, 'several children' in *Sketch*).

30. Hervey MSS, West Suffolk R.O. 941.56.72, W. to 5th Earl of Bristol, 4 Nov. 1815.
31. Hull MS Diary, 2 Feb. 1818.
32. *Ib.* 3 Feb. 1818.
33. *Ib.* 31 Jan. 1818.
34. *Ib.* 3 Feb. 1818.
35. *Ib.* 17 Feb. 1818.
36. Friends' House Lib. MSS, Gurney Papers, Notabilities 37.3, W. to Eliz. Fry, 17 Feb. 1818.
37. Nat. Lib. Scotland MSS, 3519, 9–23, W. to James Grahame, 8 June 1809.
38. Lengthy correspondence between Marsden and W. is in Bodleian; a number of W. letters to Marsden are in Library of New South Wales.
39. See *Parl. Deb.* XXXIX (1817) c. 452. See also, Roberts MSS, W. to Roberts, 21 April 1819.
40. Nat. Lib. Scotland MSS, to Grahame, as above.
41. Friends' House Lib. MSS, Gurney Papers, W. to J. J. Gurney, 12 Feb. 1819.
42. Greville, Charles, *Memoirs* (1888 ed.) I, p. 17.
43. Hull MS Diary, 1 April 1818.
44. Teignmouth, Lord, *Reminiscences of Many Years*, I, p. 254. See also Coupland, R., *Wilberforce*, pp. 344–5 and Furneaux, R., *William Wilberforce*, pp. 367–8.
45. *Parl. Deb.* XXXVI, c. 1248.
46. Brougham, Lord, *Statesmen*, I, p. 271.
47. Harford MSS, Harford's Private Memoranda.
48. Brougham, *op. cit.*, p. 272.
49. Melville, L., *William Cobbett*, I, pp. 106–7.
50. Hull MS Diary, 15 March, 14 June 1817.
51. BM Eg. MSS 1964.75, W. to Lady O. Sparrow, 30 Dec. 1817.
52. Houghton Lib. MSS, Harvard, W. to Southey, 27 May 1818. 2 letters to Wordsworth are in Wordsworth museum, Grasmere.
53. Shaver, Moorman and Hill, *op. cit.*, II, pp. 482–3, 494.
54. Southey, R., *Life and Corr.* IV, p. 317.
55. Southey, R., *Letters*, p. 99.
56. Bod. b.1. contains Samuel's Diary of the Lakes visit.
57. Hull MS Diary, 8 Jan. 1819.
58. *Ib.* 10 Jan. 1819.
59. *Ib.* 10 March, 28 March 1819.
60. Church Missionary Society MSS, Venn Papers, W. to H. Venn, 11 March 1818, and several other letters on the subject. Venn became a distinguished missionary statesman.
61. Hull MS Diary, 11 March 1819.
62. *Ib.* 11 April 1819.
63. BM Eg. MSS 1964.61, W. to Lady O. Sparrow, N.D.
64. Fitzwilliam (Northants) MSS, Box 99, W. to Lord Milton, 27 Sep. 1819.
65. *Ib.*

66. Wallas, G., *Francis Place*, p. 147.
67. See *The Spirit of the Age* (1825), pp. 331–4. This long and oft-quoted critique of W's public character is based on too many false premises and erroneous deductions to be of biographical value except as an example of the Radical view of W.
68. Hull MS Diary, 19 June 1817.

26 *Queen Caroline*

1. L V, p. 67 (evidently taken from W's notes as the words do not appear in *Parl. Deb.*, New Series I cc. 1213–28).
2. BM Add MSS 56541 (vol. 20), f. 40 Broughton Papers, Hobhouse (Broughton) Diary, 7 June 1820, see also Greville, *Memoirs*, I, p. 30.
3. Bod. d.16.227, W. to Robert, W., N.D. but endorsed '6 July' (i.e. 1820), see also Roberts MSS, W. to S. Roberts, 13 July 1820, quoted L V, pp. 62–5.
4. Hobhouse MS Diary, 21 June 1820, as above, f. 43b.
5. Hull MS Diary, 20–21 June 1820.
6. Bod. d.13.57, Queen Caroline to W., 20 June 1820.
7. Hobhouse MS Diary, 21 June 1820, as above, f. 43b.
8. Hull MS Diary, 21 June 1820.
9. Hobhouse MS Diary, as above, f. 43b.
10. Cookson, J. E., *Lord Liverpool's Administration*, p. 241.
11. Hull MS Diary, 22 June 1820.
12. Greville, C., *Memoirs*, I, p. 31.
13. Hobhouse MS Diary, 22 June 1820, as above, f. 44b.
14. Teignmouth, Lord, *Reminiscences of Many Years*, I, p. 256.
15. Hull MS Diary, 23 June 1820.
16. Hull MS Diary, 24 June 1820; Greville, *Memoirs*, III, p. 38.
17. Hobhouse MS Diary, 24 June 1820, as above, f. 45.
18. Forster, E. M., *Marianne Thornton*, p. 19 (from a letter of reminiscence from Marianne T. to her niece, E. M. Forster's mother).
19. UCL MSS, Brougham Papers.
20. Hull MS Diary, 6 July 1820.
21. Bod. c.3.166, Simeon to W., 22 Sep. 1820.
22. Knutsford, Lady, *Zachary Macaulay*, p. 356.
23. Hull MS Diary, 12 July 1820.
24. Bod. d.16.117, W. to Mrs. W., 1 July [1820].
25. BM Eg MSS 1964.99, W. to Lady O. Sparrow, 25 July 1820.
26. Rhodes House MSS, W. to Buxton, 7 Aug. 1820.
27. Bod. d.16.117, as above.
28. L V, pp. 71–2.
29. *Cobbett's Weekly Political Register*, XXVIII, c. 233 (12 Aug. 1820).
30. Bod. d.16.145, W. to Bankes, 11 Nov. 1820.
31. Duke MSS, W. Papers, W. to Harford, 4 Nov. 1819. See also to H., 3 Sep. 1812, 13 Oct. 1821. W. bought Wick Wick in 1812.
32. Hare A.J.C. (ed.), *Life and Letters of Maria Edgeworth*, (1894) II, p. 57.

33. Colvin, C. (ed), *Maria Edgeworth: Letters from England 1813–44* (1973), p. 251.
34. Calthorpe MSS, William Spooner to Lord Calthorpe, 17 May 1821.
35. Rhodes House MSS, W. to Buxton, 23 Nov. 1832.
36. For Acland's character, see Harford, A., *Harford Annals*, p. 21, H. More to John Harford, 18 Sep. 1821.
37. See *Complete Peerage*, III, p. 206 note (a).
38. Bod. d.10.26, Mrs. W. to Samuel W., N.D [?1817].
39. Rhodes House MSS, 24 May 1821. The letter is printed in the Life of Buxton and elsewhere.
40. Calthorpe MSS, W. to Calthorpe, 26 Dec. 1821.
41. *Ib*. W. to Calthorpe, N.D. For Barbara's funeral see Bateman, J. *Daniel Wilson*, I, pp. 209–10.
42. Bod. d.16.173, W. to Robert W., 3–9 March 1822.

27 Unable to Finish It

1. Hull MS Diary, 6, 13, 14, 15 Aug. 1822; BM Loan 57, Bathurst Papers, W. to Bathurst, 14 Aug. 1822.
2. Harewood MSS, W. to Canning, 22, 31 Oct.; Canning to W., 24 Oct. 1822 (copy).
3. Univ. of Michigan MSS, Croker Papers, W. to Croker, 16 Aug. 1823.
4. See Crofton, Thomas, *A Walk from London to Fulham* (1860).
5. Harewood MSS, W. to Canning, 14 Oct.; Canning to W., 19 Oct. 1822 (copy).
6. *Ib*. W. to Canning, 21 Jan. 1825.
7. Harewood MSS, Canning to W., 31 Oct. 1822 (copy) and W. to Canning, 28 Jan. 1823.
8. Huntington MSS, Locker Papers, W. to E. H. Locker, 25 March 1823.
9. Harewood MSS, W. to Canning, 26 March 1824. See Soulsby, H. G., *The Right of Search and the Slave Trade*, pp. 35–8.
   The point was gained finally by the Webster–Ashburton Treaty, 1842.
10. Harewood MSS, W. to Canning, 29 April 1823.
11. Bod. d.13.131, Canning to W., 30 April 1823.
12. W. to Clarkson, 29 Oct. 1794, quoted Davis, D. Brion, *Slavery in an Age of Revolution*, p. 413.
13. Bod. d.16.122, W. to Stephen, 29 Oct. 1820.
14. Hull MS Diary, 8 April 1818.
15. *Ib*. 9 April 1818.
16. Bod. d.16.114, W. to Babington, 29 June 1820.
17. L V, p. 171.
18. U.C.L. MSS, Brougham Papers, W. to Brougham, 13 March 1823.
19. *Ib*.
20. Anti-Slavery Society, *Substance of the Debate . . . on 15 May, 1823*, p. 137.
21. *Ib*. p. 41.
22. *Cobbett's Weekly Political Register*, 30 Aug. 1823, XLVII cc. 513–15.
23. *Ib*. c. 516.
24. *Ib*. cc. 520–1.

25. Checkland, S. G., *The Gladstones*, p. 192.
26. Roberts MSS, W. to S. Roberts, 31 Oct. 1827.
27. Duke MSS, W. Papers, W. to Harford, 10 Aug. 1819.
28. Harewood MSS, W. to Canning, 13 Jan. 1824.
29. *Ib.* Canning to W., 11 Oct. 1823 (copy).
30. Huntington MSS, Macaulay Papers, W. to Macaulay, 13 Oct. 1823.
31. For Smith, see Cecil Northcott, *Slavery's Martyr* (1976).
32. Michigan Univ. MSS, Croker Papers, W. to Croker, 30 Jan. 1824.
33. For an attack on Trustee Savings Banks and W's part in founding, see *John Bull* IV, p. 204.
34. L V, p. 214 and see F. S. Turner, *All Heaven in a Rage* (1964).
35. L V, p. 217.
36. Hull MSS, W. to Henry W., 5 June 1824.
37. *John Bull*, IV, p. 188.
38. Forster, E. M., *Marianne Thornton*, pp. 128–9, and 1st Report of Anti-Slavery Society, pp. 98 ff.
39. Huntington MSS, Macaulay Papers, W. to Macaulay, 2 July 1824.
40. India Office Lib. MSS, Raffles Papers, B III 42, W. to Sir Stamford Raffles, 26 Feb. 1825.
41. Duke MSS, W. Papers, Mrs. W. to Mrs. J. Harford, 5 Feb. 1825.
42. Thurso MSS, Sinclair of Ulbster Papers, Sir John Sinclair to W., 5 Oct. 1824 (copy).
43. Boston MSS, W. to James Montgomery, 6 Jan. 1826.
44. Duke MSS, Smith Papers, W. to W. Smith, 5 Feb. 1825.
45. Bod. d.13.67, Buxton to W., 6 Feb. 1825.

28 *The Path to the Abbey*

1. Bod. d.11.19, Robert W. to Sam W., Feb. 1825.
2. Forster, E. M., *Marianne Thornton*, p. 136.
3. Osborn MSS, W. to Lord Stowell, 31 Oct. 1825.
4. U.C.L. MSS, Brougham Papers, W. to Brougham, 3 Oct. 1825; Duke MSS, W. Papers, Brougham to W., 10 Oct. 1825.
5. Forster, *op. cit.*, p. 130; Anti-Slavery Society, 2nd Annual Report, pp. 55–7.
6. Calthorpe MSS, W. to Calthorpe, 1 March 1826.
7. Abel Smith MSS, Herts R.O., D.EAs. 4415, W. to Abel Smith, 5 Dec. 1827. For the whole story see Newsome, D., *The Parting of Friends*, pp. 131–5.
8. Bod. d.16.226, W. to Robert W., 6 July 1820.
9. Cambridge Univ. Lib. Add MSS, Sir James Stephen, MS Diary, 13 May 1845 (I owe this reference to the kindness of Canon M. M. Hennell).
10. Hull MSS, W. to Henry W., 21 Sep. 1825.
11. Bod. d.16.245, W. to Robert W., 18 March 1828.
12. Hull MSS, W. to Henry W., 6 May 1825.
13. Newsome, *op. cit.*, p. 128.
14. Duke MSS, W. Papers, W. to Harford, 23 April 1829.
15. Hull MSS, W. to Henry W., 17 July 1830.

16. Duke MSS, W. Papers, W. to William Gray, 31 Dec. 1830. The theory advanced by Ford K. Brown and repeated by Furneaux, that W's Evangelicalism became muted at the end of his life finds no support in the MS sources. He was never a slavish adherent to any *party* within Evangelicalism.

17. Thornton MSS, 7674.H.8, W. to Charles Forster, 12 March 1828.

18. PP, pp. 275–6.

19. Friends' House Library MSS, Gurney Papers, W. to J. J. Gurney, 8 July 1826.

20. The phrase is in Bod. d.16.117, W. to Mrs. W., 1 July [1820].

21. Bod. c.1.82, W. to Eliz. W., N.D.

22. Bod. c.11.27, Robert W. to Sam W., 12 May 1827.

23. Bod. c.1.178, W. to Sam W., 21 May 1827. The slave-owner's name nowhere appears in the MSS.

24. Rhodes House MSS, W. to Buxton, 23 March 1826.

25. *Ib.* 20 April 1826.

26. *Ib.* 22 Dec. 1832.

27. Wilberforce cash book in Duke MSS, quoted Furneaux, William Wilberforce, p. 439.

28. Duke MSS, Smith Papers, W. to W. Smith, 24 July 1829.

29. U.C.L. MSS, Brougham Papers, W. to Brougham, 10 May 1827.

30. Bod. d.13.237, J. J. Gurney to W., 12th month, 7th day 1826.

31. Forster, op. cit., p. 138.

32. Teignmouth, Lord, *Reminiscences of Many Years*, I, p. 245.

33. Duke MSS, W. Papers, W. to Harford, 9 Nov. 1827.

34. BM Eg MSS 1964.135, W. to Lady O. Sparrow, 22 Feb. 1830.

35. Calthorpe MSS, W. to Calthorpe, 11 Aug. 1827.

36. *Ib.*

37. Nowell C. Smith, *Letters of Sydney Smith* (1953), I, p. 469.

38. Forster, *op. cit.*, p. 130.

39. India Office Lib. MSS, Raffles Papers, DE 742.B III.44.50, W. to Raffles, 30 July 1825, 6 March 1826.

40. BM Eg MSS 1964.135.

41. Furneaux, *op. cit.* p. 436, quoting Wrangham MSS.

42. Hull MSS, W. to William Edwell, 31 March 1830.

43. BM Eg MSS 1964.135 as above.

44. Duke MSS, W. Papers, Brougham to W. [1829].

45. Calthorpe MSS, Rev. J. Sargent to Calthorpe, 23 Nov. 1829.

46. Abel Smith MSS, Herts R.O. A.S.4417, W. to Abel Smith, 1 March 1830.

47. Bod. c.2.124, W. to Sam W., 25 Feb. 1831.

48. Bod. c.3.217, W. to Babington, 10 Jan. 1831; f. 222, 14 March 1831; Newsome, *op. cit.*, p. 136.

49. L V, p. 326n.

50. Bod. c.3.221, W. to Babington, 14 March 1831.

51. Duke MSS, Smith Papers, Mrs. W. to W. Smith, 17 Aug. 1833.

52. U.C.L. MSS, Brougham Papers, William W. to Brougham, 20 Oct. 1833.

53. Bod. c.3.228, W. to Stephen, 20 June 1831.

54. Bod. c.3.221, W. to Babington, 14 March 1831.

55. Bod. c.2.137, W. to Sam W., 8 April 1831; Duke MSS, Smith Papers,

W. to W. Smith, 5 May 1832; Fitzwilliam (Northants) MSS, W. to Milton, 26 April 1831.

56. Fitzwilliam (Wentworth Woodhouse) MSS, W. to Milton, 28 May 1831.
57. UCL MSS, Brougham Papers, W. to Brougham, 28 April 1831.
58. St. John's, Cantab., MSS, W. to Mrs. T. F. Buxton, 27 March 1833.
59. Roberts MSS, W. to S. Roberts, 14 March 1831. See PP, p. 155 for a letter from Lord John Russell thanking for sympathy, year uncertain.
60. Rhodes House MSS, W. to Buxton, 21 April 1831.
61. *Ib.* 24 May 1832.
62. Duke MSS, Smith Papers, W. to W. Smith, 23 Aug. 1832.
63. Huntington MSS, Macaulay Papers, W. to Macaulay, 26 Aug. 1832.
64. Lincolnshire Papers, W. to Lord Carrington, 23 March 1832. Furneaux (p. 448) errs in saying she died at Highwood, which had been left the previous year.
65. Newman MSS, Birmingham Oratory, Note by Newman on MS of W. to Newman, 21 April 1831.
66. W. to Lord Carrington as above.
67. Roberts MSS, W. to S. Roberts, 1 Jan. 1833.
68. BM Eg MSS 1964.140, W. to Lady O. Sparrow, 6 Feb. 1833.
69. Rhodes House MSS, W. to Mrs. Buxton, 17 Nov. 1832.
70. Teignmouth, *op. cit.*, I, p. 245.
71. Rhodes House MSS, W. to Buxton, 9 April 1833.
72. L V, p. 354.
73. C II, p. 527 (date should read 25 May).
74. Rhodes House MSS, W. to Buxton, 11 June 1833.
75. Duke MSS, Smith Papers, W. to W. Smith, 25 June 1833.
76. Gurney, J. J., *Familiar Sketch*, pp. 37–43.
77. Duke MSS, Smith Papers, Mrs. W. to W. Smith, 17 Aug. 1833.
78. Jay, W., *Autobiography*, p. 317.
79. For W's last days see Hull MSS, Mrs. W. to W. Edwell, 29 July 1833; and L V, pp. 370–3, based on MS by Henry W.
80. Foot, M. R. D. (ed.), *The Gladstone Diaries*, 1968. I: 25 July 1833.
81. L V, p. 370. Gratus, J., *The Great White Lie*, castigates this gift but his polemic reads the attitudes of the late 20th century into the situation of 1833.
82. Dukes MSS, Baines Papers, J. B. Macaulay to Edward Baines, 30 July 1833.
83. L V, p. 373.
84. The letter signed by M.P.s is in the Bodleian.
85. L V, p. 375 gets the date of the funeral wrong as 5 Aug.! DNB repeats the error.
86. Gurney MSS, MS Diary of Hudson Gurney, M.P., 3 Aug. 1833. He mentions the Dukes of Sussex and Gloucester as pall bearers.

Note on Transcription of Manuscript Sources

Wilberforce was much addicted to abbreviations. To save his eyes he shortened many words, especially as he grew older and blinder. His sign for *and* sometimes looked like a flattened orange. For *the*, he frequently used the nearly extinct conventional sign written *ye* but read as *the*; unfortunately, the modern reader has been brain-washed by Ye Olde Worlde cult and cannot help treating *ye* as if it were the archaic second person plural.

He capitalized frequently although the practice was disappearing; to the modern reader this imparts an Emphasis where None is Intended. Wilberforce's punctuation was erratic: copious when on his best behaviour, more usually sparse. He denoted his paragraphs by a dash or a slight shift in line of writing. His postscripts wander all round edges and upside down.

All this looks right in manuscript but is tedious to read in print. I have therefore spelt out abbreviated words and altered punctuation where necessary. With these exceptions my quotations from *mss* and printed transcripts of *mss* are exact.

Manuscript Sources

For Catalogue numbers, where relevant, see References and Notes.

BODLEIAN Library, Oxford, Dept. of Western MSS: Wilberforce Papers, c. 600 items, including 6 volumes of general correspondence, both by and to W.; 3 volumes of family correspondence; 1 volume of miscellaneous papers including loose diary sheets; 'Fragments of My Father's Conversation' (notebook by S. Wilberforce).

A few items are in the Clarendon Papers and the Noble Papers.

BOSTON, Mass., Public Library, 64 miscellaneous letters by W., and 6 related MSS.

BRITISH MUSEUM (now British Library) c. 300 Wilberforce letters in the following collections of Papers:

Auckland   Melville
Bentham   Sparrow
Clarkson   Wellesley
Grenville   Windham
Hardwicke   Young
Liverpool

A few are in Huskisson, Peel, Ripon, Rose, and Misc. References to W. are in the Holland Papers and in Cole's *Athene Cantabrigiensis*, Vol. 20.

Abolition Committee: *Fair Minute Books*.

Diaries of John Cam Hobhouse, Lord Broughton.

BUXTON 30 Wilberforce letters to Sir T. F. Buxton at Rhodes House, Oxford.

CALTHORPE 25 letters from W. to 3rd Lord Calthorpe, and references in other family letters. Owned by Brigadier Sir Richard Anstruther-Gough-Calthorpe, Bt. Deposited at Hampshire Record Office.

DUKE UNIVERSITY (William R. Perkins Library) North Carolina.
   c. 600 items by, to, or about Wilberforce including 194 Wilberforce letters, in the following collections of Papers:
   Wilberforce (162), William Smith (24). Remainder in Buxton, Campbell, Easthope, Leonard, Russell, Staunton, Wellesley.
   Croker's Carrington Memorandum (Croker Papers).
   Fuller Letter Book (Easthope Papers).

FITZWILLIAM MSS of 4th Earl and 5th Earl (Lord Milton).
   A few W. letters but many references to him. Owned by Earl Fitzwilliam, deposited partly at Sheffield City Libraries (Wentworth Woodhouse Muniments) and partly in Northamptonshire Record Office.

HAREWOOD PAPERS 65 items in correspondence between W. and Canning. Owned by Lord Harewood, deposited with National Registrar of Archives, Leeds City Library.

HARFORD 22 W. letters, with other references, in papers of John Harford, Bristol City Library. (Note: further letters to Harford are in the Duke MSS, Wilberforce Papers.)

HENRY E. HUNTINGTON LIBRARY, San Marino, California 88 Wilberforce letters in the following collections of Papers:
   Locker (13)
   Macaulay (47)
   Montagu (24)
   and 4 others.

LEVESLEY MS Notebook of Prayers and Meditations believed to be in W's hand, marked 'March 1788'. Loaned by the Rev. T. H. Levesley of Ilkley, Yorks.

PORTEUS MS, Lambeth Palace Library 'Occasional Memorandum and Reflexions' by Beilby Porteus, Bishop of London. References to W., Slave Trade, Proclamation Society etc. also: 'Three Favourite Residences', MS in Maidstone Museum.

ROBERTS 56 W. letters to Samuel Roberts. Owned by Sir Peter Roberts, Bt., deposited at Sheffield City Library.

ST. JOHN'S COLLEGE, CAMBRIDGE 23 W. letters; Examination Book; related material.

STANHOPE 46 W. letters, to Pitt, Edward Eliot, and Bishop Pretyman (Tomline); Kent Record Office.

THORNTON MS Diary of Henry Thornton (brief and spasmodic). Notebooks containing copies by his daughter Marianne of letters of Thornton to and from his wife, letters by W., etc. Also her own MS memoirs. In University Library, Cambridge. Many references to W. throughout.

UNIVERSITY COLLEGE, LONDON c. 40 W. letters and related material in Brougham Papers and Bentham Papers.

WILBERFORCE HOUSE, HULL 30 W. letters to Henry W.; political and family letters. Diary volume, 9 Feb. 1814 to 19 Jan. 1823 (with gaps) 272 pp. foolscap.

WYVILL 122 letters between W. and Christopher Wyvill. North Yorkshire Record Office.

A substantial number of Wilberforce and related MSS are scattered in many collections. The following have been the most useful to this book:

LETTERS: to Sir Thomas Acland at Devon Record Office
  to Admiral Lord Barham in possession of Lord Gainsborough
  to 3rd Earl Bathurst, on loan to British Museum
  to Scrope Bernard in possession of Mr. John Spencer-Bernard
  to 1st Marquess Camden, in Kent Record Office
  to 1st Lord Carrington (and W's accounts with Smith, Payne and Co's Bank), in the Lincolnshire Papers in possession of Brigadier A. W. A. Llewellen-Palmer
  to James Currie, in Liverpool City Library
  to 1st Lord Erskine, in possession of Lord Buchan
  to Elizabeth Fry and Joseph Gurney, at Friends' House Library
  to David Hartley, at Berkshire Record Office
  to Charles, 2nd Earl Grey, at Durham University
  to Edward Hawker, at Oriel College, Oxford
  to 1st Earl of Harrowby, in possession of Lord Harrowby
  to 1st Lord Kenyon (also his Diary), in possession of Lord Kenyon
  to Lord Henry Petty, 3rd Marquess of Lansdowne, in possession of Lord Lansdowne at Bowood
  to 1st Lord Muncaster, at John Rylands Library, Manchester
  to James Monroe, at New York Public Library
  to Spencer Perceval, in possession of Mr. David Holland
  to William Pitt, in Chatham Papers, Public Record Office (also other papers among PRO MSS)
  to Sir Stamford and Lady Raffles, at India Office Library
  to Mary Sargent, at West Sussex Record Office
  to Granville Sharp, in possession of Colonel A. B. Lloyd-Baker
  to Henry Addington, 1st Viscount Sidmouth, at Devon Record Office

to Thomas Perronet Thompson, at Hull University Library
to Henry Addington, 1st Viscount Sidmouth, at Devon Record Office
to Thomas Perronet Thompson, at Hull University Library
to Henry Venn (and other Venn papers), at Church Missionary Society
to 1st Marquess of Westminster, in possession of the Duke of Westminster
to Samuel Whitbread, in Bedfordshire Record Office

Also Letters:

at the Bible Society, London
in the Clements Library, University of Michigan
in the Lewis-Walpole Library, Farmington, Conn.
in the Osborn Collection, Yale University

Dolben Papers, at Northamptonshire Record Office
Diaries of Hampden Gurney and Joseph John Gurney, in possession of Mr. Richard Gurney
Kinghorn Papers, in possession of Mr. Charles Jewson
Lowther Papers, at Cumbria County Record Office (owned by Lord Lonsdale)
Diary and letters of Lord Macaulay, at Trinity College, Cambridge
Sinclair of Ulbster Papers, in possession of Lord Thurso
Waldegrave Papers, in possession of Lord Waldegrave

Wilberforce letters will also be found at: the Record Offices of the Counties of Bedford, Gloucester, Hertford, Stafford, West Suffolk and Humberside; Arundel Castle; Birmingham Public Library; Birmingham Oratory; British Library of Political Science; Chatsworth House; Natural History Museum; National Maritime Museum; Queens' College, Cambridge; Saint Mary of the Angel's Church, Moorhouse Road, London, W.2; Wordsworth Museum, Grasmere; Scottish Record Office; National Library of Scotland; and in private hands; National Library of Ireland; National Library of Australia; Library of New South Wales; Library of Congress; Historical Societies of Massachusetts, New York and Pennsylvania; Berg Collection, New York Public Library; Pierpont Morgan Library; Universities of Atlanta, Cornell, Harvard (Houghton Library), Howard, New Jersey (Rutgers) and Virginia; Swarthmore College, Pennsylvania; the Archives of the United Methodist Church at Lake Junaluska, North Carolina; and in private hands.

The papers of Henry Bankes, Sir Thomas Bernard, Dean Milner and Sir Richard Hill, which all must have contained Wilberforce MSS, are lost, though many of his letters to Bankes and to Milner are in the Bodleian. Wilberforce's letters to 1st Lord Teignmouth were lost by the sons, to 2nd Lord Teignmouth's sorrow. Many of the letters to Clarkson were torn up or mislaid by Clarkson himself.

Select Bibliography

AFRICAN INSTITUTION, *Reports*, 1807, et seq.

ANSTEY, ROGER, *The Atlantic Slave Trade and British Abolition, 1760–1810*, 1975.

ANTI-SLAVERY SOCIETY, *Reports of the Society for the Mitigation and General Abolition of Slavery*, 1824, 1825, 1826.

ASPINALL, A., *Early English Trade Unions*, 1949.
Later Letters of George III. 5 vols, 1962–70.
Letters of George Prince of Wales. 8 vols, 1963–71.

AUCKLAND, ROBERT, 3rd Baron, *Journal and Correspondence of William Lord Auckland*, 1860–2.

BAGOT, JOCELYN, *George Canning and His Friends*, 1909.

BAKER, JAMES, *Sir Thomas Bernard*, 1819.

BARING, MRS. H., *Diary of William Windham*, 1866.

BARNES, THOMAS, *Parliamentary Portraits*, 1815.

BETHELL, LESLIE, *The Abolition of the Brazilian Slave Trade, 1807–1869*, 1970.

'BETTERING SOCIETY' (Society for Bettering the Condition of the Poor) *Reports*, 1798 et seq.

BROUGHAM, LORD, *Historical Sketches of Statesmen . . . in the time of George III* (1859 edition, Vol. I).
Life and Times of Henry, Lord Brougham by Himself, 3 vols, 1871.

BROUGHTON, LORD (ed. Lady Dorchester), *Recollections of a Long Life*, Vol. VI, 1911.

BROWN, FORD K., *Fathers of the Victorians*, 1961.

BURGESS, J. H. M., *The Chronicles of Clapham*, 1929.

BURKE, EDMUND, *Correspondence*, ed. R. B. McDowell and John H. Wood, Vol. VII, 1968, Vol. IX, 1970.

BURN, W. L., *Emancipation and Apprenticeship*, 1937.

BUXTON, SIR T., *Memoirs*, ed. by his son, 1872.

CARUS, WILLIAM, *Charles Simeon*, 1847.

CASTLEREAGH, VISCOUNT, *Memoir and Correspondence*, ed. by his brother, 12 vols, 1848–53.

CHANCELLOR, E. B., *Knightsbridge and Belgravia*, 1909.
Memorials of St. James's Street, 1922.

CHATTERTON, HENRIETTA LADY, *Memorials of Lord Gambier*, 3 vols, 1861.

CHECKLAND, S. G., *The Gladstones*, 1971.

CHRISTIE, IAN R., *The End of Lord North's Ministry, 1780–82*, 1958.
Wilkes, Wyvill and Reform, 1962.

CLARKSON, THOMAS, *History of the Abolition of the Slave Trade*, 2 vols, 1807.
Strictures on a Life of William Wilberforce, 1838.

COBBETT, WILLIAM, *Political Register*, 1802–1835.

Codrington Correspondence, ed. Robson Lowe, 1951.

COLE, HUBERT, *Christophe, King of Haiti*, 1967.

COLVIN, CHRISTINA (ed.) *Maria Edgeworth: Letters from England, 1813–44*,
1973.

Complete Peerage.

COOKSON, J. E., *Lord Liverpool's Administration*, 1975.

CORWIN, ARTHUR, *Spain and the Abolition of Slavery in Cuba, 1817–1886*, 1967.

COUPLAND, SIR REGINALD, *Wilberforce*, 1923 (reissued 1945).

COURTENAY, JOHN, *Characteristick Sketches of Distinguished Speakers in the House
of Commons*, 1808.

CRUMPE, SAMUEL, *Inquiry into the Nature and Properties of Opium*, 1793.

D'ARBLAY, MME (Fanny Burney), *Letters and Diaries*, ed. C. F. Barrett, 7 vols,
1842–6 (refs to 6 vol. edition, 1904).

DAVIS, DAVID BRION, *Slavery in an Age of Revolution*, 1975.

DAVIDSON, BASIL, *Black Mother*, 1961.

DERRY, JOHN, *Charles James Fox*, 1972.

Dictionary of National Biography.

DOONEN, ELIZABETH, *Documents Illustrative of the Atlantic Slave Trade*, 4 vols,
1930, reissued 1965.

Edinburgh Review.

EHRMAN, JOHN, *The Younger Pitt: The Years of Acclaim*, 1969.

FARINGTON, JOSEPH, *Diaries*, ed. James Grieg, 6 vols, 1922–6.

FORSTER, E. M., *Marianne Thornton*, 1956.

FURNEAUX, ROBIN, *William Wilberforce*, 1974.

FYFE, CHRISTOPHER, *A History of Sierra Leone*, 1962.

GLADSTONE, W. E., *Diary*, ed. M. R. D. Foot, 1968.

[GLASSE, SAMUEL], *A Narrative of Proceedings . . . towards a National Reformation, by a County Magistrate*, 1787.

GRATUS, JACK, *The Great White Lie*, 1973.

GREVILLE, CHARLES, *Memoirs*, ed. H. Reeve (8 vol. edition, 1888).

GRIMSHAWE, T. S., *Memoirs of Rev. Legh Richmond*, 1828.

GRIGGS, E. L., *Thomas Clarkson*, 1936.

GROVES, J. W., *Old Clapham*, 1887.

GURNEY, J. J., *Familiar Sketch of the late William Wilberforce*, 1838.

GUTTRIDGE, G. H., *David Hartley, M.P.*, 1926.

HALLETT, ROBIN, *The Penetration of Africa*, Vol. I, 1965.

HAMMOND, J. L. and B., *The Town Labourer, 1760–1832*, 1917.

HARFORD, JOHN, *Recollections of William Wilberforce*, 1864.

Harford Annals, ed. A. M. Harford. Privately printed, c. 1906.

HASTINGS, MAURICE, *Parliament House*, 1950.

HAY, DOUGLAS, LINEBAUGH, PETER, *et al, Albion's Fatal Tree*, 1975.

HAYTER, ALETHEA, *Opium and the Romantic Imagination*, 1968.

HAZLITT, WILLIAM, *The Spirit of the Age*, 1825.

HEADLAM, CUTHBERT, *The Letters of Lady Harriot Eliot*, 1914.

HEASMAN, KATHLEEN, *Evangelicals in Action*, 1962.

HENNELL, MICHAEL, *John Venn and the Clapham Sect*, 1958.

HINDE, WENDY, *George Canning*, 1973.

HISTORICAL MANUSCRIPT COMMISSION REPORTS:
  Ailesbury (15th, VII, 1898)
  Carlisle (15th, IV, 1897)
  Rutland (15th, IV, 1896).

HODGSON, ROBERT, *Life of Bishop Beilby Porteus* (in Vol. I of his *Collected Works*, 1816).

HOLE, CHARLES, *The Early History of the Church Missionary Society*, 1896.

HOWSE, ERNEST, *Saints in Politics*, 1952.

HUNTER ARCHAEOLOGICAL SOCIETY, *Transactions*, VIII, 1963.

INGLIS, BRIAN, *Poverty and the Industrial Revolution*, 1971.

JAEGER, M., *Before Victoria*, 1956.

JAY, WILLIAM, *Autobiography*, ed. G. Redford and J. A. James, 2nd ed., 1855.

John Bull, 1821–

JOHNSON, L. G., *General T. Perronet Thompson*, 1957.

JONES, M. G., *Hannah More*, 1952.

KENYON, GEORGE, *Lloyd, 1st Lord Kenyon*, 1873.

KNUTSFORD, LADY, *Zachary Macaulay*, 1900.

LASCELLES, E. C. P., *Granville Sharp*, 1928.

LA TROBE, C. IGNATIUS, ed. J. A. La Trobe, *Letters to My Children*, 1851.

LEIGHTON-BOYCE, J. A. S. L., *Smiths the Bankers*, 1958.

LLOYD, CHRISTOPHER, *The Navy and the Slave Trade*, 1949.

MATHIESON, W. C., *British Slavery and its Abolition, 1823–38*, 1936.

MARRYATT, JOSEPH, *Thoughts on the Abolition of the Slave Trade and civilization of Africa*, 1816.

MEACHAM, STANDISH, *Henry Thornton of Clapham*, 1964.
  Lord Bishop (*S. Wilberforce*), 1972.

MELVILLE, LEWIS, *William Cobbett*, 1913.

MILNER, MARY, *Isaac Milner*, 1842.

[MORE, HANNAH], *Thoughts on the Manners of the Great*, 1787.

MORRIS, HENRY, *Charles Grant*, 1904.

MULLINGER, J. B., *St. John's College*, 1901.

MUNCASTER, LORD, *Historical Sketches of the Slave Trade*, 1792.

NAMIER, L. and BROOKE, J., *History of Parliament: The Commons, 1754–90*, 3 vols, 1964.

NEWS, CHESTER, *Henry Brougham to 1830*, 1964.

NEWSOME, DAVID, *The Parting of Friends*, 1966.

NEWTON, JOHN, *Thoughts upon the African Slave Trade*, 1788.

NORRIS, ROBERT, *A Short Account of the African Slave Trade*, 2nd edition, 1789.

OWEN, JOHN, *History of the British and Foreign Bible Society*, 3 vols, 1816.

PALMER, ALAN, *Alexander I*, 1974.

Paterson's Roads, 18th edition, ed. E. Mogg, 1826.

Parliamentary Register, ed. John Debrett, 45 vols, 1780–96.

Parliamentary History (1066–1803), ed. W. Cobbett, 36 vols, 1806–20.

Parliamentary Debates, ed. W. Cobbett and T. Hansard (after 1812 by Hansard alone), 41 vols, 1803–1820.

New Series, ed. T. Hansard, 25 vols, 1820–30.
(see also *The Senator*).

PEARSON, JOHN, *Life of William Hey*, 2 vols, 1823.

PELLEW, GEORGE, *Life and Correspondence of Addington, 1st Viscount Sidmouth*, 2 vols, 1847.

PLACE, FRANCIS, *Autobiography*, ed. Mary Thale, 1972.

POTTLE, FREDERICK A., and SCOTT, G. (ed.) *Private Papers of James Boswell*, Vol. XVI, 1932.

Proclamations, Hand List of, 1714–1810, Bibliotheca Lindesiana, 1913.

PYM, DOROTHY, *Battersea Rise*, 1933.

RADZINOWICZ, L., *A History of English Criminal Law*, 3 vols, 1949–56.

RAMSAY, JAMES, *Essay on the Treatment and Conversion of Slaves in the British Sugar Colonies*, 1784.

An Inquiry into the Effects of Putting a Stop to the African Slave Trade and of Granting Liberty to the Slaves in the British Sugar Colonies, 1784.

Objections to the Abolition of the Slave Trade, with Answers, 1788.

ROBERTS, WILLIAM, *Memoirs of the Life and Correspondence of Mrs. Hannah More*, 4 vols, 1834.

ROBINSON, HENRY CRABB, *Diaries*, ed. Morley, 2 vols, 19?.

Exposure of Misrepresentations . . . in the Preface to the Correspondence of William Wilberforce, 1840.

Rolliad, Criticisms on the, 4th ed. Part the Second, 1790.

ROSE, GEORGE, *Diaries and Correspondence*, ed. L. V. Harcourt, 2 vols, 1860.

ROSE, J. HOLLAND, *Pitt and the National Revival*, 1911.

Pitt and the Great War, 1911.

SANDS, P. C., and HAWORTH, C. M., *A History of Pocklington School*, 1950.

SCOTT, R. F. (ed.), *Admissions to the College of St. John the Evangelist, Cambridge*, Pt. IV, 1931.

SELINCOURT, ERNEST DE, and SHAVER, CHESTER L. (eds.), *Letters of William and Dorothy Wordsworth*, 2nd ed., I, 1967.

Senator, The, or Clarendon's Parliamentary Reporter, 28 vols, 1790–1801.

SHAVER, C. L., MOORMAN, MARY, and HILL, A. G., *Letters of William and Dorothy Wordsworth*, II, 1971.

SIDNEY, EDWIN, *Life of Sir Richard Hill*, 1839.

SOULSBY, H. G., *The Right of Search and the Slave Trade in Anglo-American Relations*, 1933.

SOUTHEY, ROBERT, *Life and Correspondence*, ed. C. C. Southey, 4 vols, 1849–50.

Letters, ed. J. Wood Warter, 1846.

STANHOPE, GHITA and GOOCH, G. P., *Life of 3rd Earl Stanhope*, 1914.

STEPHEN, SIR GEORGE, *Anti-Slavery Recollections*, 1854.

STEPHEN, JAMES, *Memoirs*, ed. Merle E. Bevington, 1954.

STEPHEN, SIR JAMES, *Essays in Ecclesiastical Biography*, 2 vols, 1849 (refs to 1 vol. ed. 1872).

STIRLING, A. M. W., *Annals of a Yorkshire House*, 2 vols, 1911.

The Ways of Yesterday, 1930.

TEIGNMOUTH, CHARLES SHORE, 2nd Lord, *Reminiscences of Many Years*, 2 vols, 1878.

THOMAS, P. D. G., *The House of Commons in the 18th century*.

THORNTON, R. D., *James Currie and Robert Burns*, 1963.

THORPE, ROBERT, *A Letter to William Wilberforce*, 1815.

TIMBS, JOHN, *Club Life of London*, 2 vols, 1866.

TOBIN, J., *A Rejoinder to the Rev. James Ramsay*, 1787.
  An Address to the Rev. James Ramsay, 1788.

Transatlantic Slave Trade from West Africa, The, Seminar at Centre of African Studies, Edinburgh, 1965.

TREVELYAN, G. M., *Lord Grey of the Reform Bill*, 1920.

Victoria County History: East Riding. Vol. I: The City of Kingston upon Hull, ed. K. J. Allinson, 1969.

WALLAS, GRAHAM, *Francis Place*, 1898.

WATSON, J. STEVEN, *The Reign of George III, 1760–1815*, 1960.

WELLINGTON, 1ST DUKE OF, *Supplementary Despatches*, ed. by his son, Vol. IX, 1862.

WHITNEY, JANET, *Elizabeth Fry*, 1937.

WILBERFORCE, ANNA MARIA, *The Private Papers of William Wilberforce*, 1897.

WILBERFORCE, ROBERT ISAAC and SAMUEL, *The Life of William Wilberforce*, 5 vols, 1838.
  Correspondence of William Wilberforce, 2 vols, 1840.

WILBERFORCE, WILLIAM, *A Practical View of the Prevailing Religious System of Professed Christians in the Higher and Middle Classes of this Country contrasted with Real Christianity*, 1797.
  A Letter on the Abolition of the Slave Trade, addressed to the Freeholders of Yorkshire, 1807.
  A Letter to His Excellency the Prince of Talleyrand Perigord on the subject of the Slave Trade, 1814.
  An Appeal to the Religion, Justice and Humanity of the British Empire in behalf of the Negro Slaves in the West Indies, 1823.

WOOD, A. SKEVINGTON, *Thomas Haweis*, 1957.

WOODWARD, SN. LLEWELLYN, *The Age of Reform, 1815–1870*, 2nd ed., 1962.

WRAXALL, SIR NATHANIEL, *Historical and Posthumous Memoirs of My Own Time*, ed. H. B. Wheatley, 5 vols, 1884.

WYVILL, CHRISTOPHER, *Political Papers, chiefly respecting the Attempt . . . to effect a Reformation of the Parliament of Great Britain*, 6 vols, 1794–1802.

YOUNG, ARTHUR, *Autobiography*, ed. M. Betham-Edwards, 1898.

ZIEGLER, PHILIP, *Addington*, 1965.

Index